D1706825

33

BION OF SMYRNA THE FRAGMENTS AND THE *ADONIS*

BION OF SMYRNA

THE FRAGMENTS AND THE *ADONIS*

EDITED WITH INTRODUCTION AND COMMENTARY BY

J. D. REED

Friedrich Solmsen Fellow, Institute for Research in the Humanities, University of Wisconsin at Madison

CAMBRIDGE
UNIVERSITY PRESS

Published by the Press Syndicate of the University of Cambridge
The Pitt Building, Trumpington Street, Cambridge CB2 1RP
40 West 20th Street, New York, NY 10011-4211, USA
10 Stamford Road, Oakleigh, Melbourne 3166, Australia

First published 1997

Printed in Great Britain at the University Press, Cambridge

A catalogue record for this book is available from the British Library

Library of Congress cataloguing in publication data

Bion, of Phlossa near Smyrna.
Bion of Smyrna: the fragments and the Adonis / edited with introduction and commentary by J. D. Reed.
p. cm. – (Cambridge classical texts and commentaries; 33)
ISBN 0 521 57316 5 (hardback)
1. Country life – Greece – Poetry. 2. Adonis – Poetry. 3. Pastoral poetry, Greek. 4. Lost literature – Greece. I. Reed, J. D. II. Series.
PA3944.B4A6 1997
881′.01 – dc20 96–21684 CIP

ISBN 0 521 57316 5 hardback

AO

CONTENTS

PREFACE

It was in April of 1986 that I, as a junior at Yale, browsing in the Classics library at the top of Phelps Hall, came upon a slim, marbled volume whose spine bore the simple gilt inscription "Bion". Avid for any of the treasures that pedagogy had heretofore withheld from me, I opened it and read the first lines of the *Epitaph on Adonis*, which immediately seemed to me peculiarly indulgent of a type of romantic melancholy, at the same time wild and restrained, whose satisfaction I had so far missed in ancient literature:

> Αἰάζω τὸν Ἄδωνιν, "ἀπώλετο καλὸς Ἄδωνις".
> "ὤλετο καλὸς Ἄδωνις", ἐπαιάζουσιν Ἔρωτες.

I was subsequently disappointed to find that although Bion was a familiar figure to students of ancient literature from the Renaissance through the nineteenth century, our own century had largely neglected him. The *Adonis* had provoked valuable commentaries (most recently those of Fantuzzi and Hopkinson), but they seldom delved deeply into the questions that most interested me, the poet's historical stance and the source of his particular qualities. On his seventeen fragments no proper commentary existed at all. And so I had to satisfy my curiosity through my own research, which led to the present work. My main goal is to place Bion in literary history between the poets he admired and those whom he inspired, and to make clear both his debt to tradition and his originality; particular attention is given to a coherent tradition within Hellenistic poetry that I have termed "late bucolic", of which Bion was a major exponent. I hope that he will emerge with a claim to a greater reputation than he has now, and that these pages will prompt a greater interest in his work, both for its own merits and for its value for the study of Greek and Latin literature.

I could not have completed this project without the help of many friends. First I must record my gratitude to my graduate advisers at Stanford, Susan Stephens, Edward Courtney, and Kenneth Dover, under whose wise guidance I first began working on Bion's poetry. Donald Russell, Peter Parsons, and Adrian Hollis kindly arranged for me to spend a splendid Michaelmas term at Oxford in 1991; they and Martin West read part or all of the commentary as it was then, pointing me on to new paths and freeing my work of many imperfections. The editors of Cambridge Classical Texts and Commentaries, Michael Reeve and James Diggle, gave invaluable help. The care and alertness of my editors at the Cambridge University Press saved me from many blunders. Among the many others who generously gave their advice and assistance I must mention Alan Cameron, Frank Coulson, Eleanor Dickey, Mark Edwards, Marco Fantuzzi, John Gould, Denise Greaves, Peter Hicks, Sarah Iles Johnston, Richard Matthews, Antony Raubitschek, Daniel Selden, Stephen Tracy, and Michael Wigodsky; the shortcomings that remain are my own.

Columbus, Ohio
February 1996

INTRODUCTION

I BION'S LIFE

Our testimonia are few:

Suda II.697.22–4 Adler (s.v. Θεόκριτος): ἰστέον δὲ ὅτι τρεῖς γεγόνασι βουκολικῶν ἐπῶν ποιηταί, Θεόκριτος οὑτοσί, Μόσχος Σικελιώτης, καὶ Βίων ὁ Σμυρναῖος, ἔκ τινος χωριδίου καλουμένου Φλώσσης. The precision over Bion's home town commands credence. Phlossa, otherwise unknown (its name, with -ss-, sounds Anatolian), may have been one of the villages out of which Smyrna was reconstituted after the συνοικισμός by Antigonus and Lysimachus (cf. Strabo 14.1.37).

The Palatine corrector on *A.P.* 9.440 (= Moschus 1; text from P. Waltz and G. Soury, *Anthologie grecque* VIII (Budé, Paris 1974) 43): οὗτος ὁ Μόσχος ποιητής ἐστι τῶν καλουμένων βουκολικῶν ποιημάτων, ὧν πρῶτος Θεόκριτος, δεύτερος αὐτὸς ὁ Μόσχος, τρίτος Βίων Σμυρναῖος. The Palatine corrector and the compilers of the *Suda* (roughly a half-century later) no doubt drew on the same source.

The anonymous Ἐπιτάφιος Βίωνος ([Moschus] 3), written in commemoration of Bion's death,[1] implies that he died prematurely (cf. his ταχὺς μόρος in line 26) and states that he was poisoned (109–12). In lines 70–1 Bion is made a countryman of Homer, mourned by the river Meles; i.e. Smyrnaean.[2]

A fourth witness may be Diog. Laert. 4.58, where in a list of the "ten Bions" the seventh is a μελικὸς ποιητής. Since no other record exists of a lyric Bion, this may be a

[1] On this poem, wrongly attributed to Moschus in the Renaissance, see sections IV and VIII below.

[2] Bion's connexion with Sicily in [Moschus] 3 is of course a fiction generically marking his poetry as bucolic; cf. A. Barigazzi, *Maia* n.s. 19 (1967) 292.

mistake for βουκολικὸς ποιητής (so Knaack in *RE* 3.482). Diogenes' list may come from Demetrius of Magnesia (cf. e.g. 1.38; see J. Mejer, *Hermes* 109 (1981) 449–51), who, as a contemporary of Cicero and Atticus (*Ad Att.* 8.11.7), lived late enough to include our Bion.

In sum: Bion's place of origin was the opulent merchant city of Smyrna, καλλίστη τῶν πασῶν (Strabo 14.1.37).[3] In addition to the testimonia given above he is Σμυρναῖος in the tituli to two of his fragments in Stobaeus. His date is uncertain. He is placed third and last in the canon of bucolic poets,[4] after Moschus, who as a colleague of Aristarchus must have been at Alexandria in the mid second century B.C.[5] Henry 3 warns that the list may not be chronological, but Bion's work does show the influence of Theocritus and Moschus. Around the turn of the century Meleager seems to show knowledge of the *Epitaph on Adonis* and the ninth fragment (see section VIII below).[6] The *Epitaph on Bion* alludes to the *Adonis* and at least to the sixteenth fragment (perhaps others; see section IV below) and is imitated in turn by Catullus.[7] Bion thus flourished sometime

[3] Another Bion of Smyrna, son of Philotas, is listed as a Panathenaic victor on *IG* II² 2314 col. I.19 and 25 (dated to 182 B.C. by S. Tracy, *Hesperia* 60 (1991) 218–20; cf. *SEG* 41.114). See also G. Petzl, *Die Inschriften von Smyrna* (Bonn 1982–91) nos. 524.1 (grave inscription for Apion, son of Bion) and 688.i.18 (contribution by Metrobius, son-in-law of Bion), both from the last two centuries B.C.

[4] On the ancient critical habit of codifying the standard authors in each field, which was established by the late second century B.C., see Pfeiffer 204–8; the bucolic triad was probably set in the mid to late first century B.C., the first period of major scholarly interest in bucolic.

[5] Μόσχος, Συρακούσιος, γραμματικός, Ἀριστάρχου γνώριμος. οὗτός ἐστιν ὁ δεύτερος ποιητὴς μετὰ Θεόκριτον, τὸν τῶν βουκολικῶν δραμάτων ποιητήν (*Suda* III.413.19–21 Adler); cf. A. Blau, *De Aristarchi discipulis* (diss. Jena 1883) 24–5. See Pfeiffer 211 for Aristarchus' dating.

[6] On the date of Meleager's *Garland*, most likely to be set in the 90s B.C., see now Cameron (1993) 49–56.

[7] Catull. 5.5–6 "nobis cum semel occidit brevis lux | nox est perpetua

between the mid second and mid first century B.C., probably in the earlier part of this period.

That Bion's anonymous eulogist calls his own poem one of "Ausonian grief" ([Moschus] 3.94) – in contrast to the laments of other nations, including Syracuse – has led many to believe that the poet was Italian and had met his subject during a sojourn of the latter in Italy. Henry 4–6 thus connects Bion with Greek poets like Philodemus and Crinagoras who found patronage in Rome; this movement is first visible in the later second century (Archias and perhaps Antipater of Sidon came to Rome a little before 100 B.C.). The Smyrnaeans were early and strong supporters of Rome in the East, and doubtless cultivated clientships with prominent Roman families, motivating visits westward. It is unknown, however, whether the "Ausonian" eulogist knew Bion personally, and if so whether Bion travelled to Italy or he to Bion.

II BION BUCOLICUS

Of our poet's work there survive the ninety-eight lines of the *Adonis* and seventeen fragments ranging from one to eighteen lines; all are written in hexameters and in a poetic Doric. These last-named formal characteristics recall Bion's status in the ancient canon of bucolic poets and the label βουκολικά given to his anthologized fragments. Hexameters and Doric dialect are typical of the poems that have come down to us under the label "bucolic"; yet other features of that type have eluded Bion's modern readers. Pastoral themes, for example, have seemed absent

una dormienda" reproduces not just the idea but the wording and phrasing of [Moschus] 3.103–4 ὁππότε πρᾶτα θάνωμες, ἀνάκοοι ἐν χθονὶ κοίλᾳ | εὕδομες εὖ μάλα μακρὸν ἀτέρμονα νήγρετον ὕπνον. Cf. section VIII below.

from his poetry.[8] His major surviving poem, the *Epitaph on Adonis*, is an emotive mythological vignette; of his fragments only the second is cast, in typical bucolic manner, as a dialogue between (presumably) rustic characters. To the consternation of critics one could counter that Bion's excerptors took the quotable bits out of context; as we shall see, a close reading of the fragments discloses their thematic, as well as formal, affinity to the bucolic poetry of Theocritus and his followers. But qualms over Bion's status as "bucolic" result more fundamentally from a misunderstanding of the poetic tradition instigated by Theocritus and carried on, with evolution in style and subject matter, for two centuries. Modern criticism of Greek bucolic, looking back through the spectacles of the modern genre of pastoral, has suffered first from a blindness to the range of Theocritus' work and secondly from an almost complete neglect of the poetry of his followers, the remains of Moschus and Bion and the pseudo-Theocritean idylls in our collections. This must stop, if study of bucolic and of its development from Theocritus to Virgil is to be historically and contextually based. Theocritus did create a new type of poetry, but the range of its subject matter and mood is greater than most critics have allowed; furthermore later poets, emulating Theocritus, used the same formal characteristics (notably dactylic hexameter and poetic Doric) for a still wider, yet defined, range of poems. It will be the work of this section to vindicate for Bion, through a study of his fragments, his place in the bucolic tradition.[9]

The origins and usage of βουκολικός as a generic label

[8] Cf. Knaack in *RE* 3.1009 "es sind nur erotisch-sentimentale Tändeleien und Spielereien"; E. A. Barber in *The Oxford Classical Dictionary*[2] (Oxford 1970) 168 "The bucolic element is very slight"; Gutzwiller 176 "only a veneer of country matters remains".

[9] The length of the *Adonis* and its divergence from typical bucolic themes merit separate discussion for it; see section III below. Fr. 1, on the myth of Hyacinthus, will be dealt with in section IV.

are unclear and largely irrelevant to a modern study of ancient practice (as opposed to a study of its reception by ancient critics).[10] Theocritus gives us no clues; nowhere in his work are we required to take the term and its cognates in any but their literal senses, referring to the herdsmen who are his characters, their musical activity, and so on.[11] The ancient grammarians sometimes use it for any poem ascribed to a "bucolic" writer, regardless of style or content; sometimes they restrict it to works displaying pastoral or rustic matter. This inconsistency is to be expected. New types of poetry, emerging from the heat of Alexandrian inventiveness after literature had already been categorized and named, were often not given new generic labels; it has been left to modern scholars, with their special needs and modern notions of literary genre, to name them (e.g. the "epyllion"). In any case, we are not talking about an essential category of literature like the "pastoral" studied by twentieth-century literary critics, determined by subject matter and mood. Recent scholars have criticized the ahistorical folly of looking at Theocritus' pastoral idylls (1, 3, 4, 5, 6, 7, 11) separately from the equally Doric and mimetic *Id.* 2, 10, 14, and 15 (and from his other works) and thereby studying a single theme at the price of ignoring his Alexandrian preoccupations with generic mixture and unheroic subject matter.[12] Likewise, among Theocritus'

[10] I do not mean, of course, that practice and reception – let alone poets and critics – can always be distinguished so sharply.

[11] See the refrain in Theoc. 1; 1.20; 5.44, 60; 7.36, 49. Likewise in [Theoc.] *Ep.* 2.2 = *A.P.* 6.177.2 βουκολικοὶ ὕμνοι are just the songs played by Daphnis while he tended his cows. See commentary on fr. 10.5.

[12] See esp. D. Halperin, *Before Pastoral: Theocritus and the Ancient Tradition of Bucolic Poetry* (New Haven 1983) and G. O. Hutchinson, *Hellenistic Poetry* (Oxford 1988) 142–6; cf. A. Bulloch, *TAPA* 122 (1992) 333: "If we want to understand how Theocritus works as a poet we are going to have to drop notions of a pastoral genre ... and follow the signals which Theocritus gives us throughout his oeuvre."

followers we should look not just at the pastoral [Theoc.] 8, 9, 20, and 27, but at the poems showing the same formal features but with entirely different themes, like [Theoc.] 19 and 23, Moschus 1, and Bion's *Epitaph on Adonis*.

In the present study we are interested in Bion's stance within a tradition of poetry whose practitioners looked back particularly to certain works of Theocritus[13] and marked their affiliation by certain formal features, particularly a poetic Doric dialect (always evolving) and a particular metrical style (always evolving). "Late bucolic", as used here, comprehends Moschus (the fragments and *Runaway Love*, not *Europa*), Bion, and poems showing strong similarity to them in metre, dialect, and diction: [Moschus] 3, [Bion] 2,[14] [Theoc.] 19, 20, 23, and 27.[15] In those features they form quite a coherent group – but not in theme. Pastoral represents perhaps the strongest strain; indeed, that pastoral motifs found a special home in bucolic is shown by the habitual influence of bucolic poets on other writers of pastoral, e.g. in the numerous epigrams that use the dialect and themes of bucolic, or in Longus' borrowings from Theocritus and Bion. On the other hand, poems like Moschus 1, [Theoc.] 19, and [Theoc.] 23 concern erotic themes totally unconnected with the countryside. We need a terminology to reflect the different traditions being per-

[13] Notably *Id.* 1–7, 10–11, 14–15 – all in poetic Doric, all in hexameters, all dealing with rustic or everyday life. I accept *Id.* 8–9 as the work of a follower or followers of Theocritus. Of course, later bucolic poets also show influence from other idylls of Theocritus, as from other Greek poets.

[14] On the authorship of this poem, the *Epithalamius of Achilles and Deidameia*, see section IV below.

[15] Although I should hesitate to press the strict chronological value of the label "late bucolic", the likelihood is that these poems all belong to the hundred years between the mid second and mid first centuries B.C. The dates of Moschus, Bion, and [Moschus] 3 have been established in section I above; Ovid imitates [Bion] 2 (*A.A.* 1.681–704; see Hollis (1977) *ad loc.*) and [Theoc.] 23 (*Met.* 14.698–761; see Copley 138–9), which themselves imitate Bion.

petuated in this poetry, so in this study "bucolic" refers to the tradition signalled by formal features, "pastoral" to themes of herdsmen and rustic life. "Bucolic" thus includes Moschus 1, but not *Europa* (Moschus 2); [Moschus] 3, but not *Megara* ([Moschus] 4); [Theoc.] 23, but not [Theoc.] 25. It typically includes pastoral and rustic themes, but also others that for one reason or another its practitioners saw fit to arrogate or assimilate to their poetic line. It excludes pastoral literature that is not *formally* marked as part of that line, e.g. Longus' *Daphnis and Chloe* and certain parts of Nonnus' *Dionysiaca* (let alone Hesiodic or Near Eastern poetry dealing with herdsmen); these are valuable for tracing the development of pastoral motifs, but our emphasis is different. It is hoped that this distinction in terminology will not seem too artificial and will prove useful for distinguishing the different lines of influence converging in our poet's work.

Late bucolic presents a controlled diversity, poems of several thematic types united by their metre, their dialect, and their common retrospection to the mimetic Doric idylls of Theocritus. Bion's own surviving work is a cross-section of this tradition; with care we can see how his fragments and the poems from which they were taken continue the bucolic line. First, pastoral is a major theme. In fr. 5 someone is told that it is best to know how to fashion one's panpipe oneself: we probably have a bit of dialogue between an older herdsman and a less experienced one. In fr. 11 the speaker, on his way to serenade a shepherd, looks up and prays to the evening star to give him light. The blankness that surrounds other fragments – only the thirteenth is likely to be a complete poem (see below) – may once have set pastoral scenes. Over and over we meet unidentified speakers, ungrounded utterances, unexplained references, and other signs that we are dealing with excerpts chosen for their rhetorical niceties, or for other reasons apart from representativeness. In frr. 9 and 10, details like the conventionally rustic name Lycidas and the terms βοῦτα and βουκολίασδον warn us to imagine fictional rustic contexts for the first-person narration. This point must be made forcefully, since many critics are too ready to take these two context-less snippets, with undue positivism, as the programmatic declarations of Bion himself.[16] They come rather from the mouths of herdsmen explaining why they now sing only of love, and we should beware of identifying those personae with that of the poet who created them.[17]

At least frr. 5, 9, 10, and 11, then, are demonstrably pastoral. That their herdsmen–speakers are not heavily characterized as such is in Bion's style. Take the comast in fr. 11. In his third idyll Theocritus had a goatherd keep a κῶμος at the door of his cave-dwelling beloved; the romantic theme was humorously incongruous in the countryside, and Theocritus made much of this contrast by emphasizing the rusticity of the goatherd's surroundings without diminishing his genuine ardour (cf. lines 1–2 κωμάσδω ποτὶ τὰν Ἀμαρυλλίδα, ταὶ δέ μοι αἶγες | βόσκονται κατ' ὄρος). Bion plays down the rustic realism and plays up the romance (at least in this prayer, which is likely to have set the tone for the κῶμος, if the poem went on to describe it).[18] The speaker is less of a character; that

[16] Especially fr. 10: see commentary on fr. 10.5. Most recently, Gutzwiller 179 sees Bion's fragments as "revelations of his private creed", even imagining fr. 16, clearly the Cyclops' lament over his love for Galatea, as a heartfelt utterance by the poet in the Cyclops' persona. There is little difference between her approach and W. Morton Fullerton's naive biographical reading of Bion in *The Nineteenth Century* 28 (1890) 410–24.

[17] As does the author of the *Epitaph on Bion*, casting the βουκολικὸς ποιητής as a βουκόλος; but his purposes are not ours. In [Theoc.] 9.29, where the narrator is a practitioner of rustic song, we should still see him as a construction of the poet, not the poet himself.

[18] See Arland 46: "Diese Gegenüberstellung zeigt, wie Bion alles in eine andere Sphäre versetzt und seinen Vorbildern ihre Wirklichkeit nimmt." Cf. his suspicion (p. 38) that in the bucolics of Moschus "das

is, Bion de-emphasizes the features that differentiate him from Bion's readers and emphasizes the role with which all can identify, that of the romantic lover. This style of characterization may be typical of late bucolic: it is that of the speakers of Moschus fr. 1 and [Bion] 2, and is already discernible in [Theoc.] 8 and 9.[19] In the age of Louis XIV, Longepierre contrasted the porcelain suavity of Moschus and Bion with the rude vitality of their forerunner: "[I]l seront plus du goust de nostre siecle, qui auroit peine, je croy, à s'accoûtumer à l'extrême simplicité qui regne en plusieurs endroits de Theocrite."

The only fragment that shows the dialogue-form familiar in bucolic is the longest, fr. 2, a discourse on the seasons between Cleodamus and Myrson, presumably rustic characters. Myrson's answer to Cleodamus' question – which season he likes best – is a series of generic reflections. The aphoristic line 9, κρίνειν οὐκ ἐπέοικε θεήια ἔργα βροτοῖσι, suggests pastoral dialogue or monologue as the original context of the aphorisms in frr. 4, 5, 6.2, 7, 12.1, 15, and 17. In Theocritus' idylls such proverbs simulate the ordinary conversation of ordinary people, humorously emphasizing their reliance on clichés and the like[20]; in the lack of strong characterization Myrson's solemnity sounds merely gently pious (contrast the colourful superstitions of the goatherd in Theoc. 3.28–39). Lines 7–8 are richly, even absurdly epic ("tell me what thy heart chooseth"), but where the rusticity of a Theocritean character would contrast sharply with the high-flown diction, Cleodamus is all blandness.

Leben der kleinen Leute vom Lande keine, oder wenigstens keine wesentliche Rolle gespielt hat." Or at least was not the centre of dramatic attention, as in Theocritus.

19 But the rustic speakers in [Theoc.] 20 and 27 are quite pungently characterized.

20 Cf. Aristot. *Rhet.* 1395A6–7 οἱ γὰρ ἀγροῖκοι μάλιστα γνωμοτύποι εἰσί. Not surprisingly, proverbs were a staple of that ancestor of bucolic, literary mime (Fabiano 521).

As in fr. 11, the distance between Bion's characters and the reader is diminished; they are hardly characters, but mouthpieces for rhetorically expressed commonplaces.

Bion's poem on the Cyclops' courting of Galatea (known from both fr. 16 and lines 58–63 of the *Epitaph on Bion*) may also fall in the category of "pastoral" because of its presumptive rustic setting; in any case, Theocritus in *Id.* 11, adapting the theme from fourth-century dithyramb,[21] had sanctified it as "bucolic". Bion must have somehow made it his own, since his version seems to have gained some fame,[22] and was perhaps the source of some of our other fragments. The proverbs in frr. 4 and 17 comport well with the persistence of the Cyclops' hopes (fr. 16.3–4); fr. 14, as Schmitz 39 notes, expresses the kind of complaint that the Cyclops we know from Theocritus might make over his love. Fr. 3 celebrates song as a cure for love, a theme that was specially part of this story since Philoxenus, and it may be Polyphemus who calls upon the Muses to "bear up" (i.e. help him to endure) Love in line 1; compare fr. 3.2 μοι ἀεὶ ποθέοντι with fr. 16.3–4 τὰς δὲ γλυκείας | ἐλπίδας ὑστατίω μέχρι γήραος οὐκ ἀπολείψω (the φάρμακον in fr. 3.3 will then be a balm for one who will never fall out of love rather than a final cure). One hesitates to assign any of these fragments to Bion's *Cyclops* when one considers the emphasis in all bucolic – indeed in all Greek poetry – on perseverance and unrequited love, but fr. 3 seems likely to be Bion's new twist on the old theme.

We can thus account for all of these fragments as speeches from the mouths of country folk or other of the typical creations of a bucolic poet; but themes other than pastoral are codified in the late bucolic tradition. Fr. 13,

[21] See Philox. *PMG* 815–24; Didymus on Demosth. *Phil.* 11, col. 12.59–62.

[22] In addition to [Moschus] 3, [Bion] 2.2–3 may refer specifically to Bion's version.

sixteen lines on a young bird-limer who tries to catch Eros, is the only fragment likely to be a complete poem: there is no first-person narration, the narrative is self-contained and complete, and a sort of punch line closes the poem. Its rustic setting connects fr. 13 to the pastoral matter of much bucolic, but as far as content goes the signal point of generic connexion is actually the amatory fable, rounded by a closing conceit. The themes allegorized here, the elusiveness of love and its power over unwilling humans, ally this poem to Moschus 1 (*Runaway Love*, in which Aphrodite offers a kiss to whoever brings back the miscreant Eros), which it echoes frequently, and especially to [Theoc.] 19, an eight-line poem in which Eros is stung by a bee while filching honey from a hive (at the end Aphrodite laughingly chides him, "Are not you small too, yet capable of dealing great wounds?").[23] The swift, colourful rhetorical style of [Theoc.] 19 and Bion fr. 13 is the same,[24] as are their narrative structures: each protagonist has a disconcerting adventure, resorts to an authority figure, and indicates (δεῖξεν in each case) to him or her the cause of complaint, whereupon the authority figure (γελάσασα in [Theoc.], μειδιάων in Bion) concludes the poem with a pithy remark. Another point of similarity: in both poems the offending θηρίον is κακόν ([Theoc.] 19.1 and 5, Bion fr. 13.13).

Hellenistic poets standardized a number of different forms for narratives of this type: first the epigram, later the Anacreontic piece. In Moschus 1, [Theoc.] 19, and Bion fr. 13 we find that allegorical amatory themes and

[23] The comparison of Eros to a bee – uniting sweet honey with a painful sting – appears in epigram (Mel. *A.P.* 5.163; cf. Marc. Arg. *A.P.* 5.32, *Anacreont.* 6.1–2); it may go back to Archaic lyric (B. MacLachlan, *Phoenix* 43 (1989) 95–9).

[24] Compare e.g. the sequence of actions connected by καί in [Theoc.] 19.3–4 with that in Bion fr. 13.9–10.

epigrammatic closure have entered the bucolic tradition.[25] Elsewhere in Bion's remains – as in the bucolics of Moschus – we can detect the epigrammatic style in longer poems, e.g. in the pointed rhetoric and allegories about the deities of love that characterize frr. 3, 9, 10, and 14. Compare fr. 10 with Moschus frr. 2 and 3: in all three an amatory mythological scenario leads up to a pithy conceit; Bion, however, personalizes the fable (as also in frr. 3 and 9), with the speaker allegorizing his own experience. This especially recalls the rococo effect of Meleager's frequent encounters with the god of love.

Fr. 8 is harder to place in the tradition as we know it. The speaker declares that if his poems are good, the ones he has already written will suffice on their own for his fame; if they are not good, what is the point of his composing any more? He goes on to draw a contrast between writing poetry and *living*, equating poetic efforts to any kind of consuming ambition, and finally condemning the vanity of all human endeavour in view of the short span of life we have been allotted by Fate. These hedonistic, pessimistic verses do not sound like the usual utterance of the herdsmen–poets of bucolic: they practise their art at leisure, and proud though they may be of their attainments they do not, like this speaker, agonize over poetry as over a full-time labour whose rewards often seem doubtful, and that hinders them from enjoyment of life. Poetry here is not bound indissolubly to love, as in frr. 3, 9, and 10; in fact love is never mentioned. If the original poem depicted the complaints of a professional or court poet, such as Bion himself, issuing from the mouth of a cowherd or shepherd

[25] Bucolic-as-epigram reaches its apex in [Theoc.] 23, essentially a love-epigram stretched to sixty-three lines, including a melodramatic paraclausithyron, a suicide, poetic justice dealt by a falling statue of Eros, and a concluding couplet of wittily phrased, generally applicable wisdom (modelled on Moschus fr. 2.8; compare [Theoc.] 23.3 with Moschus fr. 2.5). See F. O. Copley, *TAPA* 71 (1940) 52–61.

singing beneath a tree at some hot noon-hour,[26] we should compare Theoc. 7.39–41 and 91–3, where Simichidas confesses his inferiority to two real poets, Sicelidas (Asclepiades) and Philetas, and claims that his fame "has reached the throne of Zeus" (Ptolemy?) – in short, briefly portrays himself as just such a poet as Theocritus himself was. Another possibility is that fr. 8 comes from a poem like Theoc. 16, a meditation on the poet's own art addressed to his patrons or audience and represented as issuing from his own mouth[27] (though in these gloomy, reflective lines there is little incentive for potential patrons).

The poetic theory implicit in fr. 8 is unlike that in frr. 3, 9, and 10, which toy with the conventions of poetic inspiration and choice in ways that prefigure the *recusationes* of Romans of the next century.[28] In fr. 8 the typically Hellenistic ideal of poetry as labour is subjected to another Hellenistic trope, the diatribe, with its characteristic excoriation of the vanity of human effort. Bion's soliloquy aims the clichés of the diatribe at the hoary motif of poetic κῦδος, calling into question that Archaic ideal in its Hellenistic form of hard-won renown. Unlike other diatribes, where a speaker tries to alter the lifestyle of his fellow mortals by acerbic criticism and ridicule, Bion's is part of an internal dialogue, implicitly directed at the speaker himself (such self-scrutiny is also very Hellenistic). And whereas poetic diatribes are usually found couched in forms amenable to this type of public harangue – e.g. invective, satire, or philosophical exposition (see commentary on fr. 8.8–14) – Bion's reflexive diatribe enriches his meditation on poetry by expanding it to larger, more conventional preoccupations.

[26] A close parallel is the crisis of a later herdsman–poet, the "uncouth swain" of Milton's *Lycidas* (64–70).

[27] Hermann suggests that fr. 6 comes from such a poem.

[28] On the revision of Callimachean doctrine that lies behind Bion's treatment (as behind the Romans') see commentary on fr. 10.12–13.

Of frr. 1, 2, 11, 13, and 16 none, in my opinion, is likely to come from the same poem as any other. If one were in the habit of reconstructing whole works from fragments one could posit five idylls of Bion that could be called, after their apparent subjects, Ὑάκινθος, Νομεῖς, Κῶμος, Ἰξευτής, and Κύκλωψ; at the very least we can be sure that our Bionean fragments represent at least five different poems. The remaining twelve could come from any of the irreducible five or from different poems. Thus several (as discussed above) might belong to the Cyclops idyll; frr. 9 and 10 might represent the different explanations of conversing herdsmen as to why each sings only of love; the lovelorn speaker of fr. 11 might adduce in his suit the *exempla* listed in fr. 12; fr. 7 might prompt fr. 5 (or vice versa). Theoretically we could have, with the *Adonis*, evidence for as many as eighteen poems of Bion of Smyrna.

Bionean bucolic is characterized by the felicitous expression of common ideas tinged with an idealized rusticity. Its tone is usually delicate (of the fragments only fr. 1, on the death of Hyacinthus, prepares us for the torridity of the *Epitaph on Adonis*), but for subjects and tropes it ranges wide, and we can trace a wide range of influences on Bion. The epigrammatic wit popular in his time pervades his poetry, as it did that of Moschus before him. We can trace at a distance the influence of Hellenistic philosophy in fr. 17, in Myrson's homely creed in fr. 2, and in the diatribal elements throughout fr. 8.[29] Since Knaack's 1897 article (*RE* 3.481–2; cf. Fantuzzi (1985) 142) it has been held that Bion laboured mightily under the influence of Nicander of Colophon, on account of certain myths handled by both poets (see on fr. 1, *Ad.* 66). To my mind the evidence for

[29] If Bion wrote a poem on Orpheus, as has been suspected (see section IV below), it might have reflected current Orphic doctrines. Eratosthenes' poetry provided a precedent for philosophic treatment of mythology (see Solmsen).

Bion's response to Nicander is inconclusive; much more palpable are his responses to e.g. Choerilus of Samos (in fr. 4), Callimachus, Moschus, Theocritus, and Homer. He can confront these poets, offering reworkings of them to readers whose literary memories were suffused with them, and still produce something distinctive, and strong enough to attract and influence later poets (see section VIII below).

III BION ΑΔΩΝΙΑΖΩΝ

Bion's major surviving poem is not directly attributed to him before Joachim Camerarius in 1530 (see p. 78 below), but the attribution is virtually beyond question. In metre and dialect it is a late bucolic poem very similar to Bion's fragments, whose attribution is direct (stylistic discrepancies between the fragments and the *Adonis* are explicable by their different themes and narrative purposes). The author of [Moschus] 3, the *Epitaph on Bion*, treats this poem as if it were by his subject (see commentary on the title). Although we may never be certain, it is henceforward assumed that the poem is Bion's.

The *Epitaph on Adonis* is an evocation of the Adonia, the ritual mourning for Adonis, and presents a typically Hellenistic mixture of mimetic and diegetic narration.[30] The best-known specimens of this mixture are Callimachus *H.* 2, 5, and 6, wherein the poet conjures up the whole scene – the dancers, the celebrants, the ritual objects, whatever is proper to the day – in the persona of a festival leader giving orders and issuing summons in preparation for a local religious ceremony. Callimachus seems to capture in hexameter hymns the liveliness and immediacy of the festival odes of the great age of Greek lyric: compare for

[30] I use the terms developed by M. A. Harder, *CQ* n.s. 42 (1992) 384–94 for Callimachus' hymns.

instance his appeal to the reader οὐχ ὁράᾳς; (*H.* 2.4) with ἦ οὐχ ὁρῇς; in Alcman's first partheneion (*PMG* 1.50). But whereas the Archaic or Classical poets, Alcman or Sappho or Pindar, when writing for such an occasion do not always feel compelled to mention the circumstances as they occur (the dancers and rituals being obvious to anyone who heard the words), the Alexandrian poet includes everything, always conscious that his words will for most hearers be entirely separate from the event that occasioned them.[31] Text and referent are tightly identified. The urgency of the moment is there even for us.

Bion goes a step farther, leapfrogging the constructed world referenced by Callimachus' mimetic hymns and making the referent of the festival itself the subject of his poem. His speaker does not direct her[32] calls and instructions to participants in the rites, but to the goddess herself, as if present at the original event that the yearly celebration commemorates.[33] The first line makes the narrator – and every reader of the poem – a mourner of Adonis; the second line places the mourner not in the real world of the annual lamentation, but in the mythical world where Adonis has died:

αἰάζω τὸν Ἄδωνιν, "ἀπώλετο καλὸς Ἄδωνις".
"ὤλετο καλὸς Ἄδωνις", ἐπαιάζουσιν Ἔρωτες

(then come instructions to the goddess). All the elements of the festival are in place, but with the deities themselves

[31] "Die Wahrnehmung wird betont, gerade weil sie (grob gesagt) nicht da ist" (Friedländer 36). Cf. Albert 47–8 and the articles by C. Calame and M. Depew in M. A. Harder *et al.*, edd., *Callimachus* (Hellenistica Groningana 1, Groningen 1993). P. Bing, *The Well-Read Muse* (Göttingen 1988) discusses the Hellenistic understanding of poetry as a written medium.

[32] The sex of the narrator is indeterminate, but since women performed the ritual lamentation one thinks immediately of a woman.

[33] Similarly, Theoc. 18 apparently contains a hexameter version of a ritual re-enactment of Helen's marriage song, aetiologically set on

instead of women lamenting a supine figurine. We are *there*, not just at the Adonia, but witnesses to the very death of Adonis and the grief of Aphrodite. The repeated cries of mourning are being cried out for the first time now; the familiar epithets καλός and ἁβρός are being applied to Adonis for the first time. Bion sets out to envision on the basis of the yearly festival what the original event must have been like, and his narration becomes an interpretation of the rite and its tacit aetiology. We must expect every detail in the story Bion tells to foreshadow a detail of the Adonia, and we must see behind the mood of the poem a like mood of the festival – at least as experienced by the poet who put it into words – and a desire to explain and interpret it.

Detached from its performative context, the Callimachean mimetic hymn gains new compass for artistic development; freed even further from the spatial and chronological facts of the rites, which he transforms into myth-telling, our poet races through the scenery that each suggestion conjures up. Where Callimachus carves out a kind of τέμενος in space and time, Bion's imagery is kinetic and cinematic. Scenes loom before us and then dissolve bewilderingly. In lines 3–4 "wird das Bett Aphrodites hingezaubert, ohne daß das Wort λέκτρον fällt" (Friedländer 36); in 68 a few deft touches place the goddess amid the impenetrable brambles of the mountainside; a line or two later she is back in the divine bedchamber. The scene described in lines 7–14, beginning with the static κεῖται, is strikingly ecphrastic, and at first it seems that we are getting

the mythical scene. Fantuzzi's subtle and suggestive argument (*Lingua e stile* 15.3 (1980) 433–50; cf. Fantuzzi (1985) 152–65) that the *Adonis* represents a secondary stage in the Hellenistic contamination of genres (a mixture of Callimachean mimetic hymn with the traditional dirge) may entail too reductive a concept of genre. The dirge-like elements in the *Adonis* are better accounted for as proceeding from the particular nature of the Adonia.

a play-by-play account of the whole situation: the goddess has done as she was bidden and has come in mourning garb to the place where Adonis lies breathing his last. From line 19 on, however, she is running to find him as if 7–14 had never happened; we are out of chronological order, with the futile kiss in 13–14 looking forward to the longed-for kiss in Aphrodite's central speech. It appears that 7–14 briefly describe the whole scene – Adonis' condition, Aphrodite's anguish, the kiss she is losing – and then lines 16–62 go through it all again in more detail.[34] The jumbled details of the laying-out (lines 70–85) show the same impressionistic style of narration. The whole effect is dreamlike, or as if the narrator were seeing the events take place confusedly as in a crystal ball.

Our evidence for the ritual lament for Adonis is scanty and confused. The cult of the beautiful dying youth, beloved of the goddess of love, originated as a seventh-century B.C. Greek adaptation of the yearly lamentation for the Mesopotamian god Tammuz (the Sumerian Dumuzi), adopted by Greek women from women of Syro-Palestine (as his Western Semitic name shows: see commentary on *Ad.* 1) who had come to practise the summer Tammuz-lament privately along with the late winter and spring festivals of the dying gods of their own cities (e.g. Melqart in Tyre, Eshmun in Sidon).[35] In Greece the divine grandeur of Tammuz and his connexion with the agricultural cycles of the community were lost: all that is left is the women's lament. Our earliest Greek testimony are the Adonis-songs of Sappho, of which remain frr. 140A L–P κατθνα⟨ί⟩σκει, Κυθέρη', ἅβρος Ἄδωνις· τί κε θεῖμεν; | καττύπτεσθε, κόραι,

[34] The alternative interpretation, that 40–62 look back to 13–14 (Albert 91), makes Aphrodite's race through the forest an aimless expression of grief after she has found and kissed Adonis (13–14) rather than a search for his body, which is how later writers seem to have interpreted it (see citations on *Ad.* 20 and 66).

[35] Burkert (1979) 105–8.

καὶ κατερείκεσθε κίθωνας and 168 ὦ τὸν Ἄδωνιν.[36] Our evidence comes mainly from Athens of the fifth and fourth centuries B.C., where the Adonia were celebrated at home with a combination of lamentation and merriment, exclusively by women and outside of state sponsorship and supervision.[37]

What complicates the picture is that once Adonis was naturalized, Greek-speakers used his name and that of his rites for a variety of similar non-Greek mythological figures and the ritual laments associated with them.[38] The male Ἀδωνιασταί celebrating τὴν πομπὴν τῶν Ἀδωνίων κατὰ τὰ πάτρια in the Piraeus in the late fourth century B.C. were Cypriot expatriates of Phoenician extraction.[39] The famous Adonia at Byblos, described by Lucian *Dea Syr.* 6–7, were an ancient Phoenician rite, only nominally Greek,[40] in which the entire city took part. The Ptolemaic Adonia described in Theoc. 15, although sharing many details with the Attic festival, are likely to be quite syncretistic; the *Inswasserwerfen* of the effigy of Adonis in line 133 (see Schol. *ad loc.*) is taken from that of Osiris in native

36 Cf. Dioscor. *A.P.* 7.407.7–8, Paus. 9.29.8. The bit of Aeolic verse that ends Sappho's eponymous stanza came to be called the Adonean after its part in her Adonis-odes. On their performance see J. Herington, *Poetry into Drama* (Berkeley 1985) 56–7; West (1992) 339–40; A. Lardinois, *TAPA* 124 (1994) 65–6.

37 A good account of the Attic Adonia is still needed; for now see Atallah 98–104, 211–55; J. J. Winkler, *The Constraints of Desire* (New York 1990) 188–209; Reed (1995). M. Detienne, *Les jardins d'Adonis* ([Paris] 1972), widely referred to, is highly suggestive but too selective and idiosyncratic to be reliable.

38 Cf. Will 94: "Adonis a quitté, en effet, et à une date relativement ancienne, ses terres ancestrales pour conquérir le monde grec et, au moment de la grande expansion de l'hellénisme, il connaîtra de nouveaux voyages."

39 *IG* II[2] 1261 = *SIG*[4] 1098 and *IG* II[2] 1290.

40 Since at least the early third century B.C., when Clitarchus *FGrH* 137 F 3 places a Greek version of Adonis' birth (that of Panyassis fr. 22A *EGF*) in Byblos. Cf. Lycophr. 831–3.

Egyptian cult.[41] St Jerome on Ezech. 8.14 should sound a warning: "quem nos Adonidem interpretati sumus et hebraeus et syrus sermo Thamuz vocat" (25.82 Migne). Since it is unacceptable (though often done) to assume diachronic and cross-cultural uniformity in the myths and rituals connected with the name of Adonis, we must beware of adducing just any testimony as evidence for the Attic festival, or conversely of assuming that the women of Classical Athens represent universal practice. When our information on the Adonia is uncorroborated by clearly Attic sources, we should remember the chronological and geographic diversity of Adonis.

Bion's poem, in fact, presents several details traceable to ritual but not to any known Attic rite. The exclamations "Adonis is dead" and "Cease from your mourning" may have Near Eastern parallels, as noted in the commentary on *Ad.* 1 and 98. The narrative itself – the mourning goddess searches through the wilderness for the deceased, finds the body and delivers a lament over it, then brings it back to her palace for the lying in state – follows a pattern evident over thousands of years in sacred texts aetiologizing the lamentation for Near Eastern gods like Sumerian Dumuzi (= Akkadian Tammuz), Egyptian Osiris, and Ugaritic Ba'al.[42] In each case (thus perhaps in Bion's poem

[41] Cf. Plut. *De Is.* 356C. Dioscor. *A.P.* 5.53.4 and 193.4 are also evidence for this practice in the Ptolemaic Adonia.

[42] Dumuzi: T. Jacobsen in H. Goedicke and J. J. M. Roberts, edd., *Unity and Diversity* (Baltimore 1975) 67; *id.*, *The Treasures of Darkness* (New Haven 1975) 63–7; B. Alster in K. Hecker and W. Sommerfeld, edd., *Keilschriftliche Literaturen* (Berlin 1986) 19–31; C. Penglase, *Greek Myths and Mesopotamia* (London 1994) 130–6 (comparing Demeter's search for Persephone). Osiris: Plut. *De Is.* 357A–358B (perhaps reflecting the ritual at Byblos); cf. the Egyptian accounts of Isis' search for Osiris cited by Griffiths 315. Ba'al of Ugarit: *ANET*[3] 139; N. H. Walls, *The Goddess Anat in Ugaritic Myth* (Atlanta 1992) 67–74. No version contains all the elements I cite; the Ugaritic version is closest to Bion's Adonis myth. Aphrodite's search for the (dead) Adonis is also

as well) the legend reflects the ritual mourning and laying-out of the effigy in the temple of the goddess. The marriage of the goddess and her lamented consort, which is mourned in *Ad.* 87–90, was ritualized for Isis and Osiris, for the divine pair at Byblos, and for Mesopotamian Dumuzi/Tammuz. The famous cult at Byblos may also have inspired the "last kiss" motif in *Ad.* 12–14 and 44–50: the nearby village of Aphaca, where stood the sanctuary of the goddess and the reputed tomb of her beloved, was known as the spot where she embraced him for the last time.[43]

Although Bion, concentrating on recreating the myth, is not as interested as Callimachus in local or antiquarian particulars, it seems that the *Epitaph on Adonis* reflects one of the great civic cults of the Near Eastern dying gods, and may have been commissioned and composed with a Hellenistic version of such a festival (like that hosted by Arsinoë in Theoc. 15) in mind. Seventeenth- and eighteenth-century commentators envisioned a pageant, a re-enactment of the myth, interpreted poetically for a festival audience[44]; Wilamowitz (1900) 10–16 sees only "die Fiction des Festes", with the poet himself, garbed in the traditional raiment of the rhapsode, mounting the podium before a theatre audience and evoking for them the rich scenes of

found in Prop. 2.13.53–6 (with echoes of Bion), Ptolemy Chennus ap. Photius *Bibl.* 152B, St Cyril *Comm. Is.* 2.3 (see on *Ad.* 19, 53), John of Gaza *Anacr.* 6 (Bergk 347–8), and in a rhetorical fable found in many versions (see on *Ad.* 66).

[43] *Et. magn.* s.v. Ἄφακα, characteristically using the Greek names Aphrodite and Adonis (but the Semitic word-play on *ʿpq* "embrace" and *ʾpq* "Aphaca" suggests a local tradition). See E. Lipiński, *Orientalia Lovaniensia periodica* 2 (1971) 14. Bion's Aphrodite leads into her wish for a last kiss with the plea μεῖνον Ἄδωνι ... ὥς σε περιπτύξω (*Ad.* 43–4).

[44] E.g. Longepierre on line 97: "On peut entendre ici par le mot de *Venus*, la Déesse même, ou celle qui dans ces fêtes joüoit son personnage."

death and lamentation in their mythological setting. We know so little about the festival of Adonis, and especially about his public, state-sponsored Hellenistic festivals, that one cannot be sure; the freedom Bion shows in subordinating ritual detail to diegetic concerns may reflect a purely literary project.[45] Comparison with Theoc. 15.100–44 – explicitly a mimetic hexameter representation of an Adonis-hymn – might be misleading. Bion's poem is in no way a hymn; hymnal elements (e.g. encomium of Adonis or Aphrodite), although implicit, do not govern the poem rhetorically, nor is anything requested of the deity addressed. Bion uses that Theocritean Adonis-song (a hymeneal, not a lament) only as a springboard to the real Theocritean influence behind his poem, the lament for Daphnis in Theoc. 1[46]: the precedent of Theoc. 15 allows our poet to lift Adonis into the spotlight from his two lines in Daphnis' speech (Theoc. 1.109–10), while the lament from Theoc. 1 re-forms the Adonis-song from Theoc. 15 as a dirge. A better parallel is suggested by Sappho's mimetic Adonis-song – or better, Adonis-drama – in fr. 140A (quoted above), where the speakers *are* Aphrodite and other female mourners (nymphs?). If more of that composition were available we could better judge whether Bion took his inspiration from the Aeolic poet or even conceived of his work as a hexameter adaptation of what she had done in lyric; but a common tradition of festival recitation may

[45] That Bion emphatically rejects the resurrection that was celebrated in some Near Eastern dying-god cults and syncretistic Adonis cults (see commentary on *Ad.* 53, 96, 98) may suggest an extra-cultic destination for his poem; but the poet may be polemically promoting one "true" cult myth in which Adonis does not come back to life (cf. the religious polemic in Callim. *H.* 1.6–11).

[46] Verbal echoes of it abound (cf. on e.g. 18 and 19) and its motifs reappear in the later poem: the lamentation of nature, the pageant of mourning deities, the attempt to bring back the deceased (Theoc. 1.138–40 ~ *Ad.* 94–5). See Porro.

lie behind both Greek poems. Bion's treatment of the myth is both typically Hellenistic and as old as the Near Eastern ritual texts that it imitates.

The originality of Bion's treatment of the myth of Adonis lies more in his metalepsis of ritual than in the story itself; as parallels listed in the commentary make clear, Bion mainly follows a standard version (see e.g. on 7, 91, 96). Any part of the myth of Adonis that does not bear directly on the festival is omitted (e.g. Adonis' birth from the myrrh tree, known from Panyassis fr. 22A *EGF* and elsewhere) or alluded to in passing (the death while hunting in 7–8 and 61, the rivalry between Aphrodite and Persephone in 54 and 96, Adonis' parentage in 91). One does not need to know much to understand the story as Bion relates it: only that Aphrodite loves Adonis, and now he is dead.[47] The narrative breaks into "three broad panels" (Estevez 37): the announcement to Aphrodite and her search for the body of Adonis (1–39); her speech over the corpse, culminating in the miraculous growth of flowers (40–67); and the funeral preparations (68–96). These scenes are disposed symmetrically, using ring-composition and chiasmus; the technique is typically Hellenistic, discernible in miniature epics and other short stretches of narrative from the time of Callimachus into the Roman period.[48] More interesting than the rough tripartite division of the poem into scenes is its chiastic structure (see commentary on lines 68 and 79), framed by the parallel exhortations to Aphrodite in 3–5 and 97–8, which articulates the dynamics of the narrative: the movement from

[47] Although this manner of narration, unadorned by recondite facts and other examples of erudition, may seem atypical of Hellenistic story-telling, it is the style of e.g. the miniature epics Moschus 2 (*Europa*) and [Moschus] 4 (*Megara*); cf. Campbell (1991) 7–9.

[48] See Bulloch 47–8 on Callim. *H.* 5; Schmiel 262–6 on Moschus' *Europa*; Courtney (1985) 92–9 on Catullus and his Hellenistic predecessors.

the palace to the wilderness and back, from mourning to cessation of mourning.[49]

Also typically Hellenistic is Bion's narratological method, tied to his choice of subject matter. The ritual lament for Adonis was a festival of *women*; it is noteworthy that two of Callimachus' three mimetic hymns, the fifth and sixth, evoke women's festivals (and remember the Adonia in Theoc. 15, attended and explicated by the two female protagonists). The focus on lamentation, too, especially in lines 41–61, recalls the important role of Greek women in delivering the formal lament at funerals.[50] It is typically Hellenistic to construct a female viewpoint through which to tell a story: other examples are Theoc. 2, [Moschus] 4, even Theoc. 24 (and cf. the great popularity of Erinna's *Distaff*).[51] This fact is to be connected to a persistent interest in matters outside the realm of the male citizenry – not always a systematic or scientific interest, to be sure, but a sympathetic fascination on the part of Hellenistic Greek men with their opposites. Note the studies of the poor or the socially marginal in e.g. Theocritus and Herodas, and in Hellenistic art the interest in the low, the exotic, and the grotesque: such portrayals could have given urban Greek-speaking males living in the new world created by Alexander the opportunity to define themselves – thoughtfully or fancifully, explicitly or unconsciously – against what they were not, through the creation of an *alter ego*. Highly suggestive in this regard is Bion's frequent assimilation of Aphrodite to Adonis (see commentary on *Ad.* 25),

[49] This grand chiastic structure is prefigured in miniature by the chiasmus in lines 1–2.

[50] See esp. the study of Alexiou, and more recently G. Holst-Warhaft, *Dangerous Voices: Women's laments and Greek literature* (London 1992). Note, however, the blend of literary motifs in Aphrodite's lament (cf. commentary on *Ad.* 42–61).

[51] Cf. A. W. Bulloch, *MH* 41 (1984) 228 on Callim. *H.* 5: "Callimachus has induced us into imagining ourselves to be Argive women."

connected with his "Stabat Mater" treatment of the goddess: she provides a focus for our sympathy that the inert boy cannot accommodate.[52] The *Epitaph on Adonis* is narrated entirely from a woman's viewpoint. Our attention first shifts explicitly from Adonis to Aphrodite in line 17, but the events of the poem are described constantly from her point of view.

At the centre of this treatment is a tension between the sexes, whose normal roles seem reversed: the powerless boy, deprived of voice and sense (cf. lines 10, 14, 96), is torn between two mighty goddesses, one of whom holds him in indissoluble bondage while the other controls our view of the scene. It is a commonplace in scholarship on Adonis to regard him as a figurative antithesis of what a Greek man should be: his death by the boar epitomizes failed hunting, his position as the kept boy of Aphrodite deprives him of traditional male virtues, and so on.[53] To this theory let it be objected immediately that no extant version of the myth clearly suggests treatment of Adonis as contemptible, or as anything but a brave young hunter who met a tragic end. Greek men, appropriating in art and literature the dying youth annually lamented by their wives, could indeed have disparaged him as the antithesis of what they themselves should *be*, but seem more often to have assimilated him to what they *wanted*: an idealized παιδικά, as in the painting and sculpture that give him the smooth muscular body, the beardless profile, and the flowing hair of the perfect ephebe, what Kenneth Dover has

[52] Cf. Estevez 37 on Aphrodite's lament: "This is not to say that we ever lose sight of her young lover's suffering or that sympathy for the goddess ever displaces sympathy for him, but we grieve for her at this point as much as we grieve for the dying youth." On the "Stabat Mater" motif see T. Gould, *The Ancient Quarrel Between Poetry and Philosophy* (Princeton 1990) 68, 292.

[53] See e.g. S. Ribichini, *Adonis: Aspetti "orientali" di un mito greco* (Rome 1981), Fantuzzi (1985) 98–9.

termed a "pin-up".[54] Bion seems to sentimentalize and idealize – not disparage – Adonis' fair skin, his ἁβροσύνη, and his position as Aphrodite's younger and subordinate beloved (see esp. on lines 7–8, 10, 18, 79); herein he follows a style of objectifying beautiful young men that stems from Archaic poets to the aristocracy like Ibycus and Anacreon. We are made to see Adonis through the eyes of his lover: any study of Bion's Adonis must consider this narratological fact and its significance given the sexual and artistic data of Bion's culture.

IV POEMS POSSIBLY BY BION

Hints of Bion's lost work may be discerned in [Moschus] 3, the anonymous lament for Bion, where in addition to numerous verbal imitations of the *Adonis* (and so perhaps of lost poems) we find fanciful descriptions of Bion as a cowherd and in other roles from his own poetry, which becomes autobiography in retrospect. In 65–6 "kisses of boys and maidens" are equated to δῶρα τὰ Μοισᾶν; this must refer to the amatory content of much of Bion's poetry. Lines 80–4, listing the matter of Bion's song, include pastoral subjects like Pan, the making of a panpipe (perhaps a reference to the poem that contained fr. 5), and the milking of a cow, as well as more on Bion's amorous bent: "he taught the kisses of boys" (i.e. was an authority on them), "cherished Eros in his bosom",[55] and "provoked Aphrodite" (see van Groningen 299; H. J. Rose, *The Eclogues*

[54] Dover *GH* 6. For such depictions see *LIMC* 1.2 s.v. Adonis. Cf. I. Wehgartner, *JDAI* 102 (1987) 185–97; Reed (1995) 342–4.

[55] [Moschus] 3.83–4 καὶ τὸν Ἔρωτα | ἔτρεφεν ἐν κόλποισιν. This may refer specifically to fr. 10, in which the speaker undertakes to teach Eros music, but is more likely a poetic reference to Bion's general preoccupation with amatory themes. Cf. Mel. *A.P.* 5.214.1 and 12.132.9–10 for the phrase τρέφειν Ἔρωτα.

of Vergil (Berkeley 1942) 13–14). These hints broadly corroborate the impression of Bion's work that we have obtained from inspection of his fragments.

[Moschus] 3.58–63, which make Bion more loved by Galatea than the Cyclops (alluding to fr. 16),[56] parallel 67–9, where the dead Bion's kiss is more welcome to Aphrodite than that of the dead Adonis. Following similar comparisons of Bion to Orpheus in [Moschus] 3.17–18 and 117–26, some have suspected a poem on Orpheus and Eurydice (Skutsch 59–60; G. Knaack, *Hermes* 40 (1905) 336–40; cf. commentary on fr. 6.2); to judge from the putative allusions by Pseudo-Moschus, it would have included Orpheus' performance before Persephone and the recovery of Eurydice, and perhaps a lament by the swans of the river Strymon (as Skutsch 59 deduces from the corrupt passage [Moschus] 3.14–16).[57] Since the *Epitaph on Bion* uses many phrases and even half-lines from the *Adonis*, it doubtless contains unidentifiable verbal echoes from Bion's lost poems. Lines 60–3 τὸν μὲν ἔφευγεν | ἁ καλὰ Γαλάτεια, σὲ δ' ἅδιον ἔβλεπεν ἅλμας, | καὶ νῦν λασαμένα τῶ κύματος ἐν ψαμάθοισιν | ἕζετ' ἐρημαίαισι seem an especially likely place to look for words adapted

56 Galatea is said to tend Bion's cows. Holland (pp. 270–1) is sure that Bion is here depicted in the role of Acis (the cowherd who rivalled Polyphemus for the love of Galatea and whom Polyphemus murdered, known to us from Ovid *Met.* 13.750–897 as part of this story), and that Bion's lost poem thus included Galatea weeping for the dead Acis as she weeps for Bion here. The fancies of Pseudo-Moschus, however, can perhaps be explained by his personification of Bion as a cowherd; his having "delighted" her (58) need mean no more than that he was so fine a singer that he pleased everyone (as he did the nightingales and swallows in line 46).

57 It is of some interest that C. M. Bowra, *CQ* n.s. 2 (1952) 113–26 sought to reconstruct a Hellenistic Greek poem on Orpheus from which Virgil and Ovid (both frequent borrowers from Bion) will have drawn; it will have included a lament by nature and Orpheus' persuasion of Persephone (pp. 116–17), both alluded to by [Moschus]. Cf. J. Heath, *TAPA* 124 (1994) 189–90.

from those of Bion's own Cyclops (e.g. λασαμένα τῶ κύματος ἐν ψαμάθοισιν | ἕζεο). With [Moschus] 3.120 Σικελικόν τι λίγαινε καὶ ἁδύ τι βουκολιάζευ (urging the dead Bion to sing to Persephone, like Orpheus) compare [Bion] 2.1 Σικελὸν μέλος ἁδὺ λιγαίνειν: both may be adapting a phrase from Bion.[58]

Fr. 1, four lines on the frantic efforts of Apollo to revive the dead Hyacinthus, suggests that Bion wrote in the bucolic form another mythological poem like his *Epitaph on Adonis*. That the description is not given purely to illustrate a generalization (in fact the generalization in line 4 is added in service of the description) implies that Bion's story of Apollo and Hyacinth formed not just a passing reference, but the subject of a poem of some note. Ovid's conjoined imitations of fr. 1.3–4 and *Ad.* 53 in his tale of Hyacinth (*Met.* 10.189, 202–3) at least suggest that the two Bionean poems were similar, and that our poet wrote at least two poems concerning the grief of deities who lost their mortal favourites to death.[59] Apollo's reactions to the stricken boy are much like Aphrodite's to Adonis (*Ad.* 40–2), down to the verbal repetitions that seem to evoke a sense of panicked urgency. If there are allusions to this poem in [Moschus] 3.6 νῦν ὑάκινθε λάλει τὰ σὰ γράμματα and 26 σεῖο, Βίων, ἔκλαυσε ταχὺν μόρον αὐτὸς Ἀπόλλων,[60] Bion must have described Apollo's lamentation and the miraculous growth of the hyacinth flower: Aphrodite's lamentation over Adonis and the miraculous growth of flowers in *Ad.* 42–61 and 64–6 are alluded to in exactly the same manner in [Moschus] 3.68–9 and 5. The ritual background of the myth of Hyacinthus could have

[58] In extant bucolic the verb λιγαίνω is confined to these two passages and [Moschus] 3.81.

[59] Cf. Nonnus *D.* 11.241–2 (~Bion fr. 1.2–3) and 325–7 (~*Ad.* 53) in the lament over Ampelus.

[60] Skutsch 58.

suggested the same mimetic–diegetic treatment that Bion gives to Adonis.

Certain idylls transmitted anonymously in the bucolic corpus have been attributed to Bion. Ursinus (1568) gave Bion the *Epithalamius of Achilles and Deidameia*, now known as [Bion] 2. Metrical technique, dialect, vocabulary, and amatory content are consistent with Bionean authorship; the speakers' names, Myrson and Lycidas, are found in Bion's poetry (frr. 2.1 and 9.10). But the structure (an epic narrative within a pastoral dialogue) and the rhetorical style of the poem are quite different from those of Bion's extant work. The tale of Lycidas in lines 10–32 breaks readily into segments of five or six lines: the origin of the Trojan war, the transvestism of Achilles on Scyros, the love for Deidameia that belied his womanly attire, his disingenuous proposition that they sleep together (at this point the poem breaks off in our manuscripts). Each theme is exploited for a few rhetorical turns, then dropped. Bion's manner is more organic and carefully wrought: he allows each idea to build on the one before it, and keeps a single theme in view throughout a passage (cf. e.g. fr. 9; on this feature of Bion's style cf. section VII.4 below). He is never so baldly rhetorical. The author of the *Epithalamius* has more in common, in this respect, with Moschus or the author of the *Epitaph on Bion*.

Of other anonymous late bucolic idylls, allusions to the *Adonis* in [Theoc.] 20 and 23 suggest authorship by followers of Bion rather than by Bion himself (see section VIII below).[61] [Theoc.] 19 has been compared in section II above to Bion fr. 13; it may argue for Bionean authorship that their similarities lie not merely in such overt features

[61] [Theoc.] 23 was first explicitly attributed to Theocritus by Demetrius Triclinius in the early fourteenth century (as its attribution in R shows), [Theoc.] 19, 20, and 27 in MSS or early printed editions around 1500.

as phrasing or plot motifs, but in the creation and handling of like situations (cf. above on Bion's similar treatments of Apollo's crisis in fr. 1 and Aphrodite's in the *Adonis*). Valckenaer, followed by Hermann and Meineke, positively identified [Theoc.] 19 as Bion's. Gallavotti gave him [Theoc.] 27 (the *Oaristys*), a pastoral poem in which a youth rapes a maiden. Its outstanding feature is that it is told in stichomythia, with a few lines of narration at the end (the beginning, which is lost, may have initiated the frame); although the device recalls the alternating singing contest in Theoc. 5 and much bucolic dialogue in general, it derives formally from drama and should be connected to the generic hybridization of [Bion] 2.[62] There are verbal similarities between [Theoc.] 27 and [Bion] 2,[63] and if we could clarify the direction of imitation we might get closer to either poem's relationship to Bion; but much more work needs to be done on the ways late bucolic poems respond to each other and to Theocritus (and other predecessors) before we can speculate with any confidence on their interrelationships, let alone their authorships.

C. Gallavotti, *RFIC* 69 (1941) 233–58 attaches Bion's name to the hexameter fragment in P. Rainer 29801 = Heitsch 17 (late third century A.D.; printed on pp. 168–9 of Gow's Oxford text of the bucolics), a jocular conversation in epic dialect between Silenus and Pan and Pan's crafting of a syrinx; he cites the high literary quality of the piece (including the refined hexameter style cultivated by Bion, among others) and extant hints that Bion wrote a poem on

[62] The evidence for dating [Theoc.] 27 "well inside the Christian era" (Gow *Theoc.* II.485) amounts to a prosodic solecism in 55 (see Molinos Tejada 201) and a use of the opt. in 25 that seems unparalleled until Nonnus.

[63] [Theoc.] 27.1 τὰν πινυτὰν Ἑλέναν Πάρις ἥρπασε βουκόλος ἄλλος ~ [Bion] 2.10 ἅρπασε τὰν Ἑλέναν ποθ' ὁ βωκόλος; [Theoc.] 27.68 φώριος εὐνή ~ [Bion] 2.6 λάθριον εὐνάν (cf. Nonnus *D.* 45.257). That the allusion to Helen and Paris is more at home in [Bion] 2 is not necessarily relevant.

the same subject, especially [Moschus] 3.80 Πᾶνα δ' ἔμελπε (like any bucolic poet: cf. Theoc. 1.3, 16, 123–30; Moschus fr. 2) and 82 καὶ σύριγγας ἔτευχε. The latter allusion may rather point – if it refers to a specific poem at all, and not just to a typical activity of the characters of bucolic – to Bion fr. 5. Gallavotti (*art. cit.*, pp. 253–4) toys with deriving fr. 5 and the papyrus from a single poem, emending the Doric of the fragment to match the Ionic of the papyrus, but concludes that fr. 5 is probably not part of the papyrus poem, since Stobaeus apparently excerpts only from Bion's βουκολικά, not from Ionic poems. This may in fact not be a problem, in view of the looseness with which ancient critics used the term "bucolic". A poet working in Bion's tradition, however, would be unlikely to write a poem on Pan except in Doric. A story about the rustic gods, amusingly plying the crafts typical of rustics, would have drawn our poet to the same formal attributes (including dialect) as the mythological vignettes in Moschus frr. 2 and 3, not to mention the more typical pastoral dialogues.

The Rainer poem illuminates the distinction between what we have termed pastoral and bucolic: the first is a theme, found in many types of literature and art; the second is a poetic tradition marked by certain formal features but flexible as to mood and content. The author of Pan and the syrinx borrows pastoral motifs from bucolic (the names, including Daphnis, in A 14–15; echoes of Theocritus), but like e.g. Longus and Nonnus embeds them in a different form. Bion would probably have wished to connect this story formally with his Doric works, and with the formally bucolic tradition.

V DIALECT

Bion's modern editors have made him both more and less Doric: more, by steadily Doricizing the epic forms that they have believed crept into his text through fifteen centuries of scribal inattention, and less, by steadily (at least since the nineteenth century) banishing the "hyperdorisms" like φίλαμα for φίλημα that they have deemed unworthy of their poet's erudition. In deciding between two MS readings, or between the MS reading and a modern conjecture, the touchstone must always be Bion's own poetry (and one must remember that his dialect may have varied from poem to poem, as did Theocritus') and more generally the other works of late bucolic. No safe criterion, since all of late bucolic has come to us in a linguistically confused condition; still, some conclusions can be reached. Bion's language is basically that of epic, flavoured by a version of the Doric that Theocritus used for the idylls that inspired bucolic.[64] Theocritus' dialect was an artful mixture of Doricisms – taken from various local and literary dialects[65] – and Doricized epicisms, contrasting sharply and, in his time, fashionably with his heroic verse-form (as did his rustic and quotidian subject-matter). Later bucolic poets, less interested in that contrast, use a stylized, conventionalized version of this Doric – more a generic marker than an artistic tool. Their dialect may be compared with the even lighter conventional Doric employed in the choral passages of Attic tragedy or in some Hellenistic epigrams. The differences between the late bucolic dialect and that of common epic usually do not go deeper than differences in pronunciation (reflected e.g. in long alpha for Ionic eta) and a few stock vocabulary items. The ultimate choice be-

[64] On the Doric of Theocritus see Gow *Theoc.* I pp. lxxii–lxxx, Dover *Theoc.* pp. xxvii–xlv, Fabiano (who deals with more general questions of diction and style), Molinos Tejada.

[65] Features of bucolic dialect that are neither Doric nor Homeric, though they may have been current in particular local varieties of Doric, can usually be traced to the conventional literary Doric of lyric poets like Alcman and Pindar, or to analogy; see commentary on e.g. frr. 3.1 Μοίσας, 6.2 κρέσσονα, 9.5 μελίσδῃ; *Ad.* 53 ἐμμί, 84 φορέοισιν.

tween bucolic and epic may well have been made by criteria as whimsical and irrevocable as the poet's ear at the moment of composition,[66] but in the hope (no more than that) that Bion was consistent in his dialect and in the belief that non-epic forms are at least marginally more likely to suffer corruption than their more familiar epic equivalents, I have accepted the following Theocritean elements that bear on the emendation of Bion's text:

Long alpha for Attic/Ionic eta. This is the commonest feature of the most unambitiously Doric poetry, and especially since the MSS show it in most instances I have seen fit to restore it everywhere: frr. 2.6; 4.1; 9.7; 10.2; 13.5, 9; 14.4; 16.2; *Ad.* 25, 33, 35, 56, 58, 59, 60, 64, 66, 82, 92, 97.[67] In *Ad.* 61 ἐμήναο, however, eta seems to follow late bucolic convention: cf. [Theoc.] 20.34; Moschus frr. 1.5, 2.2.

Doric -ω for -ου in 2nd decl. gen. sing. There is MS evidence at frr. 8.4 and 12, 9.2, 12.2 (twice) and 6, 13.15, 16.4; *Ad.* 11, 91. Thus -ω at 2.1, 5.2, 12.5, and 17.1 is probably right. Note also -ω- from compensatory lengthening in fr. 13.1 κῶρος, *Ad.* 96 Κώρα; thus probably fr. 8.1 μῶνα (cf. Theoc. 2.64, 18.8; [Theoc.] 20.45), *Ad.* 34 ὤρεσι (cf. 7, 32).

Doric -ως for -ους in 2nd decl. masc. acc. pl. MS evidence at frr. 2.14, 8.10, 13.5 and 8; *Ad.* 36, 81; thus probably in frr. 10.11, 12.5; *Ad.* 20.

Doric -μες for -μεν in 1st pers. pl. verbs. MS evidence in frr. 2.3, 8.10 and 12; thus probably in 7.1, 8.14.

Doric -οντι for -ουσι in 3rd pers. pl. verbs where nu movable is not required to avoid hiatus. MS evidence at frr. 8.2, 9.2 and 4 (twice) and 6; *Ad.* 32, 34, 91. Thus probably also at *Ad.* 22 and 33. The

[66] On the possible role of euphony in choosing dialect see Dover *Theoc.* p. xxxv, who cites e.g. the papyrus reading Theoc. 2.10 νῦν δέ μιν, where the epicism may be explained by dissimilation of consonants. That the euphony there (if such it is) could have motivated the copyist just as well as the author reminds us of the treacherousness of our task.

[67] Often a discreet eta appears in R over a Doric or pseudo-Doric alpha: 31 ἁ μορφά, 45–6 φίλασον (twice), 46 and 49 φίλαμα, 58 τριπόθατε, 86 αὐτὰν τάν, 93 Διώνα. These should be considered glosses (by Triclinius) rather than corrections: cf. R's superscript eta over 76 ἄνθεα, clearly a gloss. See commentary on 59 χήρα. They are mostly ignored by R's apographa.

standard form appears at *Ad.* 2, 15, 28, 62, 86 (ἐπαιάζουσιν Ἔρωτες) and 19, 80, 95, but note the appearance of Aeolic -οισιν at 84 and 94, perhaps an experiment.[68]

Aeolic -οισα for -ουσα in feminine participles. Cf. commentary on fr. 3.1, but note that the papyrus evidence for Theocritus shows a displacement of -ουσα by -οισα with time (Molinos Tejada 158–62). For Bion, MS evidence at fr. 10.2, *Ad.* 92; thus probably fr. 9.11 and *Ad.* 23. Notice *Ad.* 24 βοόωσα, an epic form perhaps used for special effect.[69]

Doric forms of whole words like νιν for epic μιν (thus emendation at frr. 10.9, 13.14; *Ad.* 14, 25, 77, 80, 95, 96; μιν in fact predominates in Bion's transmission,[70] but νιν would have been especially vulnerable to corruption) and τῆνος for κεῖνος (cf. frr. 9.4 and 6, 11.5, 14.7, 16.2; *Ad.* 11, 76; thus emendation is due in *Ad.* 18). I have accepted less compelling Doricisms in fr. 2.4 ὄκα, in view of τόκα in line 12 (but not Brunck's ὄκα in *Ad.* 30, for lack of evidence in that poem), and fr. 10.5 ἀπῆνθεν. Brunck, a great Doricizer, prints ἐνθ- for ἐλθ- also at frr. 2.2, 8.8, 13.14 and 16; also ἐμίν for ἐμοί wherever prosody allows: frr. 2.15, 8.2, 9.11, 10.3 and 10, 11.4. Wachsmuth conjectures τρώματα at fr. 1.4 (see commentary). The rarity or absence of these forms in late bucolic, however, suggests that they are exotica and should not be restored without MS authority (even MS authority may not be good enough: how do we know that ἀπῆνθεν in fr. 10.5 is not the work of a learned copyist?). Aeolic ἐμμί in *Ad.* 53 (see commentary *ad loc.*) suggests its restoration in line 56. Note the isolated form αἰές in fr. 4.1.

The unparalleled Doric or pseudo-Doric καθιξεῖ in fr. 13.16 (see commentary *ad loc.*) would seem to require the perispomenon accentuation of the Doric contract future, but I have shrunk from printing (with Brunck) frr. 13.13 ἐσσῆ (cf. Theoc. 10.5 for the form), 16.4 ἀπολειψῶ, *Ad.* 12 ἀποισεῖ (cf. Theoc. 3.11, 15.133), 49 φυλαξῶ (cf. Theoc.

[68] Ahrens restores -οισιν for -ουσιν and many other Aeolic forms throughout the *Adonis*, imagining influence from Sappho (see Ahrens (1854) 43–7).

[69] On such effects see Dover *Theoc.* pp. xxxv–xxxvi. For another place where a literary reminiscence or allusion might impede restoration of a bucolic form see fr. 13.11 n.

[70] The MSS have νιν at frr. 13.9, 14.6; *Ad.* 21, 72.

1.63), since Bion's intentions in a time when written accents were an optional aid for readers must remain unclear.

I have also accepted literary Doricisms that substitute long alpha for eta where etymology does not justify doing so, but that seem to have become traditional in the conventional poetic Doric used by the later bucolic poets. Fantuzzi (on *Ad.* 12, n. 121) rightly objects to the editorial principle that permits such forms in the anonymous works of the bucolic corpus but corrects them in poems whose authorship we know. φίλαμα and aor. ἐφίλασα are unambiguously attested in Moschus, Bion,[71] [Moschus] 3, [Bion] 2, and [Theoc.] 20 and 23 (cf. Molinos Tejada 40–1, 45–6). I have also accepted τριπόθατος (emended by Ahrens to -ητος) in fr. 2.15 and *Ad.* 58, since although the form reappears only in [Moschus] 3.51 (a likely echo of Bion) it is very probably formed on the analogy of words from φιλέω (note the semantic connexion). On fr. 14.1 ἅμερε see the commentary. I have rejected, however, transmitted forms like frr. 12.2 Θασεύς, 13.3 ἐνόασε (cf. *Ad.* 40 ἐνόησεν), and *Ad.* 26 στάθεα (cf. 5 στήθεα) that appear only here.[72]

It is not obvious why the *Adonis*, which does not deal with herdsmen or any other conventional theme of bucolic, was cast in the same dialect as Bion's fragments. Is its Doric meant to recall the Archaic festival odes (like those of Alcman and Pindar) that it approaches in other ways? Does the poem specifically evoke an Adonis festival in a Doric-speaking community? Unlikely: what is most relevant is that the *Epitaph on Adonis* is written not exactly in Doric, but in the dialect of late bucolic, which serves to

[71] For the record, the following editors have restored the standard form: *Ad.* 12 φίλημα Ald.[1], 13 φίλημα Morel, 14 θνᾴσκοντ' ἐφίλησεν Meineke, 45–6 φίλησον (twice) Ahrens, 46 φίλημα Paris. gr. 2812A post corr., 49 φίλημα Ahrens.

[72] At *Ad.* 88 δοίμαν (for δ' ὑμήν) suggested δ' ὑμάν to its fifteenth-century editors.

affiliate the poem to a certain tradition (the same may be said of its metre; see section VI below). Formally – generically – this is a bucolic poem. Why Bion wished to place mimetic mythological narrative in this tradition is another question, related to his stance toward his precursors. The question may be only superficially answered by appeals to "generic experimentation" or "mixture"; more pertinent is the new place within his tradition that a poet stands to win when the expectations raised by formal features are defeated by the subject matter of his poem.

VI METRE AND PROSODY

Bion's work survives in 214 hexameters (two of them incomplete), enough to permit general observations about his metrical style, if not firm conclusions. A cursory look at his metre will reveal a cultivation of the refined hexameter technique associated especially with Callimachus (see esp. Hollis *Hec.* 15–23, West *GM* 152–7). The metre and prosody of Theocritus' bucolic poetry are in many respects closer to Homeric than to Callimachean practice, and effect an expectation-defeating contrast between venerable verse-form and unheroic subject-matter; as in many respects, later Greek bucolic diminishes this contrast. The Callimachean hexameter was a model for late bucolic,[73] as for later Hellenistic poetry in general, and in the following survey I compare Bion's practice with other late bucolic authors; again, it is important to remember the small size of our sample, but the metrical consistency of late bucolic is high.

[73] As demarcated in section II above, this category comprehends (in addition to Bion) Moschus I and his three hexameter fragments; [Theoc.] 19, 20, 23, 27; [Moschus] 3; [Bion] 2. Together these productions amount to 404 full hexameters; with Bion, 616.

I. DACTYLS AND SPONDEES. Of a possible thirty-two combinations of dactyls and spondees Bion's fragments use only thirteen, the *Adonis* only twelve (even fewer than the twenty used in Callimachus' *Hymns*). The preferred patterns show a predominance of dactyls: 85 percent of his lines (90 percent in the *Adonis*) begin with the five patterns DDDD, DDDS, DSDD, SDDD, or SDDS.[74] Bion's extant work presents six lines (2.8 percent) with spondaic fifth feet (frr. 13.1, 14.3; *Ad.* 18, 25, 27, 34); each ends with a tetrasyllabic word (cf. commentary on fr. 14.3) and each begins with either DDDD (fr. 14.3, *Ad.* 25 and 27) or SDDD (fr. 13.1, *Ad.* 18 and 34), with spondees absent before the bucolic caesura (always present) or as far as possible from line-end. Each such σπονδειάζων has a feminine third-foot caesura (Callimachus' σπονδειάζοντες are more likely than other line-patterns to have masculine caesura: Hollis *Hec.* 18–19). The only other such line in surviving late bucolic is [Theoc.] 27.29 ὠδίνειν τρομέω· χαλεπὸν βέλος Εἰλειθυίης, with the same norms, except for its masculine caesura.

Bion's high dactylicity is a product of the Callimachean tradition (Theocritus contracts more bicipitia than Homer, especially in his bucolic poems: West *GM* 154[75]), but here he goes further than Callimachus himself. Bion's marked avoidance of spondees was first observed by Buecheler (1875) 34: "quemadmodum vero a disciplina Bionis facilis progressus fuit ad severiores Nonni leges, ita a Callimacho Bionem hac re maxime distare video, quod qua ille plerumque, eadem hic semper moderatione tardiorum pedum usum restrinxit". The resulting fluidity of the Bionean line has excited the attention of many readers. Fantuzzi often refers to Bion's "scorrevolezza", and the admiration of

[74] Fantuzzi (1995) 255 notes Bion's tendency to restrict vowel-contractions to the necessarily spondaic sixth foot (e.g. fr. 13.12 ἔρχευ, with φείδεο at line-opening).

[75] Cf. Fantuzzi (1995) 251–2, who especially cites *Id.* 1, 2, 4, and 5, noting the higher dactylicity of *Id.* 3 and 7.

John Addington Symonds is almost dithyrambic: "The verse bounds with tiger leaps, its full-breathed dactyls panting with the energy of rapid flight" (II.274).

Bion's preferences, in fact, are those of all late bucolic. No late bucolic poem or fragment uses more than thirteen metrical patterns, and apart from the seven σπονδειάζοντες (representing two patterns) only fourteen are represented in all the late bucolic corpus. These patterns favour dactyls: few lines have three spondees before the last foot[76]; none has four.

2. PRINCIPAL CAESURAS. The bucolic caesura – word-end after resolved fourth biceps – occurs in about 70 percent of Bion's lines (63 percent in Callimachus: West *GM* 154), with no great difference between the fragments and the *Adonis*. As in Callimachus, there is always a caesura in the third foot (the main caesura); feminine in 66.4 percent of his lines in the fragments, 80 percent in the *Adonis* (74 percent in Callimachus: West *GM* 153). 88 percent of lines with masculine third-foot caesura also have bucolic caesura (cf. Callimachus' 90 percent: Hollis *Hec.* 19); of the exceptions (frr. 2.14; 3.1, 2; 8.10; 12.2, 6) all but fr. 12.2 have word-end after the fourth princeps (a requirement for Callimachus: Maas *GM* §93) and all but frr. 12.2 and 3.1 follow the masculine caesura with a resolved third biceps (the proper name in 12.2 may account for both irregularities there).[77]

Bion's rate of bucolic caesura is in roughly the same range as that of Moschus (74.1 percent), [Theoc.] 19 (87.5 percent), [Theoc.] 20 (84.4 percent), [Theoc.] 23 (66.7 percent), [Theoc.] 27 (71.2 percent), [Moschus] 3 (78.6

[76] Bion fr. 8.9, *Ad.* 74; [Bion] 2.4, 27; [Moschus] 3.49, 74, 123 (doubtful); [Theoc.] 23.17, 18; 27.37, 60, 62. None in [Theoc.] 19, 20, or Moschus' bucolic poetry.

[77] Elsewhere in late bucolic these norms are violated at [Moschus] 3.75 and 121 and frequently in [Theoc.] 27.

percent), and [Bion] 2 (83.9 percent). Here late bucolic practice coincides with that of Theocritus in his bucolic idylls (74 percent: cited by West *GM* 154 from C. Kunst, *De Theocriti versu heroico* (Diss. phil. Vindob. 1, Vienna 1887), excluding the non-pastoral *Id.* 2, 14, 15). The rate of feminine third-foot caesura in Bion's fragments, 66.4 percent, is in the same range as in Moschus (63 percent),[78] [Theoc.] 19 (62.5 percent), [Theoc.] 20 (62.2 percent), [Theoc.] 23 (69.8 percent), [Theoc.] 27 (58.9 percent), [Moschus] 3 (62.7 percent), and [Bion] 2 (61.3 percent). Contrast Theocritus' 50–2 percent in the bucolic poems (West *GM* 153). Again, the departure from the Theocritean model reflects the steady growth of Callimachean influence over the Greek hexameter.[79]

3. OTHER WORD-DIVISIONS. Since the 1942 paper of O'Neill it has been recognized that to a remarkable degree hexameter poets restricted words of certain metrical types to certain positions in the line, and that this development of the pre-Homeric oral tradition was adhered to by Hellenistic poets, reaching a zenith of regularity in Callimachus' 97.34 percent (O'Neill 117). Bion's localization of the elements of the epic vocabulary follows convention 92.7 percent of the time in the fragments and 93.6 percent of the time in the *Adonis*, about the same as the 92.91 percent that O'Neill calculates for Theocritus. One should not place too much weight on the figures for Bion, since the remnants of his *oeuvre* come nowhere near the one thousand lines recommended by O'Neill 107 as the "minimal reliable basis" for such statistics, but the phenomenon

[78] Actually, 79.3 percent in Moschus 1, only 50.3 percent in the three fragments (which is about the average of Bion frr. 8 and 13, amounting to about the same number of lines).

[79] [Theoc.] 9, seemingly composed in imitation of Theocritus but before Moschus, still shows only 52.8 percent feminine third-foot caesuras as well as a laxer, rougher prosody.

helps explain Bion's constant echoes of earlier composers in the epic metre. That nearly every word of his can be found in the same metrical position in the works of his predecessors[80] betrays a thorough immersion in them as well as a mastery of hexameter technique.

This technique can be traced in Bion's adherence to Callimachean rules for word-division. Naeke's law (prohibiting word-break after a contracted fourth biceps) is violated only by non-lexical words (especially καί) closely connected in sense to what follows,[81] as is Hermann's bridge (prohibiting word-break after fourth trochee). Hilberg's law (prohibiting word-break after a spondaic second foot) is violated at frr. 9.9, 10.1, and 17.2, each time with a monosyllabic enclitic or postpositive in second biceps (as sometimes allowed by Callimachus; cf. Hollis *Hec.* 20). Giseke's law (which prohibits a word beginning before the second foot from ending with the second foot) is violated once (*Ad.* 62 ὧδ' ὀλοφύρατο). At *Ad.* 46 Bion violates a tendency against allowing a single word to begin after the fourth princeps and end with the fifth (the violation in fr. 8.13 ὅτι θνατοί is mitigated by weak word division); cf. Hollis *Hec.* 21, West *GM* 155.

Our poet does not observe Callimachean strictures concerning the trochaic division of the second foot, one of the most sensitive spots in the Greek hexameter because of its immediate proximity to the main caesura (Wifstrand 68). Wifstrand observes that Callimachus has only thirty instances of a trochaic word in the second foot before feminine third-foot caesura; he finds mitigating circumstances for each case (weak word division or strong sense-break after the first biceps "wodurch die Zäsur im 2. biceps geschwächt wird"). Bion does this all the time[82]: there are

[80] Fantuzzi offers copious parallels in his commentary on the *Adonis*.
[81] On *Ad.* 70 see commentary.
[82] Fantuzzi (1985) 149 notices examples in the *Adonis*.

23 examples in his mere 214 surviving lines, of which 10 may be excused for the reasons Wifstrand cites (for example, καλὸς Ἄδωνις in *Ad.* 2 etc. cohere closely enough to avoid the sense of a break). Others are palliated by a syntactic division at the main caesura, either punctuated (as in *Ad.* 60) or not (as in *Ad.* 14, where two syntactic units – main clause and dependent clause – fall neatly on either side of the caesura). This still leaves frr. 10.10, 13.10, *Ad.* 8 and 93. Meyer's first law, prohibiting a word beginning before the second foot from ending with the second trochee, is broken only twice by Callimachus (Hollis *Hec.* 19–20, West *GM* 155); Bion offers eight examples, which a stricter application of criteria reduces to *Ad.* 83 (conceivably also the corrupt fr. 6.2; frr. 9.5 and 10.13 are of a type permitted by Callimachus: Hollis *Hec.* 138). Bion similarly plays havoc with Meyer's second law (prohibiting iambic-shaped words before masculine third-foot caesura), breaking it at frr. 2.7, 14, 16, 17; 8.1; 13.9, 14; and *Ad.* 82. This law is often termed weak (West *GM* 155; Hollis *Hec.* 20: "[T]here are enough ... exceptions to make this 'rule' no more than a general preference"), but in its stricter formulation – prohibiting a trochee-shaped word in the second foot before masculine third-foot caesura – the rule is quite binding. Wifstrand 65–6, citing as mitigating circumstances a close connexion between the two words before the caesura and a strong sense-break after it, can find only one violation in all of Callimachus (*Ep.* 23.3 = *A.P.* 7.471.3, beginning ἄξιον οὐδὲν ἰδών). Even when we have excused, among Bion's examples, frr. 2.16 and 17, 13.9 and 14, and *Ad.* 82 as involving weak word division or strong sense-pause at the caesura, we are left with frr. 2.7 and 14, 8.1.

In his fragments Bion shows about the same rate of adherence to Callimachean norms as other bucolic poets of his time. Note the violations of Naeke's law in [Theoc.] 27.60 and 64; of Hilberg's law in [Theoc.] 20.44; of Giseke's law in [Theoc.] 23.58. There is a slight violation of Hermann's bridge at [Bion] 2.28. A word beginning after the fourth princeps ends with the fifth at Moschus 1.12 and fr. 2.3, [Theoc.] 23.43. Word-break at the second trochee occurs at [Theoc.] 23.37; 27.27 and 33; [Moschus] 3.6, 106, 109 (doubtful); [Bion] 2.12 (with allowance, as always, for mitigating conditions: thus Moschus 1.23 βαιὰ λαμπὰς ἐοῖσα τὸν ἅλιον αὔτὸν ἀναίθει is forgiven, since the main caesura divides two syntactic units). Here late bucolic practice is similar to that of Theocritus in certain of his bucolic poems; cf. Fantuzzi (1995) 225–40, who notes Theocritus' inobservance of Meyer's laws (although he does not allow for as many mitigating circumstances as I do).[83]

Bion's only monosyllabic line-end, in fr. 2.7, is preceded by bucolic caesura coinciding with a strong sense-break (as in Callimachus: Hollis *Hec.* 21, West *GM* 156). [Theoc.] 23.13 and 32 and Moschus fr. 1.2 follow the same norms (in Moschus fr. 1.3, ending μ' ἅλς without strong sense-break at the bucolic caesura, elision mitigates the harsh effect).

4. THE MEETING OF VOWELS BETWEEN WORDS. Bion avoids hiatus even more fastidiously than Callimachus (on whom see Hollis *Hec.* 22). More than half of the instances of hiatus in Bion's surviving poetry (frr. 2.9 and 10, 12.5 and 7, 13.7 and 10; *Ad.* 9) are accounted for by a lost digamma long honoured in the epic tradition (Maas *GM* §133, West *GM* 156). Other examples can be excused by tradition (see commentary on *Ad.* 90) or justly emended away (fr. 8.13; *Ad.* 26, 73). The un-Callimachean hiatus at bucolic caesura in fr. 13.4 (see commentary) is paralleled in late bucolic by [Theoc.] 19.5 and [Theoc.] 23.48; perhaps

[83] Fantuzzi includes in his "bucolic" category (based on pastoral content and "tenore") *Id.* 1, 3, 4, 5, 6, and 7, without distinguishing rates of adherence for the individual poems. He notes that the technique of *Id.* 2 is close to this group.

also by [Theoc.] 19.8 and [Bion] 2.11. Bion's are the norms of late bucolic, but unwonted types of hiatus occur in [Theoc.] 23.3, 42 (both doubtful); 27.44 (Ἀκροτίμη ἐσσί, perhaps for Homeric effect).

Bion readily elides indeclinable words; among declinable words he elides με and πάντα (see commentary on fr. 10.13) and the following verbs: frr. 7.1 οἶδα (in a Homeric reminiscence), 8.13 λαθόμεσθα (possibly corrupt); *Ad.* 78 ὤλετο, 82 ἔβαλλε (see commentary). His one elided noun is *Ad.* 59 δώματ' (MS δῶμα); he does not elide adjectives in his extant work (but see commentary on *Ad.* 14). Elsewhere in late bucolic I have noticed the following elisions of nouns, adjectives, and verbs: Moschus fr. 2.4; [Theoc.] 19.3, 20.2 and 18, 23.50 and 59, 27.2, 40, 44, and 48; [Moschus] 3.49, 54, 63, and 123 (perhaps corrupt); [Bion] 2.24 (in Lennep's emendation). Ten of these instances are verbs, three are nouns, one is an adjective ([Theoc.] 27.2 ἑκοῖσ' Ἑλένα). On restriction of elision in Hellenistic hexameters cf. West *GM* 156.

Correption in Bion (excluding correption of non-lexicals like καί and monosyllabic enclitics) is commonest at the bucolic caesura and at the end of the fifth foot (five times each); he also employs it at the end of the first foot (three times) and at the feminine third-foot caesura (twice). He has ten cases with -αι, two with -ει, and one each with long -α, -οι, and -ῳ. These are the norms of late bucolic.

5. PLOSIVE+LIQUID. A liquid following a plosive at word-opening never lengthens the preceding syllable (cases like *Ad.* 90 ἔτι πλέον involve a coherent word-group). The same combination within words or coherent word-groups normally does (in princeps except at *Ad.* 39); there are notable exceptions at frr. 8.4, 13.13 and 14, 16.4, and *Ad.* 98.[84]

[84] This rule does not necessarily apply to the names Κύπρις and Ἀφροδίτη; on Meleager's similar practice cf. D. Page in *Miscellanea di studi alessandrini in memoria di Augusto Rostagni* (Turin 1963) 545.

Fr. 13.9 τέχναν and *Ad.* 43 δύσποτμε, where the nasal does not lengthen the preceding syllable, are interesting exceptions to Bion's norms.[85] These are roughly the norms of late bucolic; in [Theoc.] 27.28 and 50 a final short vowel is lengthened by an initial plosive + liquid.

Related is the phenomenon, common in Homer, of short vowels lengthened before a liquid, nasal, or sigma (cf. West *GM* 15–16). This occasionally occurs in princeps in Hellenistic poetry (cf. West *GM* 156), but is rare in late bucolic: I find instances only in Bion fr. 10.8 (see commentary) and [Theoc.] 27.49, beginning τί ῥέζεις.

It will be observed that although Bion's fragments and his *Epitaph on Adonis* agree in most metrical features (notably in the high proportion of dactyls), the *Adonis* shows a somewhat more refined style. Its dactylicity is indeed somewhat greater than that of the fragments, and its proportion of lines with feminine caesura – 80 percent – is remarkably high, especially compared with the fragments' 66.4 percent. A poem like the *Adonis* may have attracted features of a metrical style more typical of mythological narrative: West *GM* 153, citing Kunst, contrasts the proportion of feminine caesuras in Theocritus' "bucolic" idylls (50–2 percent) to that in the "epyllia" (72 percent). The anomalous concentration of σπονδειάζοντες in *Ad.* 18–34 (Aphrodite's search through the mountain glens) may also find an explanation here, since prominent writers of mythological narrative in the century or two preceding Bion had cultivated this mannerism (e.g. Eratosthenes and Euphorion, perhaps following Antimachus: West *GM* 154). Allowing for the paucity of our evidence and for such differences in subject matter as might influence metrical practice, we may conclude that there is no metrical objec-

[85] Gow's conjecture ἄγρυπνον in Moschus fr. 1.13 would be the only other such instance in late bucolic.

tion to single authorship of the fragments and the *Adonis*.[86] In this regard it is also worth remembering that the fragments differ among themselves in metrical style, and that excerpts from longer poems may represent stretches where a special effect was desired: the third-foot caesuras of fr. 9, for example, are 100 percent feminine, while those of fr. 11 are only 25 percent feminine.

VII SOME ASPECTS OF STYLE

Bion's surviving poetry everywhere evinces a limpid elegance. Without seeking out the learned glosses, obscure allusions, and challenging syntactical complexes that characterize much Hellenistic poetry, our poet maintains an artistry consonant with a sophisticated audience. Bion's is a jewelled style, replete with bold expressions[87] and epigrammatic conceits that give him a veneer of typically Hellenistic preciosity. I have selected a few of his stylistic features for more complete discussion than sporadic mention of them in the commentary will afford.

1. REPETITION AND VARIATION. Poets in general like to repeat words and sounds, but one can discern a specially Hellenistic tradition. Some of Callimachus' examples (cf. Lapp 54–70) provide obvious precedents for Bion's (fr. 11.1–2, *Ad.* 42–3); another influence is earlier bucolic poets

[86] Differences in subject matter also account for the slight differences in vocabulary between the two parts of Bion's *oeuvre*; Matthews (1990) 38–43 makes too much of these. The mutilated state of the fragments also distorts our perception of Bion's style (cf. section VII.3 below).

[87] E.g. fr. 11.2 νυκτὸς ἄγαλμα and especially in the emotionally heightened language of the *Epitaph on Adonis*: 11 ῥόδον, 12 θνᾴσκει καὶ τὸ φίλαμα, 22 ἱερὸν αἷμα δρέπονται, 41 μαραινομένῳ περὶ μηρῷ, 44 χείλεα χείλεσι μείξω, 48 τὸ δέ σευ γλυκὺ φίλτρον ἀμέλξω, 49 ἐκ δὲ πίω τὸν ἔρωτα, 73 τὸν ἱερὸν ὕπνον ἐμόχθει, 78 ὀλλύσθω μύρα πάντα.

(e.g. Moschus: see on *Ad.* 12–13, 51), who adopted repetition of words and sounds along with other of Theocritus' mannerisms as a feature of the genre (on this tradition see Gebauer 35–69; on Theocritus' use of repetition see Dover *Theoc.* xlv-l). A typology of Bion's repetitions would include simple superfluous repetition (as in *Ad.* 16 ἄγριον, 94 Ἄδωνιν), epanalepsis (see on fr. 1.3), anaphora (e.g. frr. 2.12–13, 11.1–2; *Ad.* 40–1, 65–6), and homoeoteleuton (e.g. fr. 3.1–2; *Ad.* 12–13, 95–6). Note the fancy double repetition with epanalepsis and chiasmus in *Ad.* 71 καὶ νέκυς ὢν καλός ἐστι, καλὸς νέκυς, οἷα καθεύδων. In the *Adonis*, words and phrases often occur in the same metrical position two lines in a row (see commentary on *Ad.* 29). Like Theocritus, Bion repeats phrases throughout his poetry in subtler ways: cf. fr. 8, where πολὺ πλείονος in 12 echoes πολὺ πλείονα in 3. His line-openings are sometimes echoed more strikingly than traditional word-placement alone can explain (cf. *Ad.* 4 and 45, 9 and 47, 12 and 58). The similarities between certain lines in the *Adonis* underscore thematic changes (see commentary on 68 and 79).

Like patterns of separation of noun and modifier (see below), patterns of repetition are disposed around certain points in the hexameter: line-opening, the main caesura, the bucolic caesura, and line-end. One element is at line-opening and the other after the bucolic caesura in fr. 1.3 χρῖεν δ' ἀμβροσίᾳ καὶ νέκταρι, χρῖεν ἅπασαν ... (cf. 17.1) and *Ad.* 77 ῥαῖνε δέ νιν Συρίοισιν ἀλείφασι, ῥαῖνε μύροισιν; after bucolic caesura and at the opening of the next line in *Ad.* 43–4 ὥς σε κιχείω, | ὥς σε περιπτύξω and 72–3 τοῖς ἐνίαυεν, | τοῖς μετὰ τεῦς.... Anaphora and homoeoteleuton arrange repetition of words or sounds in the same metrical position in successive lines; cf. e.g. frr. 2.12–13, 3.1–2. *Ad.* 42–3 and 50–1 show a pattern, developed by Hellenistic poets from Homeric practice, wherein "words other than proper names, occurring in the fifth and sixth feet of the hexameter, are repeated at the beginning of the next line" (Williams 705); note that both Bionean examples have close parallels elsewhere in Hellenistic poetry (see commentary *ad locc.*).

This system of breaks in the line also structures half-echoes or variation of noun-case or wording, as in fr. 2.5 ἢ καὶ χεῖμα δύσεργον – ἐπεὶ καὶ χείματι πολλοί ... or *Ad.* 29 ὤλεσε τὸν καλὸν ἄνδρα, συνώλεσεν ἱερὸν εἶδος (cf. frr. 2.17, 3.1, 8.6, 11.3; *Ad.* 6 etc.). Such patterns often break a line into parallel statements: cf. fr. 9.2 ἢκ θυμῷ φιλέοντι καὶ ἐκ ποδὸς αὐτῷ ἕπονται and *Ad.* 24 Ἀσσύριον βοόωσα, πόσιν καὶ παῖδα καλεῦσα (cf. 98).[88] Fr. 15 builds a chiasmus around the bucolic caesura: μορφὰ θηλυτέραισι πέλει καλόν, ἀνέρι δ' ἀλκά. A delayed echo helps bring a passage to a close in *Ad.* 14, where φίλασεν at line-end picks up τὸ φίλαμα, repeated before the main caesura in 12–13 (and note the homoeoteleuton in those two lines).

Elsewhere in late bucolic Moschus, [Bion] 2, and [Theoc.] 23 are especially in accord with Bion's style of repetition: note especially Moschus 1.9–10, 18–19, and fr. 1.1–2; [Bion] 2.6, 21 (chiasmus), 28, and 29; [Theoc.] 23.28–9 and 62–3. Rhythms of repetition and variation pervade [Moschus] 3, probably as much under the influence of Theoc. 1 as of Bion's *Adonis*. The stichomythia of [Theoc.] 27 lends itself to anaphora and other types of localized cross-verse repetition.

In the *Adonis* verbal repetition specially evokes the ritual cries at the Adonia and emulates the sobbing, throbbing atmosphere of mourning. We hear the cries of αἰαῖ, the calling of Adonis' name (cf. esp. 94), the reiterated news that "fair Adonis is dead", often as a quasi-refrain (see commentary on lines 1–2). A haunting lyricism has not escaped the notice of readers; Albin Lesky feels that the

[88] On Theocritus' and Callimachus' disposition of rhetorical cola around the normal breaks in the hexameter, elaborated from Homeric practice, see Conrad 117–29.

Epitaph on Adonis "erreicht mit ihrer lebhaften Bewegung syntaktisch einfacher Kola, mit ihren Klangwirkungen und dem refrainartig wiederholten Klagevers die Wirkung leidenschaftlichen Sanges."[89]

Under this heading a few words may be said about expressiveness and alliteration. These are very much a matter of individual susceptibility (cf. the cautionary remarks of Fehling 78–80), and not every reader will hear in *Ad.* 18–19 the very baying of the hounds and the shrill cries "αἰαῖ!" of the mountain nymphs, or relish the hollow, re-echoed *oh*'s and *ah*'s of the wailing opening of the Adonis poem, broken off by the sudden effusion of frontal vowels and breathy aspirates in line 3. We should remember, however, that euphony – the pleasing arrangement of phonemes – was a focus of critical theorizing since at least the fourth century B.C. (e.g. by Aristoxenus and Theophrastus, perhaps preceded by Licymnius; see Wilkinson 9–10) and was elevated by Crates of Mallos, in the century or half-century before Bion, to the sole criterion of poetic excellence.[90]

2. ENJAMBMENT AND END-STOPPED LINES. Enjambment, the continuation of a syntactical unit beyond line-boundary, a typical feature of narrative (e.g. Homeric) verse, was cultivated and elaborated by Hellenistic poets (on Callimachus' *Hymns* see G. R. McLennan, *Hermes* 102 (1974) 200–6). Bion uses enjambment artfully: note especially how the enjambed figure in *Ad.* 7–8 introduces two more enjambed lines, impelling the reader breathlessly, as it were, through the initial description of the dying Adonis. *Ad.* 88–90 make special use of the device. But Bion is equally a master of the opposite effect, that of end-stopped lines (cf. Wilamowitz (1900) 38–9). This is connected to his

[89] A. Lesky, *Geschichte der griechischen Literatur*² (Bern 1963) 778.

[90] On Crates see E. Asmis, *Phoenix* 46 (1992) 138–69.

preference for verse-medial sense-pauses at the main caesura,[91] and may reflect late Hellenistic taste specifically (Wilamowitz (1900) 39; cf. Wilkinson 194 on Catullus 64, Courtney *FLP* 151 on Cicero, Lyne 23 on *Ciris*). It is common in late bucolic. Coincidence of sense-pause and verse-boundary in Bion can produce a sense of quaintness or naivety, as when combined with anaphora at fr. 2.11–14 (cf. fr. 10.7–8), or of barely restrained emotion, as in *Ad.* 37–9 (cf. fr. 1.1–2). In frr. 3, 9, and 12 end-stopped lines are structured in orderly pairs or parallel patterns; in the first two (and probably fr. 12) a generalization is embellished, then applied to the speaker's own situation. Compare the structure and sentiment of Moschus frr. 1, 2, and 3, of which the last two are especially marked by end-stopped lines.

3. WORD-PATTERNING. Hellenistic poets exploited and elaborated Homeric patterns of separation of a noun and its modifier, disposed around the major caesurae of the hexameter; on this tendency, already pronounced in the early Alexandrians and later carried farther by the "neoterics" and later Latin poets, see Conrad.[92] In such patterns of separation Homeric practice tends to place the noun first, whereas Hellenistic poets (especially Apollonius) tend to place the modifier emphatically first, thus making of these patterns an elegant means of showcasing a description. There is a striking example in a vocative address at *Ad.* 43 (with adj. at line-opening and Ἄδωνι before the main caesura). So in the pattern

—x/——x,

[91] Thus Thomson's punctuation at *Ad.* 24 yields a rhythm more characteristic of Bion than the traditional punctuation.

[92] A revision of his Harvard (1964) doctoral dissertation, which was summarized in *HSCP* 69 (1965) 195–258. On Hellenistic influence on Latin technique see also H. Patzer, *MH* 12 (1955) 77–95; T. E. V. Pearce, *CQ* n.s. 16 (1966) 298–320; D. O. Ross, *Style and Tradition in Catullus* (Harvard 1969) 132–7.

with one element before the main caesura and the other at line-end (known to German-speaking researchers as "Sperrung"), Bion places the modifier first and the noun second (fr. 12.3, 5, 6), as do Theocritus and Apollonius (Conrad 77–8, 95–108).[93] In the pattern

x —/x ——

(with one element at line-opening and the other after the main caesura; cf. *Ad.* 19 and 88) Bion places the noun first, following the more conservative practice of Theocritus (Conrad 113–14). In the pattern

—/-x- — x

(with one element somwhere between main caesura and bucolic caesura and the other at line-end) Bion, like Apollonius and Theocritus, follows Homer in preceding the noun with an unstriking, often traditional epithet (frr. 1.2, 13.2; *Ad.* 9, 82; cf. Conrad 76–7, 111).[94]

Where Bion stands out is in the highly decorated enjambed pattern in *Ad.* 7–8 and in his *clusters* of "Sperrung" in fr. 12.3–6 and of "golden lines" in fr. 11.1–2. The verse-patternings known as the "golden line" involve two nouns and their adjectives framing the hexameter in various collocations, usually with another word intervening. In early Greek the closest example seems to be *Il.* 15.685 ὣς Αἴας ἐπὶ πολλὰ θοάων ἴκρια νηῶν; in the Hellenistic period see e.g. Theoc. 16.62 (cf. 18.29); Callim. *H.* 4.14, 6.9 (with Hopkinson); Ap. Rh. 1.917, 3.1215[95]; Euphor. fr. 86 *CA*. The device becomes extremely popular in Latin poetry

[93] See also Moschus 2.5, 6, 20, 57, 75, 120, 145. We are talking about hexameters here; note that Alexandrian elegists like Hermesianax seem loth not to equip their pentameters with Sperrung.

[94] Also the practice of Moschus 2.1, 4, 28, 42, 45, 46, 100, 111, 121, 160.

[95] Both concentric; but cf. Conrad 84 (citing numerous examples): "Interlocked word-order has become with Apollonius a feature of high epic style."

from the time of Catullus on (F. Caspari, *De ratione, quae inter Vergilium et Lucanum intercedat, quaestiones selectae* (diss. Leipzig 1908) 86–93; Wilkinson 215–17), and in later Greek is favoured especially by Nonnus (Wifstrand 139–40).[96]

These word-patterns are relatively uncommon in Theocritus' bucolic idylls; Bion's prominent use of them in frr. 11 and 12, from poems that were possibly or manifestly about rustic life, thus attests the elevation of bucolic, like his metrical and prosodic refinement and other features of his style. This is true of late bucolic generally. Examples of the first pattern diagrammed above are [Theoc.] 27.67[97] and [Moschus] 3.4, as well as the refrain of [Moschus] 3. The second pattern occurs in Moschus 1.20, [Bion] 2.6 and 19, and [Theoc.] 23.24, which differ from Theocritus and Bion in placing the modifier first, and [Moschus] 3.49 and [Theoc.] 23.32, with noun first. The third pattern is commonest: Moschus fr. 1.7; [Moschus] 3.7; [Theoc.] 19.1, 20.18, and 23.1, 19, 45, 48, 57, and 60, always with the modifier first (often καλός or κακός). There are "golden lines" at [Moschus] 3.9 and [Theoc.] 20.25, and enjambed patterns of separation at [Theoc.] 23.58–9 and [Moschus] 3.62–3, 121–2.

Note also that although Matthews (1990) 42–3 sees the use of "Sperrung" in fr. 12, contrasted with its absence in the *Epitaph on Adonis*, as evidence of stylistic differences between Bion's fragments and the *Adonis*, one cannot generalize about the style of the fragments, which theoretically could represent seventeen different poems. The concentrations of

[96] On the more general phenomenon of verses framed by an adjective and its noun see Conrad 81–2, 111–13 (on Apollonius and Theocritus); Wifstrand 133–9. Cf. Moschus 2.117. Some MSS have an example of this at [Moschus] 3.67 (see commentary on *Ad.* 74 στυγνόν).

[97] This line immediately follows the end of stichomythia and introduces the conclusion of the poem; there are no such patterns in the section of stichomythia.

artistic word-patterns in frr. 11 and 12 have a special effect that Bion may have employed with discretion.[98]

4. EXPOSITORY STRUCTURE. Here I want to point to a particular rhythm, partly dependent on repetition, that sometimes characterizes Bion's development of ideas. Take fr. 3:

> Μοίσας Ἔρως καλέοι, Μοῖσαι τὸν Ἔρωτα φέροιεν.
> μολπὰν ταὶ Μοῖσαί μοι ἀεὶ ποθέοντι διδοῖεν,
> τὰν γλυκερὰν μολπάν, τᾶς φάρμακον ἅδιον οὐδέν.

The motion is curiously spiral: each return to a word (Μοῖσαι, μολπάν) is a launching-place to the next idea, until the culminating point is reached. One feels the same whirling, drilling movement in fr. 1, where three independent clauses (the third one longest) lead progressively to the point, and in fr. 16, where two participial phrases dependent on the main verb βασεῦμαι in line 1 lead to Galatea, mention of whom in turn leads to the Cyclops' formulation of his feelings. In the *Adonis* we can see it in context in Aphrodite's lament (especially 42–53), where each formulation of her grief and frantic desire leads to another as she gropes toward final expression, only to move on to another series.[99] A rewarding technique: the requisite variations evolve without allowing the poetry to stagnate, and the rush of expression never breaks free from the character's thought.

Herein we can see both Bion's debt to his tradition (bucolic and more largely Hellenistic) and his originality. One finds something of the same rhythm in Moschus, perhaps Bion's model in this regard as in much else. Compare Moschus 1.18–19

[98] Literary parallels suggest that these two fragments could come from the same poem; cf. the introduction to fr. 12.

[99] Note that this movement occurs in passages dealing with anxiety produced by love, either unrequited love or love frustrated by death.

τόξον ἔχει μάλα βαιόν, ὑπὲρ τόξῳ δὲ βέλεμνον.
τυτθὸν μὲν τὸ βέλεμνον, ἐς αἰθέρα δ' ἄχρι φορεῖται

with *Ad.* 45–6

ἔγρεο τυτθόν, Ἄδωνι, τὸ δ' αὖ πύματόν με φίλασον·
τοσσοῦτόν με φίλασον ὅσον ζώῃ τὸ φίλαμα . . .

The rhythm in both is the same; words and ideas are echoed in the same way and in the same places. But in contrast with the Moschan passage, which simply piles conceit upon conceit, Bion's *goes somewhere,* with each idea building upon the one before to further Aphrodite's thought. Again, compare Aphrodite's whole speech (*Ad.* 42–61) with Europa's in Moschus 2.135–45, which is largely a catalogue of witticisms arising from the singular occasion of a girl's being carried across the sea on a bull's back. The rhetorical turns and points in Aphrodite's speech serve a larger purpose than the immediate needs of their lines: they push the lament forward by introducing new themes that are then developed. Recall the "organic" style by which we distinguished Bion from the poet of the *Epithalamius of Achilles* in section IV above. This forward-moving repetition of ideas should be identified as a form of epanalepsis (cf. commentary on fr. 1.3): Bion's master-trope endows what could have been plodding passages with emotional tension and satisfying resolution. If Bion got his expository technique from a rhetorical style prevalent in late Hellenistic poetry (one might invoke the epigrammatism that pervades much poetry of this period, including his own), he seems to have developed it for his purposes, and in his hands the wit of late bucolic acquires a special motion.

5. THE TONE OF THE *ADONIS*. Here I mean a less tangible, less quantifiable impression made by our author's style (and thus harder to trace in literature), but one much remarked on. By the later eighteenth century the admiration for Bion's *préciosité* expressed by Longepierre (p. 9

above) gives way to the impatience of the Rev. Richard Polwhele, who discovers amidst the beauties of Bion's poem "indications of a vicious taste", indeed, "the most unpardonable of all poetic errors": "Allured by the richness of ornamented imagery, the poet too frequently overlooks the simplicity of nature."[100] By the later nineteenth century readers were identifying the poem's artificiality with an insincere emotionalism. Gilbert Murray expresses what many seem to have felt: "The *Dirge* is a magnificent piece of work in its way; florid, unreal, monotonous, almost oriental in its passionate and extravagant imagery, it exactly suits the subject for which it was composed. There is very likely no genuine emotion whatever at the back of it; but it carries the imagination by storm, and was calculated to leave such persons as Gorgo and Praxinoa [the protagonists of Theoc. 15 who hear the Adonis-song at the palace of the Ptolemies] in floods of tears."[101] J. W. Mackail is more harsh: "The Adonis-dirge is so uninspired that it suggests something produced by machinery."[102] These critics are reacting to what they see as an un-Greek monotony and extravagance in the poem: "almost oriental" in Murray's words; Mackail calls Bion "imitative and Asiatic" (p. 235), and some have explained these traits by the proximity of the poet's homeland to the supposedly emotion-loving and less rational cities of the East.[103]

[100] R. Polwhele, *The Idyllia, Epigrams, and Fragments of Theocritus, Bion, and Moschus, with the Elegies of Tyrtaeus* (Exeter 1786) 338. Cf. F. G. Eichhoff, *Etudes grecques sur Virgile* I (Paris 1825) 6: "Bion remplaça la simplicité de son prédécesseur par une afféterie puérile qui dépare ses jolies productions" – exactly the opposite of Longepierre's estimation.

[101] G. Murray, *A History of Ancient Greek Literature* (New York 1897) 385. F. Susemihl, *Geschichte der griechischen Literatur in der Alexandrinerzeit* I (Leipzig 1891) 234 calls the poem "manierirt, schwülstig und voll schillernder Rhetorik."

[102] J. W. Mackail, *Lectures on Greek Poetry* (London 1910) 236.

[103] Cf. Beckby 361, speculating on Oriental influence "der ihm vielleicht

One must hesitate to make such ethnic distinctions, since on the testimony of Aristophanes (*Lys.* 393) an Attic matron could get as worked up over the death of her god as any woman of Babylon or Byblos. The allegation of "extravagant imagery" is also difficult to sustain. Contrast Bion's lines 7–10, the description of the dying Adonis, with the same passage in Harold Acton's adaptation of the poem:

> Low on the hills he lies, the lovely bleeding one,
> His throat aflash with faint stunned strands of light.
> Low on the hills he lies and breathes his life away
> And from his thigh of milk-white azure gashed,
>   Slit by the cruel tusk,
> The ruby blood drips down his skin of snow.
> Beneath his brows stars set in crystal deep
> (Once memories, hungers glinted in their pools),
> Are glazed dim, opaque and lustreless,
> The blue orbs burn no more beneath translucent lids.[104]

This suggests what Murray and Mackail heard and complained of, but poor Bion looks positively dowdy next to Acton's finery. What is plain old "white" to "milk-white azure"? The simple ὑπ' ὀφρύσι δ' ὄμματα ναρκῆ, whose uncommon imagery and provocative phrasing one perhaps thought so splendid when one first read it, has come to Acton by way of Keats and the French Symbolistes, and the effulgence of the resulting four lines quite outshines the original. Where in Bion do we find anything like "his throat aflash with faint stunned strands of light", with its audacious personification of a phenomenon almost impossible to visualize? If you want this kind of thing in Greek, go to Aeschylus or Pindar, not Bion. In some ways his poem is absolutely restrained. Simple declarative statements (e.g. αἰάζω τὸν Ἄδωνιν) do most of the work,

von seiner kleinasiatischen Heimat her eingewurzelt war". John Addington Symonds also refers to the poem's "Asiatic fury", though approvingly (II.274).

104 "Lament for Adonis" in *An Indian Ass* (London 1925) 7–12.

rather than description or simile,[105] and there is a kind of "objectivity" to it all: the narrator gives no explicit clues to how each scene is to be taken, but rather simulates reality in an impressionistic way, telling nothing that could not be perceived by the reader's senses were he actually present. *Epitheta* merely *ornantia* are few on the ground. Except for the lament of Aphrodite, the poem suffuses its emotion not so much through what is said as through calculated repetition, accumulation of modifiers, asyndeton, and other formal devices; otherwise the language shows a kind of restraint more effective than lengthy expression.[106]

Yet Acton's treatment of the poem is in some way only an intensification, in terms of post-Romantic English poetry, of Bion's own mood. Beckby 361–2, comparing Bion's *Adonis* with the torrid gigantomachy on the nearly contemporary altar of Zeus at Pergamum, remarks, "Es zeigt..., daß der Bogen seiner Gefühlswelt weit gespannt war.... Als sicher darf man daher annehmen, daß er mit den glänzenden Mitteln seiner poetischen Kunst die Herzen seiner Zuhörer zu packen und aufzuwühlen verstand...." This poem appeals to all the senses, its "objectivity" only making their experience more immediate: the contrast of white flesh and dark blood, the shrill cries of the mourners, the smooth sheets and the harsh thorn bushes, the alabasters of exotic fragrance emptied over the corpse of Adonis; and it is perhaps Bion's mastery over a world of the senses that entrances some readers, and disturbs those who expect poetry to be more detached. The tone of the *Adonis* is essentially narratological in origin:

105 "Die Ausdrucksweise ist einfach und schmucklos, und verzichtet auf viele Beiwörter" (Mumprecht 40). Fantuzzi (1985) 140 invokes the high ratio of nouns to attributive adjectives in both the *Adonis* and the fragments as evidence of single authorship.

106 From the scholia on the *Iliad* we know that ancient readers were sensitive to emotion expressed through unemotive language (e.g. on 17.300–3; see J. Griffin, *CQ* n.s. 26 (1976) 161–87).

the poem positions the reader behind the eyes of Aphrodite and simply presents the sensations that occur to her.[107] This type of image-based narration should probably be characterized as late Hellenistic: Schmiel 270 finds something similar in Moschus' *Europa*, and it is certainly present in the *Aeneid*, often in passages traceable directly to Bion's *Adonis* (see section VIII below).

VIII BION'S INFLUENCE

At no period between the early first century B.C. and the mid sixth century A.D. (see section IX below) do we miss signs that Bion was being read and admired. What follows is a summarized, chronological survey of Bion's influence, intended to guide the interpreter of the allusions and imitations by later authors cited ubiquitously in the commentaries. In the following I assume that the borrowing of phrases or even whole lines, let alone ideas, from predecessors is a basic tactic of ancient poetics, and that if a line sounds like an imitation of a predecessor's line, it probably is one. To be sure, striking phrases could have passed into common usage; thus e.g. Bion fr. 11.2 νυκτὸς ἄγαλμα, even if originally coined by Bion, does not necessarily attest in its later users (see commentary) knowledge of Bion's poem. But recurrences of inconspicuous phrasing – of words that do not stand out for sense or style, though distinctive enough to recall a predecessor – should be regarded as conscious or unconscious echoes (e.g. Maximus 284–5 Ludwich φείδεό μοι χάλυβος, μηδ' ἐς χέρα τῆμος ἵκοιτο | ἀκμὴ ... σιδήρου ~ Bion fr. 13.12 φείδεο τᾶς θήρας, μηδ' ἐς τόδ' ἔτ' ὄρνεον ἔρχευ). In authors who clearly imitate Bion, passages that sound like imitations

[107] Emphasis on the senses highlights the pathos of Adonis' contrasting loss of sight (10), feeling (14), and speech (96).

have a greater chance of being just that; so Nonnus *D.* 29.87 ἄγριον ἕλκος probably echoes Bion *Ad.* 16 ἄγριον ἄγριον ἕλκος, since we know that Nonnus was reading the *Adonis*.

Parallels between Bion and Meleager present a challenge to the literary historian: who whom? Though the possibility exists that Meleager and Bion were contemporaries, Mel. *A.P.* 5.171.3–4 εἴθ' ὑπ' ἐμοῖς νῦν χείλεσι χείλεα θεῖσα | ἀπνευστὶ ψυχὰν τὰν ἐν ἐμοὶ προπίοι is more likely an imitation of Bion than vice versa. Bion *Ad.* 44, ending χείλεα χείλεσι μείξω, is explicable as a revision of Theoc. 12.32 προσμάξῃ γλυκερώτερα χείλεσι χείλη, following a tradition of polyptota with μείγνυμι (see commentary). Meleager combines the kiss-motif with the quaffing of the soul; both motifs arise organically from Aphrodite's speech in *Ad.* 44–9, whereas Meleager unites them for the purpose of epigrammatic decoration, straining his symposiastic theme.[108] Now compare Mel. *A.P.* 5.177.1 κηρύσσω τὸν Ἔρωτα τὸν ἄγριον with Bion fr. 9.1 ταὶ Μοῖσαι τὸν Ἔρωτα τὸν ἄγριον. The common phrasing could be fortuitous, or Bion could be echoing Meleager. But Meleager's epigram is an imitation of Moschus 1, and it would be a nice piece of Meleagrian wit to allude to the more recent bucolic poet while imitating his predecessor.

Archias *A.P.* 5.59.1–2 "φεύγειν δεῖ τὸν Ἔρωτα." κενὸς πόνος· οὐ γὰρ ἀλύξω | πεζὸς ὑπὸ πτηνοῦ πυκνὰ διωκόμενος might well imitate Bion fr. 14.7 ἐς τί δέ νιν πτανὸν καὶ ἑκαβόλον ὤπασας ἦμεν | ὡς μὴ πικρὸν ἐόντα δυναίμεθα τῆνον ἀλύξαι; The idea of no escape from Eros' swift wings is not especially common (see commentary), and the

[108] But the principle that of two similar passages the one that is apter in its context is the original must be applied with great caution; see G. Most in M. Whitby *et al.*, edd., *Homo Viator: Classical Essays for John Bramble* (Bristol 1987) 202–4, comparing Virg. *Aen.* 4.60 and Catull. 66.39 (cf. Bion's treatment of Callimachus in *Ad.* 59).

wording of the two passages is similar. Archias' epigram seems to have been in Meleager's *Garland*, and therefore should predate the 90s B.C. (cf. *GP* II.432–5). It is attractive, though probably idle, to speculate that Antip. Sid. *A.P.* 7.218.11–12, where Eros wails in response to Aphrodite's lamentation over Laïs, was suggested by the antiphonally lamenting Erotes in Bion's *Adonis*. Whether or not these epigrammatists imitate Bion or vice versa bears on on our poet's date; the next useful piece of evidence is Catullus' imitation of [Moschus] 3 (cf. below), but an imitation by Antipater, Meleager, or Archias pushes Bion back before 100 B.C.

In Bion's own field, [Theoc.] 20 shows his influence in the recollection (35–6) that Aphrodite τὸν Ἄδωνιν | ἐν δρυμοῖσι φίλασε καὶ ἐν δρυμοῖσιν ἔκλαυσεν, certainly an allusion to Bion's version of the story (cf. esp. *Ad.* 13–14 – the famous kiss – and 68). Verbal parallels in [Theoc.] 20 may also show Bion's influence.[109] [Theoc.] 23 is egregious for its frequent echoes of the *Adonis* (cf. on *Ad.* 1, 11, 17, 43, 45, 48, 52); lines 2 and 57 echo frr. 14.5 and 1.2. [Bion] 2, the *Epithalamius of Achilles and Deidameia*, recalls Bion in the name Myrson (see on fr. 2.1) and in the metaphor at lines 18–19 τόσον ἄνθος | χιονέαις πόρφυρε παρηίσι (see commentary on *Ad.* 11 and 27).

Our poet's influence is flaunted most conspicuously by the author of [Moschus] 3, the *Epitaph on Bion*.[110] This poem (whose *terminus ante quem* is set by the quasi-translation of

[109] Cf. 19 and 32 ἐμμί (~*Ad.* 53, 56), 21 τὸ πάροιθεν in a context of lost beauty (~*Ad.* 27), 29 πλαγιαύλῳ (~fr. 10.7), 34 μήνατο (~*Ad.* 61), 45 ἀνὰ νύκτα (~*Ad.* 73).

[110] Attributed μόσχου (ἢ add. man. sec.) θεοκρίτου in Vindob. philol. gr. 311 (late fifteenth century: Bühler 2 n. 1); cf. Fritzsche 1. Camerarius in his preface (1530) suspects Moschus to be the poem's author without giving a reason, but Buecheler (1875) 40 disproves the ascription on chronological grounds; see also C. Gallavotti, *BPEC* 16 (1968) 65–9. The most thorough study of the text and transmission of [Moschus] 3 is now Hicks 185–214.

lines 103–4 in Catull. 5.5–6) is a bucolic adaptation of the epicedion form, including praise of the deceased and testimony to the warm personal feelings of the speaker for him (a precedent is Thyrsis' lament for the legendary cowherd Daphnis in Theoc. 1.64–142). Bion himself is imagined to have been a cowherd, and the poem is divided into sections by a refrain – ἄρχετε, Σικελικαί, τῶ πένθεος ἄρχετε, Μοῖσαι – very like those of Thyrsis. This poem's constant borrowings from the *Epitaph on Adonis* and possible allusions to Bion's other poetry (certainly to fr. 16) have been discussed in section IV above. In lines 95–7 the poet calls himself Bion's disciple and heir to Bion's "Doric Muse". In metre, language, style, and content, however, he seems no closer to Bion than to Moschus or to the rest of late bucolic;[111] in his pointed rhetorical style he is especially close to the *Epithalamius of Achilles and Deidameia* (cf. section IV above). When the anonymous eulogist calls himself Bion's heir he is simply reflecting the reputation Bion will have had after his death as the master bucolic poet. Theocritus is mentioned in line 93, but Moschus is nowhere: Bion's achievement has (temporarily) expunged him from literary memory. Any bucolic poet of this time will have considered himself Bion's heir.

Did the author of the *Eclogues* hold our poet in such esteem? I have been unable to detect any Bionean influence on Virgil's bucolics apart from an echo of fr. 2.17 (see commentary *ad loc.*, and on fr. 2.5–6 for some parallels – possibly echoes – in the *Georgics*). With that exception, and with that of the possible imitation of fr. 2.14 in one of the *Priapea*, the Romans do not show knowledge of the fragments until Ovid's echoes of frr. 1.4, 10.4, 11.3, and 12.2–7 in various of his works; but there is no question that they were reading the *Adonis*. I accept Catull. 3, the poem

[111] See Mumprecht 39–43.

on Lesbia's dead sparrow, as influenced by the *Epitaph on Adonis*, first in its appeal to "Veneres Cupidinesque" to lament the deceased (like Bion's Erotes), and especially in lines 13–14 "at vobis male sit, malae tenebrae | Orci, quae omnia bella devoratis", which adapts Aphrodite's complaint to Persephone in *Ad.* 55 that πᾶν καλὸν ἐς σὲ καταρρεῖ (cf. commentary on *Ad.* 1 ὤλετο καλὸς Ἄδωνις). Prop. 2.13.53–6 (see Papanghelis 65–70), Ovid *Met.* 10.720–24, and [Tib.] 3.9.7–8 evoke the Adonis myth in Bionean terms (see commentary on 10, 20, 40–2, and 61); more evidence for the *Adonis* as an authoritative version of the myth may come from the Pompeian wall paintings cited in the commentary on lines 81–5.

The appeal Bion's rhetoric and imagery had for the Romans is especially manifest in Virgil and Ovid, both of whom, for example, use Aphrodite's despair at being immortal (*Ad.* 53) for their similarly frustrated characters. Bion's combination of sensual beauty and violent death seems to have appealed to Virgil, who adapts lines 10–11 for his description of Camilla's death and other passages for his dead youths (see on *Ad.* 40–2, 71, 75, 79, 81–5; the description of Euryalus in *Aen.* 9.433–4 "pulchrosque per artus | it cruor" may take inspiration from *Ad.* 9–10). Ovid in *Am.* 3.9.7–8 "ecce puer Veneris fert eversamque pharetram | et fractos arcus et sine luce facem" ingeniously combines *Ad.* 81–2 with Tib. 2.6.15–16 "acer Amor, fractas utinam tua tela sagittas | si licet, extinctas aspiciamque faces", and must assume in his readers enough knowledge of the *Adonis* to follow the allusion. It looks as if the Adonis poem, already prized by Bion's Greek successors, had been "discovered" by Latin poets by the time of Catullus and thereafter become a standard text for cultivated Romans. I have not found any certain echoes of Bion in Latin after [Tib.] 3.9.7–8; that is, after the early first century A.D.

Throughout the Imperial period the *Epitaph on Adonis*

was familiar to educated Greek speakers. During the first few centuries of our era we can count among its imitators Rufinus (lines 11, 27; perhaps 20), Gregory of Nazianzus (42, 44), and the novelists.[112] A widespread knowledge of the *Adonis* (perhaps as a school text) is suggested by echoes of it in quasi-literary texts like grave inscriptions (see on *Ad.* 71, 97). Line 22 inspired an aetiology of the rose that became popular with Imperial rhetoricians, grammarians, and poets (see on *Ad.* 66). Chief among Bion's late epigones was Nonnus of Panopolis, whose *Dionysiaca* show what an epic poet of a rhetorical bent could do with Bion's imagery. His borrowings are cited everywhere in the commentary (see e.g. on *Ad.* 4, 9, 16, 19, 21, 25–7, 40, 53); notably Bionean are his laments for the dead Ampelus (11.248–350) and Hymnus (15.273–419).[113] Among other imitators of this period and later are the Homeric adaptation of the Book of Psalms ascribed to Apolinarius of Laodicea (perhaps *Ad.* 58 and 89–90; cf. Golega 60) and Colluthus (*Ad.* 24 and 88).

To the Roman period belongs the "anacreontic" poem Εἰς νεκρὸν Ἄδωνιν (Gow OCT 166–7), whose theme and occasional bucolicisms (e.g. 7 ποτανοί, 31 φιλᾶσαι) are atypical of the *Anacreontea* and are taken, along with verbal echoes (see e.g. on *Ad.* 74 and 81–5), from Bion's poem. The poem turns on a novel conceit: brought in chains to Aphrodite by the Erotes, the boar who fatally gored Adonis confesses that he only meant to kiss Adonis' irresistible thigh, and gives himself over to condign punishment.[114] It should be connected with the adaptation of [Theoc.] 19

112 For possible or certain imitations by Achilles Tatius, Longus, and Heliodorus see commentary on lines 11, 39, 47, 49.

113 On Bion and Nonnus see G. D'Ippolito, *Studi Nonniani* (Palermo 1964) 99, 143–4.

114 The poem found favour in the Renaissance, e.g. Shakespeare, *V&A* 1109–10, 1117–18; see F. T. Prince, *The Arden Edition of ... Shakespeare: The Poems* (Harvard 1960) 59.

in *Anacreont.* 35[115]: both are composed of fluent hemiambics, metrically punctilious except for the solecism ὖλαν in Εἰς νεκρὸν Ἄδωνιν 44, but neither shows the preference to accent the penultimate syllable of the line that is already apparent in the late fourth century and becomes obligatory in the sixth.[116]

These writers' evident familiarity with the *Adonis* makes one wonder how it was treated by ancient scholars and critics. If the poem ever had a commentary, no trace of it is left in the bucolic collection that we possess (the interlinear glosses in R are the work of Triclinius or his circle). Hesychius records two forms that seem to appear nowhere else in extant Greek literature: ἀποίσει· ἀπενέγκῃ (cf. *Ad.* 12 ἀποίσει) and ἐξεκέδασεν· ἐξεπέτασεν (cf. *Ad.* 88 ἐξεπέτασσε). The latter gloss fits Bion's usage (the shaking out or undoing of the wedding garlands), and in the former the curious subjunctive of ἀπενέγκῃ could have been prompted by μήποτε in the Bionean context. If these refer to Bion, they must have come from commentaries on him. The information on Bion given by the *Suda* and the Palatine corrector on Moschus 1 (see section 1 above) must have come ultimately from a commentary, though perhaps one on Theocritus.

Although the *Epitaph on Adonis* may well have been posterity's favourite – since most imitated – Bionean poem, we should remember that extant literature may, and probably does, echo lost parts of Bion. It is not true that there is no evidence outside of the anthologists for knowledge of Bion's other work in late antiquity (as is stated or implied by Wilamowitz (1900) 31–2, Fantuzzi (1985) 144,

[115] Wilamowitz *Textg.* 80 thinks that *Anacreont.* 35 is "eine Parallele, keine Imitation" of [Theoc.] 19, which he dates to late antiquity; but in style and substance that short idyll perfectly fits the bucolic poetry of Bion and his followers and surely belongs to their period.

[116] West *GM* 167 and 169; F. Hanssen, *Philologus* Suppl. 5 (1889) 210–14. Cf. Wilamowitz *Textg.* 70–1.

and Matthews (1990) 35, especially with regard to Nonnus).[117] The following authors' imitations of Bion's fragments are to be regarded as certain: one of the authors of the *Apotelesmatica* of [Manetho][118] (see commentary on fr. 2.18; cf. frr. 8.6, 12.5), Longus (frr. 2.5–6; cf. frr. 10.7–8, 13.6), Maximus (fr. 13.12; cf. fr. 12.5), Nonnus (frr. 1.3–4, 10.7–8, 14.6; cf. on fr. 8.5), Pseudo-Apolinarius (fr. 1.2). Other passages in Bion's fragments have clear parallels in Roman-era texts, although it is hard to tell whether the parallels are direct imitations or whether Bion's striking expressions had passed into the common store (cf. on frr. 8.6, 9.9, 11.2).

IX THE TEXTUAL TRANSMISSION

The story of the early transmission of bucolic poetry as a whole, let alone of the dispersal and dissolution of Bion's poetic corpus, has yet to be told.[119] No papyrus of Bion has been recovered.[120] Our first piece of hard evidence is *A.P.* 9.205, an epigram by Artemidorus of Tarsus (early to mid first century B.C.; cf. Cameron (1995) 190) announcing his collection of bucolic poetry: Βουκολικαὶ Μοῖσαι σποράδες ποκά, νῦν δ' ἅμα πᾶσαι | ἐντὶ μιᾶς μάνδρας,

[117] Note that Wilamowitz *Textg.* 106 n. 3 rightly identifies Nonnus *D.* 37.173 στεφανηφόρον ὕδωρ as an imitation of Moschus fr. 3.2–3 = Stob. 4.20.55 ... κοτινηφόρον ὕδωρ, | ἕδνα φέρων καλὰ φύλλα καὶ ἄνθεα ... (both on Alpheus and Arethusa).

[118] The author of books 2, 3, and 6 (in the received numeration), who is of Hadrian's time (see W. Gundel and H. Gundel, *Astrologumena* (Wiesbaden 1966) 159–61). The author(s) of the remaining three books, of much later date, does not seem to borrow from Bion (but cf. on fr. 12.7 and *Ad.* 79 for verbal parallels).

[119] See Gow *Theoc.* I pp. lix–lxii , assessing the opinions of Wilamowitz (*Textg.*).

[120] P. Mil. Vogliano inv. 1102, which contains the left half of fr. 14, has proved a forgery; see C. Gallazzi, *ZPE* 34 (1979) 55–9.

ἐντὶ μιᾶς ἀγέλας (see Gow *Theoc.* I pp. lx–lxi). Artemidorus lived in an age when our author was celebrated by followers of his tradition; depending on what he meant by "bucolic" and "all" he might have included Bion. That Stobaeus takes his excerpts of Moschus and Bion from their "βουκολικά" suggests that their works at one time circulated in collections with that title.

The principal MSS that preserve the *Epitaph on Adonis*, V and R, together with their apographa, comprise a subgroup of the Laurentian family of bucolic MSS[121] that preserves a cluster of eight poems unknown to the rest of the transmission of Greek bucolic, whether on papyrus or in codex: [Theoc.] 20, 21, Moschus I, [Theoc.] 19, the *Adonis*, the anacreontic poem Εἰς νεκρὸν Ἄδωνιν, [Theoc.] 23, and [Bion] 2.[122] The implication is that this group was incorporated from an independent sylloge, whose other contents – if any – might have included the poems whence Bion's fragments were excerpted by anthologists.[123] [Bion] 2 breaks off after the second foot of line 32: no doubt the sylloge originally finished this poem and went on to others. The inclusion of Εἰς νεκρὸν Ἄδωνιν (as a sort of epilogue to the *Epitaph on Adonis*) dates the whole to no earlier than late antiquity, but since six of the other seven are in the late bucolic manner,[124] the ancestor of the collection seems to have been composed when the distinction between late

121 On the three families of bucolic MSS – Ambrosian, Laurentian, and Vatican – see Gallavotti *Theoc.* 243–60; cf. Gow *Theoc.* I p. xxxiii n. 3.

122 In this order. Only X contains all eight (copied from V before V was mutilated); R's stingier offering is due to the selectivity of Triclinius (see below). Moschus I is also transmitted elsewhere (see below).

123 On the existence of this collection see Wilamowitz *Textg.* 69–84, Matthews (1994).

124 [Theoc.] 21 does not cohere closely to late bucolic in metrical style, dialect, or content, but is at least post-Theocritean (Gow *Theoc.* II.369–70).

bucolic and earlier was fresh.[125] The fragmentary poems of Moschus and Bion might have been part of the sylloge, as might [Moschus] 3, which is transmitted in the same MSS as the cluster of eight (as well as elsewhere), but outside of it. Another late bucolic poem, [Theoc.] 27, which lacks a beginning and ends with two lines applicable to a programmatic close to a bucolic collection, could conceivably have been the end of the sylloge, broken off from it at some time. It is preserved only in Paris. gr. 2726 (D, late fifteenth century: Hicks 189). All poems in the sylloge were originally unequipped with ascriptions[126] (which could suggest belief in single authorship[127]) and scholia. That the group contains some of the most corrupt bucolic poems in our corpus (including the *Adonis*) also sets it apart and suggests the misadventures it met with before joining the larger bucolic transmission.

Evidence for the composition and transmission of this sylloge is lamentably thin. It may be, as Wilamowitz suspected, that by late antiquity the *Adonis* had been established in such collections of bucolic poetry, while Bion's complete idylls had been excerpted, anthologized, and lost. Even in the early fifth century A.D. anthologists like Stobaeus and Orion may have drawn on previous anthologies rather than on whole texts of Moschus and Bion. Against

[125] Wilamowitz (1900) 33–4 ascribes the survival of these poems to a fluke, flatly opining that their quality in itself did not merit it, and thinks that a contemporary of Bion was the original collector; but such a reader as Ovid (who borrows from the *Adonis*, [Bion] 2, and [Theoc.] 23) may have felt differently about their value.

[126] Except perhaps for Moschus 1, whose authorship is attested in X (Μόσχου Ἔρως δραπέτης) and perhaps V before damage; but the source of this ascription may lie outside the bucolic transmission (see below).

[127] Matthews (1994) 46–8 raises the suggestion that the collectors considered Bion to be the author of all these poems; in that case the sylloge will not have included [Moschus] 3, which is self-evidently not by Bion.

Wilamowitz (1900) 32, however, it must be pointed out that late authors do borrow from Bion's fragments as well as from the *Adonis* (see section VIII above) – perhaps finding them in anthologies; but it would be rash to assert that they knew only the poetry that we can trace in theirs. Imitations of the *Adonis*, the Hyacinth poem, and fr. 10 by the circle of Agathias may argue that as late as the mid sixth century a Bionean corpus, including some works that did not make it into our bucolic collections, was available to inspire poets as excerpts scattered through anthologies probably would not have done. Note the imitations by Leontius (fr. 1.1), Agathias himself (fr. 10.8; perhaps fr. 9.9), and perhaps Macedonius and Paul the Silentiary (*Ad.* 44). The loss of Agathias' *Daphniaca*, which must have drawn on all the bucolic Agathias knew, greatly obscures our view.

A likely moment for the incorporation of the late bucolic sylloge into a larger bucolic collection (and its transcription from majuscule to minuscule, introducing chaos into e.g. *Ad.* 35) is the Byzantine revival of literary studies that began in the ninth century and provoked such enterprises as the great epigram collection of Cephalas, and evidence for knowledge of its contents then would be welcome. As it happens, [Theoc.] 23.28–32 appear in Bodleianus Barocc. 50, a tenth-century miscellany; its text does not attest a transmission separate from our full text (Wilamowitz *Textg.* 75).[128] In the later twelfth century Nicetas Eugenianus *D.C.* 3.311 καὶ σὺ μισεῖς στέργοντα καὶ οὐ ποθέοντα ποθεῖς με conflates Theoc. 6.17 καὶ φεύγει φιλέοντα καὶ οὐ φιλέοντα διώκει with [Theoc.] 23.62–3 χαίρετε τοὶ φιλέοντες ... | στέργετε δ' οἱ μισεῦντες..., which may suggest that he found them already in the same collection (for Nicetas'

[128] Gallavotti *Theoc. ad loc.* thinks that [Theoc.] 23.28–32 are imitated by Constantine Manasses (d. 1187) *A.C.* fr. 149.9–11 Mazal.

extensive use of Theocritus see Conca's index, pp. 285–6).[129]

Moschus 1 (*Runaway Love*) and Bion fr. 13 are imitated together by Constantine of Sicily *Anacr.* 5 (Bergk 351–4), on whose date (early tenth century) see Cameron (1993) 245–53. Cameron documents Constantine's borrowings from Moschus 1, which he argues the author saw in an epigram anthology like that of Cephalas (note that Moschus 1 = *A.P.* 9.440). Cameron further argues (p. 249) that "it was probably via Cephalas that Moschus 1 entered the Bucolic tradition": the earliest bucolic MS in which it appears is Laurentianus xxxii.16 (S), into which it was copied in 1280 by Maximus Planudes, compiler of the famous Planudean anthology of epigrams (where it also appears); moreover, the text of Moschus 1 in S coincides with that in the *Anthology*. But the transmission of Moschus 1 in the bucolic manuscript V (whence X) is independent of S: it shows a different (and superior) text,[130] and it falls squarely within our sylloge, surrounded by poems not transmitted elsewhere. In S it follows Moschus 2, which explains why Planudes incorporated it (Moschus 2, like Moschus 1 in the *Anthology*, was always attributed).[131] The *ascription* of Moschus 1 in X – where it alone of the sylloge bears an author's name[132] – might well have come from the tradition of the *Anthology*, but the presence of the poem in V/X goes back to the sylloge of late bucolic and had nothing to do with Cephalas' epigram collection.

Constantine was jointly inspired by Moschus 1 and Bion fr. 13. The theme of his ᾠδάριον ἐρωτικόν – the speaker

[129] Nicetas' story of Eros and the bee (4.313–24) comes not from [Theoc.] 19, but from *Anacreont.* 35.

[130] Wilamowitz *Textg.* 76–7.

[131] Cf. Hicks 194. A group of late fifteenth-century MSS with Moschus 1 in this position are related to S (Hicks 200).

[132] As also possibly in V, which no longer possesses the beginning of the poem.

pursues Love, only to be attacked by his quarry – is *implicit* in Moschus 1 (esp. 26–9), but is the very point of Bion fr. 13 and surely comes from there (cf. commentary on fr. 13.2). Constantine's Eros is no runaway, but – as in Bion fr. 13 – an enticing prize: ὃν ἰδὼν ἐγὼ τότ' ἔσχον | ἐπιθυμίαν κρατῆσαι, | κραταιραῖς πέδαις τε δῆσαι, | θαλεροῖς νέοις τε δεῖξαι (11–14). The implication is that he saw the two poems together somewhere – perhaps in the late bucolic sylloge, which in that case will have contained and subsequently lost fr. 13. Alas, the two poems also appear together in Stobaeus (4.20.56–7), and this is most probably the source of their joint influence on Constantine. Stobaeus excerpts only Moschus 1.7–10 and 16–17, but Constantine could have found the whole in Cephalas, with the juxtaposition in Stobaeus simply providing his first inspiration. Thus he is not a witness to the bucolic transmission. It must be confessed that as far as the evidence goes, the group of which the *Epitaph on Adonis* is part could have been subsumed into the larger bucolic collection at any time up until the early fourteenth century.

Here it may be noted that there is no reason to trust the allegation that Bion's poetry, along with that of certain other authors, was deliberately collected and burned by the Byzantine emperors under the influence of their clergy ("the only Pretence for their severe sentence, was their writing in too amorous a strain"[133]). This rumour is due to Petrus Alcyonius, the assistant to Aldus Manutius, who in his Ciceronian dialogue *Medices legatus, sive de exsilio* (Venice 1522), Book 1, has one of the speakers recount, "Audiebam etiam puer ex Demetrio Chalcondyla graecarum rerum peritissimo Sacerdotes Graecos tanta floruisse auctoritate apud Caesares Byzantinos, ut integra illorum gratia complura de veteribus graecis Poëmata combusserint,

[133] T. Cooke, *The Idylliums of Moschus and Bion* (London 1724) 9; cf. Beckby 362.

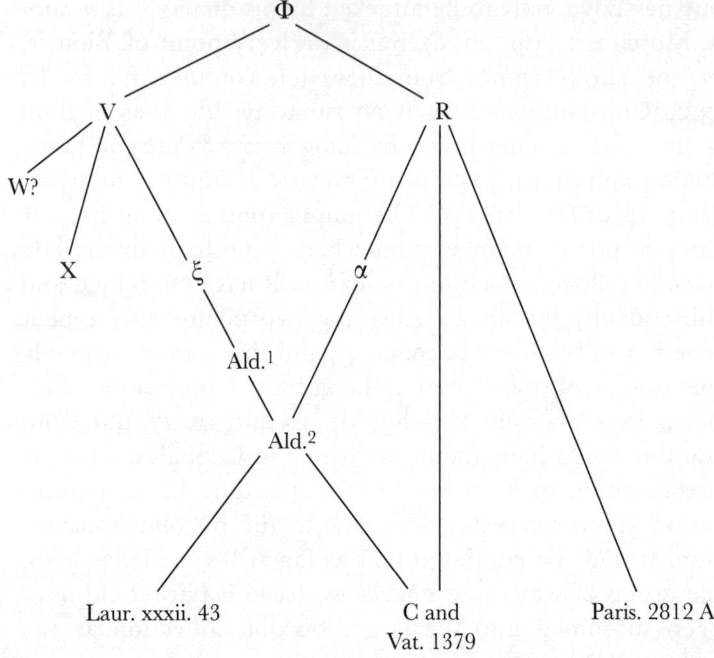

The later MS tradition of the *Epitaph on Adonis*. The designation of the minuscule archetype as Φ goes back to Hiller and Wilamowitz. Hicks uses ξ for the V-derived exemplar of the first Aldine.

in primisque ea ubi amores, turpes lusus, & nequitiae amantum continebantur, atque ita Menandri, Diphili, Apollodori, Philemonis, Alexis fabellas, & Saphûs, Erinnae, Anacreontis, Mimnermi, Bionis, Alcmanis, Alcaei carmina intercidisse." This is the Renaissance looking for someone on whom to blame the loss whose enormity it has only just realized; there is no evidence that the Byzantines sought out and destroyed pagan literature, however amorous.[134]

Little did Petrus know that even as he wrote, Bion's

[134] See L. D. Reynolds and N. G. Wilson, *Scribes and Scholars*[3] (Oxford 1991) 51.

most celebrated poem was already back in circulation, though its true authorship was to go undetected until three years after Petrus perished in the 1527 sack of Rome. The *Epitaph on Adonis* reached the Italian revival of learning anonymously in two MSS, Vaticanus gr. 1824 (**V**)[135] and Parisinus gr. 2832 (**R**), descended from the same hyparchetype. According to Gallavotti (1982, esp. p. 15; cf. Hicks 12), both V and R were copied in Thessalonica in the early fourteenth century under the supervision of Demetrius Triclinius and represent successive stages in his work on the text of Theocritus. V is the earlier of the two. Its watermarks date to 1297–1318 (Gallavotti (1982) 12 n. 8, Hicks 11 n. 60).[136] It lacks R's conscious emendations and contains more simple errors than R (at e.g. *Ad.* 52, 64); its neatness suggests that the majority of these errors are not the result of carelessness, but reflect the condition of the exemplar.

R's watermarks postdate 1316 or even 1328 (Hicks 13 n. 79)[137]; that its *Adonis* is not descended from V's seems evident from divergences in their readings that are best explained as different treatments of a common source (e.g. 24 πόδα V: παῖδα R; 83 λέβητος V: λέβησι R; cf. 82).[138] In contrast to the more sincere (and more corrupt) V, R shows many emendations for the sake of metre or sense (e.g. at *Ad.* 31, 36, 70–1, 77, and 83–4), undoubtedly the

135 I use the sigla of Gallavotti, based on those of Wilamowitz. For a comparison of different editors' sigla see Appendix B.

136 The portion of V containing Aeschylus (known as Fb) was copied "in the immediate vicinity of Triclinius" before *c.* 1317 (West (1990) 349).

137 Thus R. Aubreton, *Démétrius Triclinius et les recensions médiévales de Sophocle* (Paris 1949) 21–2 is wrong to date R between 1308 and 1320. On this MS see Omont. Wilamowitz (followed by Gow and others) calls it Tr after Triclinius, but that designation artificially distinguishes the provenances of the two principal MSS.

138 A candidate for being the common source is Paris. gr. 2722, which Gallavotti (1982) 8 (cf. 15) believes once contained the *Adonis* and constituted a preliminary stage of the Triclinian recension of the bucolics.

work of Triclinius.[139] R has been very sloppily and hastily written with a thick, runny nib, and is full of interlinear glosses – also the work of Triclinius or his circle, as their absence from V shows. Triclinius had evidently discovered a bucolic MS that had escaped previous editors in this field (Planudes, Moschopulus), one – perhaps by now the only one – that contained our sylloge, and in a single swoop saved nearly all of surviving late bucolic from extinction. This was not, of course, his intention: he excluded Moschus 1, [Theoc.] 19, and Εἰς νεκρὸν Ἄδωνιν from his final redaction (represented by R), apparently aiming for a strictly Theocritean collection and regarding those poems as alien to Theocritus; to make clear his intention, he explicitly ascribed to Theocritus all the unattributed poems – including the *Adonis* – he saw fit to include (Hiller 58–60, Wilamowitz *Textg.* 70, Matthews (1994) 28 n. 16). That his earlier, unselective redaction survived in V is a bit of luck.

From V is descended the portion of Vaticanus gr. 1311 (**X**, last quarter of the fifteenth century) that contains the *Adonis* (Ahrens (1874) 591; Hicks 12–13); I note improvements it contains on lines 17 and 50. Another apographon of V, Laurentianus Conv. Soppr. 15 = W (mid fourteenth century: cf. Gallavotti (1982) 8–9), may once have contained the *Adonis*, since in its present condition it breaks off at [Moschus] 3.15, before the sequence that it shares with V reaches our poem. In 1496 appeared the *editio princeps* of Bion's masterpiece, edited by Aldus Manutius in a collection of "Theocritus", Hesiod, and other Greek poetry. Theoc. 1–18 had already been printed by Bonus Accursius in 1480 or 1481; the Aldine Theocritus (dated February 1495, according to the Venetian style of beginning years with the first of March: Hicks 139) contains a larger selec-

[139] But R is not Triclinius' autograph: F. Garin, *RFIC* 47 (1919) 76 n. 1; C. Gallavotti, *RFIC* 63 (1934) 355 n. 2; cf. Gallavotti *Theoc.* 256, N. Wilson, *GRBS* 22 (1981) 397.

tion of the bucolic corpus. Its *Adonis* is descended from that of V. Ahrens (1874) 591 n. 71 decided that the edition was based on X (cf. Hiller 8–9, Gallavotti *Theoc.* 307), but a recent investigation points rather to a sibling of X, now lost (Hicks 138–49; cf. commentary on *Ad.* 72). The composition of the first Aldine may be still more complicated, since it shares a few readings with R (e.g. 24 παῖδα, 37 τὰν Κυθέρειαν).

In a second printing (with the same date, but presumably issued later) Aldus revised some of the idylls, including the *Adonis*, using a manuscript like R (whence readings like 31 Κύπριδος, 70–71 τὺ δὲ ... ἔσσι).[140] Hiller 8 believes that this exemplar was Vaticanus gr. 1379 (a descendant of R: Hiller 15–39), but the order of the poems in the Vaticanus and certain other considerations seem to point conversely to influence from the second Aldine on its scribe (Hicks 149–70). Its *Adonis* contains a few corrections that may be traced to the second Aldine (e.g. 95 σφ^σι^ῖν), and it shares with the Aldines the division of MS ἐσσέ into ἐς σέ at 55. Its corrections ὑμὴν ὕμηᵛ in 88–9 may derive from, but are superior to, the pseudo-Doric ὑμὰν ὑμάν of the Aldines. Thus for his second printing Aldus used a now lost apographon of R. It should be regarded as the source of new readings in the second Aldine like 36 καὶ ἀνὰ πτόλιν οἰκτρὸν ἀείδει, 44 περισμήξω, 55 καὶ Ἄρη, 82 ἄγε, 84 φορέησιν: discrepancies both between V and Ald.[1] and between R and Ald.[2] are to be credited to Aldus' exemplars since, as Hicks 146–9 stresses on the evidence of Aldus' own preface, Aldus himself does not emend the text of the bucolics ("Quod incorrectum est si lateat raro vel potius nunquam emendatur. Si vero prodit in publicum, erunt multi qui castigent, saltem longa die").

R's version of the poem was also copied, in the years

[140] There also seems to have been a preliminary issue of the revised Aldine in which the *Adonis* was unchanged (Hicks 153, 169–70).

around 1500, into Ambrosianus (104) B 75 sup. (**C**) and Parisinus gr. 2812A.[141] C is normally cited for metrical improvements in lines 11 χείλεος and 59 δώματ', but as it shares both with the second Aldine, it is probably a case like Vat. gr. 1379: a copy of R postdating the Aldines and occasionally influenced by them. I have therefore credited those emendations to the second Aldine (i.e. the apograph of R used by Aldus). The Parisinus offers some acceptable Doricizations of the received (banalized) text: *Ad.* 33, 60, 92, 97.[142] Its *Adonis* is no passive copy, but shows emendation at e.g. 36 ἀνάπαλιν ἐπ' οἰκτρὸν and 84 ἔδησε (for ἔλυσε!); it insistently adds the article in 1, 37, 38, 63, 67 ἀπώλεθ' ὁ καλὸς Ἄδωνις, 7 κεῖται ὁ κ. Ἄδ., and 92 ὤλεθ' ὁ κ. Ἄδ. This MS does not seem to show influence from the Aldine editions here. Laurentianus xxxii.43 is basically a copy of the second Aldine for the bucolic idylls after Theoc. 18 (Ahrens (1874) 593, Hiller 9, Hicks 171–8). In the *Adonis* it shows some readings that otherwise appear first in the second Aldine (e.g. 36 καὶ ἀνὰ πτόλιν οἰκτρὸν ἀείδει, 44 περισμήξω, 82 ὃς δ' εὔπτερον ἆγε) and in fact departs from the Aldine text mainly in trivial matters of spelling.[143] Parisinus Coisl. gr. 351, copied in September 1516 by the fourteen-year-old Hector Pyrgoteles, shows influence from both Aldines and from elsewhere (Hicks 190–1).

R was apparently owned at this time by the Byzantine

[141] That these are descended from R here is demonstrated by Hiller 6–8, 33–5. See also Gallavotti *Theoc.* 256, 287–8. Paris. gr. 2812A is sometimes mistakenly referred to as 2512 or 2512A. It was owned by one Abram Peces (Hicks 15).

[142] It must be said that this copyist also banalizes some of R's Doricisms (e.g. 14 θνῄσκοντ', 42 πήχεας, 81 ὀιστοὺς), in each case mistaking for a correction R's superscript η or ου, and commits many other lapses.

[143] Gallavotti *Theoc.* 280–1 (following F. Garin, *RFIC* 42 (1914) 275–82) erroneously says that this MS contains notes in the hand of Politian, who died more than a year before the first Aldine appeared; see Hicks 173–5.

exile and eminent Greek scholar Janus Lascaris (Omont 197 n. 1), and it was doubtless at his instigation that it was so often copied. Hicks 15 wonders whether Lascaris had C compiled as a fuller version of R, adding e.g. Εἰς νεκρὸν Ἄδωνιν as well as Theoc. 30, which only C contains and which Lascaris seems to have discovered on Mt Athos. Lascaris, in fact, might be suspected of even deeper complicity in the propagation of the *Epitaph on Adonis*. He made two trips to Greece in the later fifteenth century, collecting manuscripts for his patron Lorenzo the Magnificent from such places as Thessalonica and Constantinople; many of them stayed in his possession after Lorenzo's death in 1492, and Aldus is known to have drawn on them for his editions.[144] This is speculative, and is not critical for the text of the *Adonis*, but it may be Lascaris who was responsible for bringing both V and R to Italy and getting their contents published, perhaps himself contributing to the text.

The next important editions, that edited by Euphrosynus Boninus (Frosino Bonini)[145] for the Juntine press in Florence (1516)[146] and that of Zacharias Callierges in Rome (1516),[147] introduce numerous new readings of varying acceptability, some allegedly taken from a MS no longer in existence. Letters prefaced to the Juntine state that Bonini collated a copy of the bucolics edited by himself with one

[144] See M. Lowry, *The World of Aldus Manutius* (Cornell 1979) 244, 281–2.

[145] On this pupil of Politian see J. H. Cotton, *La bibliofilia* 71 (1969) 157–75, who, however, misrepresents the circumstances of his work on the bucolic poets (p. 166), making Pandolfini the editor. On Bonini's work for the Giunti see W. A. Pettas, *The Giunti of Florence* (San Francisco 1980) 49–52.

[146] The book bears the date 10 January 1515, but the Florentine year did not begin until 25 March (Gow *Theoc.* 1 p. xlvi n. 1).

[147] Published five days after the Juntine. A previous sixteenth-century edition, that of Egidius Gourmont (Paris *c.* 1508), reproduces the text of the second Aldine.

he received from Filippo Pandolfini; this latter was a copy edited by Marcus Musurus (the Cretan scholar, resident in Venice, who occupied the chair of Greek at the University of Padua during 1503–9) and supplemented by him from an ἀρχαιότατον βιβλίον at that time in the possession of Paulus Bucephalus (or Bucarus; i.e. Paolo Capodivacca) of Padua.[148] Callierges is silent about the source of his new readings, but the large number of them that he shares with the Juntine points ultimately to the same source; his own connexion with Musurus went back at least to his 1499 edition of the *Etymologicum magnum*, which Musurus prefaced.

Many of these readings reappear under the heading "Emendationes in nonnulla loca Theocriti depravata. Ex codice antiquissimo" in two sixteenth-century MSS, Salmanticensis 295, in the hand of the Spanish humanist Fredenandus Nonius Pincianus (Hernán Núñez de Guzmán), and Bruxellensis 18974, in that of the Jesuit Andreas Schott. Under the heading ἐπιτάφιος ἀδώνιδος one finds the following:[149] [69] ἐρῆμα, ἑτοίμα [for ἑτ-] γρ. [68] μήρεο γρ. μύρεο [70] τὺ δὲ γρ. τὸ δὲ [82] ἔβαιν' ὅς γρ. ἔκαιν' ὅς [87] φιαῖς ὑμεναίοις γρ. φλιαῖς ὑμέναιος [93] δοξολέγοντι γρ. δ' ὀξὺ λέγοντι. In each case the reading of the second Aldine (which also provided the form of the title and the sequence of the idylls in the "Emendationes") is glossed with one that appears in the Juntine (82), the Calliergian (69, 93), or both (68, 70, 87). As Gallavotti (1981) demonstrates, these readings all go back to the work of Marcus Musurus on the Paduan MS – perhaps mixed with the work of everyone else involved, although the

[148] See Hiller 3–4, Gow *Theoc.* I pp. xlv–xlvi. The existence of the "ancient manuscript" is corroborated by a scholium on *A.P.* 9.435 = Theoc. *Ep.* 14, which some have traced to Musurus (see Gow *Theoc.* II.538–9, Gallavotti (1981) 118–19).

[149] I quote the facsimile of Núñez printed in A. Tovar, *AFC* 4 (1947–9) 87, adding line numbers. Cf. Gow *Theoc.* I pp. xlvi–xlvii, Bühler 13–15, Gallavotti (1981).

absence of some readings new to the 1516 editions[150] suggests Musurus as sole source of the "Emendationes" (some new readings common to Call. and Junt. that are omitted by the "Emendationes" – e.g. 20 ἀλάληται, 55 πᾶν καλὸν – may also be Musuran). They may derive from notes taken from his lectures.[151] None attests a transmission independent of our two principal MSS: they either reflect MS readings we already possess[152] or are emendations of them, doubtless by Musurus.[153] Given the licence with which scholars of that time spoke of "very old books", the text of the *Epitaph on Adonis* contained in Capodivacca's ἀρχαιότατον βιβλίον will have been a recent copy derived from V or R.[154]

Because of the mistaken ascription of Triclinius the poem at this point was assumed to be by Theocritus: the metrist Pseudo-Draco cites *Ad.* 27 as Theocritus'[155]; Erasmus *Adag.* 3.2.36, on the *cestus* of Venus, names Theocritus as the author of *Ad.* 60. In 1530 Joachim Camerarius (i.e.

150 E.g. 12 ἀφήσει, 18 ὠρύσαντο, 22 τείροντι, 46 ζώει, 89 ᾄδεται (Call.); 35 ἐρυθαίνεται, 82 δὲ πτερὸν, 83–4 λέβητι ... χρυσείῳ (Junt.). These may thus be the work of Callierges and Bonini.

151 Cf. Hicks 203, interpreting Pandolfini's epistolary preface to the Juntine: "[Musurus] dictated ... the readings from his 'ἀρχαιότατον βιβλίον', as Filippo says, correcting the many corrupt places in the previously printed editions. These readings were then recorded by his hearers, presumably straight into their Aldines."

152 68 μύρεο is found in R; μήρεο in V, whence the Aldines. 82 ἔκαιν' suggests a misreading of minuscule -β-: V and R (and the Aldines) have ἔβαιν'. 70 τὸ δὲ could be a misreading of Triclinius' τὺ δὲ, if not an emendation (anticipating Morel's τόδε).

153 I accept those in 87 and 93. 69 ἑτοίμα, widely accepted until Ahrens (1854), is an attempt to make sense of a corrupt line; see commentary *ad loc.*

154 Not every poem in this lost MS was so negligible; its text of [Moschus] 3 may have been witness to a valuable tradition not attested elsewhere (Hicks 202–5).

155 [Draco] *De metris* p. 102.20 Hermann. For his dating (he seems to use the edition of Callierges) see Ahrens (1854) 26–7, L. Cohn in *RE* 5.1662–3.

Kammermeister) tentatively ascribed the poem to Bion, noting the allusion in [Moschus] 3.68–9 to the kiss given by Aphrodite to Adonis in *Ad.* 13–14. In the preface to his edition he opines that ἐν τοῖς ἑπομένοις εἰδυλλίοις εἶναι δοκοῦσι τινὰ οὐ πεποιημένα ὑπὸ τοῦ Θεοκρίτου ὡς τὸ ἐπικήδειον εἰς ἄδωνιν ὅπερ τις εἶναι τοῦ βίωνος φάμενος οὐκ ἂν, ὡς οἶμαι ἁμάρτοι μακρὸν τοῦ ἀληθοῦς; and in his introduction to the poem, μνήμη γὰρ ποιεῖται τοῦ ἀδώνιδος φιλήματος ἐν τούτῳ τῷ ἐπιταφίῳ, τοῦ καὶ πρότερον ἐν τῷ εἰς βίωνα.[156] This is as persuasive an argument as one could ask for, and the ascription is supported by metrical and linguistic similarities between the *Adonis* and the fragments assigned to Bion by the anthologists (see sections v and vi above). Camerarius' hypothesis was reprinted in the prefaces or notes to subsequent editions of the bucolics over the next thirty-five years,[157] until the breakthrough edition of Adolphus Mekerchus (Adolph Meetkercke) in 1565. Here for the first time Bion's surviving poetry – a selection of the fragments gleaned from Stobaeus (13, 10, 9, 8, and 16)[158] and the *Epitaph on Adonis* – was published together under his name (with the collected works of Moschus).[159] The monumental 1566 edition of Stephanus made the ascription standard.

Meanwhile the thirteen fragments of Bion anthologized in Stobaeus' latter two books were being edited and printed, first by Sigmund Gelen in a collection of gnomes

[156] I preserve the eccentricities of Camerarius' diction and accentuation.

[157] Notably in the three printed by Peter Brubach (Frankfurt). His 1558 edition contains influential notes on the *Adonis* by Gulielmus Xylander (Wilhelm Holtzmann).

[158] Mekerchus prints fr. 11 under Moschus' name, following Stephanus' peculiar ascription (cf. Mekerchus 30). Stephanus gives fr. 11 to Bion only in his 1577 edition.

[159] Cf. his dedication, p. 3: "Moschi & Bionis delicatissimorum poëtarum Graeca Idyllia, quae hactenus partim in tenebris delituerunt, partim variè dispersa iacuerunt, in unum fascem collegimus."

appended to the hymns of Callimachus (Basel 1532),[160] then more completely by Victor Trincavellus in his Ἰωάννου τοῦ Στοβαίου ἐκλογαὶ ἀποφθεγμάτων (Venice 1536). Trincavellus printed from a MS like Vindobonensis philol. gr. 67 (**S**, early eleventh century: Hense I p. vii),[161] which contains only frr. 4–11, 13, 15, and 16; the publication of frr. 12 and 14 had to wait until the second edition of Conrad Gesner (1549), who used Escurialensis 90 (Σ II 14) (**M**), a late eleventh- or early twelfth-century codex that eventually came into the possession of Diego Hurtado de Mendoza, the envoy of the Holy Roman emperor in Venice.[162]

Frr. 1, 2, and 3 belong to the first two books of Stobaeus, the so-called *Eclogae*, whose *editio princeps* was the edition of Willem Canter, *Ioannis Stobaei Eclogarum libri duo* (Antwerp 1575). Canter used an apographon of the fifteenth-century codex Parisinus gr. 2129 (**P**). Seven years before, however, Bion was fortunate in the publication of *Carmina novem illustrium feminarum* by Fulvius Ursinus (Fulvio Orsini), who supplemented the nine poetesses of his title with male lyric, elegiac, and bucolic poets. As curator of the Farnese library in Rome, Ursinus had access to the more sincere of our two principal sources for the *Eclogae*, Farnesinus bibl. nat. Neapolit. III D 15 (**F**, fourteenth century), and printed frr. 1, 2, and 3 from it.[163] His texts are superior to those of Canter (who does not emend Bion's text except to corrupt it further), and frr. 1 and 2 had been improved upon by

160 Καλλιμάχου Κυρηναίου ὕμνοι, μετὰ τῶν σχολίων. Γνῶμαι ἐκ διαφόρων ποιητῶν φιλοσόφων τε καὶ ῥητόρων συλλεγεῖσαι, published by Hieronymus Froben. Cf. Hense I p. xxvi. Gelen includes frr. 4–6 and 8–11 (pp. 91–4, 156, 168, and 215).

161 My sigla for Stobaeus are those of Wachsmuth and Hense.

162 Related to M, and containing the same Bionean material, is the fourteenth-century Parisinus gr. 1984 (**A**), which lay unused until Grotius' 1623 edition, according to Hense I p. lxiii. On M and A see Hense I pp. xxix–xxxviii.

163 See his notes on pp. 349–51. On F and P see Wachsmuth I pp. xxv–xxvii and ch. 3 of his *Studien zu den griechischen Florilegien* (Berlin 1882).

Crispinus in 1569–70. That Ursinus was already publicizing his trove before publication is evident from a letter written to him from Antwerp by the Flemish humanist Geraart Falkenburg (whom Ursinus had asked to find a publisher), dated 7 August 1567: "Eidyllium Bionis Εἴαρος, ὦ Μύρσων, ἢ χείματος ἢ φθινοπώρου, etc. mirifice me delectat. Gratissimum mihi erit, si alterum Moschi vel Bionis eidyllium, quod mihi legendum dabas, descriptum, quando tibi erit commodum, mecum communicaveri[s]."[164] Falkenburg's enthusiasm for Bion, it may be noted, is manifest also in his Ἰωάννου Φλημίγγου Ἐπιτάφιος, a prosodically execrable but warmly felt epicedion on his countryman John Fleming, modelled, like Shelley's *Adonais* later, on both Bion's *Epitaph on Adonis* and the pseudo-Moschan *Epitaph on Bion.*[165]

A sixth witness to the fragments, Parisinus gr. 1985 (**B**), whose readings I (like Hense) have taken from Gaisford's edition,[166] has a complicated origin and an uncertain status in a critical apparatus to Bion. It is a MS of the mid sixteenth century, copied by a learned man who had access to Trincavellus' edition and a Stobaeus codex related to M and A, and who may have incorporated his own conjectures and those of his contemporaries.[167] Three of its new readings for Moschus (fr. 1.10 ἁ πλάνος and 13 ἃ τέρπει and ἄγρικον) as well as Bion fr. 9.3 ἀείδῃ are suggested by Stephanus in the end-notes to his 1555 trans-

[164] P. de Nolhac, *La bibliothèque de Fulvio Orsini* (Paris 1887) 436–7.

[165] First printed with the *Vertumnus* of John Beck of Gorp (Antwerp 1580) and later in Vulcanius (1584) 63–9. I owe my awareness of this oddment of the Northern Renaissance to Richard Matthews, who reprints it with extensive annotation in the supplement to his 1991 dissertation.

[166] But Wachsmuth 1 p. xxx warns that Gaisford "haud raro *A* et *B* notas duorum Parisinorum in adscribendis lectionibus confudit" (similarly Hense 1 p. xxv).

[167] See Gaisford (1822) 1 p. vii, Hense 1 p. xxv, and Hense in *RhM* 41 (1886) 65.

lation.[168] This raises the suspicion that another reading in B, fr. 13.12 τόδε τὤρνεον, which Stephanus prints without comment in his 1566 edition, is the work of Stephanus himself, whose attentions have benefited Bion also at *Ad.* 34, 55, and 95. Three other noteworthy readings in B, frr. 5.2 ἄλλου and 12.1 ἀντεράωνται (both printed first in 1568 by Ursinus) and 8.4 ἄμμιν (printed first in 1623 by Grotius), are simple orthographical corrections.[169] The exchanges of scholars in this period are impossible to trace, but it seems likely that the copyist of B took at least fr. 9.3 ἀείδῃ from Stephanus' published work.

There is a chance that we shall one day find more Bion in a papyrus or a neglected MS. Fr. 17, unknown to Stobaeus, reposed unpublished in the epitome of the *Antholognomicon* of Orion until Schneidewin's 1839 *editio princeps* of that work, preserved in Vindobonensis philol. gr. 321 (fourteenth century; transcribed for Schneidewin by H. C. Schubart).[170] It was first published with Bion's other poetry by Hermann (1849). Some of his poetry may already be present to us, unrecognized as the *Adonis* once was (see section IV above for possible examples of crypto-Bionism).

A brief history of scholarship on Bion at this point will enable the reader to assess the judgements of past editors cited in the critical apparatus and commentary. Since Mekerchus and Stephanus presented the fragments united with the *Epitaph on Adonis* as a single corpus, the task of reconstitution proceeded until by the end of the sixteenth century our poet was poised to enter, in the glory of his own name, the next four centuries of European literature

[168] Cf. his 1566 edition pt. 2 pp. l–li, where he seems to claim the emendations in Moschus as his own, mentioning the 1555 translation.

[169] Other emendations in B are frr. 8.3 μείζονα for πλείονα, 9.5 and 8 κῆν for ἦν (cf. 3), 9.10 αὐτὸν for αὖτ' ἐς, and 10.11 πόθη for πόθως. I have not found these readings anywhere else.

[170] On Orion (better known for his *Etymologicon*) and the transmission see Schneidewin 35–9 and C. Wendel in *RE* 18.1084–5.

and art.[171] Emendation of the texts progressed slowly but steadily throughout the seventeenth century, and although no edition stands out between those of Stephanus (1566, 1577, 1579) and Valckenaer (1779), Bion was particularly well served by Daniel Heinsius (1604), Hugo Grotius (1623), and Caspar von Barth (1624). He was edited in several often reprinted collections of minor Greek poetry in this period, e.g. those of Whitford and Winterton.

The mid and later eighteenth century witnessed an efflorescence of commented editions of Bion in conjunction with Moschus. In addition to Schwebel (1746), Heskin (1748), and Manso (1784), listed in the bibliography, mention should be made of J. A. Schier, *Bionis et Moschi Idyllia* (Leipzig 1752); T. C. Harles, *Bionis Smyrnaei et Moschi Syracusani quae supersunt* (Erlangen 1780); L. H. Teucher, *Bionis et Moschi Idyllia* (Leipzig 1793); and F. Jacobs, *Bionis et Moschi reliquiae* (Gotha 1795).[172] Note also Eritisco Pilenejo (the pseudonym of L. A. Pagnini), *Teocrito, Mosco, Bione, Simmia greco-latini* (Parma 1780). These commentators constantly cite each other and Baron de Longepierre, whose 1686 edition (with French verse translation) prefigured theirs in its lively, charming apparatus of notes and fanciful dis-

[171] I seem to detect the influence of Bion in Shakespeare's *Venus and Adonis* (829–34 ~ *Ad.* 38; 871–4 ~ *Ad.* 22; 931–4 ~ *Ad.* 51–2 and 54–5). H. Tuzet, *Mort et résurrection d'Adonis* ([Paris] 1987) offers a history of Adonis in European literature, taking account of the influence of Bion's version (e.g. on Marino and Shelley); cf. W. P. Mustard, *AJP* 30 (1909) 274–6. Pound's *Canto* 47 attempts a sort of Frazerian reading of Bion's poem. C. Kramer, *Neophilologus* 7 (1921) 171–81 examines Bion's influence on André Chénier (esp. fr. 11 and the *Adonis*). In art, de' Rossi's *Adone morente* in the Museo Nazionale in Florence, with its tangle of fallen limbs and boar's sharp-tusked muzzle, looks like a sculptural interpretation of the word-picture in *Ad.* 7–8. Cf. the supplement to Matthews (1991), pp. 39–57.

[172] Jacobs follows Brunck and Valckenaer (see below) in paying more attention to textual problems.

quisitions on Bion and Moschus. They have left but few traces in later editions, including the present one, but for all their naivety and outdated modes of criticism they are not to be dismissed. They adduce wide-ranging comparanda from ancient and modern literature and offer fresh insights, more appreciatory than literary-critical, but usually intelligent (especially Manso's), and all the more valuable because of the dearth of criticism on Bion between their time and ours. Here too mention should be made of Friedrich Grillo's anonymously published *Idyllen aus dem Griechischen des Bion und Moschus* (Berlin 1767, repr. 1775), a translation with discursive and engaging annotation on select passages.[173]

The edition of Brunck (1772; notes in vol. III, 1776), together with that of Valckenaer (1779), which absorbed it and remained standard until the mid nineteenth century, begins a new chapter in the history of Bion's text. Previous editors had offered emendations here and there; Brunck attacks many fragments and numerous passages of the *Adonis* with emendatory fury, intent mainly on restoring dialectal uniformity, but also concerned with sense. Valckenaer records and recommends dozens of emendations, though usually consigning them to his notes – his notes, in fact, are almost exclusively textual-critical. Many are the work of Ruhnken and Luzac and testify to intense criticism of the texts of bucolic in Leiden. In England Wakefield (1795) continues this trend. He conjectures and accepts so many new readings that his text is scarcely recognisable as the Bion known to previous generations of readers; yet he scrutinises the text so closely and so intelligently that his

[173] Cf. his gallant indignation on *Ad.* 3 φάρεσι: "Uebrigens mogte ich nicht übersetzen: *Schlafe nicht auf Purpurkleidern*, weil es ein schlechtes Bild geben würde, wenn diese Göttin beim Schlafengehn allemahl ihre Kleider ausgezogen, und einer Taglöhners Frau gleich, sich auf dieselben niedergelegt hätte."

recommendations are usually of at least diagnostic value. His is the palmary emendation in *Ad.* 36. Much the same can be said of Briggs (1821), whose text, however, is more conservative than Wakefield's. Graefe's three or four pages on Bion (1815) are indispensable. Ameis, whose 1846 Didot edition records the otherwise unpublished conjectures of Bergk and others, may represent the culmination of this scholarly rigour (cf. Ameis' monograph on the article in bucolic, published the same year).

The edition of Hermann, published posthumously in 1849, pays equally close attention to textual problems, but here rigour gives way to untrammeled play with Bion's text. The liberty Hermann takes in hypothesizing lost lines and in rewriting perfectly unexceptionable passages becomes the rule for the rest of the nineteenth century, especially for German critics and especially in connection with the *Adonis*, whose text was felt to have fallen into grave disarray (see commentary on *Ad.* 1–2).[174] So promiscuous is their enthusiasm for emendation that the modern critic becomes wary of even the most chaste and self-evident of their restorations. More happily, nineteenth-century Germany also witnessed a renewed interest in the bucolic MSS, which had been largely ignored since the first Renaissance editions.[175] The new collations listed in Ahrens I (1855) xvi–xxi were followed by those of Ziegler (1868) and Hiller (1888); V and R were eventually established as paramount. Ziegler, whose text is very conservative for his age, collates only apographa of the principal

[174] Cf. Wilamowitz (1900) 34, defending the structure of the *Adonis* as transmitted: "[D]ie Namen seiner grausamsten Verstümmeler heißen erst Gottfried Hermann, August Meineke, Ludolf Ahrens."

[175] D'Orville's researches on the bucolic MSS (cf. Gow *Theoc.* I p. xxx) had already given an impetus to Brunck's and Valckenaer's work, and were later used by Gaisford and others. This early attention, however, was only to individual readings, not to the interrelationships of the MSS.

MSS, thus supplementing Ahrens. Hiller only partially succeeds in his main task, a reconstruction of the hyparchetype of V and R, but has much of value to say about the MSS and transmission. Ahrens's 1854 monograph, the first comprehensive study of the *Adonis*, can still reward its reader.

The work of Wilamowitz ends one phase and begins another. His 1900 monograph and 1905 Oxford text (2nd ed. 1910) restored the bloated, conjecture-ridden *Adonis* of the later nineteenth century to ninety-eight lines and, following the work of Hiller, established more precisely the relative values of the bucolic MSS. Wilamowitz could also take advantage of Wachmuth's and Hense's definitive work on Stobaeus. This was the model on which later twentieth-century editions were founded. Yet Wilamowitz introduced some readings that cannot be sustained; moreover, his critical apparatuses are so uninformative as to be positively misleading in places. Later editions (e.g. Gow's) are filled with citations of Wilamowitz that turn out to belong to other scholars; in the present edition he is left with only a few mentions in the apparatus: mainly Doricizations, except for his important emendation in *Ad.* 82.

Wilamowitz stands out in the mere fact of his monograph, which returns to eighteenth-century awareness of Bion's artistic and social matrix, but represents the last close work on our poet for more than two generations. The decades after 1910 saw a scattering of articles on Bion and a few editions with other bucolic poets; the most important is Gallavotti's (1946), which takes a fresh look at the MS tradition of bucolic.[176] Edmonds's Loeb (1st ed. 1912) represents a recrudescence of wanton conjecture and rewriting (coupled with the archaizing style of English

[176] Gallavotti's posthumous third edition (1993) does not represent an advance (for Bion anyway) on his first. I have not seen his second (1955).

translation that was then the hallmark of the Loeb series); Legrand's Budé (1927) is almost as bad. Gow's Oxford text (1952) is workmanlike and conservative, but does not evince special attention to Bion and the problems of his text. Beckby's edition (1975) offers nothing new, although his brief notes on Bion are memorable. On the whole, one may say that the twentieth-century tendency to canonize a few authors and relegate the unlucky many to the fringes of scholarship has created a sense of Bion's negligibility that scholars of previous centuries did not share.

In the past decade or two things have begun to change, perhaps because of new interest in the Hellenistic period. Two school anthologies of Hellenistic poetry published during the 1980s include Bion: J. Clack, *An Anthology of Alexandrian Poetry* (Pittsburgh 1982) includes a version of Gow's Oxford text of the *Adonis* with some readings from Edmonds's Loeb; Hopkinson's 1988 anthology includes both the *Adonis* and fr. 13, with notes that are often valuable and help bring new sensitivities into play. Fantuzzi's comprehensive 1985 commentary on the *Adonis* restores rhetorical and literary-critical questions to their proper place. 1987 saw the publication of M. Campbell's *Index verborum in Moschum et Bionem* (Hildesheim), which takes account of the major modern editions and many conjectures.[177] Recent doctoral dissertations have dealt with Bion: that of Macario Valpuesta Bermúdez (Seville 1990) takes all of Bion into account, including [Bion] 2; that of Richard J. H. Matthews (Bern 1991) covers the *Adonis*.[178] It is to be hoped that work of this kind will continue.

177 This index includes the miniature epics Moschus 2 and [Moschus] 4. What is still needed is a comparative study of the diction specific to late bucolic, as we have been using the label.

178 My own doctoral dissertation *The Hellenistic Tradition and Bion of Smyrna* (Stanford 1993) contained versions of the commentaries presented here, along with chapters on historical and stylistic questions.

X ABOUT THE TEXTS AND COMMENTARIES

The aim of the commentaries is simply to contextualize Bion's words for the modern reader; that is, to establish the meaning they yield against Greek poetry and against the wider usages of the Greek language, and to locate them within the dialectic of Greco-Latin literary history. I assume a general familiarity with epic grammar and diction, and focus mainly on Bion's departures therefrom, and to what traditions his style affiliates him. The aim is to gauge Bion's adherence to convention and his originality. Comparanda (linguistic and thematic) are cited primarily to give an idea of Bion's literary affinities; thus I first and foremost cite parallels in other late bucolic poetry, then in other Hellenistic poetry (especially bucolic), then in other ancient literature.

In composing the commentaries I have aimed at both thoroughness and spareness, but have preferred to err on the side of overabundance than of stinginess, especially because the interpretative and textual-critical questions in Bion have been so little discussed. This means, for example, that I discuss rejected emendations at perhaps greater length than seems necessary; but since so many of them have been rejected (or in some cases accepted) without being properly weighed, the extra space seemed worth while. I have been especially concerned to track down and record the sources of emendations. I have tried to keep the footnotes few, consigning to them tangential but interesting material like etymologies not bearing on Bion's sense, or discredited theories that may still cause misconceptions.

Secondary literature that I cite more than once is cited by author's name, with a year or an abbreviated title if confusion is likely; full information is to be found in the general bibliography. For the convenience of the reader, commentaries on authors other than Bion are also included in the general bibliography. I cite Callimachus' fragments and the *Anacreontea* by Pfeiffer's and West's numbers respectively. The only abbreviation of an ancient work that will be hard to identify is E.N.A., by which I mean the anacreontic poem Εἰς νεκρὸν Ἄδωνιν (see section VIII above).

I have not seen the manuscripts myself. I have obtained reproductions of V, R, Vat. gr. 1311, and Vat. gr. 1379 (thanks to the kindness of Richard Matthews); they are legible, and I have scrupulously checked my collations against the quite reliable collations reproduced in Ahrens and Ziegler. I owe my readings for C and Laur. xxxii.43 to Ziegler; for Paris. gr. 2812A to Dübner (ap. Ahrens (1854); cf. p. 15); for the MSS of Stobaeus to Wachsmuth and Hense; for the Vienna MS of Orion to Schubart (ap. Schneidewin). I record accents, iota subscript, and the like in more detail for the *Adonis* MSS than for those of the fragments. I have seen all the printed editions I cite. In distinguishing different readings in the critical apparatus I have preferred to use the more confrontational colon, except where readings differ only in spelling or dialect, in which case I use a comma.

The translations are meant only to give the reader the most basic sense of what the words mean in English, without regard for style. The *Epitaph on Adonis* has often received English verse translations; my own favourite is that of Jane Minot Sedgwick, *Sicilian Idyls and Other Verses* (Boston 1898) 62–6, whose unrhymed pentameters and feminine line-ends seem to me to preserve some of the music of the original.

It may be asked why I have dealt with the fragments before the *Epitaph on Adonis*, against precedent. The first reason is that the fragments represent more familiar types of poem than the *Adonis*, and so are better suited to establishing Bion's place in the tradition of Greek poetry. The second is simply that putting the fragments first may help compensate for the neglect that scholars have shown them in comparison with the longer poem, a neglect that they do not deserve.

BIBLIOGRAPHIES

1. ABBREVIATIONS

AGNF	S. Stephens and J. J. Winkler, *Ancient Greek Novels: The Fragments*. Princeton 1995.
ANET[3]	J. B. Pritchard, ed., *Ancient Near Eastern Texts Relating to the Old Testament*. 3rd ed. Princeton 1969.
ARV[2]	J. Beazley, *Attic Red-Figure Vases*. 2nd ed. Oxford 1963.
CA	J. U. Powell, *Collectanea Alexandrina*. Oxford 1925.
CEG	P. A. Hansen, *Carmina epigraphica graeca*. Berlin 1983–.
D–K	H. Diels, *Die Fragmente der Vorsokratiker*. 6th ed., rev. W. Kranz. Berlin 1951–2.
EG	G. Kaibel, *Epigrammata graeca ex lapidibus conlecta*. Berlin 1878.
EGF	M. Davies, *Epicorum graecorum fragmenta*. Göttingen 1988.
FGE	D. L. Page, *Further Greek Epigrams*. Cambridge 1981.
FGrH	F. Jacoby, *Die Fragmente der griechischen Historiker*. Berlin 1923–55.
FPL	W. Morel, *Fragmenta poetarum latinorum*. 2nd ed. Leipzig 1927.
GP	A. S. F. Gow and D. L. Page, *The Greek Anthology: The Garland of Philip and Some Contemporary Epigrams*. 2 vols., Cambridge 1968.
GVI	W. Peek, *Griechische Vers-Inschriften*. Berlin 1955.
HE	A. S. F. Gow and D. L. Page, *The Greek Anthology: Hellenistic Epigrams*. 2 vols., Cambridge 1965.
IEG	M. L. West, *Iambi et elegi graeci*. 2nd ed. Oxford 1989–92.
IG	*Inscriptiones graecae*. Berlin 1893–.
K–G	R. Kühner, *Ausführliche Grammatik der griechischen Sprache*. 3rd ed. rev. B. Gerth. Hannover 1904 (repr. 1966).
LIMC	*Lexicon iconographicum mythologiae classicae*. 7 vols., Zürich 1981–.
L–P	E. Lobel and D. Page, *Poetarum lesbiorum fragmenta*. Oxford 1955.

L–S E. L. von Leutsch and F. G. Schneidewin, *Corpus paroemiographorum graecorum*. Göttingen 1839–51 (repr. Hildesheim 1958).

LSJ H. G. Liddell and R. Scott, *A Greek-English Lexicon*. 9th ed., rev. H. S. Jones and R. McKenzie. Oxford 1968.

PCG R. Kassel and C. Austin, *Poetae comici graeci*. Berlin 1983–.

PG J.-P. Migne, ed., *Patrologiae cursus completus: Series graeca*. Paris 1857–66.

PGM K. Preisendanz, *Papyri graecae magicae*. 2nd ed., rev. A. Henrichs. Stuttgart 1973–4.

PMG D. L. Page, *Poetae melici graeci*. Oxford 1962.

RE *Real-Encyclopädie der classischen Altertumswissenschaft*. Stuttgart 1894–.

SEG *Supplementum epigraphicum graecum*. Leiden 1923–.

SH H. Lloyd-Jones and P. Parsons, *Supplementum hellenisticum*. Berlin 1983.

SLG D. Page, *Supplementum lyricis graecis*. Oxford 1974.

TLL *Thesaurus linguae latinae*. Leipzig 1900–.

TrGF B. Snell, *Tragicorum graecorum fragmenta* I. 2nd ed., rev. R. Kannicht. Göttingen 1986.

2. EDITIONS CITED

Ahrens, H. L. *Bionis Smyrnaei Epitaphius Adonidis*. Leipzig 1854.

Ahrens, H. L. *Bucolicorum graecorum Theocriti Bionis Moschi reliquiae*. Leipzig 1855–9.

Ameis, C. F. in *Poetae bucolici et didactici*. Paris 1846.

Beckby, H. *Die griechischen Bukoliker*. Meisenheim am Glan 1975.

Briggs, T. *Poetae bucolici graeci sive Theocriti Bionis et Moschi quae supersunt*. Cambridge 1821.

Brunck, R. F. P. *Analecta veterum poetarum graecorum*. 3 vols., Strassburg [1772–6].

Camerarius, J. Θεοκρίτου εἰδύλλια. Hagenau 1530.

Crispinus, J. *Vetustissimorum authorum georgica, bucolica, & gnomica poëmata quae supersunt*. [Geneva] 1569–70.

Edmonds, J. M. *The Greek Bucolic Poets* (Loeb). London 1912.
Fantuzzi, M. *Bionis Smyrnaei Adonidis Epitaphium.* Liverpool 1985.
Gaisford, T. *Poetae minores graeci.* Oxford 1814–20.
Gaisford, T. *Joannis Stobaei Florilegium.* Oxford 1822.
Gallavotti, C. *Theocritus quique feruntur bucolici graeci.* Rome 1946.
Gesner, C. *Ioannis Stobaei sententiae ex thesauris graecorum delectae.* 1st ed. Zürich 1543. 2nd ed. Basel [1549].
Gow, A. S. F. *Bucolici graeci* (OCT). Oxford 1952.
Grotius, H. *Dicta poetarum quae apud Io. Stobaeum exstant.* Paris 1623.
Hartung, J. A. *Theokrit, Bion, und Moschus.* Leipzig 1858.
Heinsius, D. *Theocriti, Moschi, Bionis, Simii quae extant.* [Heidelberg] 1604.
Hense, O. *Ioannis Stobaei Anthologii libri duo posteriores.* Berlin 1894–1912.
Hermann, G. *Bionis et Moschi carmina.* Leipzig 1849.
Heskin, J. *Bionis Smyrnaei et Moschi Syracusani quae supersunt.* Oxford 1748.
Hopkinson, N. *A Hellenistic Anthology.* Cambridge 1988.
Koennecke, O. *Bucolici graeci.* Brunswick 1914.
Legrand, E. *Bucoliques grecs* (Budé). Paris 1927.
[Longepierre, H. B. de R. de] *Les Idylles de Bion et de Moschus.* Paris 1686.
Manso, I. C. F. *Bion und Moschus.* Gotha 1784.
Matthews, R. J. H. *A Doctoral Dissertation on the* Ἐπιτάφιος Ἀδώνιδος *or Lament for Adonis.* Diss. Bern 1991.
Meineke, A. *Theocritus Bion Moschus.* 3rd ed. Berlin 1856.
Mekerchus, A. *Moschi Siculi, et Bionis Smyrnaei Idyllia.* Bruges 1565.
Morel, G. *Theocriti Idyllia XXXVI. Epigrammata XIX. Bipennis et Ala.* 2nd ed. Paris 1561.
Schaefer, G. H. *Theocritus Bion et Moschus.* Leipzig 1809.
Schneidewin, F. G. *Coniectanea critica.* Göttingen 1839.
Schwebel, N. *Bionis et Moschi Idyllia.* Venice 1746.
Stephanus, H. *Poetae graeci principes heroici carminis.* [Geneva] 1566.
Stephanus, H. *Epistolia, dialogi breves, oratiunculae, poematia ex variis utriusque linguae scriptoribus.* [Paris] 1577.
Stephanus, H. *Theocriti aliorumque poetarum Idyllia.* [Paris] 1579.
Ursinus, F. *Carmina novem illustrium feminarum.* Antwerp 1568.

Valckenaer, L. C. *Theocriti, Bionis, et Moschi carmina bucolica.* Leiden 1779.

Valpuesta Bermúdez, M. *Estudio sobre la obra literaria de Bión de Esmirna.* Diss. Seville 1990.

Vulcanius, B. *Callimachi Cyrenaei hymni, epigrammata et fragmenta, quae exstant. Et separatim, Moschi Syracusii et Bionis Smyrnaei Idyllia.* Antwerp 1584.

Wachsmuth, C. *Ioannis Stobaei Anthologii libri duo priores.* Berlin 1884.

Wakefield, G. Βιωνος και Μοσχου τα λειψανα. London 1795.

Whitford, D. *Musaei, Moschi et Bionis, quae extant omnia.* London 1659.

Wilamowitz-Moellendorff, U. von *Bion von Smyrna: Adonis.* Berlin 1900.

Wilamowitz-Moellendorff, U. von *Bucolici graeci* (OCT). 2nd ed. Oxford [1910].

Winterton, R. *Poetae minores graeci.* Cambridge 1652.

Ziegler, C. *Bionis et Moschi carmina.* Tübingen 1868.

3. GENERAL BIBLIOGRAPHY

Ahrens, H. L. "Über einige antike Sammlungen der theokritischen Gedichte", *Philologus* 33 (1874) 385–417, 577–609.

Albert, W. *Das mimetische Gedicht in der Antike.* Frankfurt am Main 1988.

Alexiou, M. *The Ritual Lament in Greek Tradition.* Cambridge 1974.

Allen, D. C. "Three Poems on Eros", *Comparative Literature* 8 (1956) 177–90.

Ameis, C. *De articuli usu apud poetas Graecorum bucolicos,* in C. W. Haun, *Jahresbericht über das Gymnasium zu Mühlhausen.* Mühlhausen 1846.

Arland, W. *Nachtheokritische Bukolik bis an die Schwelle der lateinischen Bukolik.* Leipzig 1937.

Arnim, H. F. A. von *Stoicorum veterum fragmenta.* 4 vols., Leipzig 1903–24.

Atallah, W. *Adonis dans la littérature et l'art grecs.* Paris 1966.

Barth, C. von *Adversariorum commentariorum libri sexaginta.* Frankfurt 1624.

Bechtel, F. *Die historischen Personennamen des Griechischen bis zur Kaiserzeit.* Halle 1917.

Bekker, I. *Anecdota graeca.* Berlin 1814–21 (repr. Graz 1965).

Bergk, T. *Poetae lyrici graeci* III. 4th ed. Leipzig 1882.

Bers, V. *Greek Poetic Syntax in the Classical Age.* New Haven 1984.

Bömer, F. *P. Ovidius Naso: Metamorphosen.* Heidelberg 1969–86.

Brenk, F. E. "'Purpureos spargam flores': A Greek Motif in the *Aeneid*?" *CQ* n.s. 40 (1990) 218–23.

Buck, C. D. and W. Petersen *A Reverse Index of Greek Nouns and Adjectives.* Chicago [1945].

Buecheler, F. "Bions Grablied auf Adonis", *Jahrb. f. cl. Phil.* 9 (1863) 106–13.

Buecheler, F. "De bucolicorum graecorum aliquot carminibus", *RhM* 30 (1875) 33–61.

Buffière, F. *Eros adolescent.* Paris 1980.

Bühler, W. *Die Europa des Moschos.* Wiesbaden 1960.

Bulloch, A. W. *Callimachus: The Fifth Hymn.* Cambridge 1985.

Burkert, W. *Structure and History in Greek Mythology and Religion.* Berkeley 1979.

Burkert, W. *The Orientalizing Revolution.* Harvard 1992.

Calame, C. *Alcman.* Rome 1983.

Cameron, A. *The Greek Anthology from Meleager to Planudes.* Oxford 1993.

Cameron, A. *Callimachus and His Critics.* Princeton 1995.

Campbell, M. *A Commentary on Quintus Smyrnaeus Posthomerica XII* (*Mnem.* Suppl. 71). Leiden 1981.

Campbell, M. *Moschus: Europa.* Hildesheim 1991.

Campbell, M. *A Commentary on Apollonius Rhodius* Argonautica *III 1–471* (*Mnem.* Suppl. 141). Leiden 1994.

Carden, R. *The Papyrus Fragments of Sophocles.* Berlin 1974.

Càssola, F. *Inni Omerici.* [Milan] 1975.

Chantraine, P. *Grammaire homérique.* Paris 1947.

Chantraine, P. *Dictionnaire étymologique de la langue grecque.* Paris 1968–80.

Conca, F. *Nicetas Eugenianus: De Drosillae et Chariclis amoribus.* Amsterdam 1990.

Conrad, C. *From Epic to Lyric: A Study in the History of Traditional Word-Order in Greek and Latin Poetry*. New York 1990.

Copley, F. O. *Exclusus Amator: A Study in Latin Love Poetry*. Baltimore 1956.

Courtney, E. *A Commentary on the Satires of Juvenal*. London 1980.

Courtney, E. "Three Poems of Catullus", *BICS* 32 (1985) 85–100.

Courtney, E. *The Fragmentary Latin Poets*. Oxford 1993.

Cramer, J. A. *Anecdota graeca*. Oxford 1835 (repr. Amsterdam 1963).

Cumont, F. "Les noms des planètes et l'astrolatrie chez les grecs", *AC* 4 (1935) 5–43.

Dehor, P.-J. *Hiems latina. Etudes sur l'hiver dans la poésie latine, des origines à l'époque de Néron* (Coll. *Latomus* 219). Brussels 1993.

Denniston, J. D. *The Greek Particles*. 2nd ed. Oxford 1954.

Denniston, J. D. and D. Page *Aeschylus: Agamemnon*. Oxford 1957.

Dewar, M. J. *Statius: Thebaid IX*. Oxford 1991.

Diggle, J. *Euripides: Phaethon*. Cambridge 1970.

Dodds, E. R. *Euripides: Bacchae*. 2nd ed. Oxford 1960.

Dover, K. J. *Theocritus: Select Poems*. London 1971.

Dover, K. J. *Greek Homosexuality*. Harvard 1978.

Ebeling, H. *Lexicon Homericum*. 2 vols., Leipzig 1885.

Eissfeldt, O. *Adonis und Adonaj* (Sitzb. Akad. Leipzig, phil.-hist. Kl., 115.4). Berlin 1970.

Estevez, V. A. "Ἀπώλετο καλὸς Ἄδωνις: A Description of Bion's Refrain", *Maia* 33 (1981) 35–42.

Fabiano, G. "Fluctuation in Theocritus' Style", *GRBS* 12 (1971) 517–37.

Fantuzzi, M. "On the Metre of *Anacreont.* 19W", *CQ* n.s. 44 (1994) 540–2.

Fantuzzi, M. in *id.* and R. Pretagostini, edd., *Struttura e storia dell'esametro greco* I. Rome 1995, pp. 221–64.

Fehling, D. *Die Wiederholungsfiguren und ihr Gebrauch bei den Griechen vor Gorgias*. Berlin 1969.

Forbes Irving, P. M. C. *Metamorphosis in Greek Myths*. Oxford 1990.

Fraenkel, E. *Aeschylus: Agamemnon*. 3 vols., Oxford 1950.

Frazer, J. G. *Apollodorus: The Library* (Loeb). London 1921.

Friedländer, P. "Vorklassisch und nachklassisch", in W. Jaeger, ed. *Das Problem des Klassischen und die Antike*. Leipzig 1931, pp. 33–46.

Friis Johansen, H. and E. W. Whittle *Aeschylus: The Suppliants*. [Copenhagen] 1980.

Fritzsche, T. *De carmine Moscheo cui inscriptum est Epitaphius Bionis quaestiones criticae*, in G. C. H. Raspe, *Programm der Domschule zu Güstrow*. Güstrow 1867.

Führer, R. *Formproblem-Untersuchungen zu den Reden in der frühgriechischen Lyrik* (Zetemata 44). Munich 1974.

Gallavotti, C. "Intorno al codice Patavinus di Teocrito", *ICS* 6 (1981) 116–35.

Gallavotti, C. "La silloge tricliniana di Teocrito e un codice parigino-laurenziano", *BollClass* 3 (1982) 3–22.

Gebauer, G. A. *De poetarum graecorum bucolicorum imprimis Theocriti carminibus in Eclogis a Vergilio expressis*. Leipzig [1861].

Golega, J. *Der homerische Psalter*. Ettal 1960.

Goodwin, W. W. *Syntax of the Moods and Tenses of the Greek Verb*. Boston 1890.

Gow, A. S. F. *Theocritus*. 2nd ed. 2 vols., Cambridge 1952.

Gow, A. S. F. *The Greek Bucolic Poets*. Cambridge 1953.

Graefe, C. F. *Epistola critica in bucolicos graecos*. St Petersburg 1815.

Griffiths, J. G. *Plutarch's De Iside et Osiride*. [Cardiff] 1970.

Groningen, B. A. van "Quelques problèmes de la poésie bucolique grecque", *Mnem.* 11 (1958) 293–317.

Gutzwiller, K. J. *Theocritus' Pastoral Analogies*. Madison 1991.

Hanfmann, G. M. A. *The Season Sarcophagus in Dumbarton Oaks*. 2 vols., Harvard 1951.

Headlam, W. *Herodas: The Mimes and Fragments*. Cambridge 1922.

Heitsch, E. *Die griechischen Dichterfragmente der römischen Kaiserzeit* (Abhdl. Akad. Göttingen, philol.-hist. Kl., 3. Folge, Nr. 49 and 58). Göttingen 1961–4.

Henry, N. *Introduction to and Commentary on [Moschus] III*. B. Phil. thesis. Oxford 1975.

Hermann, G. *Zeitschrift für die Alterthumswissenschaft* 4 (1837) 225–36 (review of Meineke²).

Hicks, P. G. B. *Studies in the Manuscript Tradition of Theocritus*. Diss. Cambridge 1993.

Hiller, E. *Beiträge zur Textgeschichte der griechischen Bukoliker*. Leipzig 1888.

Holland, G. R. *De Polyphemo et Galatea* (Leipziger Studien 7). Leipzig 1884.

Hollis, A. S. *Ovid: Ars Amatoria Book I*. Oxford 1977.

Hollis, A. S. *Callimachus: Hecale*. Oxford 1990.

Hopkinson, N. *Callimachus: Hymn to Demeter*. Cambridge 1984.

Irwin, E. *Colour Terms in Greek Poetry*. Toronto 1974.

Jacobs, F. *Specimen emendationum*. Gotha 1786.

Kaibel, G. "Sententiarum liber secundus", *Hermes* 17 (1882) 408–24.

Kindstrand, J. F. *Bion of Borysthenes*. Uppsala 1976.

Koechly, H. *Coniectanea in Apollonium et Oppianum*. Leipzig 1838.

Koenen, L. "The Ptolemaic King as a Religious Figure", in A. Bulloch *et al.*, edd., *Images and Ideologies*. Berkeley 1993, pp. 25–115.

Koppiers, P. H. *Observata philologica*. Leiden 1771.

Lang, C. "Bions Grablied auf Adonis", *Eos* 2 (1865) 204–23.

Lapp, F. *De Callimachi Cyrenaei tropis et figuris*. Bonn 1965.

Lattimore, R. *Themes in Greek and Latin Epitaphs*. Urbana 1962.

Lennep, J. D. *Coluthi Raptus Helenae*. Leeuwarden 1747.

Lobeck, C. A. *Paralipomena grammaticae graecae*. Leipzig 1837.

Lyne, R. O. A. M. *Ciris: A Poem Attributed to Vergil*. Cambridge 1978.

Maas, M. and J. M. Snyder *Stringed Instruments of Ancient Greece*. New Haven 1989.

Maas, P. "ὑμὴν ὑμήν", *Philologus* 66 (1907) 589–96 = *Kl. Schr.* (Munich 1973) 221–8.

Maas, P. *Greek Metre*. Trans. H. Lloyd-Jones. Oxford 1962.

Mastronarde, D. J. *Euripides: Phoenissae*. Cambridge 1994.

Matthews, R. J. H. "The Lament for Adonis: Questions of Authorship", *Antichthon* 24 (1990) 32–52.

Matthews, R. J. H. "A *Sylloge* of Minor Bucolic", *Antichthon* 28 (1994) 25–51.

Molinos Tejada, T. *Los dorismos del Corpus Bucolicorum*. Amsterdam 1990.

Mumprecht, V. *Epitaphios Bionos: Text, Übersetzung, Kommentar*. Zürich 1964.

Nisbet, R. G. M. and M. Hubbard *A Commentary on Horace: Odes Book I.* Oxford 1970.

Norden, E. *Agnostos Theos.* Berlin 1913.

Omont, H. "Notice sur le manuscrit grec 2832 de la Bibliothèque Nationale", *RPh* 28 (1904) 189–97.

O'Neill, E. G. "The Localization of Metrical Word-Types in the Greek Hexameter", *YCS* 8 (1942) 105–78.

Onians, R. B. *The Origins of European Thought.* Cambridge 1954.

Page, D. L. *Corinna.* London 1953.

Palmerius, J. *Exercitationes in optimos fere auctores graecos.* Leiden 1668.

Papanghelis, T. D. *Propertius: A Hellenistic Poet on Love and Death.* Cambridge 1987.

Parker, W. H. *Priapea: Poems for a Phallic God.* London 1988.

Pearson, A. C. *The Fragments of Sophocles.* 3 vols., Cambridge 1917.

Pease, A. S. *Publi Vergili Maronis* Aeneidos *liber quartus.* Harvard 1935.

Pfeiffer, R. *History of Classical Scholarship from the Beginnings to the End of the Hellenistic Age.* Oxford 1968.

Pierson, J. *Verisimilium libri duo.* Leiden 1752.

Porro, A. "L'*Adonidis Epitaphium* di Bione e il modello Teocriteo", *Aevum Ant.* 1 (1988) 211–21.

Reed, J. "Bion I, Lines 25–7", *CQ* n.s. 42 (1992) 538–43.

Reed, J. D. "The Sexuality of Adonis", *ClAnt* 14 (1995) 317–47.

Renehan, R. *Studies in Greek Texts* (Hypomnemata 43). Göttingen 1976.

Richardson, N. J. *The Homeric Hymn to Demeter.* Oxford 1974.

Risch, E. *Wortbildung der homerischen Sprache.* 2nd ed. Berlin 1974.

Robert, C. *Eratosthenis Catasterismorum reliquiae.* Berlin 1878.

Roscher, W. H., ed. *Ausführliches Lexikon der griechischen und römischen Mythologie.* 6 vols., Leipzig 1884–1937.

Schmidt, J. H. H. *Synonymik der griechischen Sprache.* 4 vols., Leipzig 1876.

Schmiel, R. "Moschus' *Europa*", *CP* 76 (1981) 261–71.

Schmitz, S. T. *Adnotationes ad Bionis et Moschi carmina.* Münster 1856.

Schwyzer, E. *Griechische Grammatik.* 2 vols., Munich 1939–50 (vol. II rev. A. Debrunner).

Skutsch, F. *Aus Vergils Frühzeit*. Leipzig 1901.

Smith, K. F. *The Elegies of Albius Tibullus*. New York 1913.

Solmsen, F. "Eratosthenes' Erigone: A Reconstruction", *TAPA* 78 (1947) 252–75 = *Kl. Schr.* 1 (Hildesheim 1968) 225–48.

Sommer, F. "Zur griechischen Prosodie", *Glotta* 1 (1907–9) 145–240.

Steinmayer, O. C. *A Glossary of Terms Referring to Music in Greek Literature Before 400 B.C.* Diss. Yale 1985.

Stephanus, H. *Moschi, Bionis, Theocriti, elegantissimorum poetarum idyllia aliquot*. Venice 1555.

Stier, H. *De Bionis et Moschi Epitaphiis*. Berlin 1869.

Symonds, J. A. *Studies of the Greek Poets*. 3rd ed. London 1902.

Tarán, S. L. *The Art of Variation in the Hellenistic Epigram*. Leiden 1979.

Thesleff, H. *Studies on Intensification in Early and Classical Greek*. Helsinki 1954.

Tichy, E. *Onomatopoetische Verbalbildungen des Griechischen*. Vienna 1983.

Tränkle, H. *Appendix Tibulliana*. Berlin 1990.

Tsevat, M. "The Canaanite God Šälaḥ", *Vetus Testamentum* 4 (1954) 41–9.

Verdenius, W. J. *Commentaries on Pindar* 1. (*Mnem.* Suppl. 97). Leiden 1987.

Vermeule, E. *Aspects of Death in Early Greek Art and Poetry*. Berkeley 1979.

Verrall, A. W. *The Seven Against Thebes of Aeschylus*. London 1887.

Voss, J. H. *Anmerkungen und Randglossen zu Griechen und Römern*. Leipzig 1838.

Vox, O. "A proposito di un nuovo studio sull'*Epitafio di Adone* di Bione", *QUCC* n.s. 31 (1989) 139–43.

Walther, H. *Proverbia sententiaeque latinitatis medii aevi*. 9 vols., Göttingen 1963–86.

Wendel, C. *De nominibus bucolicis*. Leipzig 1900.

West, M. L. *Hesiod: Theogony*. Oxford 1966.

West, M. L. *Hesiod: Works and Days*. Oxford 1978.

West, M. L. *Greek Metre*. Oxford 1982.

West, M. L. *The Orphic Poems*. Oxford 1983.

West, M. L. *Euripides: Orestes*. Warminster 1987.

West, M. L. *Studies in Aeschylus*. Stuttgart 1990.
West, M. L. *Ancient Greek Music*. Oxford 1992.
Wifstrand, A. *Von Kallimachos zu Nonnos*. Lund 1933.
Wilamowitz-Moellendorff, U. von *Die Textgeschichte der griechischen Bukoliker* (Philologische Untersuchungen 18). Berlin 1906.
Wilamowitz-Moellendorff, U. von *Euripides: Herakles*. 2nd ed. Berlin 1909.
Wilkinson, L. P. *Golden Latin Artistry*. Cambridge 1963.
Will, E. "Le rituel des Adonies", *Syria* 52 (1975) 92–105.
Williams, G. W. *Tradition and Originality in Roman Poetry*. Oxford 1968.
Wyatt, W. F. *Metrical Lengthening in Homer* (Incunabula graeca 35). Rome 1969.

TEXTS AND TRANSLATIONS

SIGLORUM CONSPECTUS

Sigla Stobaeana (vide pp. 78–81):
F = Cod. Farnesinus bibl. nat. Neapolit. III D 15 (s. xiv)
P = Cod. Parisinus gr. 2129 (s. xv)
A = Cod. Parisinus gr. 1984 (s. xiv)
M = Cod. Escurialensis 90 (Σ II 14) (s. xii ineuntis)
S = Cod. Vindobonensis philol. gr. 67 (s. xi ineuntis)
Gelen = Editio S. Gelenii (Basileae 1532)
Trinc. = Editio V. Trincavelli (Venetiis 1536)
B = Cod. Parisinus gr. 1985 (s. xvi)

Sigla ad *Adonidis Epitaphium* pertinentia (vide pp. 70–7):
V = Cod. Vaticanus gr. 1824 (s. xiv ineuntis)
R = Cod. Parisinus gr. 2832 (s. xiv)
X = Cod. Vaticanus gr. 1311 (s. xv exeuntis) ex V descriptus
Ald.[1] = Editio prima Aldi Manutii (Venetiis 1496)
Ald.[2] = Editio altera Aldi Manutii (Venetiis 1496)
Cod. Vaticanus gr. 1379 (circa a. 1500) partim ex R descriptus
Cod. Parisinus gr. 2812A (s. xvi ineuntis) ex R descriptus
Junt. = Editio Philippi Juntae (Florentiae 1516)
Call. = Editio Zachariae Calliergis (Romae 1516)

Virorum doctorum nomina decurtata: Ahr(ens), Cam(erarius), Crisp(inus), Gaisf(ord), Heins(ius), Herm(ann), Koenn(ecke), Mein(eke), Mek(erchus), Piers(on), Ruhnk(en), Salm(asius), Schneid(ewin), Steph(anus), Urs(inus), Valck(enaer), Vulc(anius), Wachs(muth), Wak(efield), Wass(enbergh), Wil(amowitz-Moellendorff), Wint(erton).

ΒΙΩΝΟΣ ΑΠΟΣΠΑΣΜΑΤΑ

I

Ἀμφασία τὸν Φοῖβον ἕλεν τόσον ἄλγος ἔχοντα.
δίζετο φάρμακα πάντα σοφὰν δ᾽ ἐπεμαίετο τέχναν,
χρῖεν δ᾽ ἀμβροσίᾳ καὶ νέκταρι, χρῖεν ἅπασαν
ὠτειλάν· μοιραῖα δ᾽ ἀναλθέα τραύματα πάντα.

II

⟨ΚΛΕΟΔΑΜΟΣ⟩

Εἴαρος, ὦ Μύρσων, ἢ χείματος ἢ φθινοπώρω
ἢ θέρεος τί τοι ἁδύ; τί δὲ πλέον εὔχεαι ἐλθεῖν;
ἢ θέρος, ἁνίκα πάντα τελείεται ὅσσα μογεῦμες,
ἢ γλυκερὸν φθινόπωρον, ὅκ᾽ ἀνδράσι λιμὸς ἐλαφρά,
ἢ καὶ χεῖμα δύσεργον—ἐπεὶ καὶ χείματι πολλοί
θαλπόμενοι τέρπονται ἀεργίᾳ τε καὶ ὄκνῳ—
ἢ τοι καλὸν ἔαρ πλέον εὔαδεν; εἰπὲ τί τοι φρήν
αἱρεῖται, λαλέειν γὰρ ἐπέτραπεν ἁ σχολὰ ἄμμιν.

I Stob. 1.5.7 codd. = FP Tit.: ἐκ τῶν βίωνος βουκολικῶν, εἰς ὑάκινθον 1 φοῖβον P: βίον F ἔλεν F (spiritu leni), ἕλε P 2 ἐπεμαίετο Crisp.: ἐπεβένετο F: -βώσετο P ante corr.: -βώσατο P post corr. 3 χρῖεν utrubique Urs., χρεῖεν codd. 4 μοιραῖα Herm.: μοίραιαι F: μοίραισι P ἀναλθέα Urs., -θία codd. τραύματα Herm.: φάρμακα codd.

II Stob. 1.8.39 codd. = FP Tit.: ἐκ τῶν βίωνος βουκολικῶν 1 ὦ Urs.: ὁ codd. φθινοπώρω Brunck, -ρου codd. 3 ὅσσα Urs.: ἅσσα codd. 4 ὅκ᾽ Brunck, ὅτ᾽ codd. (cf. 12 τόκα) ἐλαφρά F: -ρός P 6 τέρπονται Grotius: θάλποντας codd. ἀεργίᾳ Brunck (-γίῃ iam Urs.), -γείῃ codd. 7 εὔαδεν; εἰπὲ τί τοι φρὴν Urs.: εὔαδ᾽ ἐνεῖπε τοι τι φρὸν F: εὔα P δεν addito a man. sec. 8 σχολὰ F, -λαὶ P ἄμμιν Valck., ἡμῖν codd.

FRAGMENTS

I

Dumbfoundedness took hold of Phoebus in such great anguish.
He sought out every remedy and plied his skilful craft.
He anointed with ambrosia and nectar, anointed the whole
wound; but all wounds dealt by fate are incurable.

II

CLEODAMUS

Of spring, Myrson, and winter and autumn
and summer, which is pleasing to you? Which do you most wish to come?
Is it the summer, when everything that we labour at comes to fruition,
or sweet autumn, when hunger is slight for men,
or even laborious winter—since even in winter many people,
warming themselves, take delight in inactivity and sluggishness?
Or does lovely spring please you most? Tell which your heart
chooses, for leisure has granted us opportunity to talk.

⟨ΜΥΡΣΩΝ⟩

κρίνειν οὐκ ἐπέοικε θεήια ἔργα βροτοῖσι,
πάντα γὰρ ἱερὰ ταῦτα καὶ ἁδέα· σεῦ δὲ ἕκατι
ἐξερέω, Κλεόδαμε, τό μοι πέλεν ἅδιον ἄλλων.
οὐκ ἐθέλω θέρος ἦμεν, ἐπεὶ τόκα μ' ἅλιος ὀπτῇ.
οὐκ ἐθέλω φθινόπωρον, ἐπεὶ νόσον ὥρια τίκτει.
οὖλον χεῖμα φέρειν· νιφετὸν κρυμώς τε φοβεῦμαι.
εἶαρ ἐμοὶ τριπόθατον ὅλῳ λυκάβαντι παρείη,
ἁνίκα μήτε κρύος μήθ' ἅλιος ἄμμε βαρύνει.
εἴαρι πάντα κύει, πάντ' εἴαρος ἁδέα βλαστεῖ,
χἀ νὺξ ἀνθρώποισιν ἴσα καὶ ὁμοίιος ἀώς.

III

Μοίσας Ἔρως καλέοι, Μοῖσαι τὸν Ἔρωτα φέροιεν.
μολπὰν ταὶ Μοῖσαί μοι ἀεὶ ποθέοντι διδοῖεν,
τὰν γλυκερὰν μολπάν, τᾶς φάρμακον ἅδιον οὐδέν.

IV

Ἐκ θαμινᾶς ῥαθάμιγγος, ὅπως λόγος, αἰὲς ἰοίσας
χἀ λίθος ἐς ῥωχμὸν κοιλαίνεται.

11 τό codd.: fort. τί ἄλλων FP post corr., -ον P ante corr. 14 οὖλον codd.: οὐ λῶ Ameis κρυμώς Brunck (-μούς iam Urs.), -μός F: -μόει P 16 ἄμμε Urs. (sic): -μι codd. 17 βλαστεῖ Urs., -τη FP post corr., βάστη P ante corr.

III Stob. 1.9.3 codd. = FP Tit.: ἐκ τῶν βίωνος βουκολικῶν 1 μοῖσας P ante corr., οίσας F littera initiali a rubricatore non suppleta: μοῖσαν P post corr. 2 ταὶ P post corr., τε FP ante corr. μοῖσαι FP post corr.: μοῖσα P ante corr. 3 ἅδιον P post corr.: ἅδη P ante corr.: εὕδη F

IV Stob. 3.29.52 cod. = S Tit.: ἐκ τῶν βίωνος σμυρναίου βουκολικῶν 1 θαμινᾶς Ahr., -ῆς cod. ὅπως Herm.: ωκως cod.

MYRSON

It is not seemly for mortals to judge the works of the gods,
for all of them are holy and gratifying. But for your sake
I shall say, Cleodamus, which to me is more gratifying than the rest.
I do not wish for summer, because then the sun burns me.
I do not wish for autumn, because it produces disease in season.
Winter is cruel to bear; I fear snow and chills.
Let spring, thrice-desired to me, be here all year round,
when neither frost nor sun oppresses us.
In spring everything burgeons, everything pleasant blossoms in spring,
and night and day are equal for humans.

III

Let Eros call the Muses, let the Muses bear Eros.
Let the Muses give me song while I forever desire,
sweet song, than which no medicine is sweeter.

IV

From a constant dripping forever running, as the story goes,
even stone is hollowed into a cleft.

V

Οὐ καλόν, ὦ φίλε, πάντα λόγον ποτὶ τέκτονα φοιτῆν,
μηδ' ἐπὶ πάντ' ἄλλω χρέος ἰσχέμεν· ἀλλὰ καὶ αὐτός
τεχνᾶσθαι σύριγγα, πέλει δέ τοι εὐμαρὲς ἔργον.

VI

Μηδὲ λίπῃς μ' ἀγέραστον, ἐπεὶ χὼ Φοῖβος ἀείδειν
μισθὸν ἔδωκε †τιμὰ δὲ τὰ πράγματα κρέσσονα ποιεῖ.

VII

Οὐκ οἶδ' οὐδ' ἐπέοικεν ἃ μὴ μάθομες πονέεσθαι.

VIII

Εἴ μοι καλὰ πέλει τὰ μελύδρια, καὶ τάδε μῶνα
κῦδος ἐμοὶ θήσοντι τά μοι πάρος ὤπασε Μοῖρα·
εἰ δ' οὐχ ἁδέα ταῦτα, τί μοι πολὺ πλείονα μοχθεῖν;
εἰ μὲν γὰρ βιότω διπλόον χρόνον ἄμμιν ἔδωκεν
ἢ Κρονίδας ἢ Μοῖρα πολύτροπος, ὥστ' ἀνύεσθαι
τὸν μὲν ἐς εὐφροσύναν καὶ χάρματα, τὸν δ' ἐνὶ μόχθῳ,

V Stob. 3.29.53 cod. = S Tit.: τοῦ αὐτοῦ (ac fr. 4) 2 μηδ' ἐπὶ Grotius: μηδέτοι cod. ἄλλω Salm. (ἄλλου iam B post corr. necnon Urs.), ἄλλο cod. 3 τεχνᾶσθαι cod., fort. τεχνῆσθαι

VI Stob. 4.1.8 cod. = S Tit.: βίωνος βουκολικά 1 ἐπεὶ Gelen 215: ἐπὴν cod.

VII Stob. 4.16.14 codd. = AMS Tit.: ἐκ τῶν βίωνος βουκολικῶν 1 οὐδ' om. M ἐπέοικεν ASM post corr., ἐποιοικεν M ante corr. μάθομες Ahr., -ομεν S post corr., -ωμεν AMS ante corr. πονέεσθαι AS: πορεύσθαι M

VIII Stob. 4.16.15 codd. = AMS Tit.: τοῦ αὐτοῦ (ac fr. 7) 1 μοι codd.: μευ Ahr. μῶνα Brunck (μοῦνα iam Trinc.), μόνα codd. 4 βιότω Trinc., βιότῳ S post corr., βιώτω AM, βιώτῳ S ante corr. ἄμμιν B, ἄμβιν A, ἁμῖν MS 6 ἐνὶ μόχθω AS: ἐριμόχθω M

V

It is not right, my friend, to have recourse to a craftsman
for every purpose,
nor should you for every purpose have need of another.
But rather you yourself
craft a syrinx, for it is quite an easy task.

VI

Do not leave me unrewarded, since even Phoebus
gave the gift of song in exchange ... and honour makes
things better.

VII

I know not how—nor is it proper—to labour at what
we have not learned.

VIII

If my little songs are beautiful, even those alone
that Fate granted me aforetime will establish fame for
me.
But if these are not sweet, why should I labour at many
more?
For if wily Fate or the son of Cronus had given us
a double span of life, so as to live out one
with a view to merriment and delights, the other in
labour,

ἦν τάχα μοχθήσαντι ποθ' ὕστερον ἐσθλὰ δέχεσθαι.
εἰ δὲ θεοὶ κατένευσαν ἕνα χρόνον ἐς βίον ἐλθεῖν
ἀνθρώποις, καὶ τόνδε βραχὺν καὶ μείονα πάντων,
ἐς πόσον, ἆ δειλοί, καμάτως κεὶς ἔργα πονεῦμες,
ψυχὰν δ' ἄχρι τίνος ποτὶ κέρδεα καὶ ποτὶ τέχνας
βάλλομες ἱμείροντες ἀεὶ πολὺ πλείονος ὄλβω;
ἦ λαθόμεσθ' ἄρα πάντες ὅτι θνατοὶ γενόμεσθα,
χὡς βραχὺν ἐκ Μοίρας λάχομες χρόνον;

IX

Ταὶ Μοῖσαι τὸν Ἔρωτα τὸν ἄγριον ἢ φοβέονται
ἠκ θυμῶ φιλέοντι, καὶ ἐκ ποδὸς αὐτῷ ἕπονται.
κἢν μὲν ἄρα ψυχάν τις ἔχων ἀνέραστον ἀείδῃ,
τῆνον ὑπεκφεύγοντι καὶ οὐκ ἐθέλοντι διδάσκειν·
ἢν δὲ νόον τις ἔρωτι δονεύμενος ἁδὺ μελίσδῃ,
ἐς τῆνον μάλα πᾶσαι ἐπειγόμεναι προρέοντι.
μάρτυς ἐγὼν ὅτι μῦθος ὅδ' ἔπλετο πᾶσιν ἀλαθής·
ἢν μὲν γὰρ βροτὸν ἄλλον ἢ ἀθανάτων τινὰ μέλπω,
βαμβαίνει μοι γλῶσσα καὶ ὡς πάρος οὐκέτ' ἀείδει·
ἢν δ' αὖτ' ἐς τὸν Ἔρωτα καὶ ἐς Λυκίδαν τι μελίσδω,
καὶ τόκα μοι χαίροισα διὰ στόματος ῥέει ᾠδά.

8 ἐλθεῖν A, ἐλθῆν MS 9 βραχὺν MS: βραδὺν A μείονα A, μήονα MS 10 ἆ δειλοὶ S, ἀδειλοὶ AM κεὶς MS, καὶ εἰς A 12 βάλλομες MSA post corr., βάλλωμεν A ante corr. πλείονος Ahr., πλέο- codd. 13 ἦ λαθόμεσθ' Herm.: λαθόμεθ' ἢ MS, λαθέμεθ' ἢ A γενόμεσθα Gesner (1543), -μεθα codd. 14 λάχομες Brunck, -μεν codd.

IX Stob. 4.20.7 codd. = AMS Tit.: ἐκ τῶν βίωνος βουκολικῶν 2 ἠκ MS, ἢ 'κ A ἕπονται AS, -τα M 3 κὴν M, κ' ἢν AS ἀείδῃ Steph.: δεῖ δὴ MSA ante corr.: ὀπηδη A post corr., οἶμαι scripto in marg. 5 τις Brunck: τῶ codd. μελίσδῃ MS, -σδει A 6 προρέοντι MS, -ρρέοντι A 7 ἀλαθής Brunck, ἀλη- codd. 9 μοι A, μευ S necnon M in ras. 10 ἐς τὸν S, εἰς τὸν A: ἐστιν M 11 χαίροισα AS, -ρουσα M διὰ codd.: κατὰ Gelen 91 ῥέει Gesner (1543): ῥεῖ codd.

perhaps, once having laboured, one could receive good things afterward.
But since the gods have agreed for one span of life to come
for humans, and that one short and lesser than all things,
how long, O wretches, are we to work at toils and tasks?
And how long are we to cast our soul into profits and into crafts,
forever desiring much more wealth?
Have we then all indeed forgotten that we are mortal,
and that we have been allotted a brief time by Fate?

IX

The Muses are either intimidated by savage Eros
or they love him heartily, and they follow in his train.
And so if anyone sings with a loveless soul,
him they flee and refuse to teach.
But if anyone sings sweetly with a mind awhirl with love,
to him they hurriedly gravitate all together.
I am witness that this saying is true for everyone.
For if I sing of any other mortal or immortal,
my tongue trembles and no longer sings as before;
but if I sing anything about Eros and Lycidas,
then the song flows freely through my mouth.

X

Ἁ μεγάλα μοι Κύπρις ἔθ' ὑπνώοντι παρέστα
νηπίαχον τὸν Ἔρωτα καλᾶς ἐκ χειρὸς ἄγοισα
ἐς χθόνα νευστάζοντα, τόσον δέ μοι ἔφρασε μῦθον·
"μέλπειν μοι, φίλε βοῦτα, λαβὼν τὸν Ἔρωτα
δίδασκε".
ὣς λέγε· χἂ μὲν ἀπῆνθεν, ἐγὼ δ' ὅσα βουκολίασδον
νήπιος ὡς ἐθέλοντα μαθεῖν τὸν Ἔρωτα δίδασκον,
ὡς εὗρεν πλαγίαυλον ὁ Πάν, ὡς αὐλὸν Ἀθάνα,
ὡς χέλυν Ἑρμάων, κίθαριν ὡς ἁδὺς Ἀπόλλων.
ταῦτά νιν ἐξεδίδασκον· ὃ δ' οὐκ ἐμπάζετο μύθων,
ἀλλά μοι αὐτὸς ἄειδεν ἐρωτύλα, καί μ' ἐδίδασκεν
θνατῶν ἀθανάτων τε πόθως καὶ ματέρος ἔργα.
κἠγὼν ἐκλαθόμαν μὲν ὅσων τὸν Ἔρωτα δίδασκον,
ὅσσα δ' Ἔρως μ' ἐδίδαξεν ἐρωτύλα πάντ' ἐδιδάχθην.

XI

Ἕσπερε, τᾶς ἐρατᾶς χρύσεον φάος Ἀφρογενείας,
Ἕσπερε, κυανέας ἱερόν, φίλε, νυκτὸς ἄγαλμα,

X Stob. 4.20.26 codd. = AMS Tit.: ἐκ τῶν βίωνος βουκολικῶν 1 μοι om. A ὑπνώοντι M, -νόωντι S, -νόοντι A 2 καλᾶς MS, -λῆς A 3 ἐς om. M 4 βοῦτα codd., βῶτα Briggs 5 ἀπῆνθεν M ante corr., -λθεν AM post corr., -λθε S βουκολίασδον codd., fort. βωκ- 7 πλαγίαυλον A S, πλαυγ- M ὁ Πάν A post corr., fort. e Gesnero (1543): ὅπαν M, ὅπα S, ὄπα A ante corr. 9 νιν Ameis, μιν codd. 10 ἄειδεν MS, -δε A μ' ἐδίδασκεν A S, με δίδ- M 11 πόθως Brunck, -θους A M: πάθους S 12 ἐκλαθόμαν MS, -θέμαν A ὅσων MS, -ον A 13 ὅσσα MS, ὅσα A μ' ἐδίδαξεν MS, με δίδ- A

XI Stob. 4.20.27 codd. = AMS Tit.: τοῦ αὐτοῦ (ac fr. 10) 1 ἐρατᾶς Trinc.: ἔρωτας codd. ἀφρογενείας A, -ῇας MS

X

Great Cypris appeared to me while I was still asleep,
leading the childlike Eros by her fair hand
(he was nodding toward the ground), and spoke to me so great a word as this:
"Dear herdsman, take Eros, and for my sake teach him to sing."
Thus she spoke. And she went away, but I set about teaching Eros
all the rustic songs I used to sing – naïve, as if he wanted to learn! – :
how Pan invented the cross-pipe; Athena, the double pipe;
Hermes, the tortoise-shell lyre; sweet Apollo, the box-lyre.
These things did I teach him, but he paid my words no heed;
he himself rather sang to me of little love affairs and taught me
the desires of mortals and immortals and the deeds of his mother.
And I forgot all the things I was teaching Eros,
and I learned all the little love affairs that Eros taught me.

XI

Hesperus, golden lamp of lovely Aphrogenea,
Hesperus, my friend, holy adornment of the sable night,

τόσσον ἀφαυρότερος μήνας ὅσον ἔξοχος ἄστρων,
χαῖρε φίλος καί μοι ποτὶ ποιμένα κῶμον ἄγοντι
ἀντὶ σελαναίας τὺ δίδου φάος, ὥνεκα τήνα
σάμερον ἀρχομένα τάχιον δύεν. οὐκ ἐπὶ φωράν
ἔρχομαι οὐδ' ἵνα νυκτὸς ὁδοιπορέοντας ἐνοχλέω,
ἀλλ' ἐράω, καλὸν δέ τ' ἐρασσαμένῳ συνέρασθαι.

XII

Ὄλβιοι οἱ φιλέοντες ἐπὴν ἴσον ἀντεράωνται.
ὄλβιος ἦν Θησεὺς τῶ Πειριθόω παρεόντος,
εἰ καὶ ἀμειλίκτοιο κατήλυθεν εἰς Ἀίδαο.
ὄλβιος ἦν †χαλεποῖσιν ἐν ἀξείνοισιν† Ὀρέστας
ὥνεκά οἱ ξυνὰς Πυλάδας ᾄρητο κελεύθως.
ἦν μάκαρ Αἰακίδας ἑτάρω ζώοντος Ἀχιλλεύς·
ὄλβιος ἦν θνᾴσκων ὅτι οἱ μόρον αἰνὸν ἄμυνεν.

XIII

Ἰξευτὰς ἔτι κῶρος ἐν ἄλσεϊ δενδράεντι
ὄρνεα θηρεύων τὸν ὑπόπτερον εἶδεν Ἔρωτα

3 ὅσσον ... τόσον Ahr. ἀφαυρότερος Urs.: -ρον codd. μήνας M, μήινας S, μείνας A ἄστρων MS, -τρον A 7 ὁδοιπορέοντας Gaisf. (1822) II.460: -οντα A, -οντ' MS ἐνοχλέω MS, -χλῶ A 8 ἐρασσαμένῳ MS, ἐρασα- A ante corr.: ἐρρασσαμένην A post corr. συνέρασθαι Schaefer: συνερᾶσθαι codd.

XII Stob. 4.20.28 codd. = AM Tit.: τοῦ αὐτοῦ (ac fr. 11) 1 οἱ A post corr., ex Gesnero (1549) secundum Hense: om. M A ante corr. ἐπὴν M, ἐπὰν A ἀντεράωνται B Urs.: -άοντε codd. 2 θησεὺς M, θασεὺς A παρεόντος M, περ- A 4 ἦν om. A 5 ὥνεκα Ahr., οὕν- codd. ᾄρητο Urs.: ἄρκτο M: ἄροιτο A κελεύθως Ahr., -θους codd. 6 ἑτάρω Gesner (1549): -αίρω A, -αιρο M 7 θνάσκων A: θρά- M

XIII Stob. 4.20.57 codd. = AMS Tit.: ἐκ τῶν βίωνος σμυρναίου βουκολικῶν 1 δενδράεντι Trinc: δένδρα ἐντὶ codd. 2 ὑπόπτερον Briggs: ἀπότροπον codd. post hunc versum codd. habent ὧν ἕνεκα δὴ μέγα φαίνετο (-ται A) ὄρνεον (ὀρνέων S) αὐτῷ ex 4; deleverunt AS

dimmer than the moon as you are pre-eminent among
the stars,
be of good grace, and as I go to serenade a shepherd
give me light in place of the moon, since she
today, at the beginning of her course, has set too early.
Not for thievery
do I go, nor to harass wayfarers by night;
but I am in love, and it is right to join a lover in loving.

XII

Blessed are those who love when they are loved equally
in return.
Blessed was Theseus when Pirithoüs was at his side,
even though he went down to the house of implacable
Hades.
Blessed was Orestes among the inhospitable
[Taurians],
since Pylades had chosen journeys in common with
him.
Achilles, scion of Aeacus, was blessed when his
companion was alive;
blessed was he in death, since he avenged his baneful
fate.

XIII

A fowler, still a boy, in a grove filled with trees
while hunting birds saw winged Eros

ἑσδόμενον πύξοιο ποτὶ κλάδον· ὡς δ' ἐνόησε,
χαίρων ὥνεκα δὴ μέγα φαίνετο ὄρνεον αὐτῷ,
τὼς καλάμως ἅμα πάντας ἐπ' ἀλλάλοισι συνάπτων
τᾷ καὶ τᾷ τὸν Ἔρωτα μετάλμενον ἀμφεδόκευεν.
χὠ παῖς, ἀσχαλάων ὅτι οἱ τέλος οὐδὲν ἀπάντη,
τὼς καλάμως ῥίψας ποτ' ἀροτρέα πρέσβυν ἵκανεν
ὅς νιν τάνδε τέχναν ἐδιδάξατο, καὶ λέγεν αὐτῷ
καί οἱ δεῖξεν Ἔρωτα καθήμενον. αὐτὰρ ὁ πρέσβυς
μειδιάων κίνησε κάρη καὶ ἀμείβετο παῖδα·
"φείδεο τᾶς θήρας, μηδ' ἐς τόδ' ἔτ' ὄρνεον ἔρχευ.
φεῦγε μακράν· κακόν ἐντι τὸ θηρίον. ὄλβιος ἔσσῃ
εἰσόκα μή νιν ἕλῃς· ἢν δ' ἀνέρος ἐς μέτρον ἔλθῃς
οὗτος ὁ νῦν φεύγων καὶ ἀπάλμενος αὐτὸς ἀφ' αὐτῶ
ἐλθὼν ἐξαπίνας κεφαλὰν ἔπι σεῖο καθιξεῖ."

XIV

Ἅμερε Κυπρογένεια, Διὸς τέκος ἠὲ θαλάσσας,
τίπτε τόσον θνατοῖσι καὶ ἀθανάτοισι χαλέπτεις;
τυτθὸν ἔφαν· τί νυ τόσσον ἀπήχθεο καὶ τὶν αὐτᾷ
ταλίκον ὡς πάντεσσι κακὸν τὸν Ἔρωτα τεκέσθαι,
ἄγριον, ἄστοργον, μορφᾷ νόον οὐδὲν ὁμοῖον;
ἐς τί δέ νιν πτανὸν καὶ ἑκαβόλον ὤπασας ἦμεν
ὡς μὴ πικρὸν ἐόντα δυναίμεθα τῆνον ἀλύξαι;

3 ἐνόησε Herm., ἐνόασε codd. 5 ἀλλάλοισι MS, ἀλλή- A 6 ἀμφεδόκευεν AS, -δίκευεν M: -δίωκεν Uvarov 7 ἀσχαλάων S, -λῶν AM ὅτι Brunck: οὕνεχα codd. 8 ἵκανεν AS, -νε M 9 νιν MS: δὴ A τέχναν A, -να M, -νην S 12 τόδ' ἔτ' ὄρνεον Urs.: τόδε τ' ὄρν- M S: τόδε τὤρν- B: τόδ' ὄρν- A 14 εἰσόκα codd.: -κε Ahr. νιν Ameis, μιν codd. 16 ἔπι Wint.: ἐπὶ codd.

XIV Stob. 4.20.58 codd. = AM Tit.: τοῦ αὐτοῦ (ac fr. 13) 2 χαλέπτεις codd.: χαλέπτῃ Briggs 3 ἀπήχθεο A, ἀπέχθεο M τὶν αὐτᾷ Graefe: τιναυτα M, τίν' αὐτὰ A 4 ταλίκον M, τηλ- A τεκέσθαι Herm.: τέκηαι A, τέκναι M 6 ἐς τί M: ἔστι A

sitting on a branch of a box-tree. When he saw him,
rejoicing because he seemed a big bird to him,
he fitted all his sticks together on to one another
and waited for Eros as he hopped hither and thither.
And the boy, vexed because no success came to him,
threw away his sticks and came to an old ploughman
who had taught him this craft, and he spoke to him
and showed him Eros perched in the tree. But the old man
shook his head with a smile and answered the boy:
"Desist from this hunt, and go after that bird no longer.
Flee far away! The creature is evil. You will be fortunate
as long as you do not catch him. But if you arrive at a man's measure,
this creature who now flees and jumps away will of his own accord
come suddenly and alight upon your head."

XIV

Kindly Cyprogenea, child of Zeus or of the sea,
why do you trouble mortals and immortals so much?
I have said only a little: why were you so hateful even toward yourself
as to have given birth to Eros, such a great evil to all,
savage, unloving, with a mind unequal to his looks?
Why did you grant that he might be winged and far-shooting
so that, bitter as he is, we might not be able to escape him?

XV

Μορφὰ θηλυτέραισι πέλει καλόν, ἀνέρι δ' ἀλκά.

XVI

Αὐτὰρ ἐγὼν βασεῦμαι ἐμὰν ὁδὸν ἐς τὸ κάταντες
τῆνο ποτὶ ψάμαθόν τε καὶ ἀιόνα ψιθυρίσδων,
λισσόμενος Γαλάτειαν ἀπηνέα· τὰς δὲ γλυκείας
ἐλπίδας ὑστατίω μέχρι γήραος οὐκ ἀπολείψω.

XVII

Πάντα θεῶ γε θέλοντος †ἀνύσιμα, πάντα βροτοῖσι·
ἐκ μακάρων γὰρ ῥᾶστα καὶ οὐκ ἀτέλεστα γένοντο.

XV Stob. 4.21.3 codd. = AMS Tit.: ἐκ τῶν βίωνος βουκολικῶν
1 θηλυτέραισι Wil., -ῃσι codd.

XVI Stob. 4.46.17 cod. = S Tit.: ἐκ τῶν βίωνος βουκολικῶν
1 βασεῦμαι Urs.: βὰς εὖ καὶ cod. 2 ἀιόνα Brunck (ἠιόνα iam Trinc.), ἠόνα cod.

XVII Orion. Anth. 5.11 cod. = Vindob. phil. gr. 321 (s. xiv) Tit.: {ἐκ τῆς ὁμολογούσης} ⟨ἐκ⟩ τῶν βίωνος βουκολικῶν 1 θεῶ γε θέλοντος Schneid. p. 81: θεοῦ γὰρ θέλ- cod. 2 γὰρ ῥάστα cod.: ῥάιστα Ahr. γένοντο Ahr.: γένοιτο cod.

XV

Beauty is the grace of women, courage of a man.

XVI

But I will make my way down the hillside
yonder to the sand and to the shore, whispering,
beseeching cruel Galatea. And my sweet
hopes I shall never abandon until uttermost old age.

XVII

If God indeed be willing, everything is possible,
    everything for mortals:
for from the blessed ones things come most easy and
    not without issue.

ΑΔΩΝΙΔΟΣ ΕΠΙΤΑΦΙΟΣ

Αἰάζω τὸν Ἄδωνιν, "ἀπώλετο καλὸς Ἄδωνις".
"ὤλετο καλὸς Ἄδωνις", ἐπαιάζουσιν Ἔρωτες.
μηκέτι πορφυρέοις ἐνὶ φάρεσι, Κύπρι, κάθευδε·
ἔγρεο δειλαία, κυανόστολε καὶ πλατάγησον
στήθεα καὶ λέγε πᾶσιν, "ἀπώλετο καλὸς Ἄδωνις".
  αἰάζω τὸν Ἄδωνιν· ἐπαιάζουσιν Ἔρωτες.
κεῖται καλὸς Ἄδωνις ἐν ὤρεσι μηρὸν ὀδόντι
λευκῷ λευκὸν ὀδόντι τυπείς, καὶ Κύπριν ἀνιῇ
λεπτὸν ἀποψύχων· τὸ δέ οἱ μέλαν εἴβεται αἷμα
χιονέας κατὰ σαρκός, ὑπ' ὀφρύσι δ' ὄμματα ναρκῇ,
καὶ τὸ ῥόδον φεύγει τῶ χείλεος· ἀμφὶ δὲ τήνῳ
θνᾴσκει καὶ τὸ φίλαμα τὸ μήποτε Κύπρις ἀποίσει.
Κύπριδι μὲν τὸ φίλαμα καὶ οὐ ζώοντος ἀρέσκει,
ἀλλ' οὐκ οἶδεν Ἄδωνις ὅ νιν θνᾴσκοντα φίλασεν.
  αἰάζω τὸν Ἄδωνιν· ἐπαιάζουσιν Ἔρωτες.
ἄγριον ἄγριον ἕλκος ἔχει κατὰ μηρὸν Ἄδωνις,
μεῖζον δ' ἁ Κυθέρεια φέρει ποτικάρδιον ἕλκος.
τῆνον μὲν περὶ παῖδα φίλοι κύνες ὠρύονται
καὶ νύμφαι κλαίουσιν ὀρειάδες· ἁ δ' Ἀφροδίτα
λυσαμένα πλοκαμῖδας ἀνὰ δρυμὼς ἀλάληται

codd. = R V Tit. ἀδώνιδος ἐπιτάφιος V, θεοκρίτ(ου) ἀδώνιδος ἐπιτάφιος δωρίδι R Bioni primus adscripsit Cam. 1 ἄδωνις R, ἄδ- V 4 δειλαία R, -έα V κυανόστολε Vulc., -οστόλε codd.: -όστολα Wil. 6 ἐπαιάζουσιν R, ἐπ' αἰ- V 7 ἐν Ameis: ἐπ' codd. 8 ὀδόντι V ante corr.: ὀδόντα R V post corr. ἀνιῇ R, -εῖ V 11 ῥόδον V: ῥόδει R χείλεος Ald.², -ευς codd. 12 ἀποίσει V: R vix legitur (ἀποίσει corr. ex ἀπήσει secundum Dübner ap. Ahr.) 13 R hunc versum in margine habet ζώοντος ἀρέσκει R: ζώοντες ἄρεσκεν V 14 νιν Wak., μιν codd. θνᾴσκοντα φίλασεν Fritzsche, θνᾴσκοντ' ἐφίλ- codd. 15 ἐπαιάζουσιν R, ἐπ' αἰ- V 17 ποτικάρδιον X necnon Ald.², ποτὶ κάρδιον codd. 18 τῆνον Brunck, κεῖνον codd. ὠρύονται Herm. (ὠρύσαντο iam Call.): ὠδύραντο R, ὀδύραντο V 19 ὀρειάδες R, ὀρι- V 20 δρυμὼς R, -οὺς V ἀλάληται Junt. Call., ἀλαλεῖται codd.

EPITAPH ON ADONIS

I mourn Adonis: "Fair Adonis is dead!"
"Fair Adonis is dead!" the Loves mourn in reply.
Sleep no longer, Cypris, in crimson-dyed sheets;
wake, wretch, and black-robed loudly beat
your breast and tell to all, "Fair Adonis is dead!"
   I mourn Adonis; the Loves mourn in reply.
Fair Adonis lies in the mountains, his thigh –
white thigh – by a white tusk stricken, and he causes
      Cypris grief
as he faintly breathes his last. His dark blood runs
over his snowy flesh, and beneath his brows his eyes
      grow numb
and the rose flees from his lip, and on it
dies the kiss that Cypris will never carry away.
To Cypris the kiss is pleasing even though he is not
      alive;
but Adonis does not know that she has kissed him when
      he is dead.
   I mourn Adonis; the Loves mourn in reply.
Adonis has a savage, savage wound on his thigh,
but Cytherea carries a greater wound in her heart.
Around that boy his dear hounds bay
and mountain nymphs weep. But Aphrodite,
having let down her hair, rushes through the woods

πενθαλέα νήπλεκτος ἀσάνδαλος, αἱ δὲ βάτοι νιν
ἐρχομέναν κείροντι καὶ ἱερὸν αἷμα δρέπονται.
ὀξὺ δὲ κωκύοισα δι' ἄγκεα μακρὰ φορεῖται
Ἀσσύριον βοόωσα, πόσιν καὶ παῖδα καλεῦσα.
ἀμφὶ δέ νιν μέλαν εἷμα παρ' ὀμφαλὸν ᾁωρεῖτο,
στήθεα δ' ἐκ χειρῶν φοινίσσετο, τοὶ δ' ὑπὸ μαζοί
χιόνεοι τὸ πάροιθεν Ἀδώνιδι πορφύροντο.
"αἰαῖ τὰν Κυθέρειαν" ἐπαιάζουσιν Ἔρωτες.
ὤλεσε τὸν καλὸν ἄνδρα, συνώλεσεν ἱερὸν εἶδος.
Κύπριδι μὲν καλὸν εἶδος ὅτε ζώεσκεν Ἄδωνις,
κάτθανε δ' ἁ μορφὰ σὺν Ἀδώνιδι. "τὰν Κύπριν αἰαῖ"
ὤρεα πάντα λέγοντι, καὶ αἱ δρύες "αἲ τὸν Ἄδωνιν".
καὶ ποταμοὶ κλαίοντι τὰ πένθεα τᾶς Ἀφροδίτας,
καὶ παγαὶ τὸν Ἄδωνιν ἐν ὤρεσι δακρύοντι,
ἄνθεα δ' ἐξ ὀδύνας ἐρυθαίνεται· ἁ δὲ Κυθήρα
πάντας ἀνὰ κναμώς, ἀνὰ πᾶν νάπος οἰκτρὸν ἀείδει
"αἰαῖ τὰν Κυθέρειαν· ἀπώλετο καλὸς Ἄδωνις".
Ἀχὼ δ' ἀντεβόασεν, "ἀπώλετο καλὸς Ἄδωνις".
Κύπριδος αἰνὸν ἔρωτα τίς οὐκ ἔκλαυσεν ἂν αἰαῖ;
ὡς ἴδεν, ὡς ἐνόησεν Ἀδώνιδος ἄσχετον ἕλκος,

21 ἀσάνδαλος codd., fort. ἀσάμβ- 22 κείροντι Ald.[1], -ουσι codd. 23 κωκύοισα Brunck, -ουσα codd. ἄγκεα Ald.[2]: ἄγγεα codd. φορεῖται R: φέρεται V ante corr., φέρηται V post corr. 24 πόσιν καὶ παῖδα R: ποσὶ καὶ πόδα V 25 νιν Wak., μιν codd. εἷμα Ahr.: αἷμα codd. ᾁωρεῖτο Wil., ᾐωρ- codd. 26 στήθεα R, στάθ- V χειρῶν Ahr.: μηρῶν codd. τοὶ Ameis, οἱ codd. ὑπὸ μαζοὶ Lobeck, ὑπομαζοὶ codd. 27 τὸ πάροιθεν Ald.[1], τοπάρ- codd. 31 ἁ μορφὰ R, ἄμορφα V τὰν κύπριν V: κύπριδος R 32 ὤρεα Ald.[1], ὤρια R, ὥρια V 33 κλαίοντι Paris. gr. 2812A post corr., -ουσι codd. τᾶς ἀφροδίτας V, τῆς -δίτης R 34 ὤρεσι Steph., ὄρ- V, οὔρ- R 35 ἐρυθαίνεται Junt.: ἐρυθραίνεται codd. Κυθήρα Brunck, -ρη codd. 36 ἀνακναμῶσ' ἀνάπαλιν ἀποσοικτρὰν (ἀποικτρὸν R) codd.: corr. Wak. ἀείδει Ald.[1], ἀείδη codd. 37 αἲ αἲ V: αἲ R κυθέρειαν R: νότον V 38 om. V ante corr. 39 ἂν om. V

mourning, unbraided, unsandalled; and the thorns
cut her as she goes and pluck sacred blood.
Shrilly wailing, through long winding dells she wanders,
crying out the Assyrian cry, calling her consort and boy.
Around her floated the dark robe at her navel;
her chest was made scarlet by her hands; the breasts below,
snowy before, grew crimson for Adonis.
"Alas for Cytherea!" mourn the Loves in reply.
She has lost her fair consort; with him she has lost her sacred appearance.
Cypris had a beautiful appearance when Adonis lived,
but her beauty has died with Adonis. "Alas for Cypris!"
say all the mountains, and the trees, "Alas for Adonis!"
And the rivers weep for Aphrodite's woes,
and the springs in the mountains shed tears for Adonis.
Flowers turn red from grief. Cythera
over every hill, through every dale pitifully sings,
"Alas for Cytherea! Fair Adonis is dead."
And Echo calls back, "Fair Adonis is dead!"
Who would not have cried "alas!" for Cypris' dire love?
When she saw, when she spied Adonis' unstaunchable wound,

ὡς ἴδε φοίνιον αἷμα μαραινομένῳ περὶ μηρῷ,
πάχεας ἀμπετάσασα κινύρετο, "μεῖνον Ἄδωνι,
δύσποτμε μεῖνον Ἄδωνι, πανύστατον ὥς σε κιχείω,
ὥς σε περιπτύξω καὶ χείλεα χείλεσι μείξω.
ἔγρεο τυτθόν, Ἄδωνι, τὸ δ' αὖ πύματόν με φίλασον·
τοσσοῦτόν με φίλασον ὅσον ζώῃ τὸ φίλαμα,
ἄχρις ἀποψύξῃς ἐς ἐμὸν στόμα, κεἰς ἐμὸν ἧπαρ
πνεῦμα τεὸν ῥεύσῃ, τὸ δέ σευ γλυκὺ φίλτρον ἀμέλξω,
ἐκ δὲ πίω τὸν ἔρωτα· φίλαμα δὲ τοῦτο φυλάξω
ὡς αὐτὸν τὸν Ἄδωνιν, ἐπεὶ σύ με, δύσμορε, φεύγεις.
φεύγεις μακρόν, Ἄδωνι, καὶ ἔρχεαι εἰς Ἀχέροντα,
πὰρ στυγνὸν βασιλῆα καὶ ἄγριον· ἁ δὲ τάλαινα
ζώω καὶ θεός ἐμμι καὶ οὐ δύναμαί σε διώκειν.
λάμβανε, Περσεφόνα, τὸν ἐμὸν πόσιν· ἐσσὶ γὰρ αὐτά
πολλὸν ἐμεῦ κρέσσων, τὸ δὲ πᾶν καλὸν ἐς σὲ καταρρεῖ.
ἐμμὶ δ' ἐγὼ πανάποτμος, ἔχω δ' ἀκόρεστον ἀνίαν,
καὶ κλαίω τὸν Ἄδωνιν, ὅ μοι θάνε, καί σε φοβεῦμαι.
θνᾴσκεις, ὦ τριπόθατε, πόθος δέ μοι ὡς ὄναρ ἔπτα,
χήρα δ' ἁ Κυθέρεια, κενοὶ δ' ἀνὰ δώματ' Ἔρωτες,
σοὶ δ' ἅμα κεστὸς ὄλωλε. τί γάρ, τολμαρέ, κυνάγεις;
καλὸς ἐὼν τοσσοῦτον ἐμήναο θηρὶ παλαίειν;"

44 μείξω scripsi, μίξω codd. 45, 46 φίλασον R, -ασσον V (utrubique) 46 ὅσον R, ὅσσ- V 47 ἀποψύξῃς scripsi: ἀποψύχῃς codd. κεἰς RV ante corr.: κῦσ' V post corr. 48 ῥεύσῃ V post corr.: -σει RV ante corr. 50 ὡς Junt. Call., ὧς X: ὥς σ' codd. τὸν om. V 52 πὰρ Ameis: καὶ codd. ἁ δὲ R: ἅδ' ἁ V 55 πᾶν καλὸν Junt. Call.: πάγκαλον codd. ἐς σὲ Ald.[1]: ἐσσὲ codd. καταρρεῖ Steph.: καὶ ἄρρει codd. 56 ἐμμὶ Brunck, εἰμὶ codd. ἀνίαν Brunck, -ην codd. 57 κλαίω R, κλέω V 58 ἔπτα Wil., -η codd. 59 χήρα Mein., -η codd. κυθέρεια R, -ηα V κενοί R, καινοὶ V post corr.: κανοὶ V ante corr. δώματ' Ald.[2]: δῶμα codd. 60 τολμαρὲ Paris. gr. 2812A, -ηρὲ codd. 61 τοσσοῦτον R, τοσοῦτον V: τί τοσοῦτον Koechly ἐμήναο Brunck: ἔμηνας codd.

when she saw the gory blood upon his languishing thigh,
spreading wide her arms she keened, "Wait, Adonis,
ill-fated Adonis, wait, that I may catch up with you for the very last time,
that I may embrace you and mix lips with lips.
Wake just a little, Adonis, and kiss me again for the last time,
kiss me for as long as the kiss lives
until you breathe your last into my mouth, and into my liver
your breath flows, and I drain your sweet love
and drink up desire; and I shall keep that kiss
as if it were Adonis himself, since you, wretch, flee from me.
You flee far away, Adonis, and go to Acheron,
to a hateful and savage king. Wretched that I am,
I live and am a goddess and cannot follow you.
Take my consort, Persephone; for you are
much stronger than I, and everything fair flows down to you.
I am all ill-fated, I have insatiable grief,
and I weep for Adonis, since he has died, and I yield to you.
You are dead, O thrice-desired, and desire has flown from me like a dream.
Cytherea is widowed; the Loves throughout the palace are bereft.
With you has died my kestos. Rash one, why were you hunting?
Fair as you were, were you so mad as to wrestle a wild beast?"

ὧδ' ὀλοφύρατο Κύπρις· ἐπαιάζουσιν Ἔρωτες,
"αἰαῖ τὰν Κυθέρειαν· ἀπώλετο καλὸς Ἄδωνις".
δάκρυον ἁ Παφία τόσον ἐκχέει ὅσσον Ἄδωνις
αἷμα χέει, τὰ δὲ πάντα ποτὶ χθονὶ γίνεται ἄνθη·
αἷμα ῥόδον τίκτει, τὰ δὲ δάκρυα τὰν ἀνεμώναν.
αἰάζω τὸν Ἄδωνιν, "ἀπώλετο καλὸς Ἄδωνις".
μηκέτ' ἐνὶ δρυμοῖσι τὸν ἀνέρα μύρεο, Κύπρι·
οὐκ ἀγαθὰ στιβάς ἐστιν Ἀδώνιδι φυλλὰς ἐρήμα.
λέκτρον ἔχοι, Κυθέρεια, τὸ σὸν νῦν νεκρὸς Ἄδωνις·
καὶ νέκυς ὢν καλός ἐστι, καλὸς νέκυς, οἷα καθεύδων.
κάτθεό νιν μαλακοῖς ἐνὶ φάρεσι τοῖς ἐνίαυεν,
τοῖς μετὰ τεῦς ἀνὰ νύκτα τὸν ἱερὸν ὕπνον ἐμόχθει.
παγχρύσῳ κλιντῆρι πρόθες καὶ στυγνὸν Ἄδωνιν,
βάλλε δέ νιν στεφάνοισι καὶ ἄνθεσι· πάντα σὺν αὐτῷ,
ὡς τῆνος τέθνακε, καὶ ἄνθεα πάντ' ἐμαράνθη.
ῥαῖνε δέ νιν Συρίοισιν ἀλείφασι, ῥαῖνε μύροισιν·
ὀλλύσθω μύρα πάντα· τὸ σὸν μύρον ὤλετ' Ἄδωνις.
κέκλιται ἁβρὸς Ἄδωνις ἐν εἵμασι πορφυρέοισιν,
ἀμφὶ δέ νιν κλαίοντες ἀναστενάχουσιν Ἔρωτες
κειράμενοι χαίτας ἐπ' Ἀδώνιδι· χὢ μὲν ὀιστώς,

64 ἁ Παφία Brunck, ἁ παφίη R, ἀπαφύη V τόσον R, τόσσον V ἐκχέει Heins.: ἐγχέει codd. 66 R hunc versum post 68 habet, signis β′ γ′ α′ adscriptis ut iustus ordo restituatur τὰν V, τὴν R 68 μύρεο R, μήρ- V 69 οὐκ Ahr.: ἔστ' codd. ἐστιν Ahr., ἔστιν codd. 70 λέκτρον R, λέκτον V ἔχοι Valck.: ἔχει codd. το σὸν R, τόσσον V νῦν Ahr. (1854): νῦν δὲ V: τὺ δὲ R ἄδωνις V: ἄδωνι R 71 ἐστι V: ἐσσί R 72 φάρεσι τοῖς Mein.: φάρεσιν οἱ codd. ἐνίαυεν Steph.: -ιαῦεν codd. 73 τεῦς Wil., σεῦ codd. ἐμόχθει V, -θη R 74 παγχρύσω codd.: -χρυσέῳ Wil. πρόθες Courtney (πόθες iam Platt): πόθει R: ποθεῖ V καὶ V: τὸν R 75 δέ νιν Wass. ap. Valck.: δ' ἐνὶ codd. στεφάνοισι codd.: στεφάνους τε Briggs (malim -ως) ἄνθεσι V: ἄνθεα Briggs 75–6 καὶ . . . τέθνακε om. R 77 νιν Brunck, μιν codd. Συρίοισιν Ruhnk. ap. Valck.: μύροισιν V: καλοῖσιν R ἀλείφασι R, ἀλί- V 78 ὀλλύσθω R, ὀλύ- V μύρ- R bis, μῦρ- V bis ὤλετ' ἄδωνις R, ὤλεθ' (-τ' post corr.) ἄδ- V 80 νιν Brunck, μιν codd. 81 ὀιστώς R, -ὸς V

Thus Cypris mourned; the Loves mourn in reply:
"Alas for Cytherea! Fair Adonis is dead."
The Paphian sheds as many tears as Adonis
sheds blood; on the ground all turn to flowers:
his blood gives birth to the rose, her tears to the anemone.
I mourn Adonis: "Fair Adonis is dead!"
No longer, Cypris, mourn your consort amid the woods.
A deserted pile of leaves is not a good bed for Adonis.
Let Adonis have your bed, Cytherea, now that he is a corpse:
although he is a corpse he is beautiful, a beautiful corpse, as if asleep.
Lay him out in the soft sheets in which he used to spend the night,
in which at your side at night he used to labour through sacred sleep.
On the all-golden bed lay Adonis out, abhorrent though he is,
and strew him with garlands and flowers: with him,
since he has died, all flowers too have wilted.
Sprinkle him with Syrian unguents, sprinkle him with perfumes.
Let all perfumes die: Adonis, your perfume, has died.
Gorgeous Adonis lies in crimson-dyed sheets
and around him the weeping Loves groan aloud,
cutting their hair for Adonis. This one was throwing on arrows,

ὃς δ' ἐπὶ τόξον ἔβαλλ', ὃς δ' εὔπτερον ἆγε φαρέτραν·
χὢ μὲν ἔλυσε πέδιλον Ἀδώνιδος, οἳ δὲ λέβητι
χρυσείῳ φορέοισιν ὕδωρ, ὃ δὲ μηρία λούει,
ὃς δ' ὄπιθεν πτερύγεσσιν ἀναψύχει τὸν Ἄδωνιν.
"αἰαῖ τὰν Κυθέρειαν" ἐπαιάζουσιν Ἔρωτες.
ἔσβεσε λαμπάδα πᾶσαν ἐπὶ φλιαῖς Ὑμέναιος
καὶ στέφος ἐξεπέτασσε γαμήλιον· οὐκέτι δ' "ὑμὴν
ὑμήν", οὐκέτ' ἄειδεν ἑὸν μέλος, ἀλλὰ καὶ "αἰαῖ
αἰαῖ" καὶ "τὸν Ἄδωνιν" ἔτι πλέον ἢ ὑμέναιον.
αἱ Χάριτες κλαίοντι τὸν υἱέα τῶ Κινύραο,
"ὤλετο καλὸς Ἄδωνις" ἐν ἀλλάλαισι λέγοισαι,
"αἰαῖ" δ' ὀξὺ λέγοντι πολὺ πλέον ἢ τύ, Διώνα.
χαἰ Μοῖραι τὸν Ἄδωνιν ἀνακλείοισιν, Ἄδωνιν,
καί νιν ἐπαείδουσιν, ὃ δέ σφισιν οὐχ ὑπακούει·
οὐ μὰν οὐκ ἐθέλει, Κώρα δέ νιν οὐκ ἀπολύει.
λῆγε γόων, Κυθέρεια, τὸ σάμερον, ἴσχεο κομμῶν·
δεῖ σε πάλιν κλαῦσαι, πάλιν εἰς ἔτος ἄλλο δακρῦσαι.

82 ἔβαλλ' ὃς Koenn. (ἔβαλλεν ὃ iam Wil.): ἔβαιν' ὅς codd. δ' εὔπτερον R: δ' ἔπτερον V: δὲ πτερόν Junt. ἆγε Ald.²: αὖ γε R: ὅς δὲ V φαρέτραν Brunck, -ην codd. 83 οἳ δὲ Graefe: ὃς δὲ codd. λέβητι Junt.: λέβητος V: λέβησι R 84 χρυσείῳ Junt.: χρυσίη V: χρυσίοις R φορέοισιν R: φορίησιν V λούει R: λύει V 85 πτερύγεσσιν V, -εσιν R 86 αἲ αἲ Lennep p. 172: αὐτὰν codd. 87 φιαῖς ὑμεναίοις codd.: corr. Junt. Call. 88 ἐξεπέτασσε codd.: ἐξεκέδασσε Piers. γαμήλιον V: καμ- R δ' ὑμήν Vat. gr. 1379 post corr.: δοίμαν codd. 89 ὕμην Vat. gr. 1379 post corr.: ὕμη codd. ἄειδεν ἑὸν Koechly: ἀειδονέος codd. ἀλλὰ καὶ scripsi: ἄλλεται codd. (ἄλλ- fort. R) 90 ἢ Higt: αἲ codd. 92 ἀλλάλαισι Paris. gr. 2812A, ἀλλήλαισι R ante corr., ἀλλήλησι V R post corr. 93 αἲ αἲ Piers.: αὐταὶ codd. δ' ὀξὺ λέγοντι Call.: δοξολέγοντι codd. ante corr., δεξ- codd. post corr. 94 χαἰ Mein.: καὶ codd. ἀνακλείοισιν Gow (ἀνακλείουσιν iam Edmonds, -κλείοισι δ' iam Ahr.): -κλαίοισιν V, -κλέοισιν R post corr. (vide Hiller p. 35), -κλέοιν R ante corr. 95 νιν Wil., μιν codd. σφισιν Ald.², σφιν codd. οὐχ ὑπακούει Steph.: οὐκ ἐπ- codd. 96 νιν Wak., μιν codd. 97 τὸ σάμερον Herm. (τοσάμερον iam Paris. gr. 2812A), τοσήμ- codd. κομμῶν Barth col. 125: κώμων codd. 98 δεῖ σε R post corr.: δεῖσαι V R ante corr.

this one a bow, another was bringing a feathered quiver.
And this one has undone Adonis' shoe, others are carrying
water in a golden bowl, another is washing his thighs,
and another fans Adonis from behind with his wings.
"Alas for Cytherea!" the Loves mourn in reply.
Hymenaeus has put out every torch at the doorposts
and torn the nuptial garland asunder. He was no longer singing "hymên,
hymên!", no longer his own song, but rather "alas,
alas!" and "Adonis!" even more than the nuptial song.
The Graces weep for the son of Cinyras,
saying among themselves "Fair Adonis is dead!"
and they shrilly say "alas!" much more than you, Dione.
And the Fates call up Adonis, Adonis,
and sing incantations for him, but he does not heed them –
not that he does not want to, but the Maiden does not let him go.
Stop your wailing, Cytherea, for today; cease from breast-beatings.
You must cry again, weep again another year.

COMMENTARY

COMMENTARY ON THE FRAGMENTS

I

From a poem, or a section of a poem, on the Amyclaean youth Hyacinth (cf. the title εἰς Ὑάκινθον, "on Hyacinth"), whose accidental death upon being hit by a discus thrown by his lover Apollo is first attested in [Hes.] fr. 171 and Eur. *Hel.* 1469–73; closer to Bion see Euphor. frr. 40–3 *CA* and Nic. *Th.* 901–6 (cf. Schol. Nic. *Th.* 585A), but versions before Ovid *Met.* 10.162–219 are very scrappy. Because of the sentiment in the last line Stobaeus included the excerpt in his chapter περὶ εἱμαρμένης. On the original context of these lines and their relationship to the *Epitaph on Adonis* see Introd. IV.

1 ἀμφασία: Doricized epic for ἀφασία "speechlessness"; to lengthen the first syllable privative ἀμ- for ἀ- is used on the analogy of ἀμβροσία, where mu is original (Wyatt 80–1). The word usually connotes astonished dismay; thus "dumbfoundedness"; cf. *Et. magn.* s.v. ἀμφασίαν· τὴν ἀφωνίαν καὶ ἔκπληξιν.[1] In Menophilus *SH* 558.6 it means "speechless astonishment". The verb is more commonly λαμβάνω in such expressions (e.g. *Il.* 17.695, *Od.* 4.704), but cf. Ap. Rh. 3.1372 τὸν δ' ἕλεν ἀμφασίη.[2]

Loss of speech is a traditional reaction to a shock: cf. *Od.* 4.704–5, *H.H.* 2.282, Callim. *H.* 5.83–4 (with Bulloch), Ap. Rh. 3.284 (with Campbell), Ach. Tat. 1.12.2 and 13.1.

τόσον ἄλγος ἔχοντα: Wilamowitz emends τόσον to τὸ σόν, making the lines an apostrophe to Hyacinth (like the same episode in Ovid *Met.* 10.185–9, which show Bionean influence: see 4 n.), and ἔχοντα to Usener's ὁρῶντα[3] (assimilating the description to that of Aphrodite over the dying Adonis in *Ad.* 40–1). The first emendation would depend on an address in the lost preceding lines, whereas MS τόσον picks up a lost description of the injury; both emendations make the ἄλγος the wound of the boy rather than the grief of Apollo. Aside from the needlessness of these changes, however, the imitation in Leont. Schol. *A.Pl.*

[1] Philostr. *Im.* 1.24.3 uses the latter term in describing a picture of Apollo at the death of Hyacinth: πεπηγέναι φήσεις αὐτόν, τοσοῦτον αὐτῷ τῆς ἐκπλήξεως ἐμπέπτωκεν.

[2] αἱρέω is common with θάμβος, e.g. *Od.* 3.372; Ap. Rh. 2.681, 4.682; Ant. Sid. *A.P.* 9.66.1.

[3] In *Hermes* 14 (1879) 163 Wilamowitz reads ἰδόντα, already proposed by Jacobs 55.

245.1 τὸν σάτυρον Διόνυσος ἰδὼν τόσον ἄλγος ἔχοντα supports the MS reading. Cf. the verse-end ἄλγε' ἔχοντ-, common in epic, e.g. *Il.* 5.895; *Od.* 5.336, 11.582 and 593, 17.142; Hes. *Op.* 133 (cf. *Il.* 17.445, *Od.* 1.34).

2 Note the asyndeton, characteristic of Bion: cf. frr. 2.14, 17; 3.1, 2; 10.7–8; 12.2, 4, 6, 7; 13.13; 14.3; and *Ad.* 51 n.

ἐπεμαίετο: lit. "grab, grope at"; here "ply", as in Bion's model *H.H.* 4.108 σὺν δ' ἐφόρει ξύλα πολλά, πυρὸς δ' ἐπεμαίετο τέχνην (cf. 511 αὐτὸς δ' αὖθ' ἑτέρης σοφίης ἐκμάσσετο τέχνην). The emendation, often attributed to Vulcanius (1584), appears first in Crispinus' edition (1569–70). F's ἐπεβένετο may descend from an original corruption to ἐπεμαίνετο. This line-end is echoed in [Theoc.] 23.57 φίλων ἐπεμαίετο (= "sought") λουτρῶν, with the same collocation of noun and modifier.

For σοφὴ τέχνη "skilful craft" see Callim. fr. 202.56, anon. *A.P.* 14.54.1 (there too of Apollo's medical skill), and esp. [Apolinar.] *Ps.* 106.55 Ludwich ending σοφὴ δ' οὐ φαίνετο τέχνη, with the same collocation of noun and modifier as here. Ovid *Met.* 8.159 "Daedalus ingenio fabrae celeberrimus artis" (cf. *Fasti* 3.383) may also be an imitation.

3 χρῖεν ... χρῖεν: on epanalepsis, emphatic repetition of one element of a syntactical complex in order to further or complete the sense, see Fehling 183–6, who notes that Hellenistic poets use the "verhältnismäßig gleichgültig" Homeric device artfully to highlight significant passages. Cf. fr. 3.2–3 μολπάν, 17.1 πάντα; *Ad.* 7–8 ὀδόντι, 42–3 μεῖνον, 71 καλός, 88–9 οὐκέτι. Cf. on *Ad.* 1–2, 21 νήπλεκτος. Among late bucolic poets Bion is especially fond of the figure; elsewhere see [Theoc.] 23.49–50 and 27.39.

χρῖεν δ' ἀμβροσίᾳ καὶ νέκταρι: Bion's formal model is *Il.* 16.680, beginning χρῖσέν τ' ἀμβροσίῃ (cf. *H.H.* 2.237, Ap. Rh. 4.871). Nectar and ambrosia, the foods of the gods, have power against death and its effects (though that power is futile here); in *Il.* 5.341–2 it is their consumption that keeps the gods immortal (cf. Hes. *Th.* 639–40, *H.H.* 3.124–9 and 5.232, Pind. *P.* 9.63). Ambrosia (lit. "deathlessness"; see Chantraine *Dict.* s.v. βροτός)[4] is usually eaten, while nectar is drunk, although authors listed by Athen. 2.39A reverse these roles: Sappho fr. 141 L–P, Alcman fr. 42 *PMG*, Anaxandrides fr. 58 *PCG* (add Schol. Nic. *Al.* 44). Here the substances seem to be unguents, as in places where

[4] On the etymology of νέκταρ see S. Levin, *SMEA* 13 (1971) 31–50; R. D. Griffith, *Glotta* 72 (1994) 20–3.

gods rub or pour them on human bodies as a divine equivalent of funerary unguents (*Il.* 16.670, 680), as a preservative against decay (*Il.* 19.38–9, [Hes.] fr. 23A.22–4), or as an immortalizing agent ([Hes.] *loc. cit.*, *H.H.* 2.237, Ap. Rh. 4.870–2, Theoc. 15.108). Cf. Onians 292–9, West on Hes. *Th.* 640, Richardson on *H.H.* 2.237.

3–4 Imitated by Nonnus *D.* 11.241–2 (Dionysus over his dead favourite Ampelus) ἀμβροσίην δὲ λαβὼν παρὰ μητέρι Ῥείῃ | ὠτειλαῖς ἐπέχευεν.

4 μοιραῖα: first attested here (if Hermann's emendation is right), the adj. does not reappear until late antiquity: [Manetho] *Apot.* 5 [6].8 Koechly, Synes. *H.* 1.606 and 3.3 in verse; Alciphron 3.37, Proclus (often), Damasc. *Parm.* 216.22 in prose. An Antonine-era inscription from the Chersonnese attests an adv. μοιραίως (E. G. Surov, *Vestnik drevnei istorii* 1960 (3) 154–5).

Hermann's reading μοιραῖα δ' ἀναλθέα τραύματα πάντα – "but all wounds due to destiny are incurable" – is based on Ovid's imitation in *Met.* 10.188–9 (Apollo and Hyacinth) "nunc animam admotis fugientem sustinet herbis. | nil prosunt artes: erat inmedicabile vulnus" (cf. I. Cazzaniga, *PP* 13 (1958) 153–4; for the motif "der Heilgott kann nicht heilen" in Ovid see Bömer *ad loc.*).[5] Keeping MS φάρμακα, Wakefield wishes to read Μοίραις ἔπ' (better Μοίραις δ' ἔπ') ἀναλθέα φάρμακα πάντα, "but all drugs are without avail against the Fates". But ἀναλθής elsewhere has a passive sense (of wounds in Nic. *Al.* 246 ἀναλθέα τραύματα, Quintus 3.84 and 4.401; often in Aretaeus), and so is inappropriate with φάρμακα, which has probably intruded from 2.

For the collocation of attributive and predicate adjs. in Hermann's emendation cf. e.g. Musaeus 212 ἔχων σέθεν ἀστέρα λύχνον, "having your lamp as my guiding star".

τραύματα: Wachsmuth's τρώματα, the normal form in dialects outside of Attic (cf. Chantraine *Dict.* s.v. τιτρώσκω), may be right; in bucolic τρῶμα occurs in [Theoc.] 21.50. But cf. τραύματα in [Theoc.] 19.6 and 8, whose dialect is closer to Bion's than that of [Theoc.] 21; note that the Doric of late bucolic is a literary convention, not a simulation of an actual dialect (cf. Introd. v).

[5] A. Barigazzi, *RFIC* 90 (1962) 297–8 believes that the sentiment goes back to Euphor. *Hyacinthus* (fr. 43 *CA*) Κώκυτος ⟨. . .⟩ μοῦνος ἀφ' ἕλκεα νίψεν Ἄδωνιν, explaining the conceit as paralleling, in its original context, Apollo's inability to alleviate the wounds of Hyacinth. See Courtney *FLP* 261–2 on the influence of Euphorion's line.

II

A dialogue on the relative merits of the four seasons. From Stobaeus' chapter περὶ χρόνου. For the comparison of the seasons cf. the debate between winter and spring in Aesop 271 Perry, where, as here, spring is given the last word. The Aesopic fable may ultimately derive from a "Disputation between Summer and Winter" current in Sumerian wisdom literature (S. N. Kramer, *The Sumerians* (Chicago 1963) 218–20); M. L. West, *HSCP* 73 (1969) 120 sees in Bion an elevated literary treatment of the folk motif.

The poem may or may not be complete. Bucolic dialogues of this type tend to go on longer than eighteen lines (cf. Theoc. 4, 5, 10), and information about the characters, given within the dialogue or in a short prologue (cf. Theoc. 6, [Theoc.] 8), is lacking here. On the other hand, the inclusion of the speakers' names in lines 1 and 11 might have supplied enough information for readers familiar with Bion's other poetry.

1–2 εἴαρος . . . ἢ χείματος ἢ φθινοπώρω | ἢ θέρεος: a kind of serial partitive genitive, equivalent to τῶν ὡρῶν τίς σοι ἡδεῖά ἐστι, conflated with a series of alternatives like ἔαρ ἢ χεῖμα κτλ. ἐστί σοι ἡδύ. Gow (1953) translates "Spring, Myrson, or winter, autumn or summer, what is thy delight in them?", but Cleodamus is rather asking Myrson to choose one of the four (cf. 7–8).

Early Greek accounts of the seasons – treating the ὥρα as "not so much a point on a continuum as the simultaneous conjunction of discrete factors" (N. Austin, *Archery at the Dark of the Moon* (Berkeley 1975) 87) – give only three, not recognizing autumn (for Homer and Hesiod see LSJ s.v. ὥρα A.I; cf. the tripartite division of Persephone's year in *H.H.* 2.399–400, etc.). Alcman *PMG* 20 adds ὀπώρα, lit. "harvest", which in *Od.* 11.192, 12.76 (cf. Theoc. 11.36), and 14.384 is distinguished as part of the summer, complementary to θέρος, without possessing the status of a season itself (cf. Thuc. 2.31.1 περὶ δὲ τὸ φθινόπωρον τοῦ θέρους τούτου; see Calame 374–6). The three-season system persists ([Aesch.] *P.V.* 454–6, Aristoph. *Av.* 709, *CA* lyr. adesp. 37.5, Diod. Sic. 1.16, [Orph.] *H.* 34.21–3, *GVI* 1897.15–22 (Egypt, second century A.D.)), but in the fifth and fourth centuries, with the growth of astronomical knowledge and observation of the solstices and equinoxes, our set of four equal seasons came to predominate, with terms denoting "the end of the harvest" serving for autumn (see on 1 below). See Hanfmann 1.87–93.

1 εἴαρος: the first word of Cleodamus' query foreshadows the answer in 15–18. The lengthened gen. and dat. sing. of ἔαρ is post-Homeric (first in [Hes.] fr. 70.13), although Homer already has the adj. εἰαρινός; see Wyatt 150–1. In Hellenistic poetry see Theoc. 7.97, 12.30, 13.26; Callim. *H.* 2.81; Rhianus fr. 76.3 *CA*; Alex. Aet. fr. 1.2 *CA*; Euphor. fr. 40.3 *CA*; etc. Cf. 15 εἶαρ.

ὦ Μύρσων: neither this name nor that of Cleodamus (11) is found in extant bucolic before Bion (but cf. Morson in Theoc. 5); later a Myrson shows up in [Bion] 2.4. See Wendel 37. On ὦ + voc. in rustic dialogue see fr. 5.1 n.

φθινοπώρω: lit. "the waning of the ὀπώρα" (cf. Pamprepius 3.53 Livrea φθι]νύθουσιν ὀπῶραι, in a poem on autumn); cf. the synonymous μετόπωρον. The term first appears in Hdt. 4.42.3 and 9.117.1; in verse see Archestr. *SH* 166.1, Callim. *H.* 6.123, Antip. Thess. *A.P.* 11.37.1, Heitsch 64.91 (anon.), Paul. Sil. *A.P.* 5.258.5.

2 πλέον: sc. "than the other three". Cf. 7, 11.

εὔχεαι ἐλθεῖν: both speakers show a naïve understanding of the seasons as gifts to be prayed or wished for (cf. ἐθέλω in 12–13 and opt. παρείη in 15), rather than simply awaited.

3 ὅσ(σ)α is internal acc. with μογέω also in e.g. *Od.* 4.152, 7.214 = 14.198, 12.189–90; Theoc. 13.66; Ap. Rh. 4.733.

Cf. Petron. fr. 38.5 Bücheler (of the autumn) "ante oculos stabat quidquid promiserat annus".

4 "When hunger is easy for people to bear", because there is enough to eat at harvest-time (for ἐλαφρός in another context of seasonal relief see Hes. *Op.* 417 with West). Contrast Alcman *PMG* 20.3–5 τὸ ϝῆρ, ὅκα | σάλλει μέν, ἐσθίην δ' ἅδαν | οὐκ ἔστι. Fem. λιμός, always masc. in Attic, is Ionic (*H.H.* 2.311, Callim. fr. 346 = *Hec.* fr. 74.1 Hollis, Herodas 2.17) and Doric (Aristoph. *Ach.* 743, Callim. *A.P.* 12.150.5, Phrynichus *Ecl.* 158 Fischer τὴν λιμὸν Δωριεῖς) and entered later prose; see O. Zumbach, *Neuerungen in der Sprache der homerischen Hymnen* (Winterthur 1955) 4–5, and cf. Hopkinson on Callim. *H.* 6.66.

ἀνδράσι: "human beings" as opposed to the immortals (LSJ s.v. II), as in e.g. the Homeric phrase πατὴρ ἀνδρῶν τε θεῶν τε.

5 δύσεργον: commentators, taking the ἐπεί-clause as explaining this word, normally translate "prohibitive to work"; cf. Hes. *Op.* 494–5 ὥρῃ χειμερίῃ, ὁπότε κρύος ἀνέρας ἔργων | ἰσχάνει, [Hippoc.] *Hum.* 16 ὁ μὲν γὰρ χειμὼν ἀργὸς ἔργων, and citations on 5–6 below. But the adj. here could equally well mean "hard to work in, laborious": "or even laborious winter – since even in winter many people enjoy themselves" (Wakefield compares for this sense Virg. *G.* 1.211 "brumae intractabilis"); then the ἐπεί-clause will explain why anyone would prefer that forbidding season. LSJ give citations for either sense. This seems to be the only attestation of the word in verse.

5–6 Hes. *Op.* 493–501 warns against winter's temptations to idleness. More indulgent, like Cleodamus, is Virg. *G.* 1.299–302 "hiems ignava colono: | frigoribus parto agricolae plerumque fruuntur | mutuaque inter se laeti convivia curant. | invitat genialis hiems curasque resolvit…"; cf. Nic. fr. 70.7 Schneider προσφιλέας χειμῶνι καὶ οἰκουροῖσιν ἀεργοῖς, Porphyrion on Hor. *C.* 3.17.16 "sic enim solent rustici hieme, cum feriati sunt", Dio Chrys. *Or.* 7.18 χειμῶνος δὲ ἐπελθόντος ἔργον μὲν οὐδὲν ἦν πεφηνὸς αὐτοῖς, Dehor 25. Longus 3.4 echoes both Bion's sentiment and its context, the comparison of the seasons: οἱ μὲν ἄλλοι γεωργοὶ καὶ νομεῖς ἔχαιρον πόνων τε ἀπηλλαγμένοι πρὸς ὀλίγον καὶ τροφὰς ἑωθινὰς καὶ νυκτερινὰς ἐσθίοντες καὶ καθεύδοντες μακρὸν ὕπνον, ὥστε αὐτοῖς τὸν χειμῶνα δοκεῖν καὶ θέρους καὶ μετοπώρου καὶ ἦρος αὐτοῦ γλυκύτερον (note the assumption that spring would naturally be favoured).

The devotion of two lines to winter, when summer and autumn had each been dispatched in one, gives a sense of closure suggesting that these three seasons belong together and that the remaining fourth, spring, is to be the favourite.

6 θαλπόμενοι: to warm oneself at the hearth is one of the pleasures of winter in Hes. *Op.* 493–4; Alcaeus fr. 338.5–8 L–P; Xenophanes D–K 21 B 22.1; [Theoc.] 9.19–21; Virg. *Ecl.* 5.70, *G.* 3.376–8 (paired with *otia*); Hor. *C.* 1.9.5–6; *Cert. Hom. Hes.* 284–5 Allen; Theophylactus *Epist.* 61 (cited by West on Hes. *loc. cit.*) ὁ γεωργὸς ἐπὶ τὴν ἑαυτοῦ ἀλέαν κατέφευγε. Cf. Dehor 36.

The dittographic nature of the MS error θάλποντας prevents a secure restoration of the verb, but Grotius' τέρπονται is excellent here, esp. with the limiting datives: "warming themselves [at the hearth], they take delight in inactivity and sluggishness". Ursinus' θέλγονται ("are beguiled" or weaker "are charmed"), overwhelmingly approved by subsequent editors, is less common in such contexts and so less likely (the slight similarity between it and the MS reading is irrelevant).

ἀεργία appears also at *Od.* 24.251, Hes. *Op.* 311; on the lengthened iota see Wyatt 160–4. ὄκνος is "hesitation", thus "procrastination, laziness"; the Stoics defined it as φόβος μελλούσης ἐνεργείας (von Arnim III.98). Both words are normally pejorative (cf. Hes. *loc. cit.* ἔργον δ' οὐδὲν ὄνειδος, ἀεργίη δέ τ' ὄνειδος); their favourable treatment here underlines the peculiarity of winter's pleasures.

7 καλὸν ἔαρ: cf. καλὸν θέρος in Theoc. 6.16, [Theoc.] 21.26. Ornamental καλός, like ἁδύς (which pervades this poem: 2, 10, 11, 17), was taken by later bucolic writers from Theocritus, whose "commonest and most conventional adjective" it is (Gow on Theoc. 1.129). Cf. [Theoc.] 9.10, 15; 27.38; Moschus fr. 3.3; [Bion] 2.24; [Moschus] 3.33.

7–8 Cf. Aristoph. *Ran.* 1468 αἱρήσομαι ὅνπερ ἡ ψυχὴ θέλει. In epic the φρήν is often the seat of the emotions, as well as of the intellect (Onians 13–14), and like θυμός can be used to mean "one's own heart", the source of one's personal affections and desires (it is the seat of the θυμός in e.g. *Il.* 13.487 ἕνα φρεσὶ θυμὸν ἔχοντες; cf. Ebeling II.447).

8 The justification of time for song, conversation, or the like is a convention of the dialogue of bucolic characters: cf. Theoc. 1.14, 3.1–2; [Theoc.] 21.34; Virg. *Ecl.* 5.12. We may guess that Cleodamus and Myrson are herdsmen or rustic labourers of some other kind, although the fragment does not make clear who they are.

λαλέειν = λέγειν, as in Theoc. 15.92, [Theoc.] 20.6 and 27.58, [Moschus] 3.6 and 47. The verb is not used for the conversation of herdsmen elsewhere in bucolic.

ἐπιτρέπω + inf. = "permit", lit. "yield" (LSJ s.v. II.1); the usage is originally prosaic and comic (Aristoph. *Ach.* 51–2, *Plut.* 1078; Men. *Dysc.* 611–12), but also occurs in Theoc. 29.35, Ap. Rh. 1.695 (there more in the sense "commit").

ἄμμιν: Stephanus (first in his 1577 edition) emends to ἁμῖν, closer to the banalized MS reading, but cf. 16 ἄμμε, fr. 8.4 ἄμμιν.

9 For the sentiment see Theoc. 26.38 μηδεὶς τὰ θεῶν ὀνόσαιτο, Callim. fr. 194.72 θεοὺς γὰρ οὐ διακρίνω. Cf. Prop. 2.28A.5 (on complaints about the season) "sed non tam ardoris culpa est neque crimina caeli...".

θεήια: attested only here. Ionic adjs. in -ήιος, originally from nouns with stems in digamma, came to provide doublets for many adjs. in -εῖος (here for Homeric θεεῖος); the extension is "early and widespread" (Buck and Petersen 45). For the seasons as the work of the gods cf. Alcman *PMG* 20.1 ὥρας δ' ἔσηκε τρεῖς (implying some divinity as subject). Hanfmann 1.117 (cf. 1.107–10) considers Myrson's answer to embody a popular reflexion of "the Stoic idea of a divine order manifesting itself in the seasons".

10 **ἱερά:** because they *are* the works of the gods (cf. on *Ad.* 22).

σεῦ δὲ ἕκατι: for the phrase cf. *Od.* 20.42 Διός τε σέθεν τε ἕκητι, Ap. Rh. 4.1087 σεῖο ἕκητι (both at line-end). Here "but for your sake". There is some bland humour at the expense of Myrson, whose piety does not prevent him from accepting Cleodamus' invitation to express an opinion.

11 ἐξερέω: at line-opening once in Homer (*Od.* 9.365; also *H.H.* 2.416); always in Ap. Rh. (1.797, 3.172 and 1084, 4.1558).

Κλεόδαμε: found nowhere else in bucolic (cf. on 1 Μύρσων), but Maximus Planudes (d. *c.* 1305) took the name hence for a pastoral hexameter poem of his own, according to M. Schneider, *Berl. philol. Wochenschrift* (1894) 616. Voc. without ὦ here may convey Myrson's deference to Cleodamus; see fr. 5.1 n.

τό: in view of 7–8 εἰπὲ τί τοι φρήν | αἱρεῖται we should perhaps restore τί here.

12 ἦμεν: a Doric inf. of εἰμί, common in bucolic (Theoc. 2.41; 3.8; 4.9; 7.28, 86, 129; 11.50, 79; 14.6, 25; [Theoc.] 8.73; 21.30; 23.23); here pleonastic with ἐθέλω. Cf. fr. 14.6.

ὀπτῇ: for the figurative meaning "warm excessively" of the heat of the summer sun cf. φρύγω in Theoc. 6.16, 12.9; [Theoc.] 9.12.[6]

13 νόσον: for the unhealthiness of autumn cf. [Hippoc.] *Aphor.* 3.9 ἐν φθινοπώρῳ ὀξύταται αἱ νοῦσοι καὶ θανατωδέσταται τοὐπίπαν, Plut. *De Is.* 364B τὸ δὲ φθινόπωρον ὑγρότητος ἐνδείᾳ καὶ φυτοῖς πολέμιον καὶ ζῴοις νοσῶδες; other causes are said to be the mixture of hot and cold weather (Galen *De temp.* 1.527 Kühn) and the fact that blood is then at its lowest level in the body, while black bile is at its highest ([Hippoc.] *Nat. hom.* 7). Cf. Hor. *C.* 3.23.8.

ὥριος is a poetic form of ὡραῖος.

ἐπεὶ νόσον ὥρια τίκτει: interpretation is hard. We might take ὥρια adverbially, "since it brings forth disease in season" (cf. Aristoph. *Pax* 800 ἠρινά "in spring"), or substantivally (= ὡραῖα, "seasonal fruits") in apposition to νόσον, "since it brings forth disease as its crop" (both interpretations are suggestions of Edward Courtney).[7] In my translation I have preferred the former interpretation, with ὥρια elegantly varying τόκα in the previous verse. For LSJ (s.v. ὥριος III) ὥρια here = ὥρα, "the season" (J. A. Hartung actually emends to ὥρα, effecting a clumsy σπονδειάζων; cf. on fr. 14.3), but Bion's would be our only instance of this meaning; moreover the repetition of the subject *cum variatione* seems pointless.

[6] Xen. *Oec.* 16.14 ἡ δὲ γῆ ὀπτῷτο ὑπὸ τοῦ ἡλίου involves technical diction (cf. Virg. *G.* 1.66).

[7] Some translate "since the seasonal fruits bring forth disease", but that belief seems unattested and difficult to explain. For the traditional causes of the unhealthiness of autumn see above.

14 "Winter is cruel to bear; I fear snow and chills." Recent editors, avoiding the strong asyndeton, have preferred Crispinus' φέρει for φέρειν and Wilamowitz's δέ for τε: "Cruel winter brings snow, and I fear chills". I have considered it likely that snow and chills are paired more closely, as in *Ninus* B.II.9–10 (*AGNF* p. 51) φόβος μὲν ἦν κρυμῶν καὶ χιόνων, Dion. Per. 669 αἰεί σφιν ψυχρή τε χιὼν κρυμός τε δυσαής, Aristid. *Or.* 23.290 ἐν χιόνι πολλῇ καὶ κρυμῷ; cf. Leon. Tar. *A.P.* 6.221.2, [Orph.] *H.* 80.2, Jo. Chrys. *Epist.* 128 and 135 (*PG* 52.688 and 693). Our poet prefers to let verse-medial sense–pause coincide with the main caesura, and asyndeton is in fact a notable feature of his style (see on fr. 1.2). Punctuating differently, some editors (e.g. Winterton, Whitford, Brunck) appose snow and chills to cruel winter and make φέρειν dependent on "I fear": οὖλον χεῖμα φέρειν, νιφετὸν κρυμώς τε, φοβεῦμαι; the line should, however, parallel the previous two, with a complaint about the season followed by an explanation (the variation in wording from 12–13 closes the list of rejected seasons).[8]

Ameis's conjecture οὐ λῶ = οὐκ ἐθέλω for οὖλον would effect even stronger parallelism to the two preceding lines, and is very attractive. The relative unfamiliarity of the un-Homeric λῶ would have caused the corruption (perhaps with unspaced οὐλῶ mistaken for a gen. and corrected to nom.-acc.). The verb is used by rustic characters (mostly in 2nd pers. sing. λῇς) at Theoc. 1.12, 4.14, 5.64; [Theoc.] 8.6 and 85; [Bion] 2.1; by the Cyclops in Theoc. 11.56.

κρυμώς: a synonymous derivative of κρύος (cf. 16), first attested in Soph. fr. 507.2 Radt, Eur. fr. 682.3 Nauck; in Hellenistic poetry see Callim. fr. 75.19, *H.* 3.115; Eratosth. fr. 16.10 *CA* κρυμαλέαι; Nic. *Th.* 382 and 681, fr. 22.1; Marc. Arg. *A.P.* 11.320.3. For the long upsilon Chantraine *Dict.* s.v. κρύος compares θύος: θυμός.

φοβεῦμαι: cf. *Ninus* B.II.9–10 (quoted above). [Virg.] *Catal.* IA.2–3 = *Priap.* 84.2–3 Bücheler (in a comparison of the seasons; cf. Parker 12–13) "una mihi est horrida pestis hiemps. | nam frigus metuo ... " may imitate Bion (cf. Dehor 325 n. 28), although there the speaker (a wooden statue of Priapus) is afraid of being chopped into kindling, not of catching cold himself.

15 **εἶαρ:** the lengthened nom.-acc. of ἔαρ, a back-formation from gen. and dat. εἴαρος, εἴαρι (see on 1), is first attested in Numenius *SH* 582.2.

[8] Hermann's φέρον for φέρειν ("I fear cruel winter, which brings snow and chills") also does away with the balance that obtained in the previous two lines.

τριπόθατον: "thrice-desired". See *Ad.* 58. On the pseudo-Doric form see Introd. v; on intensive τρι- cf. Thesleff §323.

λυκάβαντι: first attested in *Od.* 14.161–2 = 19.306–7 τοῦδ' αὐτοῦ λυκάβαντος ἐλεύσεται ἐνθάδ' Ὀδυσσεύς, | τοῦ μὲν φθίνοντος μηνός, τοῦ δ' ἱσταμένοιο, where the meaning of the word, like its etymology, is controversial (see Chantraine *Dict.* s.v.; O. Szemerényi, *JHS* 94 (1974) 150–1). It obviously designates a measure of time, and in the Hellenistic period and later the word was held to mean "year", as here and in Ap. Rh. 1.610, Leon. Tar. *A.P.* 7.198.5, Philod. *A.P.* 11.41.1.[9] Numerous late Hellenistic and Imperial grave inscriptions use it for grandiose designations of the age of the deceased, e.g. *GVI* 759.7 (Myconos, second–first centuries B.C.), 567.1 (Argos, second century A.D.), 1048.1 (Sidon, second–third centuries A.D.) [εἴ]κοσί μοι λυκάβαντες, 285.3 (Rome, second–third centuries A.D.), 696.8 (Rome, third–fourth centuries A.D.); cf. Agathias *A.P.* 7.568.1.

16 **μήτε** for οὔτε reinforces the causal sense of the ἁνίκα-clause.

17 Bion likes the repetition of πᾶς: cf. frr. 5.1–2, 17.1; *Ad.* 36, 75–6. Virgil echoes this line in *Ecl.* 3.56 "et nunc omnis ager, nunc omnis parturit arbos" (cf. Gebauer 209 and 246).

εἴαρος: gen. of time. The variation with the synonymous dat. εἴαρι is elegant; cf. Theoc. 11.58 ἀλλὰ τὰ μὲν θέρεος, τὰ δὲ γίνεται ἐν χειμῶνι, Crinag. *A.P.* 6.345.1–2 εἴαρος... νῦν δ' ἐνὶ μέσσῃ | χείματι.

βλαστεῖ: the verb (= βλαστάνω), first attested in Theophr. *C.P.* 5.4.5,[10] was formed either directly from βλαστός or on the analogy of compounds like εὐβλαστέω < εὐβλαστής, πρωϊβλαστέω < πρωϊβλαστής, ὀψιβλαστέω < ὀψιβλαστής. In verse see [Sotad.] fr. 20 *CA*, Ap. Rh. 4.1425, Nic. *Th.* 642. Brunck wishes to read MS βλάστη as Doric βλαστῇ < βλαστάω, but that form lacks the poetic attestations of the other.

18 **ἶσα καὶ ὁμοίιος:** the construction is naïve ("night is equal and day is equal" for "night is equal to day"), the variation elegant. Manso wonders why Cleodamus lists equality of day and night among the virtues of spring: "Entweder betrachtet er die Gleichheit der Tage und Nächte als die Ursache von der schönen Temperatur der Luft und des Wetters...; oder er sieht [sie] als das Mittel an, wodurch die Thätigkeit

[9] But Dio Chrys. *Or.* 7.84 seems to take it to mean "month"; cf. W. H. D. Rouse, *CR* 20 (1906) 216.

[10] At Aesch. *Cho.* 589 the MSS read βλαστοῦσι, probably a corruption of βλάπτουσι (Butler).

des Landmanns am glücklichsten genährt und seine Arbeitsamkeit weder durch Ueberspannung der Kräfte, wie in den heißen Sommertagen geschwächt, noch durch Müßiggang, wie im Winter, schlaff gemacht werde." [Manetho] *Apot.* 2 [1].39 Koechly ἴσην Ἠέλιος τεύχει νύκτ' ἄμβροτον ἠοῖ imitates this line.

For ἠώς = "day" (apart from its use merely to mark time, as in e.g. *Il.* 1.493 δυωδεκάτη γένετ' ἠώς), opposed to night and encompassing midday and afternoon, see Theoc. 7.35, 12.1; Callim. fr. 178.1; [Manetho] *loc. cit.*; [Orph.] *Arg.* 649; Quintus 13.341; Musaeus 110, 288; Apoll. Soph. s.v. ἠώς· ... ἐπὶ δὲ τῆς ὅλης ἡμέρας; Hesych. s.v. ἠώς· ὅλη ἡμέρα. This bold extension is Hellenistic; *Il.* 5.267 ὑπ' ἠῶ τ' ἠέλιόν τε, "over the whole world", "wherever the dawn and sun shed their light", is different, using ἠώς for the diachronic geographical reach, not the duration, of day.[11] Personified dawn was perhaps pictured as preceding the sun all day long and was thus identified with the day (cf. Virg. *Aen.* 6.535–6; see C. Robert, *Hermes* 46 (1911) 226). For the reverse identification, somewhat more easily comprehensible, see Aesch. *Pers.* 386 λευκόπωλος ἡμέρα (cf. Soph. *Aj.* 673), Paus. 1.3.1 φέρουσα Ἡμέρα Κέφαλον.

III

From Stobaeus' chapter περὶ Ἀφροδίτης οὐρανίας. Love contains or prompts its own cure. Bion combines two commonplaces, that love prompts the creation of song and that song heals the pains of love.[12] For the first see Eur. fr. 663 Nauck ποιητὴν δ' ἄρα | Ἔρως διδάσκει, κἂν ἄμουσος ᾖ τὸ πρίν, often echoed, as in Plato *Symp.* 196E and Nicias *SH* 566; cf. fr. 9 below. For the second see Philox. *PMG* 822, Theoc. 11.1–3 (quoted on 3 below), 17–18, 80–1; Callim. *A.P.* 12.150.1–4 (all on Polyphemus' love for Galatea).

The homoeoteleuton in lines 1–2 is noteworthy.

1 Μοίσας: Theocritus uses the Aeolic and Pindaric form of Μοῦσα "perhaps to conform to his participles in -οισα" (Gow on Theoc. 1.9;

[11] Thus Apollonius the Sophist and Hesychius (above) reflect Hellenistic tradition, though both are discussing the Homeric usage. The Iliadic phrase was borrowed by Theoc. 16.5; cf. Callim. *H.* 3.249.

[12] Bion's lines make clear the assumption behind the prologue to Theoc. 11, where commentators (cf. Gow on line 13, Hopkinson (1988) 149–50) have puzzled over why song is called a *cure* for love, yet in 13–16 is listed as one of the *symptoms* of love.

but see Molinos Tejada 57–8 on the dubious papyrus evidence); from his works it passed into later bucolic usage. For the paroxytone accentuation of Doric first decl. acc. pl. with short alpha see Gow on Theoc. 1.83 πάσας, who cites 2.160 Μοίρας and [Theoc.] 9.11 τρωγοίσας; cf. Hes. *Th.* 267 Ἁρπυίας.

φέροιεν: "may they bear Love", i.e. "allow me to bear up under love" (cf. Theoc. 2.164 ἐγὼ δ' οἰσῶ τὸν ἐμὸν πόθον ὥσπερ ὑπέσταν); less probably "remove" (Holland 251 suggests τὸν Ἔρωτ' ἀφέλοιεν, but cf. LSJ s.v. φέρω A.VI.1). It is just possible that φέροιεν here means "carry to my beloved", so that the φάρμακον in 3 will be effected by *satisfaction* of love; the lines would thus describe a serenade (cf. Theoc. 3, Bion fr. 11). The commonplace (see above), however, tells against this interpretation. A serenade is perhaps meant by Tuccianus of Carthage *Anth. lat.* 277 Riese "Cantica gignit amor et amorem cantica gignunt: | cantandumst ut ametur et ut cantetur amandum", cited by Beckby as similar to Bion's chiasmus (perhaps an imitation).

2 μολπάν: cf. 3. A grand epic word for song, reappearing in bucolic only at [Theoc.] 27.73 and [Moschus] 3.123. Cf. on μέλπω in fr. 9.8.

2–3 μολπὰν . . . τὰν γλυκερὰν μολπάν: note the epanalepsis; cf. on fr. 1.3.

3 γλυκεράν: an epithet of μολπή also in *Il.* 13.637 = *Od.* 23.145, [Manetho] *Apot.* 6 [3].369 Koechly.

Elegant variation: γλυκερός and ἡδύς are synonyms. "Sweet medicine" (cf. Theoc. 11.3, in the same context) is almost an oxymoron. Compare the metaphor of the "musaeum dulce mel" (Lucr. 1.947; cf. Themist. Περὶ ἀρετῆς in *RhM* 27 (1872) 440 = III.12–13 Downey and Norman) by which the preceptor makes palatable his astringent philosophy.

φάρμακον: it is a commonplace (esp. bucolic) to identify, or decline to identify, a cure for love: Theoc. 14.52–3, [Theoc.] 23.24, Virg. *Ecl.* 10.60, *AGNF* p. 176.13 = P. Mich. inv. 5, Longus 2.7; for song as a cure or balm for love see citations above, esp. Theoc. 11.1–3 οὐδὲν ποττὸν ἔρωτα πεφύκει φάρμακον ἄλλο, | Νικία, οὔτ' ἔγχριστον, ἐμὶν δοκεῖ, οὔτ' ἐπίπαστον | ἢ ταὶ Πιερίδες.[13] It is unclear exactly *how* singing was thought to soothe unhappy love; perhaps through the self-expression

[13] Archaic poets had been similarly concerned to posit or deny a φάρμακον against grief or death: Archil. 13.7 *IEG*, Ibyc. *PMG* 313, Pind. *P.* 4.186–7; cf. Vermeule 133–4. The redirection of the trope from mortality to love is typically Hellenistic.

and self-understanding that give one a measure of control over one's troubles.

For the line-end cf. Theoc. 11.53 καὶ τὸν ἕν' ὀφθαλμόν, τῶ μοι γλυκερώτερον οὐδέν. The verbal echo, like the commonplace expressed in Bion's lines, may suggest that this fragment came from Bion's own Cyclops poem (see fr. 16).

IV

From Stobaeus' chapter περὶ φιλοπονίας. For the adage cf. Melissus D–K 30 B 8.3, Choerilus *SH* 330 πέτρην κοιλαίνει ῥανὶς ὕδατος ἐνδελεχείῃ (much quoted and imitated, e.g. by Greg. Naz. *Or.* 18.11 (*PG* 35.997), Aristaen. *Ep.* 1.17; see L. Sternbach in *Charisteria Casimiro de Morawski septuagenario oblata* (Krakow 1922) 58–73), Aristot. *Phys.* 253B15, [Plut]. *Lib. ed.* 2D. Bion's seems to be the only example in extant Greek verse apart from Choerilus'; in Lat. cf. Lucr. 1.313, 4.1286–7; Tib. 1.4.18; Prop. 2.25.16; Ovid *A.A.* 1.475–6 and *Pont.* 1.1.70, 2.7.39–40, 4.10.5; Lupercus *Anth. lat.* 648.9 Riese. The proverb illustrates the powers of habit or persistence; similar to this and often juxtaposed to it is that involving the wearing away of metal by touching. Do we have the words of a wise advisor, or of a lover reassuring himself that his suit will eventually succeed?

The editors of Choerilus *SH* 330 explain John Philoponus' ascription of the Choerilean line to Moschus, presumably the bucolic poet, as a confused reminiscence of Bion's fragment (H. Vitelli, *Comm. in Aristot. gr.* XVII (Berlin 1888) 826, on Aristot. *loc. cit.*).

1 ἐκ: for the instrumental use (LSJ s.v. III.6) cf. fr. 10.2, *Ad.* 26.

θαμινᾶς: "continuous, coming thick and fast", corresponding to ἐνδελεχείῃ in Choerilus (above) and glossed by αἰὲς ἰοίσας. The adj. (< θαμά "often") is first attested in lyric in neut. pl. as adv. (Pind. *O.* 1.53, *N.* 3.44, *Pae.* 6.16; Philox. *PMG* 819.2); as adj. first in Callim. *H.* 6.64, Aratus 1047, Ap. Rh. 3.1266 (a related adj. with long iota or ει is attested first in *H.H.* 4.44). For its application to the steady dripping of water cf. Ap. Rh. fr. 12.21 *CA* θαμινῇσιν . . . λιθάδεσσιν (a shower of stones), Agathias *A.P.* 5.280.6 θαμινοῖς δάκρυσι, anon. *A.P.* 9.384.3 θαμινῇσι . . . νιφάδεσσι.

ῥαθάμιγγος: usually found in pl. as "drops" or "dust particles" (cf. Schmidt II.269); here "dripping" ("sprinkling" in Nonnus *D.* 2.490, 618, etc.). A poetic word (first in *Il.* 11.536), perhaps related to ῥαίνω (H. Frisk, *Griechisches etymologisches Wörterbuch* II.17 (Heidelberg 1966) 638–9).

ὅπως λόγος: on the (very common) omission of ἐστί in such phrases see Renehan 138–40.

ὅπως: if MS ωκως conceals ὄκως (printed by Gelen 168), that is probably a scribal corruption; bucolic does not use the Ionic form elsewhere.

αἰές: for this Doric form of ἀεί see *Et. magn.* 405.35 Gaisford, Theognost. *Can.* 2 (Cramer *Anec.* II.3) Λάκωνες δὲ αἰὲς φασίν; it is transmitted at Aristoph. *Lys.* 1266 (where Burges' ἀές restores the metre). It seems unattested elsewhere in literary Doric, but Gesner's αἰέν is not wanted.

2 χὰ λίθος: the noun is fem. in the simple sense "stone" also in *Il.* 12.287, *Od.* 19.494, Theoc. 7.26; for the usual sense of the feminine – stone applied to certain specific uses, like jewellery and sculpture – see Headlam on Herodas 4.21.

ῥωχμός (< ῥήγνυμι; cf. Schwyzer I.493) "gully, cleft in soil or rock" was taken by Hellenistic and later poets (Ap. Rh. 4.1545, [Opp.] *Cyn.* 3.323, Nonnus *D.* 37.397) from *Il.* 23.420 ῥωχμὸς ἔην γαίης, sometimes in the variant form ῥωγμός.

κοιλαίνεται: the usual verb in versions of this proverb (see citations above).

V

From Stobaeus' chapter περὶ φιλοπονίας. The fragment is to be considered part of a dialogue between rustic persons, one – the speaker – perhaps older and more experienced than the other (cf. on line 3 and on the old ploughman in fr. 13.8). Whoever he is, he echoes the advice of Hes. *Op.* 407–8 χρήματα δ' εἰν οἴκῳ πάντ' ἄρμενα ποιήσασθαι, | μὴ σὺ μὲν αἰτῇς ἄλλον, ὁ δ' ἀρνῆται.

1 καλόν: in the ethical sense, "right, proper". Cf. [Theoc.] 27.7, Bion fr. 11.8. For οὐ καλόν + inf. see Rufinus *A.P.* 5.69.4.

One typical bucolic character addresses another as φίλε or ὦ φίλε in dialogue also at Theoc. 5.73, [Theoc.] 21.22. F. Williams, *Eranos* 71 (1973) 67 finds that in Theocritus' rustic dialogues ὦ + voc. conveys the familiarity of a social superior (somewhat like French *tu*). Bion may follow this usage, here suggesting the speaker's authority and perhaps age. Cf. fr. 2.1, 11.

πάντα λόγον: understand ἐπί, "for", from line 2 (q.v.). Kaibel 423 calls this an "audentissimum exemplum" of the construction ἀπὸ κοινοῦ (see on fr. 8.10), spanning a change in construction from the subject inf. φοιτῆν to the jussive ἰσχέμεν (see below).

λόγον: "pretext, purpose" (LSJ s.v. III.1). If the word seems otiose here, recourse might be made to πάντ' ἀλόγως "for no reason", after Legrand[14] (corruption could have gone πανταλογως > πανταλογος > πάντα λόγος corrected to -ον); but the text makes sense as it stands.

ποτὶ τέκτονα φοιτῆν: "resort to a professional craftsman" (LSJ s.v. φοιτάω 5).

2 μηδ' ἐπὶ πάντ': sc. ἐπὶ πάντα λόγον (cf. 1). Bion's phrase recalls ἐπὶ παντί "on every occasion" (see Theogn. 325, Theoc. 14.64, Herodas 3.20 with Headlam's citations); his acc. is purposive (Kaibel 423 paraphrases "ad quidvis perficiendum"). μηδ' ἐπί for transmitted μηδέτι is the emendation of Grotius "in nott. manuscr." according to Ahrens (conjectured also by Valckenaer).

ἄλλω: Salmasius' Doric form (recorded by Grotius II.131) is more likely for MS ἄλλο than B's (and Ursinus') ἄλλου; cf. frr. 8.4 and 12, 9.2, etc.

χρέος ἰσχέμεν: from the tragedians onward ἴσχω occasionally replaces ἔχω in such idioms (LSJ s.v. ἴσχω III.1).

2–3 ἰσχέμεν . . . τεχνᾶσθαι: jussive inf. with nom.-voc. subject is esp. Homeric (Chantraine *GH* II.316–17; for the classical usage see Bers 168–81). In Hellenistic verse see Theoc. 15.16 (coni. Ahrens), 24.74; *A.P.* 7.718.3 (Nossis), 6.147.3, 7.520.3, 7.521.3 (Callim.), 7.502.3 (Nicaenetus), 11.42.3 (Crinag.). μηδέ indicates that ἰσχέμεν is to be taken as jussive, not parallel to φοιτῆν.

ἀλλὰ καί αὐτός: probably emphatically adversative: "but rather you yourself" (cf. *Ad.* 89), not "but you too. . . ."

3 τεχνᾶσθαι: Doric η < α + ε in 1 φοιτῆν and fr. 13.7 ἀπάντη (cf. *Ad.* 8, 10) may argue for emendation to τεχνῆσθαι here.

σύριγγα: the poem may have continued with a description of the making of a panpipe out of reeds and wax; [Moschus] 3.82 σύριγγας ἔτευχε (sc. Βίων), portraying Bion as having done what the characters in his poetry do, suggests that our author wrote such a poem. On the ancient Greek panpipe see West (1992) 109–12. It was a typically rustic instrument (cf. *Il.* 18.525–6 νομῆες | τερπόμενοι σύριγξι; Soph. *Phil.* 213–14 οὐ μολπὰν σύριγγος ἔχων | ὡς ποιμὴν ἀγροβάτας; Eur. *Phaeth.* 71–2 Diggle; see Steinmayer 173–4), often mentioned in bucolic (Theoc. 1.128–9, 5.4–6 etc., 6.43; [Theoc.] 8.84, 9.8, 20.28); at Theoc. 4.28 and [Theoc.] 8.18 and 23 herdsmen have fashioned their own.[15]

[14] Actually Legrand, suspecting further corruption, conjectures οὐ καλόν, ὦ φίλε παῖ, σ' ἀλόγως. . . .

[15] The panpipe is also a standard prop in other pastoral literature, e.g. Longus 2.37. The crafting of one by Pan figures in P. Rainer 29801

On δέ = γάρ, as often in Homer and elsewhere, see Denniston 169–70. τοι "brings the point home to the person addressed" (Denniston 548), in this context perhaps with surprised indignation: "see here now, it is an easy task". Elsewhere in late bucolic τοι = σοί: Moschus 1.4; Bion fr. 2.2, 7; [Moschus] 3.65, 70, 71, 93, 111.

VI

From Stobaeus' chapter περὶ πολιτείας, whose other selections offer recipes for proper government. "E capituli titulo mancum esse fragmentum apparet" (Gow), and there are other reasons to suspect a lacuna.

1 **μηδέ:** our fragment probably begins in mid-speech.

ἐπεί: Gow prints MS ἐπήν, enclosing it in daggers to signify his suspicion that corruption extends from here to ἔδωκε in 2, but since the following mention of Apollo (however corrupt it may be) is certainly meant as a reason for rewarding the speaker, a causal clause seems needed, and ἐπεί (printed by Gelen 215, perhaps from a MS) is probably right. For a mythological *exemplum* introduced by ἐπεὶ καί see Theogn. 1345.

Φοῖβος: this title of Apollo also occurs in fr. 1.1.

ἀείδειν: cf. the divine bestowal of ἀοιδή in *Od.* 8.44, 64; Hes. *Th.* 22. For δίδωμι + inf. see LSJ s.v. δίδωμι III.1. Latin examples like Enn. *Ann.* 15–16 Skutsch "[Anchises,] Venus quem pulcra dearum | fari donavit, divinum pectus habere" and Hor. *Sat.* 2.5.60 "divinare etenim magnus mihi donat Apollo" may imitate Greek expressions like Bion's.[16] The absence of a subject (in the dat. or acc.: LSJ *loc. cit.*) is troubling, and may be due to a lacuna after ἔδωκε in 2 (cf. below). Either we should understand ἐμοί or ἐμέ, if the speaker is calling attention to the high provenance of his musical gifts, won in exchange for some service to Apollo, or conjecture a name,[17] if he means to hint at a legendary pre-

(Gow OCT 168–9), not a bucolic poem; see Introd. IV. It is also a *topos* to give away or bequeath one's panpipe, often in recognition of another's musical skill (Theoc. 4.30, 5.134–5, 6.43; Longus *loc. cit.*; cf. [Moschus] 3.51–6), or to dedicate one to Pan (Longus *loc. cit.*, Dion. Per. 994–6).

[16] On Virgil's liking for *dare* + inf., most often with a deity as subject, see R. D. Williams, *P. Vergili Maronis Aeneidos liber quintus* (Oxford 1960) on *Aen.* 5.247–8.

[17] Whose? Cf. Virg. *Aen.* 12.392–4 on Iapyx, "acri quondam cui captus amore | ipse suas artis, sua munera, laetus Apollo | augurium cithar-

cedent for bestowing a reward. The semantic connection between ἀγέραστον and μισθόν recommends the latter possibility. A more drastic solution was proposed by Edmonds (see below on 2).

2 Appositive μισθόν (translatable simply as "in exchange") is common, often with a gen.[18]; cf. Eur. *El.* 231 εὐδαιμονοίης, μισθὸν ἡδίστων λόγων (on this type of "appositional" internal acc. see K–G I.284–5; Schwyzer II.86–7, 617–18; Barrett on Eur. *Hi.* 752–7). In post-Classical poetry see e.g. Ap. Rh. 4.528, Geminus *A.P.* 6.260.2, Antiphilus *A.P.* 9.222.4, Nonnus *D.* 15.401.

This line is unmetrical, and the easiest solution is to assume that some material has been lost between ἔδωκε and the aphorism beginning τιμὰ δέ. In Valckenaer's transposition ποιεῖ δὲ τὰ πράγματα κρέσσονα τιμά[19] the strong sense-break after the second trochee – a violation of Meyer's first law – would be harsh even for Bion (cf. Introd. VI.3). Grotius emends ἔδωκε to ἔδω, a root aor. that seems to be attested only in the grammarians (e.g. Herodian III.1.838.14 Lentz).[20] Edmonds attractively emends to χὠ Φοῖβος ἀείδων | μισθοδοκεῖ (after Hermann's ἀείδων | μισθὸν ἔλεν), an *exemplum* comparing the speaker to Apollo.[21]

κρέσσονα: for the Ionic form (absent from the Doric of Theocritus but common in Pindar) in bucolic cf. [Theoc.] 8.83, 20.43; Bion *Ad.* 55.

This fragment may come from a scene between two herdsmen (cf. Theoc. 1, 5, 6), one of whom has sung for the other and now, in a high-flown manner humorous in a rustic, asks for recompense.[22] Hermann

amque dabat celerisque sagittas", and the stories of Cassandra and Branchus.

[18] Wakefield conjectures ἀοιδῶν for ἀείδων "in exchange for [my/someone's] songs".

[19] Or ποεῖ. . . . For correption of the first syllable of ποιέω in the Doric of Theocritus see Gow on Theoc. 3.9; in later bucolic see [Theoc.] 21.28 (in a poem whose prosody is different from Bion's). [Theoc.] 23.11 is corrupt.

[20] Ameis says that Grotius is following François Guyet of Angers (1575–1655). Grotius simply prints ἔδω with the remark "Ita ob versum posuimus pro ἔδωκε" (II.531).

[21] Hermann's reading was anticipated by Voss 195. F. Courby (ap. Legrand II.212 n. 1, who accepts Edmonds' emendations) suggests that the "songs" for which Phoebus receives pay are his oracles – an epigrammatic conceit.

[22] Lorenzo Gambara may have interpreted it in this way when he translated the lines as addressed to Lycidas, the speaker's beloved in fr. 9.10 (his translation is printed in Ursinus 366–7).

suggests rather a poem like Theoc. 16, where the poet, speaking in his own persona, addresses a patron. Yet another context is suggested by [Moschus] 3.122–5, where the author imagines the dead Bion winning his way back from the underworld with a song: οὐκ ἀγέραστος | ἔσσεται (Meineke: ἐσσεῖθ' codd.) ἁ μολπά, χὠς Ὀρφεῖ πρόσθεν ἔδωκεν (sc. Persephone) | ἁδέα φορμίζοντι παλίσσυτον Εὐρυδίκειαν | καὶ σέ, Βίων, πέμψει τοῖς ὤρεσιν. This may be a characteristic allusion to a lost poem by Bion on Orpheus and Eurydice (see Introd. IV): πρόσθεν in 123 may refer specifically to a poem alluded to (as πρώαν in 69 refers specifically to Bion's *Adonis*), and the use of ἀγέραστος sounds like an echo of this fragment. If so, we have the words of Bion's Orpheus to Persephone; line 1 might then have recorded a gift of musical ability from Apollo to Orpheus (in one myth Apollo is Orpheus' father; according to [Clem. Rom.] *Hom.* 5.15, his lover).[23]

VII

"I do not know how – nor is it proper – to apply myself to tasks that we have not learned." From Stobaeus' chapter περὶ ἡσυχίας (the relevance of the line may lie in its potential justification of idleness). Some editors, starting with Gesner's second edition, have attached this fragment to fr. 8, which it immediately precedes in Stobaeus; Schmitz 28 believes that "hic versus inscriptionem quasi totius carminis praebet", but fr. 8 deals rather with the possible futility of one's life's work. If a context is sought, the words could have been applied to his own situation by the addressee of fr. 5.

The sentiment recalls the proverb ἔρδοι τις ἣν ἕκαστος εἰδείη τέχνην (Aristoph. *Vesp.* 1431; cf. Cic. *Ad Att.* 5.10.3, *Tusc.* 1.18.41; Hor. *Epist.* 1.14.44; Crinag. *A.P.* 9.516.1).

1 οὐκ οἶδ' οὐδ' ἐπέοικεν: cf. *Il.* 14.212 (= *Od.* 8.358) οὐκ ἔστ' οὐδὲ ἔοικε τεὸν ἔπος ἀρνήσασθαι. Ameis proposes οὐκ ἔστ', "it is not possible", for Bion also (perhaps corrupted by a wrongly corrected dittography of οὐδ'), but the variation is typical, esp. of a Hellenistic author; cf. Antip. Sid. *A.P.* 7.424.5, beginning οὐχ ἅδεν οὐδ' ἐπέοικεν.

οἶδ': on Bion's restricted elision of verbs see Introd. VI.4. Here the elision comports with the Homeric tenor of the first hemistich; cf. [Theoc.] 27.44 οἶδ'· Ἀκροτίμη ἐσσί, where the hiatus is surprising in late bucolic, but gives Homeric flavour.

[23] Valpuesta Bermúdez 286–7 also connects this fragment to [Moschus] 3.122–5.

οὐδ' ἐπέοικεν: cf. fr. 2.9.

ἃ μὴ μάθομες: the model is perhaps Callim. *SH* 239.8]ιν ἐθέλεσκον ἃ μὴ μάθον ευ[; cf. Nonnus *Ev. Jo.* 7.56, 15.98. The persons denoted by "we" here may be a group to which the speaker belongs or all mortals generally, but more probably we are dealing with a switch from 1st pers. sing. to pl., both denoting "I".

πονέεσθαι: the middle form is Homeric; "after Hom., the act. form πονέω prevails" (LSJ s.v. B; cf. fr. 8.10). For the middle voice in Hellenistic verse see e.g. Theoc. 15.115, 16.94; Callim. *H.* 3.158; Ap. Rh. 1.1185, 2.667, 3.1339.

VIII

From Stobaeus' chapter περὶ ἡσυχίας (see on fr. 7). On the original context of the fragment see p. 12.

1 μοι: possessive. The risk of corruption from ἐμοί in 2 may recommend Ahrens's μευ.

μελύδρια: this diminutive of μέλος occurs also at Aristoph. *Eccl.* 883, Theoc. 7.51 (whence Bion; cf. on 3 below). W. Petersen, *Greek Diminutives in -ιον* (Weimar 1910) 246–7 traces the suffix -ύδριον to an unattested fifth-century term *θηλύδριον, coined on the analogy of ἄνδριον; he notes its frequent use with neuter s-stems (cf. Epicharm. fr. 42.3 Kaibel σκιφύδριον, Aristoph. *Eq.* 907 ἑλκύδριον; see Buck and Petersen 100). Here as at Theoc. 7.51 the diminutive is self-deprecatory: there out of Lycidas' ironic modesty, here out of the speaker's pessimism concerning his achievements (Petersen 247 detects an original pejorative sense in the suffix and notes that "personal names in -ύδριον are always deteriorative" – though on p. 248 he considers μελύδριον here, as in Aristophanes, to be hypocoristic).

καὶ τάδε μῶνα: "even these alone".

2 κῦδος: note the traditional assumption that the goal of poetic composition is renown.

θήσοντι: for pl. verb with neut. pl. subject see on *Ad.* 32 λέγοντι; cf. fr. 17.2.

τά μοι πάρος: Ameis (in his edition; cf. *De art.* 10) conjectures τό (with antecedent κῦδος), but the speaker is specifying *which* poems will bring him fame: the ones he has already written.

ὤπασε Μοῖρα: cf. Pind. *N.* 4.41–2 (of his own art) ἐμοὶ δ' ὁποίαν ἀρετάν | ἔδωκε Πότμος ἄναξ, Hor. *C.* 2.16.38–9 "spiritum Graiae tenuem Camenae | Parca non mendax dedit". These parallels discourage the tempting emendation to Μοῖσα, proposed by Stephanus in his 1555 translation: "Quos mihi tempus ad hoc video dictasse Camoenam"; later on the last page of the Prolegomena to his 1579 edition. The mention of Fate here looks forward to lines 5 and 14. The speaker seems to imply that one is either born with talent or is not; if he himself is not, there is no point in his working for it (line 3), and he should therefore abandon a task that is not bringing him κῦδος and that is keeping him from the joys of life (cf. 6).

3 ἁδέα = καλά in line 1. Here neither adj. is merely ornamental (cf. fr. 2.7 n.), but strongly evaluative. Cf. fr. 9.5 ἁδὺ μελίσδῃ and on fr. 10.8 ἁδύς.

τί μοι: the expression τί + dat. + inf. in the sense "why should (I)...?", perhaps a development from the idiom τί πλέον... "what use is it to...?", is late and prosaic: Epictet. 2.17.14, 3.22.66; 1 Cor. 5:12; Max. Tyr. 2.10; Ael. *N.A.* 7.11.[24] In verse see also Mel. *A.P.* 5.178.2, 12.68.3–4. It may give these lines a colloquial flavour, as does the mild hyperbole in πολὺ πλείονα. Note that τί μοι πολύ does not cohere as a variation of τί μοι πλέον: in the latter idiom it is surely the *comparative* force of πλέον (not the simple sense "much") that gives the sense of advantageousness. Here πολύ is intensive with πλείονα (LSJ s.v. πολύς III.a); cf. 12 below, *Ad.* 93.

μοχθεῖν: "labour at, toil over". For transitive μοχθέω (LSJ s.v. 2) see e.g. Eur. *Hec.* 815, Aristoph. *Plut.* 518, Bion *Ad.* 73 (thus Ahrens's ποτὶ πλείονα is unnecessary). For poetic composition as labour cf. Theoc. 7.51 τοῦθ' ὅτι πρᾶν ἐν ὄρει τὸ μελύδριον (cf. 1 above) ἐξεπόνασα, where Gow remarks that the verb may "indicate the high finish in poetry demanded by Callimachus and his party". Bion's speaker implicitly opposes poetic labour to the pleasures of life (6–7 and 10 below); cf. the opposition of philosophical or poetic study to love-making in *A.P.* 5.134, 12.98 (Posid.); 12.101 and 117 (Mel.); 9.161 (Marc. Arg.).

4–7 Cf. Epicurus fr. 204 Usener γεγόναμεν ἅπαξ, δὶς δὲ οὐκ ἔστι γενέσθαι· δεῖ δὲ τὸν αἰῶνα μηκέτ' εἶναι. σὺ δὲ τῆς αὔριον οὐκ ὢν κύριος ἀναβάλλῃ τὸν καιρόν· ὁ δὲ πάντων βίος μελλησμῷ παραπόλλυται καὶ διὰ τοῦτο ἕκαστος ἡμῶν ἀσχολούμενος ἀποθνήσκει. For fantasies of a twofold life see Eur. *Supp.* 1080–6, *H.F.* 655–61; note that this is different from the idea of living one's life over again. Bion uses the motif in connection with the theme of μεμψιμοιρία or discontent with

[24] The expression τί + dat. "what business is it of (mine)?", with ἐστι or μέλει understood, is old (see West on Hes. *Th.* 35, Headlam on Herodas 2.18).

one's lot, a common target of diatribe (like that in 8–13 below): e.g. [Hippoc.] *Epist.* 17 (IX.371 Littré), Hor. *Sat.* 1.1.1–22 (cf. 1.6.93–9); see G. C. Fiske, *Lucilius and Horace* (Madison 1920) 219–28.

5 **Κρονίδας:** in late bucolic this title of Zeus recurs at [Theoc.] 20.41. For Zeus as dispenser of human life cf. Euphron fr. 5 *PCG* ὦ Ζεῦ, τί ποθ' ἡμῖν δοὺς χρόνον τοῦ ζῆν βραχύν | πλέκειν ἀλύπως τοῦτον ἡμᾶς οὐκ ἐᾷς; The indecision between Zeus and Fate as dispenser of one's life is similar to the indecision between Zeus and the sea as parent of Aphrodite in fr. 14.1: both speakers aim at accuracy through comprehensiveness.

πολύτροπος: Legrand thinks Ahrens's παλίντροπος "cessant d'être inflexible" – taking it as predicate rather than as epithet – more suitable, since the speaker seems to wish for stern Fate to bend a little; he sees an allusion to Ἄτροπος, "the unbending one", the name of one of the three Fates as early as [Hes.] *Th.* 905. Bion's speaker, however, is contrasting the uncertain fate of his poems with a more secure arrangement, and the epithet "of many turns or wiles", with overtones of fickleness and unpredictability, suits Fate well here (indeed, to Valpuesta Bermúdez 316 it "parece una corrección al tradicional ἄτροπος"). For the unfavourable sense of the adj. cf. [Phocyl.] *Sent.* 95 λαῷ μὴ πίστευε· πολύτροπός ἐστιν ὅμιλος. Nonnus *D.* 41.317 κλώθουσι πολύτροπα νήματα Μοῖραι and Quintus 12.171 Αἶσα... πολύτροπος may imitate Bion.

6 **εὐφροσύναν καὶ χάρματα:** the two words are juxtaposed also in [Manetho] *Apot.* 2 [1].243 Koechly (where I would read χάρματα for χρήμ-); *Or. Sib.* 3.770–1; [Apolinar.] *Ps.* 9.3, 31.25, 34.56, 44.35, 50.16, 69.5 Ludwich (cf. Golega 60); Nonnus *D.* 39.148. The pairing may go back ultimately to Bion.

ἐνὶ μόχθῳ: cf. 3. Circumstantial ἐνί is correct here; Wilamowitz's ἐπὶ μόχθῳ, presumably intended to parallel ἐς εὐφροσύναν καὶ χάρματα (for ἐπί of purpose + dat. see LSJ s.v. B.III.2), is unwelcome, since "labour" is not the end in view. If we were each given two lifetimes we could spend one with a view to merriment and joys, i.e. in pleasure, and the other in labour, i.e. with a view to κῦδος.[25]

7 **ἦν:** one expects κεν/ἄν, but an inf. dependent on the imperf. of a verb of possibility, which here serves as apodosis of the contrary-to-fact condition, regularly does not take the modal adverb (Goodwin §415).

[25] Briggs's conjecture ἐν εὐφροσύνᾳ καὶ χάρματι is therefore also to be resisted.

τάχα: "perhaps", as in e.g. Theoc. 4.41, 7.36; [Theoc.] 21.55, 27.57.

μοχθήσαντι: cf. 3 μοχθεῖν: the speaker's admonitions have become generally applicable, but his own work and its profitability are still uppermost in his mind.

ποθ' ὕστερον: "later, afterwards", a variation of ἐς ὕστερον (which occurs in *Od.* 12.126; Hes. *Op.* 351; Theoc. 1.145; Callim. *H.* 5.107, 6.64). ποθ' is ποτί = πρός, not ποτε (otherwise no main caesura).

For ἐσθλά used of god-given blessings cf. *Il.* 24.530 (the two urns of Zeus) ἄλλοτε μέν τε κακῷ ὅ γε κύρεται, ἄλλοτε δ' ἐσθλῷ, Plato *Resp.* 379D.

The sequence "work, then pleasure" may be related to Cynic doctrine (cf. Antisthenes ap. Stob. 3.29.65 ἡδονὰς τὰς μετὰ τοὺς πόνους διωκτέον, ἀλλ' οὐχὶ τὰς πρὸ τῶν πόνων), but was no doubt commonplace.

8–14 These lines comprise an example of the popular philosophical dialexis, characterized by haranguing rhetorical questions and socio-moral polemic, which modern scholars have specified by the name of diatribe (on the term and its history see Kindstrand 97; H. D. Jocelyn, *LCM* 7 (1982) 3–7). On the diatribe form and poetic adaptations of it see e.g. A. Oltramare, *Les origines de la diatribe romaine* (Lausanne 1926) *passim*; Kindstrand 97–9; D. L. Clayman, *Callimachus' Iambi* (*Mnem.* Suppl. 59, Leiden 1980) 69–70; B. P. Wallach, *Lucretius and the Diatribe against the Fear of Death* (*Mnem.* Suppl. 40, Leiden 1976) 6–10; K. Freudenburg, *The Walking Muse: Horace on the Theory of Satire* (Princeton 1993) 16–21. Leon. Tar. *A.P.* 7.472 comprises such a harangue, with some of the same motifs as here (e.g. the shortness of life, the necessity to remember one's mortality); its form has raised generic and formal quandaries (see *HE* II.379–80: "a collection of Cynic sentiments"; "an elegy rather than an epigram").[26] Especially like Bion's passage is Manil. 4.1–11, on which see F.-F. Lühr, *Ratio und Fatum. Dichtung und Lehre bei Manilius* (diss. Frankfurt am Main 1969) 113–15. The form is first literary in the works of Bion of Borysthenes in the third century B.C. and is especially associated with the Cynics; but the sub-philosophical commonplaces used here cannot be traced to particular schools.

8 εἰ: virtually "since", adducing support for a proposition in the form of a real condition (LSJ s.v. B.VI). In Hellenistic verse see e.g. Ap. Rh. 1.1285, Asclep. *A.P.* 7.145.3, Crinag. *A.P.* 6.350.4.

[26] Cf. Palladas *A.P.* 10.81, a six-line iambic lament on the brevity of life with some of the same themes and motifs as this fragment (e.g. the distribution of life between labour and pleasure).

κατένευσαν ... ἐλθεῖν: in Homer κατανεύω in this sense takes the future inf.

9 μείονα πάντων: hyperbole is a staple of diatribe.

10 ἐς πόσον: "how long?", a conflation of εἰς πότε and πόσον χρόνον.

ἆ δειλ- is common in Homeric expressions of compassion (e.g. *Il.* 11.440, 17.443; *Od.* 20.351); the phrase normally begins its clause, but cf. Crinag. *A.P.* 9.234.1 ἄχρι τεῦ, ἆ δείλαιε ..., echoing Bion (also on the vanity of riches).[27]

καμάτως κεἰς ἔργα: "on toils and tasks", hendiadys for "toilsome tasks" (so Gow (1953) 152); cf. fr. 16.2. The preposition εἰς is to be understood with both nouns. This construction ἀπὸ κοινοῦ, especially common with place-names, is attested first in lyric and tragedy (numerous citations in K–G 1.550, supplemented by Friis Johansen and Whittle on Aesch. *Supp.* 311 Κάνωβον κἀπὶ Μέμφιν); in *Od.* 4.475–6 ἱκέσθαι | οἶκον ἐυκτίμενον καὶ σὴν ἐς πατρίδα γαῖαν and 12.27 ἢ ἁλὸς ἢ ἐπὶ γῆς we are probably dealing instead with locative uses of the acc. and gen., although these may have encouraged the later usage. Cf. G. Kiefner, *Die Versparung* (Wiesbaden 1964) 5–16. Lapp 77 lists Callimachean instances of the figure (e.g. fr. 67.5, *H.* 2.8), Kaibel 423 instances from epigram (e.g. Antip. Sid. *A.P.* 6.111.1, 118.2); note also Moschus 2.142 χθόνα καὶ κατὰ πόντον. For a peculiarly strained example see Bion's own fr. 5.1–2. F. Leo, *Ausgewählte kl. Schr.* (Rome 1960) 1.117–19 discusses the usage in Latin.

πονεῦμες: the active form of this verb is post-Homeric (cf. fr. 7.1 n.). For πονέω εἰς "expend labour upon" see Theogn. 919, Diotimus *A.P.* 7.261.1, *GVI* 1680.1 (Egypt, third–second century B.C.).

11–12 With ψυχὰν βάλλειν ποτί, a vivid expression for "devote oneself to", cf. Eur. fr. 964.2 Nauck εἰς φροντίδας νοῦν συμφοράς τ' ἐβαλλόμην, itself a bold reversal of the expression βάλλειν τι εἰς τὸν νοῦν. Compare the similar wording in [Eur.] *Rhes.* 183 ψυχὴν προβάλλοντ' ἐν κύβοισι δαίμονος, "staking one's life ...".

ποτὶ κέρδεα καὶ ποτὶ τέχνας: almost a hendiadys, "the crafts that bring us material gain".

12 For the sentiment see e.g. Solon fr. 13.71–3 *IEG* πλούτου δ' οὐδὲν τέρμα πεφασμένον ἀνδράσι κεῖται· | οἳ γὰρ νῦν ἡμέων πλεῖστον ἔχουσι βίον, | διπλάσιον σπεύδουσι, *CA* lyr. adesp. 37.22 νῦν γὰρ ὁ χρήματ'

[27] But Crinagoras opposes poetry to the striving after material wealth (line 5); Bion implicitly equates the two.

ἔχων ἔτι πλείονα χρήματα θέλει, Juv. 14.139 "crescit amor nummi quantum ipsa pecunia crevit", Plut. *De av.* 523E τίνος οὖν ἀπαλλάττει τῶν ἄλλων κακῶν ὁ πλοῦτος εἰ μηδὲ φιλοπλουτίας; Cf. Hor. *Sat.* 1.1.92–4.

πολὺ πλείονος: cf. 3 n.

13 ἦ λαθόμεσθ' ἄρα: "Have we then truly forgotten...?" Two considerations prompt emendation of MS λαθόμεθ' ἦ ἄρα. First, the postponement of ἦ would be extremely irregular, even anomalous (Denniston 281, 283; but cf. Dioscor. *A.P.* 7.407.2). Secondly, the Doricized epic present or imperf. of the MSS is inferior to the aor. of Hermann. In addition, the hiatus in ἦ ἄρα is uncharacteristic of Bion. After Hermann's transposition, however, we are left with the unwelcome separation of the two particles by the verb (cf. Denniston 284). J. A. Hartung, who prints the improbable deliberative subj. ἦ ῥα λαθώμεθα, rejects another possibility, ἦ ῥα λελάσμεθα, as too distant from the MSS, but this may in fact be the true reading (for the epic perf. in bucolic see Theoc. 2.158).

Interrogative ἦ "schließt, entsprechend seinem konfirmativen Gebrauche ..., eine Versicherung in sich, indem es den Gegenstand der Frage als *wirklich bestehend* voraussetzt. In sehr vielen Fällen ... tritt die versichernde Kraft der Partikel noch so deutlich zu Tage, daß der Satz nur als eine in fragendem Tone gesprochene Behauptung erscheint" (K–G II.526). The rhetorical question in the previous, parallel sentence suggests one here too.

14 βραχὺν ... χρόνον: for the phrase see [Aesch.] *P.V.* 939 (of the term of Zeus' regime), Euphron fr. 5.1 *PCG* (of mortal life; quoted above on 4). Note the ring-composition: the diatribe begins (8–9) and ends with a reminder of the shortness of life.

That the last two feet of the hexameter have not been excerpted suggests that the sentence ended at the bucolic caesura, but this is not certain. An epithet for Fate (e.g. ἀθανάτοιο; cf. Epimen. D–K 3 B 19.2) would produce a type of "golden line" (see Introd. VII.3).[28] Valckenaer reports that Isaac Vossius supplied the inf. of purpose ἐμβιοτεύειν "be alive", but this verb is late and prosaic, esp. patristic (though Vossius, who worked on the *Oracula Sibyllina*, could have anticipated Wilamowitz and Geffcken in conjecturing it for βιοτεύειν at the end of *Or. Sib.* 5.503).

[28] As we have it the line illustrates the Hellenistic tendency to place the adj. emphatically first when a noun and its adj. are separated, in contrast to Homeric practice (cf. Conrad 56).

IX

From Stobaeus' chapter περὶ Ἀφροδίτης πανδήμου. An exercise on the commonplace that love inspires poetry, here to the exclusion of other sources of inspiration (4–5) and other themes (8–9). Cf. on frr. 3, 10.12–13. The commonplace that poetry cures lovesickness, on which Fantuzzi bases his interpretation of this fragment (*MD* 4 (1980) 183–6), is not found in these lines.

1–2 "The Muses either fear savage Eros or love [him] heartily, and follow on his heels." Since the rest of the fragment deals only with the Muses' devotion to lovers, editors have long emended away the possibility that the Muses fear, and therefore shun, the god of love (οὐ φοβέουσαι | ἐκ θυμῶ φιλέοντι Gesner (1543); οὐ φοβέονται, | ἐκ θυμῶ δὲ φιλεῦντι Valckenaer, first printed by Brunck). The corruptions οὐ > ἤ and ἐκ > ἠκ are difficult to account for, however, and anyway φοβέομαι here refers to the general intimidation imposed by a higher power, without the original sense of flight (so Graefe 119); cf. esp. Plato *Crito* 47C–D, where φοβεῖσθαι "respect, defer to" expands upon ἕπεσθαι, and Bion *Ad.* 57 n. Compare *AGNF* p. 176.14–15 = P. Mich. inv. 5 ἡ γῆ γὰρ φοβουμένη τὸν θεὸν (sc. Eros) οὐ φέρει, "for the earth in deference to the god does not bear [a herb to remedy love]". The Muses follow in Eros' train either because they are cowed by the superior deity or because they love him heartily.

1 ταὶ Μοῖσαι τὸν Ἔρωτα: for this line-opening cf. Callim. *A.P.* 12.150.3 (see on fr. 3) and *Anacreont.* 19.1 (for a discussion of Bion's influence on this poem see Fantuzzi (1994)).

ἄγριον: lit. "of the field" (ἀγρός) as opposed to the settlement; applied to anything the opposite of "civilized, tame", often with the suggestion of savageness and cruelty. An epithet of Eros also in Bion fr. 14.5 below, Mel. *A.P.* 5.177.1 τὸν Ἔρωτα τὸν ἄγριον (probably echoing Bion; the whole epigram imitates Moschus 1) and 12.48.1, [Opp.] *Cyn.* 2.422; cf. Plato *Resp.* 329C, Moschus 1.11. Amor is often *ferus* or *saevus* in Ovid; cf. Virg. *Ecl.* 8.47, Hor. *C.* 2.8.14.

2 ἠκ: i.e. ἢ ἐκ. Some old editions (following A) print ἢ 'κ, denoting aphaeresis (prodelision), but that is a feature of iambic and lyric verse, not normally employed in hexameters (though cf. Callim. *H.* 5.47 and 63 with Bulloch); here we are dealing with crasis. Cf. κἠκ in Theoc. 11.35, [Theoc.] 8.92. For ἐκ θυμῶ φιλ- see *Il.* 9.343, 486; [Hes.] fr. 58.4; cf. Theoc. 17.130 ἐκ θυμοῦ στέργοισα.

ἐκ ποδός: with ἕπομαι, "close behind, on one's heels" (cf. Polyb.

3.68.1, 5.74.1, 18.24.2, etc.; Dion. Hal. *A.R.* 2.33.2, 6.29.4, 10.23.2; Jos. *A.J.* 7.13).

3–6 No one can sing without Love. The commonplace that love inspires poetry (see introduction to fr. 3) here takes shape as a rococo reimagining of traditional hymnists' disavowals like *H.H.* 1.18–19 οὐδέ πῃ ἔστι | σεῖ' ἐπιληθομένῳ ἱερῆς μεμνῆσθαι ἀοιδῆς; this whole fragment in effect constitutes a hymn to Eros.[29]

3 ἀνέραστον: "unloverly", as Gow and Page translate on Callim. *A.P.* 12.148.4 (*HE* II.162); in Hellenistic poetry see also Moschus fr. 2.7. The term is favoured by Imperial prose writers (e.g. Plut. *Amat.* 752C, etc.; Longus 3.11; Heliod. 2.35.1, etc.), sometimes in the sense "loveless" (cf. Alpheus *A.P.* 12.18.1).[30]

ἀείδῃ: for the source of the emendation see p. 80.

4 οὐκ ἐθέλοντι: "they refuse"; cf. *Ad.* 96.

διδάσκειν: Schmitz 28 conjectures διώκειν, the traditional opposite of φεύγειν (see *Ad.* 53 n.) and parallel to ἕπονται in 2; but the teaching of song to singers is the special job of the Muses (cf. e.g. *Od.* 8.481, 488).

5 νόον: acc. of respect (cf. fr. 14.5).

ἔρωτι δονεύμενος: "shaken, tossed about by love". Cf. Sappho fr. 130.1 L–P Ἔρως δηὖτέ μ' ὀ λυσιμέλης δόνει, Pind. *P.* 4.219 δονέοι μάστιγι Πειθοῦς, Aristoph. *Eccl.* 954 πάνυ γάρ τις ἔρως με δονεῖ, [Opp.] *Cyn.* 2.412 βελέεσσι δὲ σοῖσι (sc. Ἔρωτος) δονεῖται, Nonnus *D.* 1.324 καὶ Κρονίδην ὀρόωσα πόθῳ δεδονημένον Ἥρη.[31] The instrumental dat. suggests that "love", not "Love", is meant, but esp. in view of the personification in 1–2, 4, 6, 10 the distinction is very fine.

μελίσδῃ: cf. 10. The verb is found in the middle–passive in Theoc. 1.2, 7.89; [Moschus] 3.51, 60, 118, 119; active at [Theoc.] 20.28; [Moschus] 3.15. The spelling -σδ- for -ζ-, an Aeolism possibly taken by Theocritus from the Doric of Alcman (Gow on Theoc. 1.2), became traditional in bucolic; cf. e.g. Bion frr. 13.3, 16.2. The spelling is a Hellenistic representation of the conservative Lesbian pronunciation of

[29] On third-person hymns (e.g. the choral versions in Aesch. *Ag.* 160–83, Hor. *C.* 1.21) cf. F. Cairns, *PCPS* 38 (1992) 3.

[30] Plato *Symp.* 204C and *Phaedr.* 250D already has ἐραστός "lovable, lovely". For variation between passive and active sense of compound adjs. in -τος cf. Mastronarde on Eur. *Phoen.* 209.

[31] The verb is also metaphorical for other types of emotional disturbance: see e.g. Pind. *P.* 6.36, Mnesimachus fr. 4.60 *PCG*, Theoc. 13.65 (with Gow).

medial zeta, which in the standard language had come to be pronounced [zz] (W.S. Allen, *Vox Graeca*[3] (Cambridge 1987) 59). Molinos Tejada 129–31 observes that in bucolic -σδ- originally signalled rusticity and became conventional mainly in words dealing with the typical bucolic themes of music and romantic leisure ("el vocabulario pastoril"), e.g. συρίσδω, ψιθυρίσδω, βουκολιάσδω (contrast frr. 1.2 δίζετο, 10.3 νευστάζοντα, 10.9 ἐμπάζετο).

6 μάλα πᾶσαι: an epic phrase: *Il.* 13.741, 17.356; *Od.* 2.306, 17.346, etc.; *H.H.* 2.417, 3.171; Theoc. 24.94; [Theoc.] 25.19, 75; Ap. Rh. 1.230, 330, etc.

ἐπειγόμεναι προρέοντι: "they hurriedly gravitate to him". When used with a person as subj., ῥέω connotes attraction beyond one's control (often with εἰς): Isocr. *Pac.* 5 ἐφ' οὓς (sc. λόγους) καὶ νῦν τὸ πλῆθος αὐτῶν ἐρρύηκεν, [Phocyl.] *Sent.* 193 μηδ' ἐς ἔρωτα γυναικὸς ἅπας ῥεύσῃς ἀκάθεκτον, Appian *B.C.* 5.76 πολὺς γὰρ καὶ ἐς τήνδε ἐρρύη, ταχὺς ὢν εἰς ἔρωτας. The compound verb is elsewhere used literally of liquids, e.g. *Il.* 5.598; *Od.* 5.444; *H.H.* 3.23, 145, 380. The prefix denotes preference here (LSJ s.v. πρό D.III.4): the Muses are drawn to the lover rather than to the loveless singer.

προρέοντι: with the single-rho form contrast *Ad.* 55 καταρρεῖ, [Moschus] 3.33 ἔρρευσε.

7 μάρτυς ἐγών begins a pentameter at Theogn. 1226.

πᾶσιν: not strictly logical, but we get the point.

8–11 "I am unable to sing of anything but love and Love." This recalls the Latin *recusatio* (see on fr. 10.12–13). Cameron (1995) 471 even takes this fragment as possibly "the principal inspiration" of such disavowals of grand themes as Virg. *Ecl.* 6.3–8, judging that "[s]inging 'of another mortal or some god' must mean attempting encomiastic or mythological poetry" (p. 456); fr. 10, however, provides as good a precedent for the *recusatio*, and in any case the trope may have been current before Bion adapted it to his speakers' straits. The connection between these lines and 3–6 (where love alone inspires poetry) is supplied by the mention in 10 of Lycidas, the speaker's beloved, both source and object of his song.

8 βροτὸς ἄλλος is a common phrase in hexameter poetry, e.g. *Il.* 2.248, 24.505, *Od.* 15.321, 24.267, [Hes.] fr. 30.23, [Theoc.] 20.20. For ἀθανάτων τινά see *Il.* 13.8, [Theoc.] 25.199.

μέλπω: a grand word (epic, lyric, tragic), alien to Theocritus but common in later bucolic: [Theoc.] 8.83; Bion fr. 10.4 as well as here; [Moschus] 3.20, 80, 94; [Bion] 2.4. It appears in [Theoc.] *Ep.* 4.12 and

5.4, which emulate the dialect and subject matter of the bucolic poets. Cf. on 3.2 μολπάν.

9 βαμβαίνει: on the rare verb see F. Lochner-Hüttenbach, *Glotta* 40 (1962) 165–8; Tichy 268. It is founded on a reduplicated stem **bam-bam* (which Schwyzer I.647 connects with βαίνω – thus "go-go"; the basic meaning may be convulsive repetitive motion) and appears first in *Il.* 10.374–5 (Dolon) ὃ δ' ἄρ' ἔστη τάρβησέν τε | βαμβαίνων, ἄραβος δὲ διὰ στόμα γίγνετ' ὀδόντων, next here. In Homer it signifies shivering and shaking from fear (cf. Schol. *ad loc.* τρέμων καὶ μετὰ σφαλμοῦ τὴν πορείαν ποιούμενος, Apoll. Soph. s.v. διὰ τρόμον οὐκ ἠρεμοῦσαν τὴν βάσιν ποιούμενος; the following reference to the chattering of teeth does not define the participle). Bion, in applying the verb to the tongue, extends its meaning to the trembling and stammering of the voice (followed by Themist. *Or.* 4.56A ἐβάμβαινε δὲ ἡ φωνή, Agathias *A.P.* 5.273.6 χείλεα βαμβαίνει φθέγματι γηραλέῳ).[32]

βαμβαίνει μοι γλῶσσα: Bion may allude to Sappho fr. 31.9 L–P γλῶσσα †ἔαγε (also imitated by Lucr. 3.155, Catull. 51.9), although the contexts are different: Sappho is referring to her inability to speak due to the presence of her beloved, Bion's speaker to his inability to sing of anyone but his beloved.

10 For δ' αὖτε responding to μέν see e.g. *H.H.* 2.137; Aesch. *Pers.* 183, *Sept.* 5, *Ag.* 553; Ap. Rh. 1.1271, 2.1072, 3.1126, etc.; anon. *A.P.* 12.156.3, 14.101.3.

ἐς . . . ἐς: "about, concerning".

Λυκίδαν: a namesake of the goatherd Lycidas in Theoc. 7; the name is also used in [Theoc.] 27.42, [Bion] 2.1, and in Virgil's *Eclogues* (cf. Wendel 37). This tradition suggests that our speaker is a herdsman in love with another (presumably juvenile) herdsman; for songs on rustic ἐρώμενοι in bucolic cf. Theoc. 5.90–9, 106–7, 134–5; 7.52–89; Bion fr. 11.4 below. The pederastic content of Bion's poetry is noted by [Moschus] 3.83 καὶ παίδων ἐδίδασκε φιλάματα (cf. 66).

μελίσδω: see on 5 μελίσδῃ.

11 καὶ τόκα: "thereupon", a frequent sense of καὶ τότε in Homer (e.g. *Il.* 1.92, *Od.* 2.108); there is no warrant for Ruhnken's emendation to αὐτίκα (ap. Valckenaer).

χαίροισα: "gladly"; Brunck III.2.88 paraphrases "sponte sua".

διὰ στόματος ῥέει ᾠδά: the model is Hes. *Th.* 96–7 ὃ δ' ὄλβιος,

[32] Cf. *Et. magn.* s.v.: εἴρηται ἀπὸ μεταφορᾶς τῶν ποδῶν ἐπὶ τῶν μὴ ἑδραίαν τὴν φωνὴν ἐχόντων.

ὅντινα Μοῦσαι | φίλωνται· γλυκερή οἱ ἀπὸ στόματος ῥέει αὐδή (= *H.H.* 25.4–5; cf. *Il.* 1.249, Nonnus *D.* 10.188). Ursinus reads αὐδά at the end of Bion's line in conformity to the traditional phrase, but the variation is typical of Hellenistic practice. In bucolic the contracted form of ἀοιδή is post-Theocritean: [Theoc.] 8.62 and 9.1, 2, 28, 32; [Moschus] 3.15, 94, 112.

X

From Stobaeus' chapter περὶ Ἀφροδίτης πανδήμου. An epigrammatic reversal: the teacher is taught (compare the hunted hunter in fr. 13.13–16).

1 **μεγάλα:** cf. Theoc. 11.16 Κύπριδος ἐκ μεγάλας, Paul. Sil. *A.P.* 9.620.2; Venus is *magna* in Tib. 1.2.79, Prop. 3.8.12. The epithet may refer to literal size as much as to divine might; for the superhuman stature of the gods see e.g. *Il.* 4.443; *H.H.* 2.188–9, 5.173–4.

ἔθ' ὑπνώοντι: the speaker means that he learned in a dream the amatory song that now uniquely composes his repertory (12–13); he thus assimilates himself to poets who claimed indoctrination by a deity in a dream: Aeschylus (Paus. 1.21.2), Callimachus (Schol. on fr. 2; cf. anon. *A.P.* 7.42, Prop. 2.34.32), Ennius *Ann.* frr. 2–10 Skutsch (cf. Persius *Prol.* 1–3), Prop. 3.3. Cf. Isoc. *Hel.* 65, Plato *Phaed.* 60E, Corinna *PMG* 657 (with Page 29), *Vita Aesopi* (G) 6–9 Perry. Similar to Bion's version is *Anacreont.* 1, where the dreaming speaker meets Anacreon, led by Eros, and the old poet gives him the garland off his head: καὶ δῆθεν ἄχρι καὶ νῦν | ἔρωτος οὐ πέπαυμαι (16–17; cf. 12–13 below). A. Kambylis, *Die Dichterweihe und ihre Symbolik* (Heidelberg 1965) 104–6 connects the motif to the reputedly heightened awareness of a sleeper's soul and its nearness to divine wisdom; M. Brioso Sanchez, *Emerita* 47 (1979) 5 n. 1, discussing *Anacreont.* 1, calls it "un equivalente a la situación de soledad que es normal en las consegraciones no oníricas". It appears in Near Eastern literature: Burkert (1992) 109. In view of this tradition eighteenth-century emendations like ἔθ' ἡβώοντι (J. F. Herel ap. Valckenaer) and ἐφηβώοντι (Wakefield) are unwarranted. Bion, playing on loftier instances of the commonplace (perhaps esp. that of Callimachus), describes a kind of burlesque dream-indoctrination, inadvertent on the part of the goddess.

ἔτι may point to an hour just before waking, "ubi somnia vera" (so Graefe 119). For the belief that the hours after midnight brought true dreams see Moschus 2.5, Hor. *Sat.* 1.10.33 (literary injunctions by a god), Ovid *Her.* 19.195–6; it may be reflected in anon. *SH* 922.1–2 and

1046. Bühler 52 n. 5 lists places where "bei einem Traum ausdrücklich eine frühe Morgenzeit angegeben wird", e.g. Plato *Crit.* 44A, Cic. *Div.* 1.59, Virg. *Aen.* 8.67–9, [Tib.] 3.4.17–18. The adv. also indicates that a broader specification of the occasion preceded the lines we have (e.g. "I learned my songs of love one night not long ago").

παρέστα: "came to me, appeared to me"; cf. the epiphany of Aphrodite to Helen in *Il.* 3.405 τοὔνεκα δὴ νῦν δεῦρο δολοφρονέουσα παρέστης;[33]

2 νηπίαχον: "childlike" (for the etymology see Buck and Petersen 681). Applied to Eros also in anon. *A.P.* 9.157.8; he is νήπιος in *A.P.* 12.47.1 (Mel.), 5.58.1 (Archias); *A.Pl.* 196.4 (Alc. Mess.), 197.3 (Antip. Thess.). The contrast between Eros' innocent childlike appearance and his mischievousness is common in epigram; cf. also Moschus 1 *passim*, *Anacreont.* 33.10–11 ὁ δ' Ἔρως "ἄνοιγε", φησίν· | "βρέφος εἰμί, μὴ φόβησαι".

3 ἐς χθόνα νευστάζοντα: lowering one's face and gaze is a sign of bashfulness (here false bashfulness), most often in amatory contexts (e.g. *H.H.* 5.156, Theoc. 2.112 (both feigned), Ap. Rh. 3.1008 and 1022, Longus 4.14, Colluth. 305, Aristaen. 1.15, Musaeus 160, Irenaeus *A.P.* 5.253.1), but also in others: *Il.* 3.217 (feigned incompetence), Ap. Rh. 1.784, Ter. *Eun.* 579–80, Virg. *Aen.* 11.480.

τόσον δέ μοι ἔφρασε μῦθον: for this form of speech-introduction cf. Leon. Tar. *A.P.* 9.99.3 ἔπος ἐκ γαίης τόσον ἄπυε and esp. Moschus 2.134, ending τόσην ἀνενείκατο φωνήν (imitated by Nonnus *D.* 38.221 and 46.282 = 48.702).

4 μέλπειν: see on fr. 9.8.

βοῦτα: textual corruption has obscured the conventions of the dialect of late bucolic, but the correct reading here may be the pseudo-Doric βῶτ- (printed by Briggs; cf. Voss 194), which is transmitted at [Moschus] 3.81 (βούτ- at [Moschus] 3.65, [Theoc.] 20.34). Likewise βωκόλος ([Bion] 2.10, [Moschus] 3.11) and βωκολιάσδω ([Moschus] 3.120) are the usual MS readings for βουκ- in late bucolic (cf. 5 below). On conventional pseudo-Doricisms in late bucolic dialect, e.g. φίλαμα for φίλημα, see Introd. v.

δίδασκε: Bion's conceit of the poet as teacher of Eros is picked up by Ovid *A.A.* 1.7–8 "me Venus artificem tenero praefecit Amori; | Tiphys

[33] For the verb in a context of poetic inspiration cf. Pind. *O.* 3.4 Μοῖσα δ' οὕτω ποι παρέστα μοι, where, however, it means "was at my side in assistance".

et Automedon dicar Amoris ego" and 17–18 "Aeacidae Chiron, ego sum praeceptor Amoris; | saevus uterque puer, natus uterque dea"; see Hollis *ad locc.* Ovid is punning on Bion's conceit: whereas Bion's herdsman is literally to be the instructor of Love, Ovid teaches *us* to love.

5 ὥς marking the end of speech is Homeric (contrast *Ad.* 62). The use of λέγειν in poetry is Hellenistic (see on *Ad.* 5).

ἀπῆνθεν: Dor. ἦνθον for ἦλθον is very common in Theocritus; in later bucolic see [Theoc.] 23.17, 20 (coni. Winterton utrubique), 58. The standard form, however, is more common in late bucolic: Bion frr. 2.2, 8.8, 13.14 and 16; [Moschus] 3.109, 117; [Theoc.] 20.39.

ὅσα βουκολίασδον: "all the rustic songs I used to sing". Perhaps βωκ- should be read (see on 4). For -σδ- see on fr. 9.5 μελίσδῃ. The verb (attested first in Theoc. 5.44 and 7.36) denotes simply the musical activity of herdsmen.[34] Bion's cowherd is not representing himself as a "bucolic" poet in the literary sense; the inventions by various deities of various musical instruments that the speaker teaches Eros in 6–8 are not themes typical of bucolic, but rather represent the preliminaries to a musical education. One should certainly resist the theory of some critics that the speaker should be identified with Bion himself, and that this fragment programmatically records our poet's own conversion from pastoral poetry to the amatory theme of the *Epitaph on Adonis*.[35] It is worth noting that even the "bucolic" or "Sicilian" Muses of [Theoc.] 9.28, [Moschus] 3.8 (etc.), and Virg. *Ecl.* 4.1, while serving the authors and their audiences programmatically by signalling bucolic genre, are invoked *within their poems* simply as inspirers of the fictional herdsman-narrators' songs. In [Bion] 2.1 the Σικελὸν μέλος requested by Myrson of Lycidas turns out to be a tale of Achilles on Scyros: again, "Sicilian" refers to the circumstances of the narrated singing, not to genre (cf. [Moschus] 3.120).

[34] The term βουκόλος was early extended to the herders of other livestock than cows; see Dover *Theoc.* lv, who adduces other verbs of uttering (e.g. φροιμιάζομαι, παροιμιάζομαι) as possible models for the Theocritean coinage.

[35] Arland 41: "Das klingt wie eine Absage an die Bukolik"; M. Fantuzzi, *MCr* 15–17 (1980–2) 159: "Fantasiosa eziologia autobiografica del trapasso della poesia bucolica a quella erotica"; cf. Matthews (1990) 37. Note that the two themes are not mutually prohibitive in Bion; they coexist in fr. 11 and seemingly in fr. 9. [Moschus] 3.80–4 lists examples of both as representative of Bion's poetry. Much of late bucolic turns toward amatory themes, without disavowing pastoral; cf. Introd. II.

6 νήπιος: here "foolish, unwitting" (as often in Homer and later); originally "with childlike innocence". Cf. the self-admitted foolhardiness of the poetic initiate in *Anacreont.* 1.14 ἐγὼ δ' ὁ μωρός. . . .

ὡς: "as if".

7–8 The brief list of εὑρεταί recalls the Hellenistic fondness not only for aetiologies, but also for catalogue poetry, wherein legends having a common theme were picturesquely summarized in succession after the model of the Hesiodic catalogues. For the introduction of this technique within other types of narrative, as here, cf. e.g. Theoc. 3.40–51, Ap. Rh. 1.496–511 (with repeated ὡς, as here), [Theoc.] 20.34–43, Virg. *Ecl.* 6.31–86 (see Williams 243–6) and *Aen.* 1.742–6, Ovid *A.A.* 1.283–340 (see Hollis *ad loc.*); precedents are the catalogues of heroines integrated into *Il.* 14.315–28, *Od.* 11.225–330. Apollonius' and Virgil's examples, like Bion's, represent song. Cf. on line 11 below and fr. 12.

With this list compare the rustic musical training of Echo in Longus 3.23: παιδεύεται ὑπὸ Μουσῶν συρίζειν, αὐλεῖν, τὰ πρὸς λύραν, τὰ πρὸς κιθάραν, πᾶσαν ᾠδήν. Although the cross-pipe is replaced by the more famously pastoral panpipe and the order of cithara and lyre is reversed, Longus may echo Bion here. Nonnus *D.* 41.372–4, a catalogue of inventors of musical instruments (Pan and the syrinx, Hermes and the lyre, Hyagnis and the αὐλός) in the form of a prophecy, imitates Bion.

7 ὡς εὗρεν πλαγίαυλον ὁ Πάν: the cross-pipe is mentioned as a rustic instrument (therefore a suitable invention of the rustic god) at [Theoc.] 20.29, Philodem. *A.P.* 11.34.5, Longus 1.4 and 4.26, Heliod. 5.14.5. It was "held transversely and played by blowing across the open end or, as in modern flutes, across a hole cut in the side" (Gow on [Theoc.] *loc. cit.*); see West (1992) 113. Bion's story of its origin is not found elsewhere; Pliny *H.N.* 7.204 makes Midas its inventor.[36] Ovid and later authorities make Pan the inventor of the syrinx (see Bömer on *Met.* 1.689–712). For another myth possibly invented or innovated by Bion see *Ad.* 66 n.

ὡς αὐλὸν Ἀθάνα: for the nature of the αὐλός, a reed instrument closest to the modern oboe, see Steinmayer 26–31, West (1992) 81–107. For the story see Pind. *P.* 12.6–8, Callim. *H.* 3.244–5, Diod. Sic. 5.73.8, Ovid *Fasti* 6.695–710, Hyg. *Fab.* 165; cf. *PMG* 758 (Melanippides) and

[36] King Juba II of Mauretania uses the term πλαγίαυλος for the φῶτιγξ, an Egyptian pipe, and makes Osiris its inventor (*FGrH* 275 F 16).

805A (Telestes). For other versions of the invention of the αὐλός see 8 n.

8 ὡς χέλυν Ἑρμάων: this extended form of Hermes' name occurs also at [Hes.] frr. 137.1, 150.31; *EG* 949.4 (Sparta, second century A.D.), 964.2 (Athens, second century A.D.), 1046.24 (Rome, second century A.D.); [Orph.] *Arg.* 383 χελυκλόνου Ἑρμάωνος (perhaps a reminiscence of Bion); often in Nonnus *D.* Agathias *A.P.* 4.3.110, beginning ὡς χέλυν Ἑρμάωνι (in a series of ὡς-clauses listing gods and their attributes), imitates Bion's whole phrase. The newborn Hermes fashioned the first lyre from a tortoise shell: *H.H.* 4.24–61, Soph. fr. 314.298–328 Radt (*Ichn.*), *AGNF* p. 75 (the early novel *Metiochus and Parthenope*; see T. Hägg, *SO* 64 (1989) 36–73). "Occasionally poets call the λύρα a χέλυς, from its material. [....T]he first genuine use of χέλυς as a metonymy seems to be at Sappho fr. 118" (Steinmayer 112). On the instrument see Maas and Snyder 79–112, West (1992) 56–9.

κίθαριν ὡς ἀδὺς Ἀπόλλων: cf. [Plut.] *De mus.* 1135F οὐ γὰρ Μαρσύου ἢ Ὀλύμπου ἢ Ὑάγνιδος ὥς τινες οἴονται εὕρημα ὁ αὐλός, μόνη δὲ κιθάρα Ἀπόλλωνος, ἀλλὰ καὶ αὐλητικῆς καὶ κιθαριστικῆς εὑρετὴς ὁ θεός. On the κίθαρις/-α or box lyre see Steinmayer 84–8, 110, 214; Maas and Snyder 53–78; West (1992) 51–6.

κίθαριν: the lengthening of a closed, short final syllable[37] before an initial vowel (see Maas *GM* §128, West *GM* 156) is so unusual for late bucolic that Grotius (II.539) may be right to suspect that κίθαριν has replaced the synonymous κιθάραν (the asyndeton in this series makes Mekerchus's restoration κίθαριν δ' ὡς[38] unlikely). Bion may allude, however, to Callim. *H.* 2.19, where the final syllable of κίθαριν (there Apollo's ἔντεα) is lengthened in second princeps before ἤ. The anomaly may thus slyly hint at the Callimachean literary themes parodied in this memoir (cf. on 1, 12–13).

For postponed ὡς see e.g. Theoc. 2.103, 5.110, 7.41, etc.; Callim. frr. 2.5, 75.70, 178.10; Moschus 1.16; Bion fr. 14.4 and *Ad.* 43. Here the variation from the three preceding clauses helps effect closure.

ἀδύς: an epithet of Apollo only here (in anon. *A.P.* 9.525.8 he is ἡδυεπής and ἡδύφρων). The same epithet in Archias *A.P.* 10.7.4 (applied to Zephyrus) and Marc. Arg. *A.P.* 5.110.3–4 (Bacchus) refers to those deities' concrete attributes, West Wind and wine; perhaps here

[37] There is no chance of long iota: short -ις was added to a borrowed stem to make a Greek noun (Buck and Petersen 14 note the productivity of this suffix in words of foreign origin). On the etymology of κίθαρις/-α see West (1992) 50 n. 5.

[38] Also in Stephanus (1566).

the sweetness of Apollo is supposed to lie in his ravishing citharody. Cf. *H.H.* 3.169 ἥδιστος ἀοιδῶν, Hermes. fr. 7.28 *CA* ἥδιστον ... μουσοπόλων; see Steinmayer 58–60 for ἡδύς in musical contexts.

9 ἐξεδίδασκον: the prefix denotes thoroughness or completion (cf. *Ad.* 49). The imperf. is conative.

ὃ δ' οὐκ ἐμπάζετο μύθων: the phrase ends *Od.* 17.488, 20.275 and 384, always with "Thus spoke so-and-so" filling the first hemistich. Cf. *Od.* 1.305, Callim. fr. 784.

10 ἐρωτύλα: LSJ take the word as an adj., but we are more justified in taking it literally as a neuter diminutive of ἔρως: "little love affairs", the theme of the god's song, enlarged upon in the next line (cf. 13).[39] Elsewhere it appears as a hypocoristic masc. noun, "darling", applied variously: Theoc. 3.7 τὸν ἐρωτύλον, "your sweetheart" (Gow); the name of a gem in Pliny *H.N.* 37.160; Eros himself (Ἔρως, Ἐρωτύλλε[40]) in *PGM* 7.478 (third century A.D.); the name of a tiny star, perhaps Alcor near Mizar in the Great Bear (Leontius *A.P.* 9.614.2, Schol. Basil. 9 (G. Pasquali, *Nachr. v. d. Königl. Gesellschaft d. Wiss. zu Göttingen*, philol.-hist. Kl. (1910) 197); see Roscher VI.875).[41] The diminutive here may be pejorative, reflecting the speaker's chagrin at unwillingly imbibing frivolous amatory matter (cf. 12–13).

καί μ' ἐδίδασκεν: for elision of με see frr. 2.12, 6.1, 10.13 below. Contrast 6 and 12 Ἔρωτα δίδασκον, where Bion omits the syllabic augment so as not to elide the name (he avoids eliding common or proper nouns). For Eros as teacher of poetry cf. esp. Eur. fr. 663 Nauck (quoted above, with imitations, in the introduction to fr. 3); as teacher of love cf. Callim. fr. 67.1, Moschus fr. 3.8.

11 ματέρος ἔργα: a witty adaptation of a standard phrase: cf. Hes. *Op.* 521 ἔργα ... Ἀφροδίτης, *H.H.* 5.1 ἔργα πολυχρύσου Ἀφροδίτης, Solon fr. 26.1 *IEG* ἔργα δὲ Κυπρογενοῦς, [Theoc.] *Ep.* 4.4 Κύπριδος ἔργα, Philip *A.P.* 9.416.1 ἔργων Κύπριδος, anon. *A.P.* 7.221.1 Κύπριδος ἔργα. On Eros as son of Aphrodite see fr. 14.4 n.

[39] Wilamowitz OCT 169 (cf. *Textg.* 79), followed by many, rashly applies the word as a generic label to this fragment and to frr. 9 and 13. For the biographical fallacy on which this interpretation rests see on 5 above; cf. Introd. II.

[40] With "hypocoristic doubling" (C. D. Buck, *Comparative Grammar of Greek and Latin* (Chicago 1933) §472.8).

[41] Erotylus is named as an author, apparently of Orphica, in *PGM* 13.945 (see H. D. Betz, ed., *The Greek Magical Papyri in Translation* (Chicago 1986) 334).

Virg. *G.* 4.345–7 "inter quas curam Clymene narrabat inanem | Volcani, Martisque dolos et dulcia furta, | aque Chao densos divum numerabat amores" suggests the kind of mini-catalogue Bion might have elaborated here, inserting a list reminiscent of the Hellenistic catalogue-poets (cf. on 7–8), among whom, for example, Hermesianax recorded the loves of mortals, Phanocles the loves of the gods.

12–13 The involuntary singing of love (cf. fr. 9.8–11) recalls the Latin *recusatio* (e.g. Virg. *Ecl.* 6.3–5, Prop. 3.3, Hor. *C.* 4.15.1–4), esp. playful instances like Ovid *Am.* 1.1, where Cupid himself prohibits the poet from themes other than love (cf. *Am.* 2.1.11–17, 2.18, 3.12.15–16). The recusational abandonment, at a deity's behest, of weightier poetic themes for lighter (often amatory) ones stems from the *Aetia* prologue (Callim. fr. 1.21–8); Cameron (1995) 454–83 emphasizes, however, the distinction between Callimachus' abjuration of a tumid style and the Romans' (and Bion's) disavowal of genres that lie beyond their powers. The closest Greek example is *Anacreont.* 23.1–4 θέλω λέγειν Ἀτρείδας, | θέλω δὲ Κάδμον ᾄδειν, | ἁ βάρβιτος δὲ χορδαῖς | Ἔρωτα μοῦνον ἠχεῖ. Fantuzzi (1994) 542, discussing Bion fr. 9, observes that this motif "is very rare in Greek literature, with the exception of the Anacreontea, where [it] stereotyped a theme by Anacreon and became an obsessive topos of the 'anacreontic' poetic ideology"; cf. P. Rosenmeyer, *The Poetics of Imitation* (Cambridge 1992) 96–106.[42]

ὅσων ... ὅσσα: for the variation in scansion cf. Philetas fr. 7.2 *CA*, Theoc. 4.39 and 12.3, Leon. Tar. *A.P.* 7.472.3, Callim. *H.* 6.30. See fr. 11.3 n.

13 μ' ἐδίδαξεν: on the elision see 10 n.

ἐρωτύλα: "little love affairs" (see 10 n.), in contrast with the εὑρήματα he sang of before.

πάντ' ἐδιδάχθην: Wilamowitz reads πάντα διδ-, but Bion neither hesitates to elide πάντα (cf. frr. 2.17 and 5.2, and esp. *Ad.* 76, ending πάντ' ἐμαράνθη) nor markedly avoids the syllabic augment. Cf. 10 n.

[42] It is worth noting (although the fact does not bear directly on this fragment) that the author of the *Epitaph on Bion* opposes Bion's work to the martial themes of Homer ([Moschus] 3.78–84; cf. esp. 80 κεῖνος δ' οὐ πολέμους, οὐ δάκρυα, Πᾶνα δ ἔμελπε...), perhaps assimilating him to an ideal that Hellenistic poets had adapted from Archaic lyric and elegy (cf. Anacr. fr. 2.2 *IEG*). Cf. [Bion] 2.2, a call for pleasing, entertaining, amatory poetry. See van Groningen 299–300, Cameron (1995) 420.

XI

An amatory prayer to the evening star, following traditional cletic form (cf. fr. 14): an address to the deity with conciliatory epithets; the salutation χαῖρε; a specific request for help. The full poem might have included a paraclausithyron (cf. line 4) or the speaker might have gone on to describe the origins of his love (cf. Theoc. 2.64–143, 11.25–9). From Stobaeus' chapter περὶ Ἀφροδίτης πανδήμου.

1–2 Ἕσπερε ... | Ἕσπερε ...: for the anaphora cf. Callim. *H.* 6.7–8, beginning Ἕσπερος ... | Ἕσπερος ... (cf. *H.* 1.87–8).

Both verses follow the vocative with variants of the "golden line", involving two nouns and their adjs. framing the hexameter (cf. Introd. VII.3); the first is concentric (*abBA*), the second interlocked (*abAB*). Bion's opening this prayer with two such lines is a *tour de force* that testifies to sensitivity to the device in this period.

1 Ἕσπερε: the evening star is chosen as recipient of this prayer for light during an amatory escapade (cf. 4–5) primarily because of its appearance at the hour of the κῶμος, but also because of its traditional associations with love. This planet, our Venus, had been considered the special star of Aphrodite since at least the fourth century B.C. ([Plato] *Epin.* 987B, Arist. *Met.* 1073B31), when the Greeks began assigning each planet to a different god after the model of the older astronomy of Mesopotamia (where the evening star belonged to the goddess Ishtar); see Cumont 7–13. But Hesperus had other connexions with love. At least as early as Sappho's time he was invoked in hymeneals (marriages took place in the evening) as presiding over the transfer of the bride to her new husband (Sappho fr. 104 L–P; cf. Catull. 61.1 and 20–35). A further amatory connexion, perhaps originating in the Hellenistic period as the αἴτιον for Aphrodite's special interest in this star, was its identification with Phaethon ("shining"), the son of Dawn carried off by Aphrodite in [Hes.] *Th.* 986–91; the identification was popularized by Eratosthenes in his *Catasterisms*, where Phaethon was metamorphosed into the planet after a beauty contest with the goddess (Robert 196–7 = Hyg. *Astr.* 2.42; see Diggle 13–15). As harbinger of night, the time of love, Hesperus is a friend to lovers in Mel. *A.P.* 5.172, 12.114; that role may also be relevant to Callim. fr. 291.3 (= *Hec.* fr. 113.3 Hollis) ἑσπέριον φιλέουσιν, ἀτὰρ στυγέουσιν ἑῷον.

It is hard to say to what extent this literary prayer reflects actual practice, but *PGM* 4.2891–942 (fourth century A.D.) is a love-spell addressed to the planet Venus (identified with its goddess). See 8 n. on the Hellenistic conceit of the stars' interest in human love affairs.

ἐρατᾶς: the adj. is unusual as a divine epithet until later, e.g. [Manetho] *Apot.* 2 [3].181 Koechly ἐρατὴ Κυθέρεια (the planet Venus), [Orph.] *H.* 40.7, 70.3; but cf. Hes. *Th.* 353 ἐρατή τε Διώνη.

χρύσεον: Bion may have chosen the epithet for its reminiscence of traditionally χρυσῆ Aphrodite (cf. *Ad.* 74 n.), but heavenly bodies are often "golden": cf. Sim. *PMG* 581.3 (the moon); Eur. *El.* 54 (stars), *Ph.* 176 (the moon); Marc. Arg. *A.P.* 5.16.1 (the moon), 9.270.1 (stars); anon. *A.P.* 9.710.4 (the Pleiades). Radiance is the point of comparison; colour is irrelevant, as also in poetic comparisons of hair to gold (cf. Ion's memoir of Sophocles, *FGrH* 392 F 6: οὐδὲ τόδε σοι ἀρέσκει ἄρα ... ὁ ποιητής, ἔφη, ὁ λέγων χρυσοκόμαν Ἀπόλλωνα· χρυσέας γὰρ εἰ ἐποίησεν ὁ ζωγράφος τὰς τοῦ θεοῦ κόμας καὶ μὴ μελαίνας, χεῖρον ἂν ἦν τὸ ζωγράφημα).

φάος Ἀφρογενείας: the formula "star of so-and-so", with the presiding deity in the gen., is typical. The (at least nominal) identification of planets with their gods – our Mercury, Venus, Mars, etc. – is attested only from the first century B.C. on, "erst als die astrale Mystik immer mehr Gewalt bekommen hatte" (F. Boll *et al.*, *Sternglaube und Sterndeutung*[5] (Darmstadt 1966) 48; cf. Cumont 36 "Les désignations abrégées ... furent celles des faiseurs d'horoscope"); see e.g. Cic. *N.D.* 2.119, Antiochus of Athens, Dorotheus of Sidon.

For φάος "lamp" used of a heavenly body cf. Dorotheus p. 399.28–9 Pingree εὖτέ γε μὴν φαέεσσι δυσὶν νωμήτορες ἐσθλῶν, | Ἠελίῳ Μήνῃ τε. . . .

Ἀφρογενείας: this title of Aphrodite, from the story of her sea-birth, is Hellenistic: Mnasalces *A.P.* 9.324.1, Moschus 2.71, Antip. Sid. *A.P.* 7.218.11, *CA* ep. adesp. 9.iii.5. A later version is Ἀφρογενής. Cf. the folk-etymology of the goddess's name in Hes. *Th.* 195–8 τὴν δ' Ἀφροδίτην | ... κικλήσκουσι ... οὕνεκ' ἐν ἀφρῷ | θρέφθη, *H.H.* 6.5, Plato *Crat.* 406C, Choeroboscus *Orth.* s.v. Ἀφροδίτη (Cramer *Anec.* II.170), *Et. magn.* 179.4–5 Gaisford, Eustath. *Il.* 413.12–13.

2 κυανέας: a poetic synonym of μέλας; Irwin 79–110 documents the semantic interchangeability of the two adjs. from Homer on (the sense "blue" is rare and strictly prosaic[43]). Cf. on *Ad.* 4 and 25. Night is often μέλαινα in epic (e.g. *Il.* 10.297, *Od.* 12.291, *H.H.* 4.67); for Bion's fancier

[43] Sim. *PMG* 567.4 κυανέου 'ξ ὕδατος and Bacchyl. 13.124–5 κυανανθέϊ πόντῳ do not refer to the blueness that we see in the sea, but are variations on μέλας as epithet of water, esp. seawater (e.g. *Il.* 2.825, 21.202; *Od.* 4.359, 6.91, 12.104).

epithet see *SLG* adesp. 458.i.1–2, Nonnus *D.* 31.133, Quintus 3.514 (cf. Timoth. *PMG* 803.1; Ap. Rh. 1.777; Musaeus 113, 232).

ἱερόν: because of the connexion of the planet with the goddess Aphrodite; cf. on *Ad.* 22, 73. At Virg. *Aen.* 8.591 the morning star "extulit os sacrum".

φίλε: "friend", here reminding the star of the obligations of friendship. Cf. Asclep. *A.P.* 5.167.6 Ζεῦ φίλε, also in a comastic prayer. Contrast φίλος in 4.

ἄγαλμα: the more abstract sense "that which gives delight" (< ἀγάλλομαι) concresces into "adornment" (on a human body in *Od.* 19.257, Alcman *PMG* 1.69, Alcaeus fr. 357.4 L–P); cf. Wilamowitz on Eur. *H.F.* 49; H. Bloesch, *Agalma* (Bern 1943) 12–16.[44] The phrase νυκτὸς ἄγαλμα recurs in two late hymns to the moon, [Orph.] *H.* 9.9 and *PGM* 4.2786 = Heitsch 59.10.3 (fourth century A.D.). Cf. Hor. *Carm. saec.* 2 (Apollo and Diana) "caeli decus"; Virg. *Aen.* 9.18 "Iri, decus caeli" and 405 (the moon) "astrorum decus"[45]; Sen. *Hi.* 410 (the moon) "noctis decus".

3 τόσσον . . . ὅσον: Ahrens's ὅσσον . . . τόσον gives a more favourable comparison, likely in a speaker anxious to conciliate his addressee, and deserves consideration. The evaluation of the brightness of the star prepares us for the object of this prayer (5). For the prosodic variation between the correlatives cf. *Ad.* 46, 64; elsewhere cf. *Il.* 8.16; Hes. *Th.* 720; Callim. *H.* 1.64, 2.42; Ap. Rh. 1.468; Antip. Sid. *A.P.* 7.413.8.[46] Cf. Bion frr. 10.12–13 and 14.2–3, *Ad.* 30–1; on juxtaposed prosodic variants in Greek verse, an artistic device since Homer, see N. Hopkinson, *Glotta* 60 (1982) 162–77.

ἀφαυρότερος: for the sense "dim, faint" of stars cf. Aratus *Phaen.* 256, 277, 569; [Manetho] *Apot.* 2 [1].4 Koechly. This is poetic; the tech-

[44] Post-Shakespearean readers may be drawn to the more concrete interpretation here by remembrance of *R&J* Act 1, sc. v "It seems she hangs upon the cheek of night | Like a rich jewel in an Ethiop's ear".

[45] "Astrorum decus" may combine Bion fr. 11.2–3. It is not impossible that this phrase, in Nisus' prayer for light as he aims at Euryalus' assailants, is a deliberate reference to Bion, ironically bringing out the amatory background of Virgil's passage. The description of the dead Euryalus in 9.433–4 may owe something to *Ad.* 9–10 (cf. Introd. VIII).

[46] Moschus fr. 2.3 ὡς Ἀχὼ τὸν Πᾶνα, τόσον Σάτυρος φλέγεν Ἀχώ, which should perhaps be emended to ὅσσ' Ἀχὼ . . . (cf. 5–6; for the corruption cf. Theoc. 22.117), would then yield another example.

nical term for a star of low magnitude is ἀμαυρός (Eudoxus, Hipparchus, Ptolemy, Schol. Aratus *locc. citt.*).

μῆνας: from an old Indo-European word for the moon, early superseded in Greek by σελήνη (see Chantraine *Dict.* s.vv. μήν and σελήνη). Gow and Page on Marc. Arg. *A.P.* 5.16.1 (*GP* II.167) call this "a rare word", citing seventeen verse attestations from Homer (*Il.* 19.374, 23.455) to late antiquity; for the Hellenistic period, however, it is well attested: Hermes. fr. 7.15 *CA*, Aratus *SH* 83.1, Ap. Rh. 3.533 and 4.55, Euphor. fr. 84.4 *CA*, Aeschrion *SH* 6.1, Alex. Eph. *SH* 21.20, Dorotheus (quoted on 1 φάος), Marc. Arg. *loc. cit.* and *A.P.* 5.110.6, *SH* anon. 908.27.

ἔξοχος ἄστρων echoes the common Homeric line-end ἔξοχος ἄλλων (*Il.* 6.194, *Od.* 5.118, etc.). The evening star is most famously superlative in *Il.* 22.318 Ἕσπερος, ὃς κάλλιστος ἐν οὐρανῷ ἵσταται ἀστήρ (cf. Sappho fr. 104B L–P, Catull. 62.26, A. Rehm in *RE* 8.1.1252); the planet Venus is in fact the brightest natural object in the sky after the sun and moon.[47] Ovid imitates Bion in *Met.* 2.722–3 "quanto splendidior quam cetera sidera fulget | Lucifer et quanto quam Lucifer aurea Phoebe"; cf. *Her.* 18.71–2, a similar comparison of the moon to the stars in a prayer for light like this one (see below on 5), and Stat. *Silv.* 2.6.36–7.

4 χαῖρε: in such exercises in propitiation not merely "Hail!" (in greeting or farewell), but a wish for the god's good humour; followed (as here) by a specific request in e.g. *H.H.* 13.3 χαῖρε, θεά, καὶ τήνδε σάου πόλιν, 15.9 χαῖρε, ἄναξ Διὸς υἱέ· δίδου δ' ἀρετήν τε καὶ ὄλβον; Callim. *H.* 1.94 χαῖρε, πάτερ, χαῖρ' αὖθι· δίδου δ' ἀρετήν τ' ἄφενός τε. See E. L. Bundy, *CSCA* 5 (1972) 49–54.

On nom. φίλος in addresses in Homer and elsewhere see M. L. West, *Glotta* 44 (1967) 139–44, who shows that it is used when good will or receptiveness is specially sought; he remarks on our passage that "φίλος offenbar mehr bedeutet als φίλε im 2. Vers" (p. 142, citing *Od.* 8.413 and Pind. *N.* 3.76 for the imprecatory formula χαῖρε φίλος). A. Svennung, *Anredeformen* (Lund 1958) 200–7 argues that the usage originated as substantival and appositional, and paraphrases "you who are my friend". Elsewhere in bucolic see Theoc. 1.61 and 149, 7.50, 15.144; [Theoc.] 27.25.

[47] Its radiance (or that of the morning star) compared with other stars is used metaphorically of a person who stands out among others in Pind. *I.* 4.25–6, Sil. Ital. 7.639–40, Stat. *Theb.* 6.578–82 (cf. Ap. Rh. 2.40–2). For such comparisons with heavenly bodies see Nisbet and Hubbard on Hor. *C.* 1.12.48.

κῶμον: a hopeful, often drunken and uproarious, nocturnal sally to the door of one's beloved, with intent to win his or her love or at least impress him or her with the ardour of one's own. On the practice, which typically concluded a drinking party, see Headlam on Herodas 2.34–7.[48] On the conventions of the κῶμος in Hellenistic epigram see Tarán 52–114; Copley 14–15 distinguishes the development of the motif in drama, where its rowdy aspects were emphasized, from its non-dramatic development, where "the revel has become a lover's pilgrimage". Bion's speaker's pastoral κῶμος to a shepherd has a precedent in Theoc. 3, where a goatherd serenades his cave-dwelling beloved Amaryllis. κῶμον ἄγω here = κωμάζω, "perform a κῶμος", not "lead a band of comasts" (as in Honestus *A.P.* 11.32.2): our speaker seems to be alone (note the singular verbs in 7–8).

5 **ἀντὶ σελαναίας τὺ δίδου φάος:** in Theoc. 2.10–11 Simaetha prays to the moon for light during a love spell; in Mel. *A.P.* 5.191.1 a comast apostrophizes the moon as ἡ φιλέρωσι καλὸν φαίνουσα Σελήνη; Leander prays to the moon for light on his first visit to Hero in Ovid *Her.* 18.59–74. Our speaker's prayer is a conspicuous variation on this *topos.* Comasts are often preoccupied with finding a light to guide their way: Antiphanes fr. 197.2 *PCG*; Alexis fr. 246.6 *PCG*; *A.P.* 12.116.4 (anon.), 117.1–4 (Mel.).

σελαναίας: this poetic doublet of σελήνη (after epic doublets like ἀνάγκη/ἀναγκαίη, based on adjs. in -αῖος) is attested first in the mid fifth century: Emped. D–K 31 B 43, Praxilla *PMG* 747.2; for the Doric form see Eur. *Ph.* 176, Plato *Crat.* 409B, Theoc. 2.165.

6 **ἀρχομένα:** i.e. the moon is new tonight.

τάχιον: short iota in comparatives in -ίων is epic (Chantraine *GH* 1.254; cf. fr. 3.3 ἅδιον), although ταχίων itself is prosaic; the normal poetic form is θάσσων.

φωρά "theft, thievery" probably occurs first in *H.H.* 4.136 (coni. Hermann; cf. 385, where the meaning is different); see also Nic. *Al.* 273, Crinag. *A.P.* 9.516.3. For the antipathy between Hesperus and thieves cf. Catull. 62.33–5 "namque tuo adventu vigilat custodia semper. | nocte latent fures, quos idem saepe revertens, | Hespere, mutato comprendis nomine Eous", where D. A. Kidd, *Latomus* 33 (1974) 30 sees influence from Bion. For other references to the nocturnal lifestyle of thieves see Hes. *Op.* 605, Eur. *I.T.* 1026, Callim. *SH* 288.63–5 (= *Hec.* fr.

[48] The term could also denote other, non-amatory types of post-symposiastic adventure; see *RE* s.v.

74.22–4 Hollis). Thieves are a potential threat to comasts: see *HE* II.486 on Posid. *A.P.* 5.213.3.

7 ἵνα: un-Theocritean in a purpose clause, but elsewhere in bucolic see [Theoc.] 27.11, 13, 47; Moschus fr. 2.8.

ὁδοιπορέοντας ἐνοχλέω: "harass wayfarers". Cf. on 6 above. ἐνοχλέω is mainly prosaic, but occurs at Theoc. 29.36, Strato *A.P.* 12.1.2, anon. *A.P.* 11.126.5.

8 καλόν: see fr. 5.1 n.

δέ τ': the sense of the combination here seems comfortably to fit the Homeric usage whereby "la particule τε signale que la phrase liée par δέ exprime un fait permanent, qui sert de digression à un élément de la phrase précédente" (C.J. Ruijgh, *Autour de "τε épique"* (Amsterdam 1971) §532); for its use in a concluding, explanatory statement like this one cf. Ap. Rh. 4.1334–6 ἦ μὲν ἑταίρους | εἰς ἓν ἀγειράμενος μυθήσομαι, εἴ νύ τι τέκμωρ | δήωμεν κομιδῆς· πολέων δέ τε μῆτις ἀρείων. Thus emendation (δέ γ' Gow, τοι Wilamowitz) is not wanted.

ἐρασσαμένῳ: note the variation from ἐράω.

συνέρασθαι: Schaefer's accentuation (yielding an unattested compound συνέραμαι) is right, since MS συνερᾶσθαι must be passive (ἔραμαι has active sense). Ahrens emends to συναρέσθαι "assist, collude with" (< συναείρομαι, with second aor. a contamination from ἄρνυμι: see LSJ s.v. ἀείρω), presumably on the ground that the speaker should not be asking for a rival; but the objection is too literal-minded: "join a lover in loving" is an elegant way of saying "assist a lover", as in *CA* lyr. adesp. 1.11–14 (the "Fragmentum Grenfellianum") ἄστρα φίλα καὶ πότνια Νὺξ συνερῶσά μοι | παράπεμψον ἔτι με νῦν πρὸς ὃν Κύπρις | ἔκδοτον ἄγει με χὠ | πολὺς Ἔρως παραλαβών. Bion's phrasing was perhaps suggested by Theoc. 29.31–2 χρή σε ... μοι τὠραμένῳ συνερᾶν ἀδόλως σέθεν, where however a requital of love is meant.

The passage from the Grenfell fragment is especially similar to Bion's in the prayer to the stars to escort the hopeful lover. The motif of the watchful stars' presiding over human love is Hellenistic (e.g. Theoc. 2.165–6, Mel. *A.P.* 5.191.1; cf. C. Segal, *Mnem.* 27 (1974) 139–42), connected with the Hellenistic fancy of Nature's interest in human events (cf. on *Ad.* 31–9).

XII

From Stobaeus' chapter περὶ Ἀφροδίτης πανδήμου. Classical Athenians, in accordance with their own expectations, and perhaps with the specific example of Harmodius and Aristogiton in mind, interpreted the

Homeric friendship of Achilles and Patroclus as a love affair (see Dover *GH* 197–8, Buffière 367–75, and D. M. Halperin, *One Hundred Years of Homosexuality* (New York 1990) 85–7, who discusses the original affinities of that heroic partnership to Near Eastern examples like Gilgamesh and Enkidu, David and Jonathan). The other two couples listed by Bion may have followed on that model; the three pairs are listed together first in Xen. *Symp.* 8.31 (in a denial that their relationships were sexual). All three pairs appear in lists of exemplary friendships at Ovid *A.A.* 1.743–6, *Pont.* 2.3.41–5, *Trist.* 1.9.27–34 (some of these seem to imitate Bion); Hyg. *Fab.* 257.1; Plut. *De amic.* 93E.

Bion's summary treatment of their stories is reminiscent of catalogue-poetry; cf. on fr. 10.7–8. In their context these *exempla* might have been invoked by one whose beloved was unresponsive (the comast of fr. 11?); for such recitations in bucolic cf. Theoc. 3.40–51, [Theoc.] 20.34–43 (cf. Virg. *Ecl.* 2.60–1). Schmitz 37–8 suggests that this fragment was part of Bion's Cyclops idyll (cf. fr. 16), but the Cyclops would probably not have adduced exclusively male–male couples in his pursuit of Galatea.

1 ὄλβιοι: on the traditional μακαρισμός or formula of beatitude ("blessed are they who ..."), used esp. in mystery cults that promised blessedness in the afterlife but also in any expression of what makes a person truly happy, see Norden 100 n. 1; B. Snell, *Hermes* 66 (1931) 75; Dodds on Eur. *Ba.* 72. The operative word is often ὄλβιος, as here: Hes. *Th.* 96 (= *H.H.* 25.4); *H.H.* 2.480; Alcman *PMG* 1.37; Theogn. 1013, 1335, 1375; Pind. *O.* 7.10, fr. 137 Maehler; Bacchyl. 5.50–1; Soph. fr. 837 Radt (τρισόλβιοι); Emped. D–K 31 B 132; Theoc. 12.34. μάκαρ is also used (cf. below on 6): Theogn. 1013, 1173; Choerilus *SH* 317.1; Eur. *Cy.* 495, *I.A.* 543–4, *Ba.* 72. Callim. fr. 178.32–3 uses both τρίσμακαρ and ὄλβιος. Here a participle and condition replace the indefinite relative clause typical of the formula.

ὄλβιοι οἱ φιλέοντες: cf. Theoc. 13.66, beginning σχέτλιοι οἱ φιλέοντες. Bion is wittily allusive: σχέτλιος is the formulaic opposite of ὄλβιος (cf. the antimacarism in Callim. *H.* 3.124), though not in the Theocritean passage. Molinos Tejada 197 finds that correption before οἱ or αἱ in bucolic is post-Theocritean; see also [Theoc.] 8.80, [Moschus] 3.102.

ἀντεράωνται: first attested in Aesch. *Ag.* 544, [Eur.] *Rhes.* 184. For the sentiment cf. Theoc. 12.16 χρύσειοι πάλιν ἄνδρες ὅτ' ἀντεφίλησ' ὁ φιληθείς, Moschus fr. 2.8 στέργετε τὼς φιλέοντας ἵν' ἢν φιλέητε φιλῆσθε, both concerning reciprocal erotic love. These parallels suggest that Bion intends φιλέω and ἐράομαι as synonyms meaning "love" in the erotic sense; the distinction between the affection (φιλία) felt by the beloved and the sexual desire (ἔρως) felt by the lover (see Dover *GH* 53), which here would make Theseus, Orestes, and Achilles the ἐρώμενοι and Pirithoüs, Pylades, and Patroclus the ἐρασταί, is unlikely to be intended, since it is normally the ἐραστής who is deemed blessed by reciprocation.

2–3 Theseus and Pirithoüs are mentioned as a heroic pair first in *Od.* 11.631. In a widespread story they together braved the perils of the Underworld in order to kidnap Persephone as a wife for Pirithoüs – without success, for Hades sat them in chairs that grew fast to their flesh and held them (Heracles later rescued Theseus). See [Hes.] fr. 280 and the early epic *Minyas* (fr. 1 *EGF*), from which the Hesiodic fragment may in fact come; Panyassis fr. 9 *EGF*; Critias *TrGF* 43 F 1–14 and Addenda p. 349; Ap. Rh. 1.101–3; Plut. *Thes.* 35; [Apollod.] *Bibl.* 2.5.12 with Frazer's note and *Epit.* 23–4. The two are first mentioned as lovers in Xen. *Symp.* 8.31 (in a denial that they were), but Buffière 374 cites earlier artistic depictions of them as a pederastic couple.

2 Θασεύς, transmitted by A, is probably a scribal error or false Dorization; the form is not attested elsewhere (in bucolic the regular form occurs at Theoc. 2.45).

3 εἰ καί: "even though", as often (Denniston 300–1).

ἀμειλίκτοιο, "impossible to appease" (< μειλίσσω), is applied to Clymenus (= Hades) in this metrical position by Damagetus *A.P.* 7.9.7; on the god's implacability cf. *Ad.* 52. Synonymous ἀμείλιχος is applied to him in *Il.* 9.158, *GVI* 1158.17 (Cos, first century B.C.), Adaeus *A.P.* 7.305.3. *Or. Sib.* [2].227–8 καὶ τότ' ἀμειλίκτοιο καὶ ἀρρήκτου ἀδάμαντος | κλεῖθρα πέλωρα πυλῶν τε ἀχαλκεύτων Ἀίδαο may echo Bion.

κατήλυθεν: this is the only instance of the epic (and lyr.) aor. of ἔρχομαι in bucolic (although it also occurs in Theoc. 12.1–2, which shares several features with bucolic).

ἀμειλίκτοιο ... Ἀίδαο effects a figure known to German-speaking researchers as "Sperrung", whereby a noun and its attribute are placed one before the main caesura and the other at line-end; other Bionean examples are in lines 5 and 6 of this fragment (cf. the "golden lines" in fr. 11.1–2). The figure is one of several patterns of separation of noun and attribute cultivated by Hellenistic poets (see Introd. VII.3). Theocritus already considers it "suited to the elevated style" (Conrad 108), employing it only in his Ionic, non-mimetic poetry.

4 †χαλεποῖσιν ἐν ἀξείνοισιν†: these are the denizens of Taurica (the modern Crimea) who wished to sacrifice the visiting Orestes and Pylades to Artemis (most famously in Eur. *I.T.*). One of the two adjs. must represent the people's name. Wilamowitz prints χαλεποῖσιν ἐν Ἀξείνοισιν, remarking that "si ponti proprium nomen erat Ἄξενος [< a folk-interpretation of Iranian *axšaēna-* "black": Chantraine *Dict.* s.v. Εὔξεινος], accolae item Ἄξεινοι appellari poterant commodissime" (OCT 175)[49]; but the feebleness of χαλεποῖσιν and the appropriateness of ἀξείνοισιν as an epithet here suggest that the former is corrupt. Wakefield emends to Χαλύβεσσιν ἐν ἀξείνοισιν, invoking a legendary people of Pontus (rather distant from the scene of Orestes' narrow escape – but [Aesch.] *P.V.* 715 locates them in Scythia).[50] What we want to read is Graefe's Ταύροισιν ἐν ἀξείνοισιν (p. 120; approved by Hermann: "videtur oblitterato nomine versus imperite expletus esse").

5 ὥνεκα: Ahrens's Doricization is supported by frr. 11.5, 13.4. The Doric of Theocritus has οὕνεκα (7.82, 11.30–1).

ξυνὰς ... κελεύθως: "shared journeys". Bion imitates Ap. Rh. 1.337 ξυναὶ ... κέλευθοι (cf. Greg. Naz. *Carm. mor.* 2.650 (*PG* 37.629) ξυνὴ δὲ κέλευθος). [Manetho] *Apot.* 6 [3].140 Koechly, ending ξυνὰς ἀνύωσι κελεύθους, and Maximus 187–8 Ludwich ξυνήν κεν ἐς Ἄϊδα παιδὶ κέλευθον | στέλλοιτ' may echo Bion. Cf. Theoc. 7.35 ξυνὰ γὰρ ὁδός, Ap. Rh. 1.101–3 Θησέα ... Πειρίθῳ ἑσπόμενον κοινὴν ὁδόν. On the collocation of attribute and noun see on 3.

ᾄρητο: Doricized ppf. third pers. sg. < αἱρέομαι, "had chosen", i.e. voluntarily undertaken. Orestes was blessed even in trouble because Pylades had accompanied him to Taurica. With the phrase αἱρέομαι κέλευθον Beckby compares Xen. *Anab.* 5.6.12 οἱ μὲν ἄνδρες ᾕρηνται τὴν πορείαν ἣν ὑμεῖς ξυμβουλεύετε.

6 μάκαρ: see on 1 above for the use of this term in formulas of beatitude; on the eschatological associations of the term with the blessed dead see Vermeule 72–3. The variation from ὄλβιος here and return to it in 7 effects closure: we have the end of this list.

Αἰακίδας: the addition of the patronymic is an epic flourish unchar-

[49] Let us say rather that that description could as well be applied to the inhabitants as to the region; a toponym from the name of the sea might be Ἀξένιοι (as Kenneth Dover observes to me).

[50] The learned reference might be thought in keeping with the elevated style of these lines (cf. 3 κατήλυθεν, 6 Αἰακίδας, the "Sperrung" in 3, 5, and 6). Closer to the MSS than Wakefield's reading is Meineke's Χαλύβοισιν (Χάλυβος for Χάλυψ is attested in tragedy); Meineke prefers, however, to read χαλεποῖσιν ἐνὶ ξείνοισιν.

acteristic of Bion and of bucolic in general (in [Bion] 2.6 Πηλεΐδαο anticipates the epic matter of the next section). For the collocation of patronymic and name, effecting "Sperrung", cf. on 3.

ἑτάρω: Patroclus. A love affair between Achilles and Patroclus (cf. line 1) is attested first in Aesch. frr. 134A–137 Radt (*Myrm.*), Plato *Symp.* 179E–180B, Aeschin. *Tim.* 141–3 (cf. introduction above). They are paradigmatic also in Theoc. 29.34 (though probably for friendship rather than for love).

7 **θνᾴσκων:** perhaps "in death" rather than "in dying"; for the perfective sense of the pres. participle see on *Ad.* 14.

ὅτι οἱ μόρον αἰνὸν ἄμυνεν: the verb = "avenged" rather than "defended" here (cf. Soph. *Phil.* 602 ἔργ' ἀμύνουσιν κακά; ἀπαμύνω = "avenge" in Asclep. *A.P.* 5.7.3); so Palmerius 818 (who implausibly takes Patroclus as subj. of ὄλβιος ἦν θνᾴσκων). Bion's choice of verb *cum variatione sensus* effects a correction of Achilles' death-wish in *Il.* 18.98–9 αὐτίκα τεθναίην, ἐπεὶ οὐκ ἄρ' ἔμελλον ἑταίρῳ | κτεινομένῳ ἐπαμῦναι ("defend"). Meineke's emendation of ὅτι οἱ to ὃ οἱ οὐ gives the sense of the Homeric passage, but no change is needed or wanted; cf. Plato *Symp.* 179E-180A (Achilles) ἐτόλμησεν ἑλέσθαι βοηθήσας τῷ ἐραστῇ Πατρόκλῳ καὶ τιμωρήσας οὐ μόνον ὑπεραποθανεῖν ἀλλὰ καὶ ἐπαποθανεῖν τετελευτηκότι.

μόρον αἰνόν: cf. *Il.* 18.465 μόρος αἰνός (Achilles' death), [Manetho] *Apot.* 1 [5].261 Koechly μόρον αἰνόν; also the Homeric compound αἰνομόρος. On the adj., "terrible, dire", see *Ad.* 39 n.

XIII

From Stobaeus' section on the ψόγος Ἀφροδίτης. A young fowler hunts winged Eros. This is likely to be our only complete poem by Bion except for the *Epitaph on Adonis* (see Introd. II).

1 **ἰξευτάς:** one who catches birds with bird-lime, ἰξός; for the procedure see on 5 below. This was a humble occupation; cf. Plato *Leg.* 823E πτηνῶν θήρας αἱμύλος ἔρως οὐ σφόδρα ἐλευθέριος. The word is Hellenistic, first attested in Lycophr. 105, *LXX* Amos 8:1–2, Agis *A.P.* 6.152.2.

ἔτι κῶρος: the phrase appears in [Hes.] fr. 146; cf. ἔτι παρθένος in e.g. Theoc. 17.134, Moschus 2.7 (prose citations by Bühler *ad loc.*).

ἐν ἄλσεϊ δενδράεντι: the spondaic ending (cf. Introd. VI.1) is due to a Homeric reminiscence: the phrase ends *Od.* 9.200 and *H.H.* 3.235, 384 (with καὶ ἄλσεα δενδρήεντα ending 76, 143, 221, 245).

2 ὄρνεα: this word is ἅπαξ λεγόμενον in Homer (*Il.* 13.64; normally ὄρνις); elsewhere mostly prosaic, but note *CA* lyr. adesp. 7.2, Tymnes *A.P.* 7.199.1, Antiphilus *A.P.* 5.307.4. Cf. 4 and 12 below.

τὸν ὑπόπτερον: an epithet of Love or love also in Eubulus fr. 40.2 *PCG*, Plato *Alcib. I* 135E (quoted on 4), Mel. *A.P.* 5.178.3. Eros is clearly depicted as winged at least since the art of the late sixth century B.C.; Archaic poets seem to describe him as flying (Sappho fr. 47 L–P, Anacr. *PMG* 379).

MS τὸν ἀπότροπον has been taken to allude specifically to Moschus 1 (Ἔρως δραπέτης); cf. Allen 177: "The runaway Eros of Moschus, though still fugitive, appears as the mysterious center, unnamed by the *personae* but recognized by the poet, of Bion's idyll." The sense "fugitive", however, could not emerge in ἀπότροπος (lit. "turned away") without a more telling context; Bion makes his undeniable debt to Moschus 1 less pointedly felt (cf. on 5, 6, 15). Legrand accepts ἀπότροπον as "to be avoided", holding that it anticipates 13 φεῦγε μακράν, but here that description has less point than "winged", which introduces the crucial comparison (see 4). Hopkinson suggests τανυσίπτερον or the like, but the more conventional and paleographically closer τὸν ὑπόπτερον is probably right. Briggs's emendation may be supported by the application of ὑπόπτερος to Eros in Constantine of Sicily *Anacr.* 5.19 (Bergk 352), which owes much to this poem: the speaker unsuccessfully chases Eros, who then turns on him and forces him to love.

3 ἑσδόμενον: on -σδ- see on fr. 9.5.

πύξοιο: why the box-tree? Known for its antipathy to Aphrodite and her realm (Cornutus *Theol. gr.* 24 Lang; cf. J. Murr, *Die Pflanzenwelt in der griechischen Mythologie* (Innsbruck 1890) 100), it may hint at the boy's unreadiness for love and foreshadow his failure to catch Eros (7), if any special meaning is intended. On the boy's liminal stance between sexual innocence and experience see Allen 177–80.

ποτὶ κλάδον: the acc. implies previous motion. Cf. *Od.* 18.395 πρὸς γοῦνα καθέζετο, 22.334–5 ποτὶ βωμόν | ἑρκείου ἵζοιτο; [Aesch.] *P.V.* 276 πρὸς ἄλλοτ' ἄλλον πημονὴ προσιζάνει.

δ' ἐνόησε: Wilamowitz reads δὲ νόησεν, but Bion neither hesitates to elide δέ nor markedly avoids the syllabic augment. MS ἐνόασε is a pseudo-Doricism, unattested elsewhere and probably a scribal error (cf. Introd. v). ὡς ἐνόησε is common in Homer, e.g. *Il.* 11.284, 15.422, 22.136; *Od.* 10.375.

4 φαίνετο ὄρνεον αὐτῷ: "seemed a big bird to him". The un-Callimachean (but quite Homeric) hiatus at bucolic caesura seems uncharacteristic of Bion (see Introd. VI.4), but the parallels in [Theoc.] 19.5 and [Theoc.] 23.48 probably render unnecessary Wakefield's φαίνεται ("His temporum variationibus nihil acceptius poëtis").[51] Valckenaer's φαίνετο τὤρνεον, "rejoicing because the bird seemed big to him", accepted by some editors, makes poor sense here: the point is not the size of Eros *qua* bird, but the boy's mistake.

For Eros likened to a bird cf. Theoc. 15.120–2, Moschus 1.16 (see on 15); *Anacreont.* 25 describes how Desire has established a nest of Erotes: βοὴ δὲ γίνετ' ἀεί | κεχηνότων νεοττῶν· | Ἐρωτιδεῖς δὲ μικρούς | οἱ μείζονες τρέφουσιν (11–14, perhaps inspired by Plato *Alc. I* 135E ὦ γενναῖε, πελαργοῦ ἄρα ὁ ἐμὸς ἔρως οὐδὲν διοίσει, εἰ παρὰ σοὶ ἐννεοττεύσας ἔρωτα ὑπόπτερον ὑπὸ τούτου πάλιν θεραπεύσεται). In certain Pompeian frescoes Venus shows Adonis a nest of little Cupids (*LIMC* III.1.964 nos. 48–9).

5 The bird-catcher's rods are called κάλαμοι (otherwise δόνακες) also in Agis *A.P.* 6.152.2, Aesop 115 and 235 Perry; cf. Hesych. καλαμοτύπος· ἰξευτής; *calamus* in Prop. 2.19.24, Martial 14.218.1, etc. (see *TLL* s.v. I.B.2.c). The method was to stick some bird-lime on the end of the first rod, then slot one into another until the combined length reached the bird; see K. Zacher, *Hermes* 19 (1884) 432–6 and esp. O. Crusius, *Hermes* 21 (1886) 487–90.

ἐπ' ἀλλάλοισι: very common in Homer in this position.

συνάπτω is used for this activity also in Aesop 115 Perry.

6 τᾷ καὶ τᾷ: "hither and thither". Construe with μετάλμενον. For the phrase see e.g. [Hes.] *Scut.* 210; Aratus 80; Ap. Rh. 3.1312; Dion. Per. 183, 637, 1072; Opp. *Hal.* 3.259; [Opp.] *Cyn.* 1.503; *A.P.* 9.808.4 (Cyrus), 10.74.4 (Paul. Sil.).

μετάλμενον: epic aor. participle < μεθάλλομαι (the psilosis is an Aeolicism: Chantraine *GH* 1.184), "jumping from place to place". In Homer the verb means "attack", with the prefix denoting pursuit; here it denotes repeated change of direction. As parallels to Bion's sense LSJ s.v. cite Appian *B.C.* 5.120 ἐμάχοντο παντοίως καὶ ἐς ἀλλήλους μεθήλλοντο; Heliod. 6.14 καὶ μεθαλλομένη ξιφήρης ἄρτι μὲν πρὸς τὴν πυρκαϊὰν ἄρτι δὲ ἐπὶ τὸν βόθρον; Them. *Or.* 22.269C ὥσπερ τὰ κυνάρια μεθαλλόμενοι δάκνουσί τε ἀλλήλους καὶ σπαράττουσι.

[51] The MSS also show examples at [Theoc.] 19.8 and [Bion] 2.11, where emendation (respectively by Porson and Heskin) has other grounds as well (respectively sense and syntax), but may be unwarranted. Cf. *Ad.* 26.

ἀμφεδόκευεν: unattested elsewhere.[52] "Observed (or lay in wait for) on all sides", i.e. in whichever direction Eros hopped. Stressing the patient watchfulness of the boy, however, ἀμφιδοκεύω is a surprisingly static verb for the bird-limer's activity. Graefe 119 recalls that his dedicatee, Count Uvarov, proposed an unattested ἀμφεδίωκε, "pursued (with the stick) in all directions". The verb would be an adaptation for hexameter verse of περιδιώκω, used of chasing birds in different directions in Strabo 6.1.8; cf. Aesch. *Ag.* 394 διώκει παῖς ποτανὸν ὄρνιν.

Bion has undoubtedly taken the birdlike hopping of Eros from Theoc. 15.122 (the Erotes) πωτῶνται πτερύγων πειρώμενοι ὄζον ἀπ' ὄζω; cf. Theoc. 29.14–15 (fickle love likened to a bird moving its nest from branch to branch) νῦν δὲ τῶδε μὲν ἄματος ἄλλον ἔχῃς κλάδον, | ἄλλον δ' αὔριον and Moschus 1.16–17 (cf. on 15). Bion's line may have inspired the scene in Longus 2.4 where Philetas tells of vainly chasing Eros around his garden; note the implicit comparison of the god to a small bird in 2.5 δυσθήρατός εἰμι καὶ ἱέρακι καὶ ἀετῷ καὶ εἴ τις ἄλλος τούτων ὠκύτερος ὄρνις.

7 ἀσχαλάων: "Ἀσχάλλων scribatur, ἀσχαλάων, an ἀσχαλόων, nihil adeo interest" (Valckenaer). The first reading need not be considered (ἀσχάλλω is less common in verse than the synonymous, dactyl-friendly contract verb). As for the "assimilated" form ἀσχαλόων (common in epic), such forms are rare in late bucolic: only in [Theoc.] 27.23 ἐμνώοντο and Bion *Ad.* 24, where βοόωσα may be intended to add epic flavour. Unassimilated forms also occur at [Moschus] 3.3 and 24, [Theoc.] 27.50, and 11 below (q.v.).

ὅτι: some editors have accepted Porson's ὅκα (ap. Gaisford *Poet. min.* II.244), but the unmetrical οὕνεχα (i.e. οὕνεκα) of the MSS, which may have originated as advice to interpret ὅτι causally, points to a causal clause. Gesner's ἕνεχ' (= οὕνεκα: LSJ s.v. ἕνεκα II) is unlikely, since elsewhere Bion observes the lost digamma of οἱ (cf. fr. 12.5 and 7, line 10 below, *Ad.* 9).

ἀπάντη: "befell", a sense of ἀπαντάω found mostly in prose and comedy.

8 καλάμως: see on 5.

ῥίψας: "having thrown *away*", a sense of the verb used esp. of weapons (LSJ s.v. ῥίπτω IV), as in Mel. *A.P.* 12.144.2.

[52] LSJ s.v. misleadingly cite [Orph.] *Arg.* 927, where ἀμφιδοκεύει is Hermann's conjecture for MS αἶψα δοκεύει (accepted by Vian in his 1987 Budé text). The subject there is the dragon guarding the golden fleece.

ἀροτρέα πρέσβυν: an "old ploughman", a character reminiscent of the Hellenistic fondness for scenes of humble life, appears also in [Theoc.] 25.1 and 51. ἀροτρεύς (= ἀροτήρ) is Hellenistic: [Theoc.] *locc. citt.*; Aratus 1075, 1117, 1125; Ap. Rh. 1.1172; Nic. *Th.* 4. A more experienced elder to whom a character has recourse also seems to figure in fr. 5 and may have been more prominent in bucolic than surviving poems attest, esp. if old Philetas in Longus' *Daphnis and Chloe* is meant to support the bucolic pedigree of that novel. One use for such a character is suggested by the way Bion's old ploughman, although he does not appear until now, focalizes the whole poem: his is already the superior viewpoint that lends irony to the boy's vain efforts in 1–6.

9 τέχναν: the failure of a stop + nasal to lengthen a preceding short syllable is unusual in late bucolic: only here and in *Ad.* 43.

ἐδιδάξατο: the use of the middle voice in the sense of the active is mainly poetic (LSJ s.v. διδάσκω I.1); cf. e.g. Pind. *O.* 8.59, [Sim.] *A.P.* 6.213.3, [Moschus] 3.95, Nonnus *D.* 48.233, Leo *A.P.* 9.201.2.

10–11 "πρέσβυς and παῖδα at successive line-ends emphasize the contrast between the qualities of youth and age" (Hopkinson).

11 μειδιάων: Brunck conjectures μειδιόων; that form occurs in bucolic at Theoc. 7.20, but cf. on 7 ἀσχαλάων.

For κίνησε κάρη "shook his head" see *Od.* 17.465 (= 17.491, 20.184); for this whole line cf. *Il.* 17.442 κινήσας δὲ κάρη προτὶ ὃν μυθήσατο θυμόν. The Homeric reminiscence may protect κάρη, but Moschus 1.12 κάρανον would support restoration of the non-Ionic form κάρα here.

12 φείδεο: "desist from" (LSJ s.v. IV). Maximus 284–5 Ludwich φείδεό μοι χάλυβος, μηδ' ἐς χέρα τῆμος ἵκοιτο | ἀκμὴ ... σιδήρου echoes this line.

μηδ' ἐς τόδ' ἔτ' ὄρνεον ἔρχευ: "and go after this bird no longer". Ursinus' τόδ' ἔτ' ὄρνεον requires less change from MS τόδε τ' ὄρνεον and makes better sense than τόδε τὤρνεον, the reading of B (perhaps due to Stephanus); note also that Bion elsewhere uses ὅδε without the article (frr. 9.7, 13.9).

13 Cf. Ach. Tat. 2.34.3 πονηρὸν τὸ θηρίον (also in a warning).

On Doric ἐντί for ἐστί see F. Bechtel, *Die griechischen Dialekte* II (Berlin 1923) 274–5, 650; it is first attested in a Rhodian inscription of around 300 B.C., but whether Theocritus used it is disputed (see Gallavotti *Theoc.* pp. lii–liv, Gow on [Theoc.] 19.6, Molinos Tejada 320–2). In late bucolic see [Theoc.] 19.6 (there too in conjunction with the word θηρίον); perhaps Moschus 1.27 (which this line echoes in several respects) φεῦγε· κακὸν τὸ φίλαμα· τὰ χείλεα φάρμακον ἐντί; Moschus fr. 1.3 and 10.

14 εἰσόκα μή νιν ἕλῃς: cf. Moschus 1.24 ἢν τύγ' ἕλῃς τῆνον (the fugitive Eros), δήσας ἄγε μηδ' ἐλεήσῃς, also on the dangers of meeting Eros at close quarters. Bion's ploughman reverses the injunction of Moschus' Aphrodite.

εἰσόκα: Dor. for εἰσότε. Note, however, that although εἰσότε + indic. "until, as long as" is attested (*H.H.* 28.14; Ap. Rh. 4.800, 1212), where it occurs with the subjunctive (*Od.* 2.99 = 19.144 = 24.134) it means "in preparation for the time when". Here the sense must be *dummodo*, "as long as you don't catch him". Ahrens conjectures εἰσόκε (on which see Chantraine *GH* II.263), but εἰσόκα should be preferred as the more unusual word.

Words meaning "until, as long as", followed by a subjunctive, may lack the modal particle (see LSJ s.vv. ἄχρι, ἔστε, μέχρι, etc.); Goodwin §620 calls this "most frequent in tragedy", but cites examples from prose as well. In Hellenistic poetry cf. Callim. fr. 388.10 ἄχ]ρι τέκῃ Παλλά[ς κῆ γάμος] Ἀ̣ρ[τ]έμιδι (with μέχρις̣ κ̣ε μέ̣νῃ in the preceding line), Bion *Ad.* 46–7.

ἢν δ' ἀνέρος ἐς μέτρον ἔλθῃς: cf. epic phrases like ἥβης μέτρον ἱκάνει at line-end, e.g. *Il.* 11.225, *Od.* 11.317, Hes. *Op.* 132, *H.H.* 2.166. Bion replaces ἱκάνω with ἔρχομαι. That a variation of the Homeric formula can be used of ships putting into harbour in *Od.* 13.101 νῆες ἐύσσελμοι ὅτ' ἂν ὅρμου μέτρον ἵκωνται suggests that μέτρον here = "term of a journey" (LSJ s.v. 3.b), with ἥβης or ὅρμου an appositive gen.; cf. F. Létoublon in *ead.*, ed., *La langue et les textes en grec ancien* (Amsterdam 1992) 93–103. ἀνήρ here is metonymical for ἀνδροτής, a synonym of ἥβη in the Homeric phrase ἀνδροτῆτα καὶ ἥβην (*Il.* 16.857, 23.363): another *variatio* by Bion.

15–16 The promise is like that of Aphrodite in Sappho fr. 1.21 L–P καὶ γὰρ αἰ φεύγει, ταχέως διώξει, but here the opposite of reassuring. With the epigrammatic "hunted hunter" motif compare the taught teacher in fr. 10.

15 ἀπάλμενος: epic second aor. participle < ἀφάλλομαι; cf. on 6 μετάλμενον.

αὐτὸς ἀφ' αὑτῶ: construe with ἐλθών in 16. ἀφ' αὑτοῦ or ἑαυτοῦ, "on his own, of his own accord", is common in Attic prose (in verse see Eur. *Med.* 202 ἀφ' αὑτοῦ *per se*); with emphatic αὐτός at e.g. Thuc.

1.122.1. Bion's line-end may echo Moschus 1.16 καὶ πτερόεις ὡς ὄρνις ἐφίπταται ἄλλον ἀπ' ἄλλω (cf. on 6 above).[53]

16 ἐλθὼν ἐξαπίνας: for the line-opening see *Il.* 5.91, 9.6, 15.325, 17.57; Nicomachus *A.P.* 7.299.2.

ἔπι: Winterton's reaccentuation of MS ἐπί is correct; his similar emendation of *Ad.* 3 ἐνί to ἔνι is not.

καθιξεῖ: this Dor. fut. of καθίζω seems not to be attested elsewhere, but is modelled on Dor. aor. ἐκάθιξα (Theoc. 1.12 and 51, 5.32).

The image here is suitably avian, but "[u]npleasant things are often described as landing on one's head" (Hopkinson), e.g. ἄτη in *Il.* 19.93, Rhianus fr. 1.17–18 *CA*; τύχη in Soph. *O.T.* 263; πότμος in Soph. *Ant.* 1345–6. Cf. the image of Love the wrestler treading on the smitten individual's head: Mel. *A.P.* 12.48.1, Parthen. *SH* 624, Prop. 1.1.4, Ovid *R.A.* 530 (cf. Gow on Theoc. 7.125).

XIV

From Stobaeus' chapter on the ψόγος Ἀφροδίτης. A complaint in prayer-form to Aphrodite spoken by one unhappy in love (cf. the prayer in fr. 11). Compare Theogn. 1386–9 Κυπρογενὲς Κυθέρεια δολοπλόκε, σοί τί περισσόν | Ζεὺς τόδε τιμήσας δῶρον ἔδωκεν ἔχειν; | δαμνᾷς δ' ἀνθρώπων πυκινὰς φρένας, οὐδέ τίς ἐστιν | οὕτως ἴφθιμος καὶ σοφὸς ὥστε φυγεῖν. Bion has complicated (and Hellenisticized) the prayer by making Eros the object of complaint. Not a complete poem, but part of a prayer designed for a specific situation: the fragment lacks closure, epigrammatically clever though the last lines may be (note that we do not hear what exactly is prayed for).

1 ἅμερος ("gentle, kindly") is a literary Doricism for ἥμερος (perhaps influenced by Dor. ἁμέρα = ἡμέρα "day": B. Forssman, *Untersuchungen zur Sprache Pindars* (Wiesbaden 1966) 41–5), already attested in Pind. *O.* 13.2; *P.* 1.71, 3.6; *N.* 8.3, 9.44 (all emended to the standard form by Schroeder) and Aesch. *Ag.* 721; in bucolic cf. [Theoc.] 23.3 and ἀνάμερος in Moschus 1.10, [Moschus] 3.111. The epithet here is conciliatory and euphemistic.

[53] MS ἄλλον ἐπ' ἄλλῳ; Meineke ascribes the emendation to Ahrens. Cf. Hdt. 1.102.2 ἀπ' ἄλλου ἐπ' ἄλλο ἰὼν ἔθνος, Leon. Tar. *A.P.* 7.736.2 ἄλλην ἐξ ἄλλης εἰς χθόν' ἀλινδόμενος, Babrius 57.3–4 ἄλλο φῦλον ἐξ ἄλλου | σχεδίην ἀμείβων; for similar expressions see Headlam on Herodas 5.85 (p. 269). Moschus in turn imitates Theoc. 15.122 (quoted above on 6).

Διὸς τέκος ἠὲ θαλάσσας: the speaker wishes to be sure he is addressing the correct deity (Cic. *N.D.* 3.59, for example, treats Aphrodite the daughter of Zeus and sea-born Aphrodite as two different goddesses). For concern at hymn-opening over the correct nativity of a god cf. *H.H.* 1.1–7, Antag. fr. 1 *CA*, Callim. *H.* 1.4–7; this convention stems from the liturgical necessity of naming a deity properly, lest it fail to pay heed (see Norden 144–7, Fraenkel on Aesch. *Ag.* 160). Compare the even greater uncertainty of the imprecator in Laevius fr. 26.1–2 *FPL* "Venerem igitur almum adorans | †sive femina sive† mas est."[54] There is thus no warrant for emendations like Gesner's ἠδὲ θαλάσσας (1549) or Hermann's οὐδὲ θαλάσσας.

Διὸς τέκος: the phrase appears in e.g. *Il.* 1.202, 2.157, 5.115; *Od.* 4.762; *H.H.* 28.17, 31.1 of various of Zeus' offspring.

2 τόσον points to the speaker's own amatory predicament, no doubt described elsewhere in the poem.

θνατοῖσι καὶ ἀθανάτοισι: for the phrase see e.g. *Il.* 12.242, 20.64, Hes. *Th.* 506, *H.H.* 4.576. Cf. fr. 10.11 θνατῶν ἀθανάτων τε.

χαλέπτεις: for the sentiment cf. Theoc. 1.100–1 Κύπρι βαρεῖα, | Κύπρι νεμεσσατά, Κύπρι θνατοῖσιν ἀπεχθής. Since this is our only instance of χαλέπτω (normally "trouble, oppress" + acc.) used intransitively for "give trouble (to)" (corresponding to ἀπήχθεο in 3), Briggs conjectures middle χαλέπτῃ ("Sed forsitan nihil mutandum"); for the middle voice + dat. "be angry at" used of Aphrodite see Ap. Rh. 3.109, Dion. Per. 484.

2–3 τόσον ... τόσσον: for the variation cf. Callim. *H.* 2.94, *GVI* 923.9–10 (Thasos, late first century B.C.). See on fr. 11.3.

3 τυτθὸν ἔφαν: cf. *Il.* 24.170 τυτθὸν φθεγξαμένη. Here the effect is "moreover": you not only trouble others, but moreover, and more important, you trouble even yourself. The phrase forestalls any anger on the part of the addressee at the rebuke: "I have not finished speaking; hear me out before you get angry" (the following words appeal to Aphrodite's sympathy).

καὶ τὶν αὐτᾷ: the line-end is sloppy for Bion, whose other σπονδειάζοντες end in single tetrasyllabic words (fr. 13.1; *Ad.* 18, 25, 27, 34), and Graefe 121, in establishing the reading, also suggests τεΐν (accepted by editors since Hermann) or τίνη (an extension of τίν known from Rhin-

[54] This formula is specifically Roman, reflecting Roman theology; cf. Courtney *FLP* 139. Servius on *Aen.* 2.351 mentions a shield kept on the Capitoline inscribed "genio urbis Romae, sive mas sive femina".

thon fr. 13 Kaibel); the close semantic coherence of the phrase, however, may excuse the anomaly (Sommer 238 n. 2). Doric dat. τίν with long iota (perhaps on the analogy of ἡμῖν and ὑμῖν: Sommer 239) occurs at Pind. *I.* 6.4 (where Snell, followed by Maehler, considers nu to be artificially protracted); Theoc. 2.20, 3.33, 5.52, 15.89; [Erinna] *A.P.* 6.352.2. For the whole phrase cf. Callim. *H.* 6.25 τὶν δ' αὐτᾷ (suspected by recent critics).

The sentiment recalls Moschus 1.21 (spoken by Aphrodite) τοὶ πικροὶ κάλαμοι (of Eros) τοῖς πολλάκι κἀμὲ τιτρώσκει (for the influence of Moschus 1 on this fragment cf. 6–7 n.).

4 **ταλίκον:** with κακόν. ὡς (=ὥστε; cf. Goodwin §608–9) is postponed (cf. fr. 10.8).

τεκέσθαι: how τέκηαι (A) and τέκναι (M) intruded is difficult to explain, but it is more difficult to imagine a reading that better gives the required sense of result than Hermann's inf. In Quintus 12.256 ὀτρύνει πάντεσσι κακὸν Τρώεσσι γενέσθαι Campbell *ad loc.* sees "an identical pattern" to that of this line, but the similar wording may be fortuitous.

Eros is held to be the son of Aphrodite (otherwise her attendant or agent) as early as Sim. *PMG* 575.1; the relationship is very popular in the Hellenistic period. Late bucolic, starting with Moschus 1 (see on 6–7 below), often toys with the conceit; cf. Bion fr. 10 (esp. line 11) and [Theoc.] 19.

5 **ἄγριον:** see on fr. 9.1.

ἄστοργον: "lacking affection". Use of the adj. in poetry is post-Classical: of uncaring or unrequiting persons in Theoc. 2.112, 17.43; Nic. *Th.* 552 (a cow); *CA* lyr. adesp. 6.9; of Death in [Theoc.] *Ep.* 16.4, *GVI* 639.6 (Athens, third–fourth *c.* A.D.).

μορφᾷ νόον οὐδὲν ὁμοῖον: perhaps suggested by Moschus 1.9 (Eros) οὐ γὰρ ἴσον νοέει καὶ φθέγγεται (see below on 6–7 for the influence of Moschus 1 on this fragment); imitated by [Theoc.] 23.1–2 ἀνήρ τις πολύφιλτρος ἀπηνέος ἤρατ' ἐφάβω, | τὰν μορφὰν ἀγαθῶ τὸν δὲ τρόπον οὐδὲν (Jacobs 51: οὐκέθ' codd.) ὁμοίω. For other complaints and warnings about the disharmony of appearance and disposition see West on Hes. *Op.* 714, citing *Od.* 8.176–7, 17.454; Tyrt. 10.9 *IEG*; Pind. *O.* 8.19.

νόον: acc. of respect (cf. fr. 13.5).

For the asyndetic triad of modifiers cf. *Ad.* 21. Similar to this pattern, a crescendo occupying a whole hexameter, are Panyassis fr. 12.13 *EGF* ἐσθλόν, ἀλεξίκακον, πάσης συνοπηδὸν ἀοιδῆς, Antip. Sid. *A.P.* 7.748.5 ἀκλινές, ἀστυφέλικτον, Ἀθωέος ἶσον ἐρίπνᾳ, [Orph.] *Lith.* 56 ἄμβροτοι, ἀτρεκέες, ῥίμφα πρήσσουσαι ἕκαστα. Cf. Moschus fr. 3.7 κῶρος δεινοθέτας κακομάχανος αἰνὰ διδάσκων (also of Eros). For a triad modifying a god's name in the previous line cf. *H.H.* 19.1–2.

6–7 These two lines elaborate a conceit exploited and popularized by Moschus 1, *Runaway Love*, whereby each physical attribute of Eros is listed and connected to an effect of love; for other examples see Eubulus fr. 40 *PCG*, Antag. fr. 1 *CA*, Mel. *A.P.* 5.177–80, *Met. and Parth.* col. II (*AGNF* pp. 85–9), Prop. 2.12, Quintil. 2.4.26, Chariton 4.7.6, Cornutus *Theol. gr.* 25 Lang,[55] Ach. Tat. 2.4.5, Servius on *Aen.* 1.663. The trope, admirably suited to rhetorical exercises, perhaps originated in the ἐρωτικοὶ λόγοι of the fourth century B.C., passing into Hellenistic poetry through rhetoric and comedy (R. L. Hunter, *Eubulus* (Cambridge 1983) 131–3).

6 "To what purpose did you grant that he might be winged and far-shooting?" The model for the line-end is Theoc. 7.128–9 ὃ δέ μοι τὸ λαγωβόλον ... ξεινήιον ὤπασεν ἦμεν, *cum variatione constructionis*: for ὀπάζω + inf. (here with subject acc.; often with dat.) cf. Pind. *O.* 9.66, Ap. Rh. 2.616, anon. *A.P.* 14.126.3. Cf. fr. 6.1 for δίδωμι + inf. Valckenaer's ἄμμιν for ἦμεν (after ἡμῖν Gesner (1549)) is misconceived, for although the divine "giving" of an evil could be paralleled (e.g. Sem. 7.72 *IEG*, Aesch. *Sept.* 256), here Eros' doubly determined long reach, not the imposing of him on unhappy mortals, is the primary object of complaint (cf. 7).

ἐς τί: for the expression see e.g. Soph. *Tr.* 403, Antip. Sid. *A.P.* 9.721.1 (coni. Jacobs), [Theoc.] 27.55, Philip *A.Pl.* 177.5.

πτανόν: applied to Eros also in Eur. *Hi.* 1275–6, Mel. *A.P.* 12.23.3, Archias (quoted below on 7), Strato *A.P.* 12.202.1, Paul. Sil. *A.P.* 5.301.2, anon. *A.P.* 9.108.2, anon. *A.Pl.* 250.1 and 251.1. Cf. fr. 13.2 ὑπόπτερον. For the rhetorical use of Eros' wings compare Moschus 1.16–17, where, however, the god is compared to a bird that hops from person to person; Bion intends rather his speed (7).

ἑκαβόλον: the adj., normally an epithet of the divine archers Apollo and Artemis, provokes surprise and an epigrammatic sense of appropriateness when applied to Eros. Antip. Sid. *A.P.* 7.29.6 mentions the god's ἑκηβολία; Nonnus *D.* 16.8 Ἔρως ... ἑκηβόλος follows Bion. For the idea cf. Moschus 1.13–14 μικκύλα μὲν τήνῳ τὰ χερύδρια, μακρὰ δὲ βάλλει· | βάλλει κεἰς Ἀχέροντα καὶ εἰς Ἀίδεω βασίλεια.

7 Ἔρως and ἔρως are conventionally πικρός: Theogn. 1353, Eur. *Hi.*

[55] A. D. Nock, *CR* 43 (1929) 126–7 suggests that Cornutus' version may come from Apollodorus Περὶ θεῶν.

727, Theoc. 1.93, Asclep. *A.P.* 12.50.4; the god wields πικροὶ κάλαμοι in Moschus 1.21, πικρὰ βέλη in [Theoc.] 23.5 and Crinag. *A.Pl.* 199.5. Cf. Eros as a γλυκύπικρον ὄρπετον in Sappho fr. 130.2 L–P, much imitated.

Archias *A.P.* 5.59.1–2 "φεύγειν δεῖ τὸν Ἔρωτα." κενὸς πόνος· οὐ γὰρ ἀλύξω | πεζὸς ὑπὸ πτηνοῦ πυκνὰ διωκόμενος may echo Bion here, as does perhaps Ach. Tat. 2.5.2 (Eros speaking) ἵπταμαι καὶ τοξεύω καὶ φλέγω· πῶς δυνήσῃ φυγεῖν; (>Nic. Eugen. *D.C.* 4.115–16). Cf. Simias *Alae* 9 and Eros' ταχιναὶ πτέρυγες in Mel. *A.P.* 5.179.10 and Mel. (or Strato) *A.Pl.* 213.1. For the general sentiment cf. [Theoc.] 27.20 οὐ φεύγεις τὸν Ἔρωτα, τὸν οὐ φύγε παρθένος ἄλλη, Longus 1 praef. πάντως γὰρ οὐδεὶς Ἔρωτα ἔφυγεν ἢ φεύξεται μέχρις ἂν κάλλος ᾖ καὶ ὀφθαλμοὶ βλέπωσιν.

XV

From Stobaeus' section ὑπὲρ κάλλους. A comparison of the proper virtues of men and women. Holland 251 speculates that this line was spoken by Bion's Polyphemus (cf. fr. 16), trying to persuade Galatea that for a male to be misshapen is no detriment. The statement, however, could have been part of a priamel serving to introduce anything the speaker considered καλόν (for priamels in bucolic see Theoc. 10.30–1; [Theoc.] 8.57–9 and 76–80, 9.7–8 and 31–2; Virg. *Ecl.* 2.63–5, 5.16–18 and 32–4; cf. Theoc. 12.3–9). Cf. Gorgias D–K 82 B 11.1 (*Enc. Hel.*) κόσμος πόλει μὲν εὐανδρία, σώματι δὲ κάλλος, ψυχῇ δὲ σοφία, πράγματι δὲ ἀρετή, λόγῳ δὲ ἀλήθεια; also Theoc. 18.29–31.

1 μορφά: "beauty". The term is un-Theocritean, but in later bucolic cf. Bion *Ad.* 31; [Theoc.] 20.14, 23.2. Beauty is the special attribute of women also in *Anacreont.* 24.9 (where φρόνημα is that of men). Cf. Cic. *Off.* 1.130 "cum autem pulchritudinis duo genera sint..., venustatem muliebrem ducere debemus, dignitatem virilem".

θηλυτέραισι: the Homeric "comparative" fem. of θῆλυς, in accordance with a common use of adjs. in -τερος, contrasts not with the positive degree of the same adj. but with a different class altogether; cf. ὀρέστερος "of the mountains" as opposed to "of the plains". "Dans l'ordre des sexes, on voit que θηλύτερος, spécifiant pour les besoins de l'énoncé la classe féminine comme distincte, s'oppose à des catégories masculines. [...L]e genre 'normal' étant le genre masculin, seule la classe opposée devait être signalée" (E. Benveniste, *Noms d'agent et noms d'action en Indo-Européen* (Paris 1948) 117–18). The substantival use is post-Classical: Matron *SH* 534.83, Phanocles fr. 1.10 *CA*, Theoc. 17.35, Nic. *Al.* 583.

ἀνέρι δ' ἀλκά: martial prowess is the special province of the male most famously at *Il.* 6.492 πόλεμος δ' ἄνδρεσσι μελήσει, contrasted by Hector with the womanly tasks that Andromache should pursue[56]; cf. Eur. fr. 880 Nauck, Virg. *Aen.* 7.444. The notion, of course, is implicit in the word ἀνδρεία. ἀλκή is used particularly of *defensive* military powers (LSJ s.v. II), e.g. the ability to defend one's homeland and fellow citizens.

On contrastive δέ not preceded by μέν see Denniston 165 (cf. *Ad.* 66).

A particularized version of this antithesis, wherein the personal charms of Aphrodite serve her in place of weaponry, is popular in late epic: Claudian *Gig.* 43–54, Nonnus *D.* 35.164–83,[57] Colluth. 162–3 τί γὰρ σακέων Ἀφροδίτῃ; | ἀγλαΐῃ πολὺ μᾶλλον ἀριστεύουσι γυναῖκες (cf. *Anacreont.* 24.9–13). Cf. Auson. *Epig.* 64 (Venus bare is already armed).[58] Note that this *topos* belies or undermines Bion's presumptive endorsement of the common dichotomy between woman as passive, man as active.

XVI

From Stobaeus' chapter περὶ ἐλπίδος; spoken by the Cyclops Polyphemus in a poem concerning his love for the sea-nymph Galatea (cf. Theoc. 11). [Moschus] 3.58–63 alludes to Bion's poem. The verbal and thematic similarities to Theoc. 2.164 ἐγὼ δ' οἰσῶ τὸν ἐμὸν πόθον ὥσπερ ὑπέσταν may suggest that Bion's lines, too, concluded an amatory lament.

1 **αὐτὰρ ἐγών:** very frequent at line-opening in epic. Emphatic ἐγών here may mark a contrast (obscured by the loss of what preceded) with other, exemplary lovers (cf. fr. 12) or with Galatea (Arland 46); with ἐμάν it hints at the speaker's yearning for self-sufficiency and for a feeling of control over his actions. Holland 250 detects a "quasi melan-

[56] Proficiency at household tasks and crafts is always woman's chief virtue in Homer, as at *Il.* 9.128–30, where ἔργα precede κάλλος in Agamemnon's enumeration of captive women's assets; Bion's substitution of physical beauty as the counterpart to manly virtue is typically Hellenistic.

[57] On the theme of female nudity as weaponry in Nonnus' *Dionysiaca* see J. J. Winkler, *In Pursuit of Nymphs: Comedy and Sex in Nonnos' Tales of Dionysos* (diss. U. Texas 1974) 157–67.

[58] Ausonius' conceit is transferred to Cupid in *Perv. Ven.* 35 (cf. 56). On the influence of Ausonius on *Perv. Ven.* see D. Shanzer, *RFIC* 118 (1990) 306–9.

cholica continentia, qua suam h.e. consuetam sibi, semper tamen irritam uiam se profecturum pollicetur Polyphemus". The melancholy of the situation, however, is imperceptible or at least undaunting to the speaker (cf. 3–4).

1–2 ἐς τὸ κάταντες | τῆνο: "down that hillside yonder". For the idiom see Xen. *Hell.* 3.5.20 εἰς τὸ κάταντες, Plato *Tim.* 77D ἐπὶ κάταντες (cf. Theoc. 1.13 = 5.101 ὡς τὸ κάταντες τοῦτο γεώλοφον). Bion's setting may be the same as in Theoc. 11.17–18, where the Cyclops sings καθεζόμενος . . . ἐπὶ πέτρας | ὑψηλᾶς ἐς πόντον ὁρῶν, and Hermes. fr. 1 *CA* δερκόμενος πρὸς κῦμα, μόνη δέ οἱ ἐφλέγετο γλήν.

2 ψάμαθόν τε καὶ αἰόνα: hendiadys for "the sandy beach" (cf. fr. 8.10). The scene of Polyphemus' suit is the ἠιών also in Theoc. 11.14, [Bion] 2.3, and [Moschus] 3.59 (the last in an allusion to Bion's version).

ψιθυρίσδων: sc. "blandishments" or the like; the verb is used of whispered talk between lovers at Theoc. 2.141, [Theoc.] 27.68. For -σδ- see on fr. 9.5 μελίσδῃ.

3 ἀπηνέα: a Homeric adj. Used of an unreceptive lover also at [Theoc.] 23.1 and 48 (perhaps after Bion).

3–4 τὰς δὲ γλυκείας | ἐλπίδας . . . οὐκ ἀπολείψω: "and I shall not abandon these sweet hopes"; but James Diggle plausibly conjectures gen. τᾶς δὲ γλυκείας ἐλπίδος, "and I shall not desist from this sweet hope".

4 ὑστατίω μέχρι γήραος: to Holland 250 these words suggest that Bion, like Theocritus, cast his Polyphemus as a youth.

ὑστατίω: an extended poetic form of ὕστατος (for such doublets see Risch §40B), first in *Il.* 8.353 and 15.634, *Od.* 9.14; later in Rhianus fr. 70.2 *CA*, Callim. *H.* 2.79, Nonnus *D.* 2.627.

Unlike his predecessors, who emphasize the cure that singing effected on the Cyclops' love (see citations on fr. 3), Bion has his Cyclops vow never to cease in his hopes, cruel as his beloved may be. We cannot know whether these lines precede a serenade that eventually, as in Theoc. 11, changes into a self-consolation that cures his love, or if they represent a new version of the ending that leaves Polyphemus uncured; if the latter is the case, we have here a declaration of unsublimated and (so the Cyclops hopes) eternal desire new to the tradition. It is tempting to guess that this theme entered Bion's treatment through a conflation of Theoc. 11 with Theoc. 2, where the conclusion of Simaetha's monologue finds her hopeful as ever (cf. introduction above). Virg. *Ecl.* 2 shows influence from both Theoc. 2 and 11 (cf. R. W. Garson, *CQ* n.s. 21

(1971) 188–9), although Virgil blends the two idylls differently, allowing Corydon the Theocritean Cyclops' cure.

XVII

The text of Orion's *Antholognomicon* (see p. 81) is printed by Schneidewin 41–58; the excerpt from Bion on pp. 47–8, in Orion's section περὶ θεοῦ. For the sentiment and phrasing of this fragment cf. the lines revered by the later Pythagoreans as the work of Linus: ἔλπεσθαι χρὴ πάντ', ἐπεὶ οὐκ ἔστ' οὐδὲν ἄελπτον· | ῥᾴδια πάντα θεῷ τελέσαι καὶ ἀνήνυτον οὐδέν.[59] The second verse of "Linus" especially recalls the second of Bion's verses[60] and may have inspired our poet, who, however, has transferred the emphasis from the ease of God's accomplishments to that of man's when divinely aided. The piety of this aphorism and its vague philosophical pedigree recall fr. 2.9–10.

Title: Meineke (ap. Schneidewin 184; cf. Meineke 426) believes that an excerpt from a comedy ἡ Ὁμολογοῦσα has fallen out.

1 θεῶ γε θέλοντος: θεῶ γ' ἐθέλοντος, which Schneidewin prints (p. 81), is farther from the MS reading, but avoids a violation of Meyer's first law (prohibiting a word beginning before the second foot from ending with the second trochee). Note, however, that Bion breaks this law at *Ad.* 83 (in addition to his predilection for such word-breaks: see Introd. VI.3), and that the violation is palliated by the strong coherence of the whole phrase. For the phrase θεοῦ θέλοντος or θεῶν θελόντων see e.g. Aesch. *Sept.* 427 and 562; Eur. *Supp.* 499 and 1146, fr. 397.1 Nauck. Cf. Theoc. 12.22–3 ἀλλ' ἤτοι τούτων μὲν ὑπέρτεροι Οὐρανίωνες· | ἔσσεται ὡς ἐθέλουσιν (with Gow's note).

θεῶ: since the rest of Bion's extant work is in bucolic dialect Schneidewin's Doric ending is probably right; the possibility remains, however, that the poem whence this fragment was excerpted was in epic dialect (note that Moschus composed in both dialects) and that MS θεοῦ should stand. It is unclear whether the title ἐκ τῶν Βίωνος βουκολικῶν

59 [Linus] fr. 9 in West (1983) 67, preserved in Iambl. *Vit. Pyth.* 139, whence Stob. 4.46.1 and (only the second line) Apostolius 15.17A (L–S II.632–3). The lines seem to have begun an early Hellenistic poem in the Pythagorean tradition (West (1983) 60–1). Ought one to think now of the poem on Orpheus that Bion may have written (Introd. IV)?

60 The first is a reworking of Eur. fr. 761 Nauck ἄελπτον οὐδέν, πάντα δ' ἐλπίζειν χρεών. Cf. Archil. fr. 122.1–2 *IEG*.

specifies the dialect (among other generic features) or is a more general term.

ἀνύσιμα: the long upsilon is a puzzle. "An dicemus profuisse poetae ausuro, quod ἀνύω sigma duplicat in futuro et quae inde ducuntur temporibus?" (Schneidewin 82). That is most unlikely. J. A. Hartung's ἀνύσμια, an unattested adj. from an unattested noun ἀνυσμός (= ἄνυσις), is not to be entertained. In any case the sense is right (cf. line 2), and we should not resort to Meineke's hesitantly proffered ὀνήσιμα (ap. Schneidewin 184). M. L. West suggests a misreading of ἁλώσιμα – or did the MS reading originate as a gloss on some synonymous adj.?

For the repetition of πάντα cf. fr. 2.17 n.; for the epanalepsis here see on fr. 1.3 χρῖεν.

2 "For from the blessed ones things come very easy and not without success" (taking the adjs. as predicative; otherwise "for very easy and not unsuccessful things come ..."). I see no semantic warrant for Ahrens's emendation of γὰρ ῥᾷστα to ῥάιστα (with a stop after ἀνύσιμα and none after βροτοῖσι), although the accentuation of MS ῥάστα could point to a corruption of ῥάιστα, with γάρ added to correct the metre. Ahrens would make the two statements parallel; if we read γὰρ ῥᾷστα, the second line is an explanation of the first.

Substantival μάκαρες = "the gods" appears in Homer only at *Od.* 10.299 (normally as epithet of θεοί), but is common elsewhere, e.g. Hes. *Th.* 33, *Op.* 136, 718; *H.H.* 5.92 and 195, 12.4, etc.; Theoc. 1.126, 13.72, 15.104, etc.; Callim. frr. 85.12, 119.1, *H.* 2.25–6, 3.65; Moschus 2.27. On the term see Vermeule 72–3 (cf. fr. 12.6 n.).

οὐκ ἀτέλεστα γένοντο: this phrase ends the line also at *Od.* 18.345. For pl. verb with neut. pl. subject see on *Ad.* 32 λέγοντι; cf. fr. 8.2. Lack of context makes it hard to see the function of transmitted opt. γένοιτο. Legrand suggests potential opt. without ἄν (see Goodwin §240–2, Bers 128–42; for bucolic examples cf. Theoc. 2.33–4, 11.52; [Theoc.] 8.20, 89, 91; Moschus 1.6; [Moschus] 3.107),[61] but as the sentence seems to be aphoristic I have considered Ahrens's gnomic aorist more likely. Cf. Callim. *H.* 2.40–1 ἐν ἄστεϊ δ' ᾧ κεν ἐκεῖναι | πρῶκες ἔραζε πέσωσιν, ἀκήρια πάντ' ἐγένοντο.

[61] For this usage in Hellenistic poetry see Bulloch on Callim. *H.* 5.103. Schneidewin's emendation of ῥᾷστα καί to ῥᾷστά κεν (p. 81) leaves the line caesura-less and nonsensical.

COMMENTARY ON THE *EPITAPH ON ADONIS*

Title: "epitaph" in my translation preserves the oddness of the Greek title. ἐπιτάφιος (sc. λόγος) normally designates an encomiastic prose oration over the dead (cf. Plato *Menex.* 236B, Arist. *Rhet.* 1365A31, Men. Rhet. 418–22, [Dion. Hal.] *Ars rhet.* 6). Bion's poem is doubtless so called simply because it concerns the death of an individual (and does, as the commentary will show, use many epicedic tropes). Compare the title of [Bion] 2, the Ἐπιθαλάμιος Ἀχιλλέως καὶ Δηϊδαμείας, which does not perform the rhetorical function denoted by the term ἐπιθαλάμιος. [Moschus] 3, the Ἐπιτάφιος Βίωνος, is a verse encomium of the dead Bion. These ill-fitting, rhetoric-derived labels are all undoubtedly late and say nothing about the authors' thematic or generic intentions.

In compiling his edition of the bucolic idylls, Demetrius Triclinius apparently regarded as Theocritean any poem without strong claim to other authorship (see Introd. IX); this poem, anonymous in the hyparchetype as in V, thus acquired the ascription Θεοκρίτου in R (misreported by some editors; cf. Matthews (1990) 35 n. 4). Models and parallels cited in the commentary will make clear the late Hellenistic origin of the poem and the impossibility of Theocritean authorship. The ascription to Bion, first made by Joachim Camerarius in a note in his 1530 edition on the basis of an allusion in [Moschus] 3.68–9 (on the death of Bion; see on line 13), is supported by metrical and stylistic similarities between this poem and the known fragments of Bion. Pseudo-Moschus, who probably wrote no more than a half-century after this poem was composed, in addition to the direct allusion (exactly parallel to his allusion to Bion fr. 16 in lines 58–63) echoes this poem everywhere in his and seems to have considered it the work of his subject.

1 αἰάζω: lit. "say αἰαῖ (for)"; cf. Soph. *Aj.* 430–3 αἰαῖ· ... νῦν γὰρ πάρεστι καὶ δὶς αἰάζειν ἐμοί | καὶ τρίς (for verbs in -άζω from interjections in -αι see Tichy 168). αἰάζω, followed by the name of the lamented, begins Aratus *A.P.* 11.437, Phaedimus *A.P.* 7.739. αἰαῖ (repeated often in this poem: 31, 37, 63, 86, 89–90, 93) must have been a familiar cry at the Adonia; cf. Aristoph. *Lys.* 393, Callim. fr. 193.37.

καλός: cf. 2, 5, 7, 37–8, 61, 63, 67, 71, 92. A standing epithet of Adonis: Nossis *A.P.* 6.275.4, Theoc. 15.127, *GVI* 815.3 = *SEG* 17.599.5 (Pamphylia, second century A.D.). He is *formosus* in Virg. *Ecl.* 10.18, Prop. 2.13.55, *Anth. lat.* 4.19 Riese; *pulcher* in Nemes. *Ecl.* 2.73; *speciosus* in *Aegr. Perd.* 27. The adj. is standard in acclamations of beautiful young men (see D. M. Robinson and E. J. Fluck, *A Study of the Greek Love-Names* (Baltimore 1937); *HE* II.105 on Aratus *A.P.* 12.129; Dover *GH* 114–22), of whom Adonis is a paragon.

Ἄδωνις: the name is from Western Semitic *'adôn* "lord" + -ις (Eissfeldt 5–6 compares Osiris, Serapis), or perhaps from *'adônî* "my lord" (Eissfeldt *loc. cit.*; F. Baethgen, *Beiträge zur semitischen Religionsgeschichte* (Berlin 1888) 42 compares Βααλτίς < *ba'altî* "my lady").[62] Cf. Atallah 303–8, Burkert (1979) 192 n. 3. This is the most common form of his name (first attested in Sappho fr. 140A.1 L–P); we also find Ἄδων (Nossis *A.P.* 6.275.4, Theoc. 15.149) and Ἀδώνιος, found on vase paintings (Atallah 303) and used by some comic writers (ap. Photius *Lex.* 35.4–7 Reitzenstein). Lat. *Adoneus* (Plaut. *Men.* 144, Catull. 28.8, Auson. *Ep.* 48.6) may come from Greek. A form with rough breathing, Ἅδωνις, approved by some grammarians (Aristarchus ap. Eustath. *Il.* 539.4, Herodian III.1. 539.20 Lentz), rests on a fictive derivation from ἁνδάνω, with influence from proper names in Ἁδ- and ϝαδ- (cf. Bechtel 21–2; H. Solin, *ZPE* 14 (1974) 273); the form is attested on a later fourth-century B.C. South Italian pelike (A. D. Trendall and A. Cambitoglou, *The Red-Figured Vases of Apulia* (Oxford 1978–82) II pl. 175.1), but cult practice assures the Semitic origin of Adonis and the unaspirated form of his name (see Introd. III).[63]

A cry "Adonis is dead!" had a place in the Adonis festival for which Sappho composed fr. 140A.1 L–P κατθνᾴσκει, Κυθέρη', ἄβρος Ἄδωνις (for the perfective aspect of the pres. see on 14 below); the announcement that "great Pan is dead" in Plut. *Def. or.* 419B–C has been thought to conceal such a ritual cry in the cult of one of Adonis' Near Eastern counterparts (S. Reinach, *BCH* 31 (1907) 5–19; J. Hani in Association Guillaume Budé, *Actes du VIII*[e] *congrès* (Paris 1969) 511–19). For the motif "so-and-so is dead" in tragedy see Alexiou 136.[64] Bion's phrase ἀπώλετο καλὸς Ἄδωνις is imitated by [Theoc.] 23.45 καλὸς δέ μοι ὤλεθ'

[62] The Greeks, in adopting the god of Western Semitic speakers (see Introd. III), seem to have taken the honorific for a proper name.

[63] V's reading ὤλεθ' Ἅδωνις in 78 encouraged Ahrens to restore the aspirated form throughout the poem (V clearly shows a rough breathing mark, *pace* Matthews (1991) 236). V also seems to have Ἁδ- in line 1.

[64] Cf. Catull. 3.3 "passer mortuus est meae puellae". V. Casadio, *MCr* 21–2 (1986–7) 337–8 finds Catullus' indebtedness to Bion also in 3.1 "lugete o Veneres Cupidinesque" (alluding to Bion's chorus of Loves) and 3.13–14 (see below on 55). Cf. R. Hunter, *MD* 32 (1994) 165–8, whose further thoughts on Catullus' use of Bion seem very speculative.

ἑταῖρος, [Moschus] 3.7 καλὸς τέθνακε μελικτάς and 18 ἀπώλετο Δώριος Ὀρφεύς (both referring to Bion himself), and by the refrain in Nonnus *D.* 15.399–414 βούτης καλὸς ὄλωλε.

2 ὤλετο: the change from ἀπώλετο is due immediately to metrical requirements, but the effect, the iteration of a compound verb by the simple with no change in meaning, can be paralleled in all styles and periods of Greek (West (1990) 96 and J. Diggle, *Euripidea* (Oxford 1994) 84 n. 64 cite discussions); it is common also in Latin and was apparently an Indo-European idiom (Renehan 11–16 and *id.*, *CP* 72 (1977) 243–8; C. Watkins, *HSCP* 71 (1966) 115–19 cites examples from Hittite proclamations of the Old Kingdom). Cf. 64–5 ἐκχέει ... χέει. Here the figure has an echo-effect (cf. 38 n.), as if the Loves had begun their response before the narrator had finished, thereby obscuring ἀπ-.

ἐπαιάζουσιν: the Loves lament antiphonally (cf. Antip. Sid. *A.P.* 7.218.11–12, where Eros wails in response to Aphrodite's lamentation over Laïs). The compound verb is first attested in Nic. *Al.* 303 ἐπαιάζουσα "mourning over"; here the prefix denotes response or accompaniment (LSJ s.v. ἐπί G.I.5; cf. Lucian *De luctu* 20 πρὸς τὸ μέλος ἐπαιάζοντες). For ἐπί used of response in cult ritual see Hopkinson on Callim. *H.* 6.1; but in the Adonia, evoked by Bion here as by Sappho fr. 140A L–P, the practice simulates a funereal lament with a leader (Bion's narrator) and a responding chorus. On the antiphonal lament see Alexiou 13, 131–60; for the use of ἐπί in lamentation cf. *Il.* 22.515; 24.722, 746, 776.

Ἔρωτες: T. G. Rosenmeyer, *Phoenix* 5 (1951) 17–18 notes the emergence, in fifth-century choral lyric, of pl. ἔρωτες "desires" in place of the singular abstract; the personification soon followed suit (Eur. *Ba.* 405; cf. Anacr. *PMG* 445). Personified love appears in Greek art in the form of winged boys, called Ἔρωτες or Ἵμεροι or Πόθοι, from at least the fifth century (see S. G. Miller, *AJA* 90 (1986) 166 for references); in the post-Classical period especially they proliferate. Because of his relationship with Aphrodite, whose companions or children they are (cf. 59), they are inevitable in scenes of Adonis.

1–2 These verses provide components of the "refrain" of this poem (5–6, 15, 28, 37–8, 62–3, 67, 86; sometimes joined by αἰαῖ τὰν Κυθέρειαν); Fehling 186 classes Bion's method of composition as an extended, Hellenistic type of epanalepsis (cf. fr. 1.3 n.). The term "refrain", however, is misleading. The search for strophic responsion articulated by a refrain like those in Theoc. 1 and 2 exercised many of Bion's nineteenth-century German editors and critics, rendering much of their emendatory labour futile; the poem does not simulate a song like those idylls (cf. Wilamowitz (1900) 16–17), but a festival atmosphere punctuated by irregular cries (cf. the repetitions of ἰὴ ἰὴ παιῆον in Callim. *H.* 2). The ritual exclamations, issued by the narrator or the responding chorus of Loves, sometimes break the poem cleanly into sections (6, 15, 67), but more often proceed directly from the narrative (5, 31–9, 89–93) or make transitions by concluding one subject before introducing another (28, 62–3, 86).[65] Cf. Estevez, esp. p. 36.

3 **πορφυρέοις:** cf. 79. Not just a colour term, but specifically "dyed with πορφύρα", a substance extracted from murex snails. Highly prized and extremely expensive throughout antiquity, the dye ranged from turquoise through violet to scarlet, but was most famously a rich crimson (hence poetic applications of the adj. to cheeks, lips, blood, etc.; cf. 27); cf. L. B. Jensen, *JNES* 22 (1963) 104–18.

ἐνί: Aphrodite is to be envisioned wrapped in the bedclothes, asleep.

φάρεσι: "bedcovers" here (cf. 72), not "outer garments" as usual; cf. Soph. *Tr.* 915–16 ὁρῶ δὲ τὴν γυναῖκα δεμνίοις ... στρωτὰ βάλλουσαν φάρη. Greek outer garments, which were simply large, rectangular pieces of fabric, commonly served as blankets (see Gow on Theoc. 18.19), so that words for one could easily denote the other; cf. χλαῖνα in e.g. *H.H.* 5.158 and even εἷμα in 79 below.

4 **δειλαία:** an extended form of the synonymous δειλός (cf. fr. 8.10), first attested in Hippon. fr. 36.4 *IEG* and *IEG* adesp. iamb. 14.2. The phrase ἔγρεο, δειλαίη begins Nonnus *D.* 47.161 (where 158 echoes *Ad.* 40–1).

κυανόστολε: attested only here and perhaps invented by Bion on the model of κυανόπεπλος (Hes. *Th.* 406; *H.H.* 2.319, 360, etc.). The poetic colour term κυάνεος (= μέλας; see on fr. 11.2) is traditional for the garments of mourning deities (see West on Hes. *loc. cit.*). Compounds in -στολος are attested from the fifth century, though not really common until the Roman era (Buck and Petersen 370–1). The proparoxytone form first printed by Vulcanius is correct; cf. H. W. Chandler, *A Practical Guide to Greek Accentuation*² (Oxford 1881) §534: "Compound adjectives, of which the second half is derived from a noun, retract the accent" (MS κυανοστόλε would be an active form from στέλλω: Chandler §512).

[65] Cf. Stier 4–5: "Nostrum vero poetam in hoc epitaphio sacris illis acclamationibus et nuntiis ex ipso Adoniorum usu petitis ephymnia composuisse videmus et ita quidem composuisse, ut ... cum ipsis rebus quae aguntur artissime cohaereant, quin etiam interdum syntactica ratione cum praecedenti sententia conjuncta sint."

Fantuzzi explains κυανόστολε as an elegant "predicate vocative" (J. Wackernagel, *Vorlesungen über Syntax*² (Basel 1950) 1.307–8 is the best discussion), produced by attraction of the predicate adj. to a second pers. verb; cf. e.g. Soph. *Aj.* 695–7, *Phil.* 827–9; Theoc. 17.66; Callim. fr. 599 (perhaps also fr. 24.9).[66] The shift from the voc. of simple address δειλαία to the predicate voc. κυανόστολε should not be suspect, and Wilamowitz's proleptic κυανόστολα (with στήθεα), which assumes the attraction to the voc. to have been a scribal error and not the intention of the poet, is not necessary.

καί is postponed (a poetic usage; see Lapp 49 for examples from Callimachus).

For the contrast between the crimson sheets and the sombre robe of mourning Fantuzzi cites Lycophr. 859–64 (women mourning Achilles will eschew πέπλους κάλχῃ φορυκτούς), Ovid *Trist.* 1.1.5 6 (to his book) "nec te purpureo velent vaccinia fuco: | non est conveniens luctibus ille color" (imitated by Martial 8.48.6). Vox 140 notes that Simonides, in his account of the sails that were to announce to Theseus' father either the safety or death of his son, opposed to the black sail not a white one but a φοινίκεον ἱστίον ὑγρῷ | πεφυρμένον ἄνθεϊ πρίνου | ἐριθαλέος (*PMG* 550A).

πλατάγησον: the basic meaning is "make a noise by striking with the hands"; Chantraine *Dict.* 911 calls the verb a "réfection de παταγέω d'après πλήσσω, πληγή" (cf. the similarly formed πλατάσσω). The simple verb is Hellenistic (συμπλαταγέω is Homeric), e.g. *A.P.* 6.218.6 (Alc. Mess.), 6.219.19 (Antip. Sid.), 7.182.4 (Mel.); for Bion's usage see *GVI* 1823.5–6 (Naucratis, second century B.C.) στέρνα ... ἐπλατάγησε τεὰ γηρόκομος γενέτις. Bion's model is [Theoc.] 8.88, ending καὶ πλατάγησε, where however the verb is intransitive and means "clapped his hands", as often.

For the female custom of beating the breast in mourning, often involving laceration by the fingernails, cf. e.g. *Il.* 18.30–1 and 50–1, 19.284–5; Aesch. *Pers.* 1054; Soph. *Aj.* 632–4, *El.* 90, *O.C.* 1609; Eur. *Supp.* 88 and 603–5, *Tro.* 794, *Or.* 1466, *H.F.* 1047–8. Cf. 25–7 and 97 below.

5 **καὶ λέγε πᾶσιν:** for the custom see on 1. The phrase inspired [Moschus] 3.17–18 εἴπατε πάσαις | Βιστονίαις Νύμφαισιν "ἀπώλετο Δώριος Ὀρφεύς", where the natural world is bidden to spread the news of Bion's own death. This whole line recalls Theoc. 2.21 πάσσ' ἅμα καὶ λέγε ταῦτα· "τὰ Δέλφιδος ὀστία πάσσω" (cf. Theoc. 10.45).

[66] For the usage in Latin poetry see Smith on Tib. 1.7.53 (adding Virg. *Aen.* 12.947; Ovid *A.A.* 1.145, 194).

λέγε: verbs meaning "to say" are normal in expressing a lament (E. Reiner, *Die rituelle Totenklage der Griechen* (Stuttgart 1938) 29–30). For laments expressed by λέγειν see 92–3; cf. the derivation of ἔλεγος from ἒ ἒ λέγειν (*Suda* II.241.18 Adler). Führer 11 notes the popularity of the prosaic λέγειν "to say" in Hellenistic poetry, and (n. 11) calls its frequency in this poem "besonders auffallend" (cf. 32, 92, 93; also frr. 10.5, 13.9).

7 κεῖται: often used of those dying or dead; cf. e.g. *Il.* 5.467, 16.541, etc., and esp. Lycophr. 981 κεῖται κάρα μάστιγι γογγύλῃ τυπείς.

ἐν ὤρεσι: Adonis' death and Aphrodite's grief are said to take place ἐν ὤρεσι in Theoc. 3.46, where the mountains are a pastoral setting[67]; here we are to think of them as the scene of Adonis' ill-fated hunt (see below). The phrase ἐν οὔρεσι is common in hexameter verse. MS ἐπ' (from the line above) would mean *on* particular mountains (cf. *Il.* 5.523); ἐν indicates the general region, "in the mountains".

μηρόν: acc. of respect. Wounds dealt by boars are typically sustained in the thigh or groin in literature as in life: cf. *Od.* 19.449–50 (Odysseus), Ap. Rh. 2.825 (Idmon), Lycophr. 487 (Ancaeus); of Adonis himself in Ovid *Am.* 3.9.16, *Met.* 10.715; E.N.A. 19 and 30; and often in artistic portrayals of his death. He is presumably bleeding to death from a ruptured femoral artery.

The story of Adonis' death by the boar, alluded to here and in 61–2, was standard by Bion's time. It is first certainly attested in the early Hellenistic period (e.g. Lycophr. 831–3), but probably arose from (comic?) contamination with a similar myth of Attis in the years around 400 B.C. See Atallah 63–74; Burkert (1979) 108; Reed (1995) 330 n. 54, 334–7.

7–8 μηρὸν ὀδόντι | λευκῷ λευκὸν ὀδόντι τυπείς: a sophisticated pattern of word-separation (cf. Introd. VII.3): a concentric enjambed collocation of two pairs compounded with polyptoton and epanalepsis (of ὀδόντι; cf. on fr. 1.3). "Interlaced word order represents the penetration of soft white thigh by hard white tusk" (Hopkinson).

8 λευκῷ: a standing epithet of boars' tusks; see Ebeling II.27 s.v. ὀδούς and esp. Lycophr. 833 (of the boar that killed Adonis).

λευκόν: "white" describes an attractively fair complexion, esp. of women (cf. 27) and boys. For the fair skin of Adonis cf. 10 below and *Anacreont.* 17.28–9 τὸν Ἀδώνιδος παρελθὼν | ἐλεφάντινος τράχηλος.

67 He is typically a herdsman in pastoral (possibly from Near Eastern literature, where his counterpart Dumuzi/Tammuz is a shepherd): Theoc. 1.109, [Theoc.] 20.35–6, Virg. *Ecl.* 10.18.

ἀνιῇ: cf. sepulchral formulas in which the deceased gives ἀνία to his survivors, e.g. *CEG* 123.2 (Thessaly, mid to late fifth century B.C.), *GVI* 312.3 (Tomis, second–third century A.D.). Nonnus *D.* 6.365 Ἄδωνις ἀνιάζων Ἀφροδίτην has a different context. The long iota in this verb (as in ἀνία: cf. 56) is Homeric; a form with short iota appears later (Theogn. 655, Theoc. 11.71, Callim. fr. 553.1, etc.).

9 **λεπτόν:** "faintly, weakly"; cf. e.g. Eur. *I.A.* 813 λεπταῖς πνοαῖς, *Or.* 224 λεπτὰ γὰρ λεύσσω κόραις (where the scholiast paraphrases ἀσθενῆ; cf. Hesych. s.v. λεπτόν· ἀσθενές). Bion's use of adv. λεπτόν + participle in this position is imitated by Nonnus *D.* 11.219, 25.47 (cf. Agathias *A.P.* 11.352.5).

ἀποψύχων: "breathing his last", Lat. *exspirans*. Lit. "breathing out" (sc. τὸν βίον, as in Soph. *Aj.* 1031; cf. ἀποπνέω); like Lat. *anima*, ψυχή originally meant "breath, wind" (Onians 93–6). Cf. 47.

μέλαν αἷμα is an epic formula (see Irwin 191 n. 82; compare αἷμα κελαινόν); cf. esp. Theoc. 2.55, ending μέλαν ἐκ χροὸς αἷμα. The description of blood as "black", strange to us, is due to a tendency, typical in the early development of a colour terminology, to describe objects according to their value (i.e. how light or dark they are) rather than their hue; thus blood is "black" against fair skin, as in a black and white photograph. See B. Berlin and P. Kay, *Basic Color Terms* (Berkeley 1969), who report that the Jalé, a people of New Guinea who have only two colour terms, one for dark and one for light, use the former to describe blood (pp. 23–4). In the language of Greek poetry this usage is an ancient survival; even Proto-Indo-European had a term for red.

10 **χιονέας:** the adj. first denotes colour (of clothing) in Asius fr. 13.3 *EGF*; first attested of a fair complexion here and in 27 below (see on 8 λευκόν), but cf. Sim. fr. 21.8 *IEG* (boyish thighs termed νιφάδες?) and Ion *TrGF* 19 F 46 νιφόεσσ' Ἑλένα. Later in e.g. [Bion] 2.19, *GVI* 746.3 (Athens, third–fourth century A.D.), often in Nonnus (more citations on 27). For χιονέα σάρξ see Rufinus *A.P.* 5.35.5. The frequency of Lat. *niveus* of attractive complexions may suggest a wider use in Greek, unless the Latin poets were specifically following Bion; cf. esp. Prop. 2.13.53–4 "niveum ... Adonem" (with Papanghelis 64), where Venus' dishevelled journey to the place where he lies (55–6) is also Bionean. Cf. Lyne on *Ciris* 170.

ὑπ' ὀφρύσι: the phrase is common in epic. See A. S. F. Gow, *CR* 58 (1944) 38–9 for the diverse possible meanings of ὀφρύς; here perhaps not "eyebrows" but "eyelids" or "eyelashes".

ναρκῇ: "lose sensation" (often "become numb"), apparently referring to his loss of sight. Here, in a list of physical details narrated not from Adonis' point of view, but from that of an observer remarking on his external appearance, the verb suggests some visible effect of his eyes' loss of their sensory powers, perhaps torpidity or glassiness.

10–11 ὑπ' ὀφρύσι ... χείλεος: imitated by Virg. *Aen.* 11.818–19 (Camilla) "labitur exsanguis, labuntur frigida leto | lumina, purpureus quondam color ora reliquit".

11 καὶ τὸ ῥόδον begins [Theoc.] 23.28, also in a context of lost beauty.

τὸ ῥόδον: boldly metaphorical for the redness of Adonis' lips (cf. Dioscor. *A.P.* 5.56.1 χείλη ... ῥοδόχροα).[68] Later examples of a rosy complexion called "rose" include [Theoc.] 23.8; *Anacreont.* 16.22–3; Rufinus *A.P.* 5.62.3–4; Ach. Tat. 1.4.3 and 19.1, 2.1.3, 5.13.1; Alciphr. 1.11.3; Nonnus *D.* 11.286 and 377–8, 16.78; cf. [Bion] 2.18–19. It is worth recalling that "flower" often denotes "beauty" (e.g. Theoc. 7.121), esp. youthful beauty that fades (cf. Lattimore 195–7); and the rose was notorious for the impermanence of its beauty: [Theoc.] 27.10, Philip *A.P.* 11.36.4, Strato *A.P.* 12.234.1–2, Ach. Tat. 2.36.2, Philostr. *Ep.* 4, anon. *A.P.* 11.53.

R's reading (glossed τὸ ἐρυθρόν) looks like ῥόδι, but the slight bulb on the lower left side of the last sign points to a hastily written compendium for ει, anticipating φεύγει. The sign is too short, low, and vertical to be the raised diagonal stroke that R sometimes uses for -ον.

φεύγει: Fantuzzi compares [Theoc.] 23.13 τᾷ δὲ χολᾷ τὸ πρόσωπον ἀμείβετο, φεῦγε δ' ἀπὸ χρώς. Rufinus *A.P.* 5.62.3–4 οὐδὲ ... τῶν ἱλαρῶν μήλων ... ῥόδον ἐξέφυγεν and Heliod. 3.19.1 καὶ τήν τε παρειὰν ἤδη τὸ ἄνθος ἔφευγε also imitate Bion's conceit.

χείλεος: sing. for pl., as in Callim. fr. 93.6, [Theoc.] 23.8 (on sing. for pl. of body parts cf. K–G 1.15). Bion's avoidance of a contracted fourth biceps before word-break makes the χείλεος of the second Aldine more probable than the χείλευς of the principal MSS. "L'errore della tradizione si spiega facilmente come iperdorismo" (Fantuzzi); the correction is doubtless a lucky banalization.

ἀμφί: lit. "around"; but ἀμφί + dat. often gives a more general sense of location (LSJ s.v. B.I.2). Translate "on".

τήνῳ: his lip.

12 θνᾴσκει καὶ τὸ φίλαμα: as if there had been a kiss on his lips ready for her to receive. For the "death" of kisses cf. [Moschus] 3.65–6

[68] Less bold are comparisons of body colouring to the rose in e.g. Callim. *H.* 5.27–8, Nonnus *D.* 4.130, Musaeus 58–9; cf. poetic adjs. like ῥοδόπηχυς.

πάντα τοι, ὦ βούτα, συγκάτθανε δῶρα τὰ Μοισᾶν, | παρθενικᾶν ἐρόεντα φιλάματα, χείλεα παίδων, where they represent the amatory poems of Bion. An unusual variety of things are said to "die" in this poem; cf. 29–31, 60, 75–6, 78.[69] In 46 the kiss of Adonis will be said to "live".

μήποτε: "In Hellenistic epigrams the distinction between μή and οὐ frequently yields to metrical convenience" (*HE* II.74). Bion too may be permitted the licence of his contemporaries, but cf. the use of μή (esp. with fut. indic.) in oaths and strong asseverations (K–G II.183–4).

ἀποίσει: with the sense of "carrying away" a treasured thing (a connotation more usual in the middle voice, as in Theoc. 1.3). Callierges' emendation ἀφήσει "forgo" is attractive in view of the next two lines, where Aphrodite does kiss Adonis; but a person can give a kiss and yet not receive one. Cf. Ovid *Met.* 8.211–12 (Daedalus) "dedit oscula nato | non iterum repetenda suo".

12–13 The repetition of τὸ φίλαμα is from Moschus 1.4–5. Cf. on 30 καλόν.

13 ζώοντος: objective gen. (or gen. absolute?). This must be the kiss mentioned in [Moschus] 3.68–9 χὰ Κύπρις φιλέει σε (Bion) πολὺ πλέον ἢ τὸ φίλαμα | τὸ πρώαν τὸν Ἄδωνιν ἀποθνάσκοντα φίλασεν, on whose testimony Camerarius first ascribed the *Epitaph on Adonis* to Bion (see p. 78). For another scene of Aphrodite still cherishing the dead or dying Adonis see Theoc. 3.48 (perhaps Bion's inspiration).

14 For ἀλλά (instead of δέ) responding to μέν see Denniston 5: "... in the main a poetical use. The strong adversative particle disturbs the equipoise between the clauses, and the second clause states a consideration which goes some way towards invalidating the first". It makes no difference whether she likes his kiss or not.

ὅ = ὅτι, "that".

θνᾴσκοντα: dead, not dying (cf. 13 οὐ ζώοντος). The pres. of θνῄσκω can have a perfective sense, referring to either the occasion of death ("have died") or the state ("be dead"): Aesch. *Cho.* 327, Soph. *O.T.* 118, Eur. *Hec.* 695, Paus. 5.7.5 τὰ μὲν ζῶντα ... τὰ δὲ θνῄσκοντα; often in grave inscriptions, e.g. *CEG* 531.ii.1 (Piraeus, fourth century B.C.), *GVI* 306.4 (Erythrae, third–second centuries B.C.) and 807.1 (Chios, first century B.C.). Cf. Goodwin §27 and K–G I.135–7 on perf. sense in the pres. of verbs like τίκτω (be a parent = have borne a child). Cf. 58.

θνᾴσκοντα φίλασεν: the emendation of Fritzsche (p. xvi) conforms

[69] The mannerism is imitated at [Moschus] 3.32–5 as well as at 65–6.

to the imitation by Pseudo-Moschus (see 13 n.) and avoids the unwonted elision of a participle (but note that Bion elides verbs in 78 and 82).

16 ἄγριον: cf. Eur. *Phoen.* 1669 τραύματ' ἄγρια, Nonnus *D.* 29.87 ἄγριον ἕλκος; in Lat. Ovid *Met.* 10.131, *A.A.* 3.572 and 744. The reduplication here is expressive of anguish; cf. e.g. Soph. *O.T.* 1330 ὁ κακὰ κακὰ τελῶν ἐμὰ τάδ' ἐμὰ πάθεα.

For the line-end cf. the Homeric line-end κατὰ μηρὸν ὀιστῷ, denoting the location of wounds (Eurypylus in *Il.* 11.662, 810; 16.27).

17 Κυθέρεια: an old name for Aphrodite anciently derived from the island of Cythera (τὰ Κύθηρα), either because she προσέκυρσε Κυθήροις (Hes. *Th.* 198) at her birth,[70] or because she was worshipped on that island with special honour (Schol. *Il.* 10.268A, Diod. Sic. 5.77.5). The inconsistency in the quantity of the "e" is puzzling, and recent investigators have proposed other derivations, with the geographical connexion due to a folk-etymology (G. Morgan, *TAPA* 108 (1978) 115–20; Burkert (1992) 189–90).

ποτικάρδιον ἕλκος: cf. Theoc. 11.15 ὑποκάρδιον ἕλκος (Bion's model), [Theoc.] 20.17 ὑποκάρδιον ὀργάν, [Theoc.] 23.5 βέλη ποτικάρδια βάλλει (Stephanus: ποτὶ παιδία β. codd.), each at line-end.

18 περί: "on all sides of", or the preposition may be adverbial here (either "round about" or "very much") with τῆνον παῖδα the obj. of both ὠρύονται (as in Bion's model, Theoc. 1.71; cf. below) and κλαίουσιν. The close connexion between περί and παῖδα recommends the former interpretation.

παῖδα: cf. 24. The word not only emphasizes Adonis' youth (he is eighteen or nineteen years old in Theoc. 15.129), but also suggests his role as Aphrodite's beloved and the junior partner in their relationship (cf. Dover *GH* 172 on the depiction of mortal ἐρώμενοι of goddesses as παιδικά). Lang 208 speaks of "jenes zärtliche Verhältniss zwischen Aphrodite und Adonis, das auf dem Altersunterschied beruht".

φίλοι κύνες: his hunting dogs. Classical grave reliefs often include the hound of the deceased (cf. J. K. Anderson, *Hunting in the Ancient World* (Berkeley 1985) 71); a second-century B.C. Etruscan funerary sculpture depicts Adonis' dog in attendance below his master's deathbed (*LIMC* 1.2.165 pl. 33). The motif of the pet in mourning is Hellenistic, connected to the general theme of Nature's sympathy (see on 31–9): in [Theoc.] *Ep.* 6.5 a shepherd's dogs bark over a dead lamb; Nonnus may have taken the mourning of Erigone's dog for its mistress

[70] Cf. Hes. *Th.* 199 on her title Κυπρογενής.

at *D.* 47.225–45 from the *Erigone* of Eratosthenes (see Solmsen 266–7). Among later authors Fantuzzi cites Ael. *N.A.* 7.10, 10.41; Dio Cassius 58.1.3; Nonnus *D.* 5.381–3; Quintus 2.578–9. A precedent is the weeping of Achilles' divine horses for Patroclus in *Il.* 17.426–40.

φίλοι: hunting hounds, usually female, are male in e.g. [Opp.] *Cyn.* The sense of the adj. here is reciprocal: Adonis treated them well, and their consequent affection prompts their grief. Cf. Solon fr. 23 *IEG* ὄλβιος, ᾧ παῖδές τε φίλοι ... καὶ κύνες ἀγρευταί. S. Lilja, *Dogs in Ancient Greek Poetry* (Helsinki 1976) 94 considers that the epithet here "gives a characteristically delicate nuance"; along with παῖδα it creates a mood of tender pathos.

ὠρύονται: Hermann's emendation of MS ὠδύραντο rightly keeps the dogs and the nymphs in the next line lamenting contemporaneously; Hopkinson also notes that "ὠρύομαι is a much rarer word than ὀδύρομαι, and is the technical term for dogs howling."[71] In a context of mourning it is liable to corruption into forms of ὀδύρομαι, as occurred in Bion's model Theoc. 1.71 (on the dying Daphnis) τῆνον μὰν θῶες, τῆνον λύκοι ὠρύσαντο. There note τῆνον μάν in the same position as Bion's τῆνον μέν; Hopkinson proposes μάν for Bion also, but μέν contrasts the presence of the dogs and nymphs around the body with the distraught wandering of Aphrodite (19 ἁ δ' Ἀφροδίτα).

19 ὀρειάδες: this poetic fem. of ὄρειος, "of the mountains", is first attested as the name of a maenad on an Attic vase of *c.* 400 B.C. (*ARV*² 1184.1; see H. Heydemann, *Satyr- und Bakchennamen* (Halle 1880) 8 n. 29); later in Antip. Sid. *A.P.* 6.219.5 ὀρειάδα ... πέτραν. Originally all nymphs were generically "of the mountains" (cf. Hes. *Th.* 129–30; in *H.H.* 5.257 tree-nymphs are ὀρεσκῷοι) and were given any adj. derived from ὄρος[72]; Bion is the first we know to use ὀρειάς. Virg. *Aen.* 1.500 first uses the term alone to mean specifically "mountain nymph, oread", as we do; this usage became normal in Latin (see *TLL* s.v.) and is found in Greek in *GVI* 1897.9 (Egypt, second century A.D.) and Nonnus *D.* 6.259. Nonnus also follows Bion in using the adj. with νύμφα at *D.* 14.206, 21.280, 42.62.

Nymphs in general (water nymphs in particular) seem to attract adjs.

[71] Cf. Theoc. 1.71 (wolves and jackals) and 2.35 (dogs), Callim. fr. 725 (a wolf), Opp. *Hal.* 1.399 (beavers), Dio Cass. 69.14 (hyenas), Triph. 611 (dogs).

[72] E.g. ὀρεστιάδες (*Il.* 6.420, *H.H.* 19.19), ὄρειαι ([Hes.] fr. 10A.17–19, formerly fr. 123.1), ὀρεσσίγονοι (Aristoph. *Ran.* 1344); see Roscher s.v. *Nymphen*, III.519.

in -άς and -ίς in the Hellenistic period: cf. Alex. Aet. 3.22 *CA*; Callim. *H.* 4.109, 256; Alc. Mess. *A.Pl.* 226.6; *A.P.* 9.327.1 (Hermocreon), 329.1 (Leon. Tar.), 823.6 ([Plato]); anon. *SH* 1022. Traditional terms like δρυάς and Ναΐς are no doubt the precedent.

Attending to dead mortals is a typical job of nymphs: Fantuzzi cites *Il.* 6.419–20 (Eëtion), Ap. Rh. 1.1066 (Clite), Virg. *Ecl.* 5.20–1 (Daphnis), Ovid *Met.* 6.394 (Marsyas; add Orpheus in 11.48–9), Sil. Ital. 1.156 (Tagus), Philostr. *Im.* 2.4.3 (Hippolytus); add Nestor of Laranda *A.P.* 9.129.5 (Cephisus; from Nestor's *Metamorphoses*). These nymphs may have a special attachment to Adonis; they recall the νυμφῶν τινες, ἃς καὶ ὀρειάδας καλοῦσι, δαίμονες, who reared him from infancy in a version of the myth reported by St Cyril *Comm. Is.* 2.3 (*PG* 70.440) and perhaps known to Bion and his audience (cf. Ovid *Met.* 10.514, *LIMC* 1.2.160 pl. 3, Servius on *Ecl.* 10.18). On nymphs' rearing of human children cf. Hes. *Th.* 347 with West.

ἁ δ' Ἀφροδίτα: the enjambment echoes Theoc. 1.82–3 ἁ δέ τυ κώρα | πάσας ἀνὰ κράνας, πάντ' ἄλσεα ποσσὶ φορεῖται, of someone searching for the dying Daphnis (cf. Porro 216). Bion uses Theoc. 1.83 in 23 and 35 for the wanderings of Aphrodite. Cf. enjambed τᾷ δ' Ἀφροδίτᾳ after sense-pause in [Theoc.] 19.4.

20 λυσαμένα πλοκαμῖδας: cf. *GVI* 1249.2 (Crete, second–first centuries B.C.) λυσάμεναι πλοκάμους, Rufinus *A.P.* 5.73.2 λυσαμένη πλοκάμους. πλοκαμίς = πλόκαμος, "a braided lock of hair"; its use in poetry is Hellenistic: Men. fr. 901, Theoc. 13.7, Euphor. frr. 94.3 and 140.3 *CA*, Menophilus *SH* 558.12. Mourning women conventionally let down their hair (often in preparation for cutting it; cf. 81): Eur. *Phoen.* 323, Catull. 64.350, Virg. *Aen.* 11.35; in Theoc. 15.134 women celebrate the Adonia λύσασαι κόμαν. Cf. esp. Prop. 2.13.55–6 "illis formosus (sc. Adonis) iacuisse paludibus, illuc | diceris effusa tu, Venus, isse coma".

ἀνὰ δρυμώς: cf. *Od.* 10.251 ἀνὰ δρυμά, Theoc. 1.117 ἀνὰ δρυμώς. δρυμός is a thicket of oak trees (δρῦς), more generally of any trees (cf. Schol. Soph. *Tr.* 766 δρῦν γὰρ λέγει πᾶν δένδρον). The Greeks take little pleasure in the pathless woods, and δρυμοί or δρυμά emphasize the hostility of wild places to human endeavor: cf. Theoc. 3.16, 13.67; in [Theoc.] 25.135 wild beasts of the δρυμός are contrasted with the pasturing herds. Cf. 68 (and the βάτοι in 21).

21 Asyndetic strings of three adjs. begin the hexameter also at *Il.* 5.746, *H.H.* 4.171 and 19.2, [Theoc.] *Ep.* 4.3, [Bion] 2.2 (doubtless in imitation of Bion); Nonnus *D.* 42.269, of Aphrodite following Adonis, imitates Bion's passage. Such triads were a special trick of tragic lyric, e.g. Aesch. *Supp.* 113, 681–2 (see W. von der Brelie, *Dictione trimembri* *quomodo poetae graeci imprimis tragici usi sint* (diss. Göttingen 1911) 8–26). Cf. fr. 14.5.

πενθαλέος = πένθιμος and πενθικός, "grief-stricken, in mourning", from πένθος, which can denote both personal grief and the public display thereof. First attested here[73]; later in *GVI* 711.8 (Andros, first century A.D.) μήτηρ πενθαλέη, [Manetho] *Apot.* 3 [2].142 and 6 [3].409 Koechly, Greg. Naz. *Carm. mor.* 17.26 (*PG* 37.783); often in Nonnus. Hexameter poets from the earliest period coin adjs. in -αλέος promiscuously, no doubt "to meet the exigencies of the dactylic metre" (Buck and Petersen 35); cf. Risch §36.

νήπλεκτος: unattested elsewhere. A grander, more poetic equivalent of ἄπλεκτος (Alc. Mess. *A.P.* 7.412.2), here used not of hair but of the person whose hair is undone (cf. Lat. *incomptus*). Some critics, offended by the redundancy with λυσαμένα πλοκαμῖδας in the previous line, have attempted alternatives; the most plausible is Brunck's νήπεκτος "uncombed" (attested only in *CA* epic. adesp. 2.30, where it refers to uncarded wool).[74] But νήπλεκτος accords far better with the funereal imagery of these lines, and the redundancy itself – the same idea phrased differently as part of a new but connected thought – is in the style of this poem (cf. e.g. 45–9, 70–4).[75]

ἀσάνδαλος: barefootedness is a funeral custom in Ter. *Phorm.* 106 (perhaps from Terence's model: see Apollodorus fr. 18 *PCG*); cf. Nonnus' imitations of this line (*D.* 5.407, 15.373, 47.216, and esp. 42.268–70 μέλπε γάμον χαρίεντος Ἀδώνιδος, εἰπὲ καὶ αὐτήν | αὐχμηρὴν ἀπέδιλον ἀλωομένην Ἀφροδίτην | νυμφίον ἰχνεύουσαν ὀρίδρομον). The resulting cuts and dirtiness are consistent with the personal neglect typical of mourning rituals. Bare feet were part of certain religious rites (Hopkinson (1984) 39–41), but the deportment of women celebrating Adonis (cf. the loosened hair, wailing, and breast-beating attributed to Aphrodite in 20, 24, 25–7) signifies mourning rather than religious veneration.

The word appears as ἀσάμβαλος in Pherecydes *FGrH* 3 F 105 (in the sense "wearing one sandal") and twelve times in Nonnus *D.*; esp. in view of Nonnus' frequent imitations of Bion, it is very possible that MS ἀσάνδαλος has replaced ἀσάμβαλος here (as in at least one MS of

[73] *EG* 372.30 = *SEG* 6.140.6, cited by Fantuzzi as earlier than Bion, is fourth century A.D.

[74] Bergk's νήπεπλος (ap. Ameis) is not supported by R's gloss ἄπεπλος, which has no ancient authority.

[75] This rhetorical technique is in effect a type of epanalepsis, and should be connected to Bion's liking for that figure (see on fr. 1.3).

Pherecydes: see Schol. Pind. II.117 Drachmann; cf. West on Eur. *Or.* 1468). σάμβαλος is an Ionic and Aeolic form of the more familiar σάνδαλος. Note, however, that Gregory of Nazianzus apparently uses ἀσάνδ- in *Carm. mor.* 10.563 (*PG* 37.721) and *Carm. de se* 12.201 (*PG* 37.1180), each time in a Bionean series of adjectives.

βάτοι: thorn bushes, like the δρυμοί of line 20, characterize the countryside as a place hostile to human activity; cf. Theoc. 1.132, 7.140.

22 κείροντι: for the sense "scratch, tear at flesh" Fantuzzi cites *Od.* 11.578 γῦπε ... ἧπαρ ἔκειρον (whence Lucian *Dial. mort.* 24.1 ὑπὸ τῶν γυπῶν καὶ αὐτὸς κειρέσθω τὸ ἧπαρ, *Dial. deor.* 5.1 ὑπὸ ἑκκαίδεκα γυπῶν ... κείρεσθαι τὸ ἧπαρ).

ἱερόν: the adj. is routinely applied to anything belonging to or concerning a deity. Cf. B. A. van Groningen, *Pindare au Banquet* (Leiden 1960) 68: "L'épithète s'emploie souvent pour charactériser une chose, un évènement, un être vivant, qui présentent un aspect mystérieux, dépassant la mesure normale de la réalité ...". Cf. frr. 2.10, 11.2; *Ad.* 73. For the phrase ἱερὸν αἷμα see Callim. *SH* 254.2 (there figurative for "descendant of the gods"; cf. Koenen 93).

αἷμα δρέπονται: lit. "pluck, cull", as one does flowers or fruit (that plants are doing the plucking is a nice reversal). For the phrase cf. Aesch. *Sept.* 718 ἀλλ' αὐτάδελφον αἷμα δρέψασθαι θέλεις, where it means something like "make a prize of a brother's murder" (Verrall 86; the verb picks up the imagery of 693 πικρόκαρπος ἀνδροκτασία). Bion, combining the metaphors of Aeschylus and Callimachus, reduces αἷμα to literality.[76]

This appears to be the only place in Greek literature up to this time where an Olympian god bleeds; that Aphrodite has any blood at all is famously contradicted by *Il.* 5.339–42, where ichor, said to be the divine equivalent of blood, runs from the wound Diomedes has inflicted on her hand.[77] Cf. 64 n.

23 ὀξὺ δὲ κωκύοισα: cf. *Il.* 18.71, beginning ὀξὺ δὲ κωκύσασα

[76] Commentators regularly compare Virg. *Aen.* 11.803–4 "hasta ... bibit ... cruorem"; the similarity (as Fantuzzi observes) is in the personification of a blood-letting instrument, but it is doubtful whether Virgil was inspired by Bion here.

[77] That ἱερὸν αἷμα is a periphrasis for ichor is unlikely; when Homer in *Il.* 5.870 speaks of the ἄμβροτον αἷμα of Ares he means the "immortal" blood of the god (punning on the sense "bloodless"? See A. Kleinlogel, *Poetica* 13 (1981) 269–72) to remind us of the account a few hundred lines before; see Schol. *ad loc.*

(Thetis); Nonnus *D.* 5.549 and 46.282 = 48.702, all beginning ὀξὺ δὲ κωκύουσα. For ὀξύς denoting a sound of higher than normal pitch cf. the term for the acute accent, ὀξὺς τόνος, and our musical "sharp".

ἄγκεα: "winding mountain dells". Related to words like ἄγκυρα, ἄγκων, with the notion of bending. μακρός, not an epithet of ἄγκεα elsewhere, is conventionally applied to tall (or long) mountains, tall trees, and long waves (see *SH* on 52.2).

φορεῖται: cf. Theoc. 1.83, where someone seeking the dying Daphnis πάσας ἀνὰ κράνας, πάντ' ἄλσεα ποσσὶ φορεῖται (cf. on 19, 36).

24 "Crying out in oriental fashion, calling her consort and boy." I punctuate following J. A. K. Thomson, *CR* 60 (1946) 61, who, citing the emphatic position of Ἀσσύριον, takes it adverbially with βοόωσα (cf. the earlier suggestion of Lang 209 ἄκρατον βοόωσα, πόσιν κτλ.).[78] This punctuation differentiates the participles semantically, improves the rhythm of the line, and effects a more pertinent antonomasia. The MSS all punctuate thus.

Ἀσσύριον: Greek often uses "Syrian" and "Assyrian" indifferently for any Near Eastern people once subject to the Assyrian empire (see T. Nöldeke, *Hermes* 5 (1871) 443–68); the ritual cries at the Adonia, here placed in the mouth of Aphrodite as the prototypical Ἀδωνιάζουσα, were known to have originated in the Near East (like the cult itself). Extravagant lamentation, moreover, is characterized as oriental from the tragedians on (cf. Garvie on Aesch. *Cho.* 423–4); E. Hall, *Inventing the Barbarian* (Oxford 1989) 44, 83–4, 131–2, and 149 connects the characterization to barbarians' reputed lack of σωφροσύνη. For a close parallel to the adverbial use of the toponym with βοάω see Aesch. *Pers.* 1054 καὶ στέρν' ἄρασσε κἀπιβόα τὸ Μύσιον.

βοόωσα: note the "assimilated" form, here perhaps for epic flavour; cf. fr. 13.7 n.

πόσιν καὶ παῖδα καλεῦσα: in Bion's periphrasis for "Adonis" Aphrodite's viewpoint is reflected, as always; on such subjective, focalized antonomasia in Homer see I. J. F. de Jong, *Mnem.* 46 (1993) 289–306. The two terms reflect different roles of the deceased: for πόσις used of the mortal consort of a goddess cf. *H.H.* 5.242, Ap. Rh. 1.1325. For Adonis as "boy" see on line 18; Ruhnken (ap. Gaisford *Poet. min.* IV.216)

[78] Most editors take Ἀσσύριον as an epithet of πόσιν. Adonis is "Assyrian" (= eastern) in Panyassis fr. 22A *EGF*; Lucian *Dial. deor.* 19.1; Nonnus *D.* 31.127, 41.157. In 91 below, as often, his father is the Cypriot king Cinyras, who had legendary origins in the east ([Apollod.] *Bibl.* 3.14.3).

compares Varro *Sat. Men.* fr. 540 "sic ille ⟨cum⟩[79] puellus Veneris repente Adon | cecidit cruentus olim". Similarly in Soph. fr. 210.73 Radt Priam mourns Eurypylus as τὸν παῖδα καὶ γέροντα καὶ νεανίαν (see Pearson 1.158, Carden 27)[80]; in Ach. Tat. 1.13.5 Charicles' father calls his newly betrothed son, killed while riding, ἱππεῦ καὶ νύμφιε; Nonnus *D.* 30.167 (Eërië to the dying Tectaphus) υἱὲ πάτερ βαρύποτμε is a startling example.

V's πόδα is a misreading of the πέδα of an exemplar, which Triclinius correctly identified as a misspelling of παῖδα; there is no warrant to emend with Hermann (1837) 232 (most recently followed by Gallavotti, Fantuzzi, and Hopkinson) to the banal adv. πολλά (taking Ἀσσύριον with πόσιν). Colluth. 69, ending καὶ παῖδα καλέσσας, surely echoes this line-end.

25–7 With the emendations of Ahrens, which I accept, these lines represent Aphrodite in a typical condition of mourning women, with robe torn and chest made bloody by her own hands. This interpretation has met with resistance (Wilamowitz (1900) scorns the "unglaubliche Geschmacksverirrung, die der laufenden Göttin ein Gewand ... um den Nabel baumeln läßt"), but the MS reading, which apparently describes Adonis lying covered with his own blood, presents serious difficulties. Reasons for accepting Ahrens's changes are set out in Reed (1992); what follows is a summary with a few additions.

The MSS say, "And around him dark blood hung to his navel, and his chest was made scarlet from his thighs, and Adonis' breasts underneath, snowy white before, turned crimson". The verb αἰωρέομαι means "hang", often with a sense of floating in the air. Blood cannot do this. Lest anyone attempt reinterpretation or emendation of the verb,[81] grave difficulty lies in the prepositional phrases signalling the route of the blood ("around him to the navel"): παρ' ὀμφαλόν awkwardly lays Adonis on his back with his knees up, so that the blood spills over his stomach to his chest, and ἀμφὶ δέ νιν, "and around him", prominently

79 Suppl. Courtney (1985) 91.

80 I owe this reference to a personal communication from Hugh Lloyd-Jones, who notes that a precedent is Andromache's calling Hector her father, mother, brother, and spouse (*Il.* 6.429–30).

81 "Spout up" (LSJ s.v. αἰωρέω) is an unattested sense. Fantuzzi revives ἠρωεῖτο "spurted forth" (cf. *Il.* 1.303 = *Od.* 16.441), which Ahrens (1854) 54 ascribes to Camerarius (perhaps more likely the work of Xylander ap. Brubach's third ed. (Frankfurt 1558)). See Reed (1992) 539.

placed at line-opening, is a jejune specification, inexplicable in a description of Adonis' flowing blood (ἀμφί + acc. does not designate location on a surface). In the next two lines the MSS make a pointless distinction between two parts of Adonis' upper torso, his chest and (snowy-white!) nipples, both elegantly encrimsoned by varying verbs (μαζός of a man = nipple, if it is to be meaningfully distinguished from the rest of his chest).[82] Finally, if Bion were turning from Aphrodite's frantic run through the woods to an update on her πόσις καὶ παῖς (24), we should want a sharper transition than he achieves with the unemphatic νιν (e.g. ἀμφ' αὐτόν; cf. τῆνον μέν in 18); δέ in 25 is also weak for a transition to Adonis, since the poet has been using it to connect Aphrodite's various displays of grief (21 and 23).

The number and variety of problems entitle us to suspect that Bion did not intend what the MSS report, and there are both internal and external indications that the lines originally described Aphrodite beating her chest in grief, as she was bidden to do in 4–5. The context suggests some culminating feature of Aphrodite's lamentation here, and two details, the mention of στήθεα and μαζοί and the reddening of white skin, are telling. Funereal beating of the head or breast is part of the Adonia in Sappho fr. 140A.2 L–P, Aristoph. *Lys.* 396, Dioscorides *A.P.* 5.53 and 193, Plut. *Alcib.* 18.5 and *Nic.* 13.7, Lucian *Dea Syr.* 6; note that Bion seems to model Aphrodite's behaviour on that of women celebrating the festival (see on 20, 21, 24). In Theoc. 15.134–5 breast-baring is part of the Ptolemaic Adonia. In imitations of these lines Nonnus applies Bion's wording to grieving women beating their chests (*D.* 5.375–8, 18.331–2, 24.185, 46.279).[83] Finally, the mention in 29–31 of Aphrodite's ruined beauty is better accounted for by a preceding description of her lacerated chest than by the bramble-cuts and mussed hair in 21–2.

The circumambulatory blood and the mention of thighs make it difficult to see Aphrodite beating her breast here. With Ahrens's corrections of αἷμα to εἷμα in 25 (anticipated by Graefe 118: "εἷμα posset dici αἰωρεῖσθαι, non αἷμα") and μηρῶν to χειρῶν in 26 all problems dis-

[82] The Loeb translation of Edmonds – "his breast took on the purple that came from his thighs, and the paps thereof that had been as white as snow waxed now incarnadine" – brings out the strangeness of the MS reading admirably.

[83] That these are imitations of Bion is made likely by the rarity of couplings of στήθεα or μαζοί and the verb φοινίσσω in Greek and by Nonnus' manifest appropriation of other Bionean imagery for his own lamenting heroines (see on 21, 40, 44).

appear and no new ones arise. We now read: "And around her the dark robe hung at her navel, and her chest was made scarlet by her hands, and the breasts underneath, formerly snowy white, became crimson for the sake of Adonis." A crescendo of the effects of mourning on the divine body: first we see the damage to her robe, then to her upper torso, then finally to her glory, the μαζοί themselves. The corruption is easily explained: a scribe with μέλαν εἴβεται αἷμα still in mind from line 9 writes αἷμα for εἷμα in 25; then he or a later scribe, mistaking the passage for a description of the dying Adonis, corrects χειρῶν to μηρῶν to conform to lines 7 and 16.

25 ἀμφὶ δέ νιν: "and around her". In her frenzy Aphrodite has ripped the robe down the middle, so that half hangs down on either side of her, held by the ζώνη. ἀμφί + acc. normally has a progressive sense when used of clothing, but cf. Ach. Tat. 1.1.10 χιτὼν ἀμφὶ τὰ στέρνα τῆς παρθένου (cf. ἀμφί μιν in Homer of stationary crowds).

μέλαν εἷμα: Fantuzzi keeps MS αἷμα, arguing that the *poeta doctus* would not call the goddess's robe μέλας after calling it κυάνεος in line 4 (q.v.); he cites West's note on Hes. *Th.* 406 that in Greek poetry it is normally mortals who wear μέλας mourning, while deities normally wear κυάνεος. This convention, however, is only that – not an ironclad law[84]; and it is precisely in the style of a *poeta doctus* to exploit the convention in the way that Bion does here. Like the blood of Aphrodite in 22 and the "death" of her beauty in 31, the workaday synonym of κυάνεος draws the goddess closer to mortality.[85] The *repetitio cum variatione* of Adonis' μέλαν αἷμα in 9 assimilates Aphrodite to her beloved as in 16–17, 31, 64–5, and elsewhere (compare also χιόνεοι in 27 to Adonis' snowy flesh in 10). The effect is to explore the limits of the goddess's humanity, suddenly and tragically to be denied in 53.

εἷμα: usually pl., but sing. in *Il.* 18.538, *Od.* 14.501, Pind. *P.* 4.232, Aesch. *Ag.* 1383, Nossis *A.P.* 6.265.3.

παρ' ὀμφαλόν: cf. Eur. *Hec.* 558–61, where Polyxena, λαβοῦσα πέπλους ἐξ ἄκρας ἐπωμίδος, | ἔρρηξε λαγόνος εἰς μέσον παρ' ὀμφαλόν | μαστούς τ' ἔδειξε στέρνα θ' ὡς ἀγάλματος | κάλλιστα. There παρά + acc. indicates progressive action ("to her navel"); here the meaning is

[84] The veil of Thetis at *Il.* 24.94 is κυάνεον, τοῦ δ' οὔ τι μελάντερον ἔπλετο ἔσθος.

[85] The suffering of divinity is portrayed as a humanization in e.g. *H.H.* 2, where the grieving Demeter takes on mortal guise and goes to live with a human family. Cf. [Longin.] 9.7 on Homer's humanization of the gods when they suffer.

simply "by (i.e. at the level of) her navel" (as the phrase is used of the location of wounds in Homer).

ᾀωρεῖτο: an admirable verb for the bunched tatters of the robe that "hung floatingly" at Aphrodite's waist. For the tearing of clothes in the process of beating one's breast cf. Sappho fr. 140A.2 L–P (mourners of Adonis), Aesch. *Pers.* 121–5, Hdt. 2.85.1, Prop. 2.13.27, Ovid *Met.* 10.722–3 (Venus for Adonis). Tearing one's clothes, of course, was a sign of mourning in itself; cf. esp. Aesch. *Pers.* 835–6 κακῶν ὑπ' ἄλγους λακίδες ἀμφὶ σώματι | στημορραγοῦσι ποικίλων ἐσθημάτων.

26 **ἐκ:** see fr. 4.1 n.

χειρῶν: for other emendations giving the same sense see Reed (1992) 541; but χεῖρες are conventional in poetic descriptions of funereal beating (e.g. *Il.* 18.30, 19.284; Soph. *Aj.* 632; Eur. *Supp.* 72, *Alc.* 87).

φοινίσσετο: φοῖνιξ is another name for πορφύρα (cf. 3 n.), a typically Phoenician product. For comparison of it with the colour of blood cf. e.g. *Il.* 4.141, 23.717; [Hes.] *Scut.* 194; Timoth. *PMG* 791.32–3; cf. πορφύροντο in 27 (the greater frequency of φοινίσσομαι in this connexion may be due to homophony with φοινός; cf. on 41).

τοὶ δ' ὑπὸ μαζοί: τοί, avoiding hiatus, is the emendation of Ameis *De art.* 3; late bucolic occasionally permits hiatus at bucolic caesura (see fr. 13.4 n.), but with τοί available Bion probably eschewed hiatus here. The division of MS ὑπομαζοί is the work of Lobeck 384: "the breasts underneath", i.e. under the στήθεα (Helius Eobanus Hessus[86] already translates "et niveae quondam sub pectore mammae").[87] The MS reading may have originated in a MS in which accents were not always marked on prepositions; V and R, however, are careful in this regard.

The blood running down from the upper part of Aphrodite's chest (στήθεα), which she is beating, reddens her μαζοί. In Greek literature mourning women normally beat their στήθεα or στέρνα, not their breasts[88] (on the distinction, here underscored by the collocation of the two nouns, see Bulloch on Callim. *H.* 5.88). A mid seventh-century B.C. terracotta from Rhodes (R. A. Higgins, *Catalogue of Terracottas in the British Museum* (London 1954) I pl. 2.14) depicts a mourner with red-painted incisions fanning downward from her upper chest. Nonnus does have

[86] Helius' translation was printed with Camerarius' edition (1530).

[87] Briggs's τῶν δ' ὕπο μαζοί – with τῶν referring to στήθεα – is clearer, but unnecessary. In the same year as Lobeck, Hermann (1837) 232 independently recommended οἳ δ' ὕπο μαζοί, unconvincingly paraphrasing πορφύροντο ὑπὸ τοῦ αἵματος.

[88] Similarly in Lat. their *pectora*, not their *mamillae*.

women beat their μαζοί (see citations above on 25–7), perhaps prompted by Bion's mention of μαζοί here; cf. also anon. *A.P.* 9.362.21, Quintus 14.278–9.

27 χιόνεοι: see on 10 above; of a woman's breasts also in anon. *A.P.* 5.84.2, Nonnus *D.* 15.261–2 ὄφρα με μαζῷ | χιονέῳ πελάσειε. Bion's image of crimson blood on snowy flesh (cf. 9–10) is adapted for descriptions of attractive blushes in [Bion] 2.19, Nonnus *D.* 4.130–2; in Lat. cf. Ovid *Am.* 3.3.6, *Met.* 3.423; [Tib.] 3.4.30 (of bloody skin in Statius *Theb.* 9.883, on which see Dewar); cf. Rufinus *A.P.* 5.35.5–6. A precedent for the colour contrast is *Il.* 4.141–7, where Menelaus' legs are compared to ivory stained with purple-dye; the Iliadic passage also inspired the threefold description and downward ensanguination in Bion's lines: cf. *Il.* 4.146–7 τοῖοί τοι, Μενέλαε, μιάνθην αἵματι μηροί | εὐφυέες κνῆμαί τε ἰδὲ σφυρὰ κάλ' ὑπένερθε.

Ἀδώνιδι: dat. of interest, "for the sake of Adonis". Buecheler (1863) 107 emends to πάροιθ' ἐπ' Ἀδώνιδι, with ἐπί "in honour of" (cf. 81), but the dat. alone is adequate; cf. e.g. Aesch. *Cho.* 152–3 ἵετε δάκρυ καναχὲς {ὀλόμενον} | ὀλομένῳ δεσπότᾳ (del. Blomfield), Theoc. 14.38 τήνῳ τεὰ δάκρυα. G. Bernhardy, *Wissenschaftliche Syntax der griechischen Sprache* (Berlin 1829) 86 n. 39 had construed it in this way before Ahrens's emendations.

πορφύροντο: the verb originally meant "billow, surge", as of the sea; by an assimilation to the dye πορφύρα (effected by the Hellenistic period; cf. Theoc. 5.125, [Bion] 2.19) it came to mean "become crimson" (the adj. πορφύρεος, of the heaving sea, without reference to colour, is already Homeric; see Chantraine *Dict.* s.vv.). The original connexion, if any, between the two terms is uncertain; see Tichy 281–5. The colour of blood is likened to that of πορφύρα at *Il.* 17.360–1 and often by Nonnus, e.g. *D.* 4.450, 28.138, 34.156; cf. Quintus 14.319.

This verb does not seem to occur in the middle voice elsewhere before Nonnus, and we should consider emendation to πορφύροντι. We should then emend MS ᾐωρεῖτο to αἰωρεῖται and φοινίσσετο to φοινίσσεται (the reading of Paris. gr. 2812A before correction; this would allow us to keep MS οἱ without hiatus); a misreading of Doric -οντι as -οντο could have prompted change of the whole sentence into the imperfect. Ahrens emended these verbs to the present, though he retained the middle of πορφύρω, printing πορφύρονται. Against emendation: Nonnus shows a predilection for Bionisms (cf. e.g. on 19, 21, 60) and might have revived this one. The use of the middle voice for the active is a typical affectation of Hellenistic poets (see *HE* II.456); here perhaps on the analogy of φοινίσσομαι.

28 αἰαῖ: the MSS spell this word αἲ αἴ (also in 31, 37, 39, 63, 89–90), as do the authors of the emendations in 86 and 93; my critical apparatus omits this fact. The now standard form was first printed in Meineke's second ed. (Berlin 1836). Cf. Fantuzzi (1985) 64 n. 260.

αἰαῖ τὰν Κυθέρειαν: the rare acc. of exclamation was used originally in ritual expressions of sorrow; cf. the popular etymology whereby the lamentatory exclamation αἴλινον was interpreted as a cry of "alas!" for a dead Linus. Later it is extended to other expressions of woe for a named person: *CEG* 512.1–2 (Piraeus, early fourth century B.C.) with ὤ, 709.6 (Halicarnassus, fourth century B.C.?) with αἰαῖ, 718 (Egypt, earlier fourth century B.C.?) with ᾤμοι; Heliod. 7.14.5 ὢ τὸν Καλάσιριν. Cf. on 32, and see Fraenkel on Aesch. *Ag.* 1146, Bulloch on Callim. *H.* 5.89–90, *HE* II.139 on Asclep. *A.P.* 13.23.5. A cry "alas for Aphrodite!" may have been traditional, though unattested in ritual; after all, this is her misfortune too (commemorated in her temple in some localities), a detail that Bion exploits in assimilating the goddess to the dead boy (see on 25 μέλαν εἷμα). Note how the natural features in 31–4 alternate laments for Adonis with laments for Aphrodite.

29 ἄνδρα: "husband", more or less (cf. Gow on [Theoc.] 8.49). Cf. 68; he is Aphrodite's ἀνήρ also in Theoc. 15.131, Julian *Symp.* 329D, E.N.A. 20 and 23.

συνώλεσεν: for the idea cf. Soph. *El.* 1149–50 νῦν δ' ἐκλέλοιπε ταῦτ' ἐν ἡμέρᾳ μιᾷ | θανόντα (vel -ι) σὺν σοί. On the variety of things said to die in this poem, often jointly with Adonis, see on 12. For the compound verb see Eur. *Hel.* 103; with ὤλεσε a half-felt paronomasia, since Aphrodite has not only "lost" her beauty, but has deliberately "destroyed" it in her grief (cf. *Od.* 18.251–2 = 19.124–5 ἦ τοι ἐμὴν ἀρετὴν εἶδός τε δέμας τε | ὤλεσαν ἀθάνατοι). Cf. [Theoc.] 27.31 ἀλλὰ τεκεῖν τρομέω μὴ καὶ χρόα καλὸν ὀλέσσω ("lose").

ἱερόν: see on 22.

εἶδος: "appearance", often with the implication of beauty, like our "looks".

30 Wakefield's θάλεν "floruit" for καλόν would give a stronger image and would accord with flower imagery elsewhere in the poem (cf. 11, 41, 64–6, 76); but it is in Bion's style to repeat a word in the same position two lines in a row (cf. 12–13, 37–8, 40–1, 45–6, 50–1, 65–6, 75–6, 95–6). For the phrase καλὸν εἶδος see *Il.* 3.44–5, Marc. Arg. *A.P.* 5.89.1.

ζώεσκεν: the iterative imperf. of ζώω occurs in Hes. *Op.* 90 and 133 and Ap. Rh. 1.1074, where the subject is collective; in Bion's sense in *GVI* 1741.7 (Athens, third century A.D. or later), 1982.31 (Attica, third century A.D.?); [Orph.] *Lith.* 151; Greg. Naz. *A.P.* 8.82.1.

31 μορφά: "beauty" (see fr. 15.1 n.).

τὰν Κύπριν αἰαῖ: for the exclamatory acc. see on 28. Its unusual position here before the interjection explains Triclinius' emendation to Κύπριδος ("the beauty of Cypris has died ...").

31–9 The catalogue of mourning natural features in these lines was inspired by the lament for Daphnis in Theoc. 1, where animals tame and wild mourn the dying herdsman. Bion, taking a hint from Theoc. 7 (see on 32 below), makes not animals but features of the landscape mourn Adonis; the personification would not have seemed as great a "pathetic fallacy" as it may to us, since the Greeks traditionally imagined every mountain, river, and tree to embody some anthropomorphic spirit or deity. This kind of universal sympathy appears occasionally in Greek literature: in Aesch. *Sept.* 901–2 στένει πέδον φίλανδρον in response to the battle's outcome; in Soph. *Aj.* 412–22 and 856–65 Ajax's farewell to the natural features of the Troad prefigures Daphnis' farewell, without making explicit the assumption of Nature's sympathy (on tragic apostrophes to the natural world see A. P. Wagener, *TAPA* 62 (1931) 78–100). Cf. also Antip. Sid. *A.P.* 7.241.7–8, anon. *A.P.* 7.717.1–2 (= *HE* lines 3870–1), Aristid. *Or.* 11.12 (quoting Pind. fr. 136A Maehler), Philostr. *Im.* 2.4.3, Greg. Naz. *A.P.* 8.129 and 249. In bucolic the trope came to fullest fruition (see J. C. Buller, *Ramus* 10 (1981) 35–52, who invokes the typically Hellenistic belief in Nature's benevolence, or at least interest in human affairs); the author of [Moschus] 3, following Theocritus and Bion, takes it to an extreme of comprehensive inventiveness. From Greek bucolic Virgil introduced such catalogues into Latin: *Ecl.* 5.24–8, 10.13; *G.* 4.461–2; *Aen.* 7.759–60.

32 ὤρεα: for human feelings or activities ascribed to mountains cf. Soph. *O.T.* 1086–95; Eur. *H.F.* 790–7, *Ba.* 726 and 1383–4; Corinna *PMG* 654; Theoc. 7.74 (quoted below); Callim. *H.* 4.118–20. See A. Gerber, *Naturpersonification in Poesie und Kunst der Alten* (*Jahrb. f. cl. Phil.* Suppl. 13, Leipzig 1883) 303–15.

λέγοντι: the rule that a neut. pl. subject takes a sing. verb was never as strong in epic language as in Attic (Chantraine *GH* II §23, Schwyzer II.607; cf. frr. 8.2, 17.2); here the plural may reflect the personification of the mountains (cf. K–G §365.a) or be due to attraction by the verb's other subject, δρύες. For λέγειν used in expressions of grief see on 5; for its introducing an exclamation cf. 93 and Dion. Per. 704 εὐοῖ Βάκχε λέγοντες.

αἱ δρύες: cf. on 20 δρυμώς. For the articulated δρύες following article-free ὤρεα cf. 26 στήθεα ..., τοὶ δ' ὑπὸ μαζοί and 66 αἷμα ῥόδον ..., τὰ δὲ δάκρυα τὰν ἀνεμώναν. For this construction in bucolic Ameis *De art.* 39 compares among others Theoc. 15.58 ἵππον καὶ τὸν ψυχρὸν ὄφιν, [Moschus] 3.23–4 ὤρεα δ' ἐστὶν ἄφωνα, καὶ αἱ βόες ... γοάοντι (the latter echoing Bion).

αἲ τὸν Ἄδωνιν: for the acc. see on 28. Cf. Sappho fr. 168 L–P ὢ τὸν Ἄδωνιν and Aristoph. *Lys.* 393 αἰαῖ Ἄδωνιν, reflecting a traditional exclamation at the festival of Adonis.

The model for this line is Theoc. 7.74 χὡς ὄρος ἀμφεπονεῖτο καὶ ὡς δρύες αὐτὸν (sc. Daphnis) ἐθρήνευν; cf. Virg. *Ecl.* 5.28. [Moschus] 3.23 (quoted above) and Nonnus *D.* 15.390 (in a Bionesque lament for the cowherd Hymnus) καὶ δρύες ἐφθέγξαντο are imitations.

33 καὶ ποταμοί: the model is Theoc. 1.118 καὶ ποταμοὶ τοὶ χεῖτε καλὸν κατὰ Θύβριδος ὕδωρ, where Daphnis bids his world farewell (cf. *Il.* 3.278). Bion is imitated by [Moschus] 3.2, beginning καὶ ποταμοὶ κλαίοιτε: Nature is called upon to do at Bion's death what Bion had shown her doing at the death of Adonis.

κλαίοντι τὰ πένθεα: cf. Callim. *SH* 240.11 πένθος ἐδάκρυσαν. The Doric form of the verb, first printed by Brunck, is read in Paris. gr. 2812A.

34 παγαὶ ... δακρύοντι: πηγαί are natural springs, the sources of streams and rivers, in contradistinction to the κρῆναι, wells and fountains, that human use may make of them (so R. E. Wycherley, *CR* 51 (1937) 2–3). The springs' natural flow is fancied as lacrimation; this line inspired the more explicit conceit in [Moschus] 3.29 Κρανίδες ὠδύραντο, καὶ ὕδατα δάκρυα γέντο (cf. Ovid *Met.* 1.584 (Inachus) "fletibus auget aquas" and 11.47–8 "lacrimis quoque flumina dicunt | increvisse suis"). A precedent is the trickling rock that the weeping Niobe became (*Il.* 24.602–17, Soph. *Ant.* 823–33, Callim. *H.* 2.22–4).

ἐν ὤρεσι: cf. 7.

35 ὀδύνας: the word is not used in earlier bucolic, but occurs at [Theoc.] 19.5, 27.26; [Mosch.] 3.94.

ἐρυθαίνεται: MS ἐρυθραίνεται is prosaic. A strained conceit: flowers turn red from grief (as human faces do from strong emotion in Soph. *Ant.* 528–9, [Theoc.] 20.16) presumably in order to serve as the crimson flowers customary at funerals (cf. Fantuzzi *ad loc.*, Brenk 222–3). The imitation in [Moschus] 3.5 νῦν ῥόδα φοινίσσεσθε τὰ πένθιμα, νῦν ἀνεμῶναι ("legt euer Trauerroth an": Buecheler (1863) 108; note the conflation of *Ad.* 35 and 66) is clearer, since roses and anemones are typically red. Wilamowitz's idea (followed by Hopkinson) that the verb here = "turn brown", i.e. "wilt", is implausible.

The tendency to personify natural features seems seldom to have been extended to flowers (cf. Longus 4.8, where uprooted flowers are extravagantly mourned over, and Nonnus *D.* 32.86–9, 42.302). The effect is sentimental, perhaps because of their smallness and prettiness. Cf. lines 75–6.

Κυθήρα: this title of Aphrodite may be first attested here (it is an epithet "Cytheran" in [Aristot.] *Mir. aud.* 843B; cf. G. Huxley, *GRBS* 8 (1967) 89); its next datable appearances are [Manetho] *Apot.* 2 [1].273; 3 [2].176; and 6 [3].301, 518, 723 Koechly in the Antonine period. Undatable are [Plato] *A.Pl.* 210.2; *Anacreont.* 15.11, 16.21, 17.15, 28.1, 35.7, 43.14, 44.9, 55.31, 60.23; anon. *A.P.* 9.606.1. The title is a metrical variant (based on the name of the island; cf. on 17) of Κυθέρη, a woman's name in Antip. Thess. *A.P.* 6.209.1 and the goddess's title in Lucian *Symp.* 41 and seven times in [Manetho] *Apot.*; this latter in turn is a doublet of Κυθέρεια (cf. e.g. Εὐρώπεια/-η, Μήδεια/-η, Περσεφόνεια/-η with Lobeck 320–2).

Because an interjection by the goddess seems incongruous amid the voices of nature mourning for her sake, J. Langhorne, *The Death of Adonis* (London 1759) 8 sees Κυθήρα as the island Cythera, consummating the list of its natural features (so too Wilamowitz, Legrand, Hopkinson, and others). The island is τὰ Κύθηρα in Greek; the first-decl. form would be a personification. No extant authority, however, sets Adonis' death on Cythera, although the legendary Phoenician associations of the island (Hdt. 1.105.3, Paus. 1.15.7 and 3.23.1, Steph. Byz. s.v. Κύθηρα) and cult of Aphrodite (see on 17) make it like localities whence mythologers traced Adonis (e.g. Byblos, Cyprus).

36 The model for the line is Theoc. 1.83 πάσας ἀνὰ κράνας, πάντ' ἄλσεα ποσσὶ φορεῖται (cf. on 19, 23).

κναμώς: "hills" below mountains; etymologically the "shins" of mountains (cf. κνήμη).

ἀείδει: an exclamation like that in 37 can be "sung": Callim. *H.* 6.39 calls an exclamation of grief and pain a κακὸν μέλος (cf. Eur. *H.F.* 751), and ἀείδω introduces interjections in 88–90 below, if only by zeugma.[89] Luzac's ἀυτεῖ (ap. Valckenaer) is therefore unnecessary (though cf. *GVI* 1502.5 (Phocis, *c.* 300 B.C.), ending οἰκτρὸν ἄυσεν). If the *island* is the subject (see on 35), whispering mournfully through all her hills and glades, we could recall that ἀείδω was used of the sounds of nature (e.g. Theoc. 7.26, Moschus fr. 1.8; cf. Theoc. 1.1–2, Lucian *V.H.* 2.5).

[89] Bion's commentators typically compare Virg. *G.* 1.378 "ranae cecinere querelam", but frogs normally "sing", as in [Aristot.] *Mir. ausc.* 70, [Moschus] 3.106; cf. F. G. Sturz, *Opuscula nonnulla* (Leipzig 1825) 303 s.v. ᾄδει.

The reading preserved by V, ἀνάπαλιν ἀποσοικτρὰν ἀείδει (whence the feeble correction in R), contains two errors, of which the first, -λι- for -ν-, is an easy misreading of the majuscule. The second, -ὰν for -όν, hardly needs to be accounted for (perhaps from ἀνά twice in this line), but it is tempting to see the mistake as lying not in the vowel, but in the word division. Might Bion have written οἴκτρ' ἀναείδει, "sings out pitifully"? The verb is unattested, but cf. ἀνυμνέω and ἀναμέλπω (e.g. [Callisth.] 1.46 οἰκτρὸν ... μέλος ἀναμέλψαι). "Sings out" may be more expressive of the following exclamation than "sings" (on ἀνα- of sounds see 80 n.).[90] Lang 209, following Luzac (see above), reads οἴκτρ' ἀναΰτεῖ.

37 αἰαῖ τὰν Κυθέρειαν: V has the incomprehensible αἰαῖ τὰν νότον, which some have thought a garbled form of the original text, with R's reading an emendation by Triclinius.[91] The presence of τὰν in V, however, raises the suspicion that νότον has somehow replaced Κυθέρειαν or some epithet referring to Aphrodite (Buecheler (1863) 108 thinks of τὰν δύσποτμον; cf. 43 and 56), and in view of lines 28, 63, and 86 R is probably right; the difficulty is in explaining the error in V.[92] On the emphatic use of one's own name see 59 n.

38 Ἀχώ: personified Echo (first attested in Eur. *Hec.* 1111) conventionally repeats the last part of an utterance: cf. e.g. Leon. Alex. *A.P.* 7.548, Gauradas *A.Pl.* 152; most ingeniously Ovid *Met.* 3.380–92. For mourning Echo cf. [Moschus] 3.30–1, Ovid *Met.* 3.507, Nonnus *D.* 15.389 (in a lament inspired by Bion; cf. on 1 and 32). Ptolemy IV Philopator (reigned 221–204 B.C.) introduced Echo in a tragedy on Adonis (*TrGF* 119 F 1).

ἀντεβόασεν: Paus. 2.35.10 uses this verb of Echo (echoing Bion?). Cf. Nemes. *Ecl.* 1.73 "reboat ... Echo".

39 The list of mourning natural features concludes with an explanatory rhetorical question – "Who would not have cried 'alas!' for the terrible love of Cypris?" – whose answer is obviously "no one" (cf.

[90] Cf. G. Panayiotou, *Hellenika* 38 (1987) 58: "The preposition ἀνά, as the first component of compound verbs of *wailing aloud*, is quite common", with examples.

[91] Nothing particularly recommends Fantuzzi's "αἰαῖ" τὸν νέον οἶτον (after Ahrens and Gallavotti), although there is enough variation in the "refrain" of this poem to permit it.

[92] That νότον is a misspelled intrusion of a marginal νόθον, intended to mark this line as misplaced or the next as spurious, as R. Peiper, *Jahrb. f. cl. Phil.* 9 (1863) 620 suggests, is unlikely.

Callim. *H.* 1.92 τεὰ δ' ἔργματα τίς κεν ἀείδοι; and 2.31 τίς ἂν οὐ ῥέα Φοῖβον ἀείδοι; Virg. *Ecl.* 10.3 "neget quis carmina Gallo?"). Longus 4.8 ἔκλαυσε δ' ἄν τις καὶ ξένος ἐπιστάς may imitate Bion (cf. on 35, 71).

αἰνὸν ἔρωτα: Aphrodite's "terrible" love for a mortal, which has necessarily failed her, is the object of lamentation (cf. 58). Fantuzzi notes that the adj. is a variation on the more common, synonymous δεινός, "dire, terrible,"[93] an attribute of ἔρως in [Hes.] fr. 298; Aesch. *Eum.* 865; Eur. *Hi.* 28, fr. 1054.1 Nauck, fr. 16.21 Page; Mel. *A.P.* 5.176.1–2. Both adjs. are connected with ἔρως in Hermes. fr. 7.83–4 *CA*, Moschus fr. 3.7. For ἔρωτα as obj. of κλαίω cf. Theoc. 2.64 πόθεν τὸν ἔρωτα δακρύσω;

τίς οὐκ ἔκλαυσεν ἂν αἰαῖ: the verb both takes an object (αἰνὸν ἔρωτα) and introduces direct speech (κλαίω can refer to both tears and noise: Schmidt 1.471–3); the interjection αἰαῖ gives the very words of the lament.[94] Cf. Aesch. *Ag.* 1144–5 Ἴτυν Ἴτυν στένουσ' ἀμφιθαλῆ κακοῖς | ἀηδὼν μόρον (Page: βίον codd.),[95] Callim. fr. 193.37–8 Ἄδωνιν αἰαῖ τῆς θεοῦ τὸν ἄνθρωπον | ἰηλεμίζειν, Phalaecus *A.P.* 13.27.7 αἰαῖ κωκύει τὸν ἑὸν γόνον ἤματα πάντα. Compare verbs of exclamation or lamentation taking a double acc., one external of the person acclaimed and one internal of the thing uttered (esp. tragic: K–G 1.321).

40–42 There are imitations in Virg. *Aen.* 11.39–42 "ipse caput nivei fultum Pallantis et ora | ut vidit levique patens in pectore vulnus | cuspidis Ausoniae, lacrimis ita fatur obortis: | 'tene,' inquit, 'miserande puer'" etc. (cf. 10.821–32) and Ovid *Met.* 10.720–1 (Venus and Adonis) "utque aethere vidit ab alto | exanimem inque suo iactantem sanguine corpus . . .".

40 ὡς ἴδεν, ὡς ἐνόησεν: the opening is reminiscent of a pattern inspired by *Il.* 14.294 ὡς δ' ἴδεν, ὥς μιν ἔρως πυκινὰς φρένας ἀμφεκάλυψεν (cf. 19.16, 20.424), where the second ὡς is demonstrative: "when

[93] On Callim. *SH* 257.21 αἰνολέων is glossed as δεινολέων; cf. Hesych. s.vv. αἰνόν, αἰνότατον.

[94] A. Ludwich's emendations in *Coniectanea ad bucolicos graecos* (Königsberg 1908) 7–8 of ἂν αἰαῖ to ἐν αἴᾳ or ἀν' αἶαν, although apt, are unwarranted.

[95] Cf. Fraenkel *ad loc.* Denniston and Page (p. 175) speak misleadingly of apposition; Ἴτυν Ἴτυν is the characteristic cry of the nightingale. See also Soph. *El.* 148, Eur. *Phaeth.* 70 Diggle (q.v.). In Heitsch 6.55 (P. Heidelb. 222, second–third century A.D.) τὸν Ἴτυν, τὸν Ἴτυν κατακλ[άεται, Itys is both obj. and exclamation.

he saw, thereupon ...."[96] Bion, however, is simply repeating "when she saw" with variation; from Homer on ὁράω and νοέω are frequently juxtaposed in a way that suggests they are felt as synonyms (e.g. *Il.* 10.550, *Od.* 13.318; cf. West on Hes. *Op.* 267). Like Bion's construction are Nonnus *D.* 47.158–9 ὡς ἴδεν ἕλκεα τόσσα καρήατος, ὡς ἴδε δειλή | λύθρον (an imitation) and Quintus 12.120 ὡς ἴδεν, ὡς ἤκουσεν...; cf. Callim. *H.* 4.200 (with Pfeiffer's restoration).

ὡς ἴδεν: a common Homeric line-opening; cf. esp. *Il.* 19.283 (Briseis coming upon the dead Patroclus). For ὡς ἐνόησεν see on fr. 13.3.

ἄσχετον: Hopkinson translates "unstaunchable", which is a possible meaning (lit. "impossible to hold back") and fits the sense here better than the "unstaunched" of Gow (1953) 145. The point is that she now sees for sure that he will die. Usually the adj. = "irresistible, uncontrollable"; cf. e.g. *Il.* 16.548–9 πένθος | ἄσχετον.

41 φοίνιον: a poetic extended form of φοινός < φόνος, "murderous, gory". A longstanding epithet of blood, e.g. at *Od.* 18.97 and esp. in tragedy. Here the adj. stresses the horror of the sight.[97]

μαραινομένῳ: we could translate "languishing". In Homer the verb is used of the extinguishing of fire (*Il.* 9.222, 23.228), later of any sapping of vitality. The application to the site of Adonis' wound is striking (compare the use for physical debility in e.g. Eur. *Alc.* 203, 236; Philod. *A.P.* 11.30.6). The normal verb for the wilting of flowers, it recalls floral imagery elsewhere in the poem (11, 65–6, esp. 76).

περί: "on" (cf. 11 ἀμφί).

The models for this line are *Il.* 4.149 ὡς εἶδεν μέλαν αἷμα καταρρέον ἐξ ὠτειλῆς and Theoc. 22.100 ὡς ἴδον ἕλκεα λυγρὰ περὶ στόμα τε γναθμούς τε (with αἷμα φοίνιον in 98–9).

42 ἀμπετάσασα: aor. participle < ἀναπετάννυμι, "fling open or spread open wide", used of sails at *Il.* 1.480, of gates at *Il.* 12.122. Aphrodite's posture is easily imaginable (and is familiar from e.g. the *Lamentation* of Giotto), but seems unattested in ancient funereal art. The

[96] For the numerous imitations see Gow on Theoc. 2.82, Hollis on Callim. *Hec.* fr. 69.2 (= fr. 260.2 Pfeiffer), both Bühler and Campbell (pp. 216–18) on Moschus 2.74, Livrea on Colluth. 257. On Latin imitations (e.g. Virg. *Ecl.* 8.41) see S. Timpanaro, *Contributi di filologia e di storia della lingua latina* (Rome 1978) 219–87.

[97] Note that the adj. does not primarily denote colour, and is not cognate with the red dye φοῖνιξ: that root appears as *po-ni-k-* in Linear B (cf. E. D. Foster, *Minos* 16 (1977) 59–60), where derivatives of φόνος (< *g^whónos*) would still have shown a labio-velar.

same form of the verb recurs in Bion's sense in Greg. Naz. *Epit.* 71.2–4 (*PG* 38.48) = *A.P.* 8.30.2–4 ἤντεο, μῆτερ ἐμή ... | χεῖρας ἀμπετάσασα φίλας τεκέεσσι φίλοισι, | Γρηγόριον βοόωσα (cf. *Ad.* 24), undoubtedly an imitation.[98]

κινύρετο: "wailed". On the verb's origins (< Homeric κινυρός) see M. Leumann, *Homerische Wörter* (Basel 1950) 241–3; Bulloch (1985) 230 n. 1. It occurs first in drama (Aesch. *Sept.* 123, fr. 47A col. 2.6 Radt; Aristoph. *Eq.* 11); later in Callim. *H.* 2.20 and often in Ap. Rh. (see Campbell on Ap. Rh. 3.259: "mothers in particular κινύρονται").

42–61 Aphrodite's lament over Adonis fuses the epic persona of the grieving wife (e.g. Andromache; cf. on 51–2, 59) to that of lovelorn female soliloquizers popular in Hellenistic literature, e.g. Apollonius' Medea, Catullus' Ariadne, Virgil's Dido, often in Ovid (descended in part from Euripides' Phaedra). See Lyne 270 on the conventional plaint of the heroine in miniature epics. On the rhetorical style of this passage see Introd. VII.4.

42–3 For the enjambed repetition of μεῖνον cf. Callim. *H.* 4.118–19 ἀλλὰ σὺ μεῖνον, | μεῖνον....

43 δύσποτμε: first attested in tragedy; rarely found elsewhere in poetry, but see Nic. *Al.* 297 and anon. *A.P.* 7.334.14. The failure of a nasal to "make position" after a stop is found in late bucolic only here and at fr. 13.9 (contrast 56 πανάποτμος); here reminiscent of tragic diction and the high style.

πανύστατον: for neut. sing. as adv., "for the very last time", cf. e.g. Soph. *Aj.* 858, Aristoph. *Ach.* 1184, [Theoc.] 23.35 (the last perhaps echoing Bion, as often).

κιχείω: poetic aor. subj. of κιχάνω, "catch up with". Aphrodite imagines the dying Adonis as fleeing from her pursuit; cf. 50–1 φεύγεις, 53 διώκειν.

For postponed ὡς see on fr. 10.8.

44 περιπτύξω: cf. Nonnus *D.* 24.207 ὄφρα περιπτύξω διερὸν νέκυν. The last embrace of Aphrodite and Adonis is mentioned in *Et. magn.* 175.6–9 Gaisford as occurring at Aphaca near Mt Lebanon (cf. p. 21).

χείλεα χείλεσι μείξω: such anatomical polyptota appear first in

[98] Gregory's unwonted metrical error in χεῖρας ἀμπετάσασα makes one wonder whether he imitated Bion more clearly by writing πήχεας ... φίλους, with χεῖρας originating as a gloss. The Palatine MS reads χεῖρας δ' ἀμπετάσασα, a hasty attempt to correct the metre.

military contexts, e.g. Tyrt. fr. 11.31–3 *IEG*, Eur. *Her.* 836 ποὺς ἐπαλλαχθεὶς ποδί, Ennius *Ann.* 584 Skutsch, Fur. Bib. fr. 10 *FPL*, Virg. *Aen.* 10.361; later in erotic, e.g. Tib. 1.8.26 "femori conseruisse femur" and Bion's model, Theoc. 12.32 προσμάξῃ γλυκερώτερα χείλεσι χείλη. Bion's μείγνυμι is metaphorical for "join" (LSJ s.v. II); cf. Theogn. 961 ὕδωρ δ' ἀναμίσγεται ὕδει codd., Asclep. *A.P.* 12.163.1 τι καλῷ μεῖξαι καλόν, Ap. Rh. 2.78 χερσὶν ... χεῖρας ἔμειξεν, Moschus fr. 3.5 κοὐ μείγνυται ὕδασιν ὕδωρ.[99] Bion is followed by Mel. *A.P.* 5.171.3 (see 50 n.), Greg. Naz. *A.P.* 8.53.4 οὔποτε χείλεα μίξας ἀνάγνοις χείλεσιν ἁγνά, Macedonius *A.P.* 5.245.5 χείλεσι γυμνοτάτοις, οὔ τινι μισγομένοις, Paul. Sil. *A.P.* 5.236.3–4 χείλεα μῖξαι | χείλεϊ σῷ. Cf. Matius fr. 12.2 *FPL* "columbulatim labra conserens labris", Marc. Arg. *A.P.* 5.128.2 χείλεά τε γλυκεροῖς χείλεσι συμπιέσας, Lucian *Amor.* 53 χείλη προσεγγίσας χείλεσιν – these might equally well imitate Theocritus.

μείξω: confusion between long iota and the diphthong ει in this verb is evident from the fourth century B.C. (K. Meisterhans, *Grammatik der attischen Inschriften*[3] (Berlin 1900) 48) and long iota eventually became regular, but as the original spelling of the aor., ἔμειξα, persists in papyri through Bion's period (E. Mayser, *Grammatik der griechischen Papyri aus der Ptolemäerzeit* I.1[2] (rev. H. Schmoll, Berlin 1970) 60 and 62; I.2[2] (Berlin 1938) 187), MS μίξω probably reflects later scribal practice.

44–50 The last kiss. There was a tradition, at least in Rome from the first century B.C. on, that a loved one was supposed to catch a dying person's last breath in a kiss (cf. Cic. *Verr.* 5.118, Virg. *Aen.* 4.684–5 with Pease, Ovid *A.A.* 3.745–6 and *Met.* 7.860–1 (cf. 12.425), [Ovid] *Cons. ad Liv.* 95–7 and 158, Justin 22.2.8, Manil. 5.623–4, Sen. *Herc.* 1339–40, Stat. *Silv.* 5.1.195–6); the idea was that the survivor should catch the dying person's fleeting soul, identified with his breath (cf. 49–50 below). The only other Greek examples seem to be *GVI* 1874.5 (Egypt, later second century B.C.) Ἄτθις, ἐμοὶ ζήσασα καὶ εἰς ἐμὲ πνεῦμα λιποῦσα and Longus 1.30 Δόρκων μὲν τοσαῦτα εἰπὼν καὶ φίλημα φιλήσας ὕστατον ἀφῆκεν ἅμα τῷ φιλήματι καὶ τῇ φωνῇ τὴν ψυχήν (the latter probably reflects less a touching deathbed ritual than a taste for Bion's imagery such as the novelists often show).

45 τυτθόν: for the temporal sense of the adv. see Ap. Rh. 2.917

[99] Note too the sexual connotations of the verb. S. A. Naber, *Mnem.* 34 (1906) 169 needlessly emends MS μίξω to Theocritus' μάξω (Valckenaer had warned against this). "Mix lips with lips" is only Aphrodite's first and tamest effort to articulate what she wants from this last encounter.

τυτθόν περ . . . ἰδέσθαι, Greg. Naz. *A.P.* 8.82.1; perhaps also Callim. *SH* 285.4 τυτθὸν ἀκοῦσαι (=*Hec.* fr. 40.4 Hollis, q.v.) and *CA* ep. adesp. 2.48 τ]υτθὰ λίπωμαι.

τὸ δ' αὖ πύματον: "again, for the last time". The latter hemistich of this line is repeated in [Theoc.] 23.40.

46 τοσσοῦτον and ὅσον are adverbial. The context gives them a temporal sense (the "quantity" of the kiss is its duration), which is picked up by ἄχρις in the next line; cf. Mimn. fr. 2.8 *IEG* ὅσον τ' ἐπὶ γῆς κίδναται ἠέλιος, *GVI* 1955.3 = the "Song of Sicilus" (Tralles, first century A.D.) ὅσον ζῇς, Ach. Tat. 4.4.8 (of a man's putting his head into the mouth of an elephant) τοσοῦτον ἐκδέχεται κεχηνώς, ὅσον ὁ ἄνθρωπος βούλεται. For the prosodic variation between the correlatives see on fr. 11.3.

ζώῃ: cf. 12, where his kiss is said to "die". Subjunctive, since ὅσον here = "as long as" (so Fantuzzi); for the lack of ἄν here and in 47 see fr. 13.14 n. Callierges' ζώει, accepted by most subsequent editors, is thus unwarranted.

47 ἀποψύξῃς: see on 9. Aor. is more likely than MS ἀποψύχῃς, esp. in view of the other aorists in this clause (ῥεύσῃ, ἀμέλξω, πίω); Adonis' completed expiration is the end in view.

ἧπαρ: the liver, representing "the innermost part", is especially appropriate here, since like our "heart" it was popularly identified since the Classical period as the seat of powerful emotions like love (Onians 84–9, Nisbet and Hubbard on Hor. *C.* 1.13.4, Courtney on Juv. 1.45); see e.g. Theoc. 11.16, 13.71, 30.10 (coni. Kraushaar); Hor. *C.* 1.25.15, 4.1.12; *Epod.* 5.37; *Epist.* 1.18.72. Cf. [Timaeus of Locri] *An. mund.* 100E τὸ δ' ἐπιθυματικὸν περὶ τὸ ἧπαρ, *Anacreont.* 33.28, Walther 1.402 no. 3428.

48 γλυκύ: a traditional epithet of love (γλυκὺς ἵμερος often in Homeric verse; cf. Alcman *PMG* 59A, Asclep. *A.P.* 12.153.3). Cf. love as "bittersweet" (fr. 14.7 n.).

φίλτρον: usually "love potion", here "love", as in Eur. *Tro.* 858–9 and *El.* 1309, *GVI* 1128.4 (Melos, third century B.C.), Moschus fr. 3.8, Mel. *A.P.* 5.212.3, Aemilianus *A.P.* 7.623.4, [Opp.] *Cyn.* 3.108, [Orph.] *Arg.* (often), Nonnus *D.* 15.400, *Anacreont.* 51.5.[100] Cf. [Theoc.] 23.1 ἀνήρ

[100] The meaning "love" may have developed not metaphorically from the meaning "love potion", but as a separate word based on the interpretation of -τρον as an abstract suffix with φιλ- (cf. Buck and Petersen 314); this would explain its having both meanings of φιλία (i.e. both familial and sexual love).

τις πολύφιλτρος ("amorous, in love"). Aphrodite uses the word designedly, likening Adonis' love to a potion that will somehow keep their love alive when he is not (cf. 49–50); the metaphor is more transparent in Plautus *Truc.* 43–5 "si semel amoris poculum accepit meri ... extemplo et ipsus periit et res et fides". Note the pun: this φίλτρον comes from a φίλημα. The anatomical meaning of the word τὸ ὑπὸ τῷ κίονι ἐν τῷ ἄνω χείλει κοῖλον (Rufus *On.* 38–9; cf. Pollux *On.* 2.90), referred to by some commentators and approved for this passage by LSJ, is unnecessary and unsuitable as obj. of ἀμέλγω, which in this sense normally refers to the thing sucked, not the thing sucked on.

ἀμέλξω: lit. "milk" (an animal); in act. or mid. vividly metaphorical for "drink, suck, drain". Cf. Aesch. *Cho.* 898 ἐξήμελξας εὐτραφὲς γάλα; of other fluids Ion fr. 26.9 *IEG*, *PMG* anon. 979 = *SH* 1001, [Theoc.] 23.25, Apollonides *A.P.* 6.239.3, Nonnus *D.* 12.321, Leont. Schol. *A.P.* 5.295.1, Macedonius *A.P.* 9.645.8.

49 ἐκ δὲ πίω τὸν ἔρωτα: for tmesis of this verb see e.g. Theoc. 2.56; ἐκ- denotes "completion, like our 'utterly'" (LSJ s.v. C.2). The basis of the metaphor is the feeling and movement of Aphrodite's mouth in action; she is identifying the yearned-for kiss with love itself. Elsewhere the metaphor refers primarily to a lover's drunken sensation of giddy happiness: Anacr. *PMG* 376.2 μεθύων ἔρωτι (cf. Ach. Tat. 1.6.1), Virg. *Aen.* 1.749 "longumque bibebat amorem,"[101] anon. *A.P.* 5.305.3 καὶ μεθύω τὸ φίλημα, πολὺν τὸν ἔρωτα πεπωκώς, *Anacreont.* 6 = *A.Pl.* 388. For kissing as drinking see Gow on Theoc. 7.70, Tarán 37–40; cf. below on 50.

φυλάξω: cf. epig. anon. (Mel.? Strato?) ap. Cameron (1993) 232 τηρῶ σοῦ τὸ φίλημα τὸ χρύσεον ὡς ἀπὸ σίμβλου | κηρίον, Ach. Tat. 2.8.1 καὶ ἐφύλαττον ἀκριβῶς ὡς θησαυρὸν τὸ φίλημα τηρῶν ἡδονῆς.

50 The reading of the principal MSS, ὥς σ' αὐτὸν τὸν Ἄδωνιν, produces a peculiar apposition – "as you yourself; as Adonis" – as if Aphrodite feared her addressee had to be reminded of his name. MS ὥς σ' is a dittography or a repetition of ὥς σε in 43–4.

Does Aphrodite mean to suck in Adonis' soul with his last breath? Bion may combine the image of the soul hovering on the lips of the dying person on its way out (see Herodas 3.4 with Headlam, Mel. *A.P.* 5.197.5) with the popular conceit that in a kiss the lovers' souls mingle,

[101] On which Servius remarks, "adlusit ad convivium. sic Anacreon: ἔρωτα πίνων" (*PMG* 450 – but this may refer not to Anacreon himself, but to one of the *Anacreontea*; for the confusion cf. Aul. Gell. 19.9.4).

for which see [Plato] *A.P.* 5.78 = Page *FGE* 162–3, Prop. 1.13.17, Petron. *Sat.* 79 and 132, Rufinus *A.P.* 5.14.3–4, Aul. Gell. 19.11 with H. Dahlmann, *Ein Gedicht des Apuleius? Gellius 19,11* (Abhl. Akad. Mainz 8.5, Wiesbaden 1979), Ach. Tat. 2.8.2 and 37.9–10, Aristaen. 2.19. See S. Gaselee, *The Criterion* 2 (1924) 349–53.[102] Mel. *A.P.* 5.171.3–4 εἴθ' ὑπ' ἐμοῖς νῦν χείλεσι χείλεα θεῖσα | ἀπνευστὶ ψυχὰν τὰν ἐν ἐμοὶ προπίοι adapts Bion's lip-mixing and love-quaffing metaphors (44, 49) to the conceit; cf. Mel. *A.P.* 12.133.5–6.

δύσμορε: the adj. is Homeric; for its application to the deceased in grave inscriptions see e.g. Phaedimus *A.P.* 7.739.5; *GVI* 1139.7 (Crete, second century B.C.), 1263.2 (Panticapaeum, second–first centuries B.C.). But the context – φεύγεις and ἔρχεαι seem gently to rebuke Adonis – recalls the Classical and later use of δύσμορος as a term of reproach, as at e.g. Soph. *Aj.* 1203, Men. *Sam.* 69 and 255, Theoc. 7.119 (where Gow notes the same use for words of similar meaning, e.g. τάλας, ἄθλιος, δύστηνος).

50–51 For the enjambed repetition of φεύγεις see [Theoc.] *Ep.* 3.5–6 ἀλλὰ τὺ φεῦγε, | φεῦγε. For the sense of the verb see on 43 κιχείω; cf. Ovid *Am.* 3.9.49 (*fugiens* = *mortuus*), *GVI* 1161.14 (Tomis, first–second century A.D.) καὶ ὁ πατήρ μου ὁ γλυκὺς θρηνεῖ ὅτι ὧδε πέφευγα.

51–2 Cf. *Il.* 22.482–4 (Andromache at the death of Hector) νῦν δὲ σὺ μὲν Ἀίδαο δόμους ὑπὸ κεύθεσι γαίης | ἔρχεαι, αὐτὰρ ἐμὲ στυγερῷ ἐνὶ πένθεϊ λείπεις | χήρην ἐν μεγάροισι (cf. 59 n.).

51 **μακρόν:** usually used of the carrying power of loud noises (e.g. *Il.* 6.66 μακρὸν ἀύσας); for the neut. sing. as adv. used of travelling (more commonly μακράν, as in fr. 13.13) cf. Callim. fr. 1.13 (suppl. Pfeiffer) and 15.

καὶ ἔρχεαι: Wakefield conjectures κατέρχεαι (cf. MS καὶ ἄρρει for καταρρεῖ in 55), noting that "multus est Bion in his ἀσυνδετοις, quae sane vehementiores affectus lugentium potenter exhibent. Vide vv. 1, 2, 29, 69, 77, 97, 98"; but καί is wanted, since ἔρχεαι εἰς Ἀχέροντα not only follows but *defines* φεύγεις μακρόν. For ἔρχεαι Pierson 53–5 conjectures οἴχεαι, noting many instances of that verb in contexts of death, e.g. Mnasalces *A.P.* 7.488.1–2 εἰς Ἀχέροντα | οἴχεαι; but ἔρχομαι is also found in such expressions (e.g. Tymnes *A.P.* 7.477.4).

102 For modern examples (e.g. Marlowe *Doctor Faustus* Act v, sc. i "Her lips suck forth my soul") see H. Stubbe, *Die Verseinlagen im Petron* (*Philologus* Suppl. 25.2, Leipzig 1933) 170; S. Mattiacci in V. Tandoi, ed., *Disiecti membra poetae* III (Foggia 1988) 203 n. 31.

εἰς Ἀχέροντα: the phrase often designates the destination of the deceased in sepulchral epigrams, e.g. *A.P.* 7.12.3 (anon.), 488.1 (Mnasalces), 648.1 (Leon. Tar.); *GVI* 1254.3 (Cyrene, third–second century B.C.), 1361.7 (Athens, second century B.C.), 1470.1 (Crete, second century B.C.). For this river representing the whole underworld (common in Hellenistic poetry: *HE* II.119) see also Soph. *Ant.* 812, Eur. fr. 860 Nauck, and esp. Theoc. 15.86 and 102 (in connexion with the death of Adonis).[103]

Fantuzzi notes that this line, along with 52 and with the repetition of φεύγεις, strongly recalls Moschus 1.13–14 μακρὰ δὲ βάλλει· | βάλλει κεἰς Ἀχέροντα καὶ εἰς Ἀίδεω βασίλεια (Wilamowitz: βασιλῆα codd.). Virg. *G.* 4.469 "Manisque adiit regemque tremendum" may imitate Bion (with "tremendum" translating στυγνόν in 52).

52 πάρ: MS καί would seem to make Acheron king of the Underworld (Ameis's motivation to emend: "nam duplex praepositio Acheronta et Plutonem distinguere videtur justo gravius"), and even if the personified river could stand for the god of the dead (a Levantine belief: Tsevat) the apposition is intolerably lame: "you are going to Acheron, a monarch both grim and fierce". A second prepositional phrase also effects a type of repetition with variation that Bion likes (cf. on 21 νήπλεκτος, 73 τοῖς). Corruption was prompted by the frequency of καί in the vicinity.

στυγνόν: "dreadful"; the basic meaning of the root is "shudder at" (cf. στυγέω and West on Hes. *Th.* 739). The adj. describes the underworld or its lord at Soph. *O.C.* 1390–1, *GVI* 1473.1 (Panticapaeum, first century B.C.); Fantuzzi compares cognate στυγερός as epithet of Hades at *Il.* 8.368, Ap. Rh. 3.810. Note the etymological connexion with the river Styx. [Theoc.] 23.19 ἄγριε παῖ καὶ στυγνέ imitates Bion here.

ἁ δὲ τάλαινα: the phrase occurs in the same position in *GVI* 1129.5 (Erythrae, first century B.C.) and Philip *A.P.* 7.186.3. For the articulated predicate see Ameis *De art.* 17; cf. Theoc. 3.24 ὤμοι ἐγών, τί πάθω; τί ὁ δύσσοος; The adj. is first attested in tragedy (masc. τάλας is Homeric).

53 ἐμμι: the Aeolic form is found in a Doric context also at Callim. fr. 197.2 (see Gow *Theoc.* I p. lxxiii n. 3); elsewhere in bucolic at [Theoc.] 20.19 and 32, later than Bion. Cf. 56.

διώκειν: cf. on κιχείω in 43. Paired with φεύγεις in the preceding line this verb recalls the traditional flight and pursuit of beloved and

[103] For a like metonymy in Mesopotamian literature see K. Tallqvist, *Sumerisch-Akkadische Namen der Totenwelt* (Stud. Or. 5.4, Helsinki 1934) 33–4.

lover: cf. Sappho fr. 1.21 L–P, Theogn. 1299, Theoc. 6.17 and 11.75, Callim. *A.P.* 12.102.5–6 (the expression is literal in *Il.* 22.158).

Aphrodite regrets her immortality in the absence of Adonis. The quasi-paradox that "death is better than a life of misery" is commonplace (e.g. Mimn. fr. 4 *IEG*; Soph. *Ant.* 461–6, *Aj.* 475–6, etc.; Hor. *A.P.* 467; Ovid *Her.* 10.82; Sen. *Phoen.* 98, *Ag.* 996). For the more sensational wish of a suffering immortal to die see already [Aesch.] *P.V.* 752–4 and fr. 193.22–6 Radt. Bion may have inspired the divine death-wishes prompted by the deaths of mortal lovers or relations in Virg. *Aen.* 12.879–84 (esp. 880–1 "possem tantos finire dolores | nunc certe, et misero fratri comes ire per umbras"; cf. U. Boella, *RSC* 27 (1979) 321–8); Ovid *Met.* 1.661–3, 10.202–3; Nonnus *D.* 11.325–7.

Aphrodite's declaration of her inability to follow Adonis may be intended to forestall an expectation that she will descend to the Underworld to retrieve him, as in a version recorded by St Cyril *Comm. Is.* 2.3 (*PG* 70.441) and perhaps known to Bion's readers (cf. 19 n.). That motif goes back to Near Eastern dying-god myths, e.g. the Ugaritic Ba'al epic wherein the goddess 'Anat, after discovering Ba'al's body and raising a lament, announces, "After Ba'al I'll descend into earth" (*ANET*^{3} 139). Cf. 98 n. on Bion's denial of an annual return like those celebrated in Near Eastern dying-god cults and Adonis cults influenced by them (Theoc. 15.102–3, 143–9; Lucian *Dea Syr.* 6).

54 πόσιν: see on line 24. The phrase τὸν ἐμὸν πόσιν appears in the same metrical position in *GVI* 1128.1 (Melos, third century B.C.).

As Fantuzzi notes, "L'esortazione di un vivo ad un dio degli Inferi – perché accolga benevolo l'anima del defunto – appare topica negli epigrammi sepolcrali ..."; he cites *GVI* 1572.1 (Thessaly, *c.* 300 B.C.) and 1576.2 (Capreae, first–second century A.D.), Leon. Tar. *A.P.* 7.67.3, Jul. Aeg. *A.P.* 7.58.2 and 59.1. It is noteworthy, however, that these all use an imperative of δέχομαι or the like; λάμβανε is more resentful, though resigned: Aphrodite is not asking her fellow goddess for benevolence. Cf. 96.

55 κρέσσων: see on fr. 6.2.

MS πάγκαλον for πᾶν καλόν is probably an intrusion of the not uncommon adj. πάγκαλος, and not, as Wilamowitz (1900) 35 n. 1 supposes, evidence of a MS tradition dating back to a time before standardized spelling eliminated cross-word assimilation. Catull. 3.13–14 "at vobis male sit, malae tenebrae | Orci, quae omnia bella devoratis" imitates Bion (see on 1). For expressions of resentment toward the rulers of the underworld see Lattimore 147–9.

ἐς σέ: Doric τέ, printed by Wilamowitz in his 1900 edition though not in his OCT, may be correct here, in view of the Theocritean model (see below); cf. 93 τύ, also in an imitation of Theocritus.

καταρρεῖ: modelled on Theoc. 1.5–6 ἐς τὲ καταρρεῖ | ἁ χίμαρος "falls to you as your due" (see fr. 9.6 n. on the sense of inevitable attraction in ῥέω); but the literal meaning recalls (esp. with 51 Ἀχέροντα) the popular belief that certain visible bodies of water flowed down to those in the land of the dead: *Il.* 2.755, Diod. Sic. 5.4.2, Strabo 5.4.5, Paus. 2.37.5. Waters like the Styx in Arcadia, the Acheron in Epirus, and the Acherusian Lake in Argolis were perhaps thought to communicate with their underworldly namesakes. See Plato *Phaedo* 111D; E. Rohde, *Psyche*[2] (Leipzig 1898) I.214 n. 2, II.12–13 n. 2; M. Ninck, *Die Bedeutung des Wassers im Kult und Leben der Alten* (*Philologus* Suppl. 14.2, Leipzig 1921) 1–4; J. ter Vrugt-Lens, *Mors Immatura* (Groningen 1960) 44–5.[104] Cf. the "harbour of Hades" in Soph. *Ant.* 1284; Leon. Tar. *A.P.* 7.264.2, 452.2, 472B; and numerous grave inscriptions. A similar image, and close to Aphrodite's complaint, is Sim. *PMG* 522 πάντα γὰρ μίαν ἱκνεῖται δασπλῆτα χάρυβδιν, | αἱ μεγάλαι τ' ἀρεταὶ καὶ ὁ πλοῦτος (cf. *CA* p. 217 ii.19).

The source of the emendation of MS καὶ ἄρρει is unclear; Stephanus (1566) prints γρ. καταρρεῖ in the margin as if he had seen it in a MS or earlier edition (his other uses of γρ. on this poem point to Callierges or the Juntine ed.). Ahrens (1854) 23 suspects the ingenuity of Ursinus, in whose 1568 text it is first printed; but note that Stephanus has been accused of attributing his own conjectures to venerable sources (see J. E. Sandys, *A History of Classical Scholarship* II (Cambridge 1908) 176–7).

56 ἐμμί: Brunck's emendation of εἰμί, based on line 53, q.v. The phrase εἰμὶ δ' ἐγώ begins Archil. fr. 1.1 *IEG* and [Hom.] *Batr.* 17.

πανάποτμος: cf. *Il.* 24.255 and esp. 24.493, beginning αὐτὰρ ἐγὼ πανάποτμος; also in [Moschus] 4.51, Nonnus *D.* 2.627.

ἀκόρεστον: "impossible to slake". The normal epic form is ἀκόρητος; Bion takes his form from tragic lyric (e.g. Aesch. *Ag.* 756 ἀκόρεστον ὀιζύν, Soph. *El.* 123 ἀκόρεστον οἰμωγάν). Found in hexameter or elegiac verse also at *GVI* 849.5 (Phrygia, first century A.D.), [Manetho] *Apot.* 6 [3].209 Koechly, Palladas *A.P.* 10.56.7, anon. *A.Pl.* 309.1.

ἀνίαν: cf. 8 n.

57 ὅ μοι θάνε echoes *Il.* 22.486 ἐπεὶ θάνες (in the same metrical position; cf. the echoes in 51–2, 59); thus ὅ probably = ὅτι "because" (cf. 14), not ὅς "who" (as R glosses it). Note the untranslatable dat. of interest, stressing Aphrodite's loss.

[104] Tsevat documents Levantine parallels to this belief.

καί σε φοβεῦμαι: "and I yield to you, defer to you". Aphrodite fears no *specific* danger from Persephone, but capitulates to her generally. This sense of the verb is rare and unknown to LSJ, but is adequately attested (see fr. 9.1 n.).[105] Cf. Plut. *Ant.* 33.3, where an astrologer tells Mark Antony that he persistently loses to Octavian at games because ὁ σὸς ... δαίμων τὸν τούτου φοβεῖται· καὶ γαῦρος ὢν καὶ ὑψηλὸς ὅταν ᾖ καθ' ἑαυτόν, ὑπ' ἐκείνου γίνεται ταπεινότερος ἐγγίσαντος καὶ ἀγεννέστερος – there φοβέομαι is defined (καί) as yielding to a power acknowledged as greater, just as Aphrodite does before the κρέσσων (55) Persephone.

58 θνᾴσκεις = ἔθανες (see on 14), in view of aor. θάνε (57) and ἔπτα.

τριπόθατε: "much yearned for, desired"; cf. *SEG* 33.1475 (Cyrenaica, first–second century A.D.) ὁ ποθητὸς Ἄδωνις, Aristaen. *Ep.* 1.8 περιπόθητος Ἄδωνις. For the adj., unattested before Bion (and perhaps applied here on the model of Theoc. 15.86 ὁ τριφίλητος Ἄδωνις), see fr. 2.15 and [Moschus] 3.51 (there of Bion himself); of Adonis also in the hymn to Attis ap. Hippolytus *Ref. haer.* 5.9.8 = Heitsch 44.2.3–5 σὲ καλοῦσι μὲν Ἀσσύριοι τριπόθητον Ἄδωνιν (early second century A.D.: T. Wolbergs, *Griechische religiöse Gedichte der ersten nachchristlichen Jahrhunderte* (Meisenheim am Glan 1971) 8, 60–3). It occurs later in [Apolinar.] *Ps.* 26.7 and 71.3.

πόθος δέ μοι ὡς ὄναρ ἔπτα: for the comparison of fleeting intangibles to dreams see *Od.* 11.222 ψυχὴ δ' ἠύτ' ὄνειρος ἀποπταμένη πεπότηται (cf. Ap. Rh. 3.446–7 with Campbell), Mimn. 5.4–5 *IEG* ἀλλ' ὀλιγοχρόνιον γίνεται ὥσπερ ὄναρ | ἥβη τιμήεσσα, [Theoc.] 27.8 τάχα γάρ σε παρέρχεται ὡς ὄναρ ἥβη. Evanescence is the chief point of comparison. Desire is conceived as a fluid, aerial substance also in Sappho fr. 22.11–12 L–P ἆς σε δηὖτε πόθος τ. [... | ἀμφιπόταται. Thus πόθος here is not concretely "beloved person" (as e.g. Edmonds and Legrand take it; Brunck prints Valckenaer's πόσις, cited already by Koppiers 77). Cf. on 60 κεστός.

ἔπτα: frr. 10.1 παρέστα and 14.3 ἔφαν argue for Wilamowitz's Dorization. Cf. the line-ending]..... ιεπτα in *SH* 902.12 (P. Hamb. II 121, second century B.C.), a fragmentary poem in bucolic dialect.

59 χήρα: R has χήρη with an alpha above the second eta, but it may

[105] Unawareness of this sense has prompted such emendations as κοὔ σε φοβεῦμαι (Barth 125, interpreting "utinam te timere possem!", as if Aphrodite were returning to the wish she hinted at in 52–3), καὶ σὲ φοβεῖται (Koppiers 77), κεἰς σὲ φορεῖται (Jacobs 53–4), and καὶ σεσόβημαι (Bergk ap. Ameis).

be doubted whether this is a correction or one of R's many instances of glossing a poetic form with the standard form. The non-Ionic form is first printed in Meineke's 2nd ed. (Berlin 1836).

ἁ Κυθέρεια: for the emphatic use of one's own name for "I" cf. *Il.* 1.240, 19.151; Aesch. *Sept.* 6; Soph. *Aj.* 98, *O.T.* 1366. Pride often motivates the device (cf. West on Hes. *Th.* 22); here perhaps the astonishing contrast between the Lady of Cythera's customary untroubled condition and her present anguish.

κενοί: "bereft" (cf. Soph. *Aj.* 986–7), parallel to χήρα, as if the Loves were orphaned by Adonis' death.

ἀνὰ δώματ': "throughout the palace". An epic phrase (as is ἀνὰ δῶμα). δώματα can be grander than mere houses, as in the divine epithet, frequent in epic, 'Ολύμπια δώματ' ἔχοντες. The elision produced by correction of MS δῶμα is Bion's only one of a noun (cf. Introd. VI.4), but may be meant to recall the epic formula, and is preferable to the un-Bionean hiatus of the MSS.

The sentiment here echoes Andromache's words at the death of Hector (*Il.* 22.483–4; cf. 24.725–6) ἐμὲ . . . λείπεις | χήρην ἐν μεγάροισι· πάις δ' ἔτι νήπιος αὔτως; the formal model is Callim. *H.* 6.105 χῆραι μὲν μάνδραι, κενεαὶ δέ μοι αὔλιες ἤδη.

60 κεστός: lit. "embroidered"; from being used in *Il.* 14.214 to describe Aphrodite's pectoral strap, endowed with powers of irresistible seduction, the adj. came to be used by itself for the strap (first attested in Callim. fr. 43.53; cf. Schol. *Il. loc. cit.*). For the nature of the article and Near Eastern parallels see C. Bonner, *AJP* 70 (1949) 1–6; C. A. Faraone, *Phoenix* 44 (1990) 222–3. Aphrodite's magic has perished – i.e. is useless, worthless – now that love has flown from her. A good parallel for the sentiment may be Prop. 1.4.25–6 "non ullo gravius temptatur Cynthia damno | quam sibi cum rapto cessat amore decus [*Kraffert*: deus *codd.*]".

τί γάρ: the explanatory force of the particle refers to the motivation of her whole speech: "I have these woes because you went hunting – why oh why did you do it?" Cf. Aristoph. *Nu.* 57; *A.P.* 5.3.5 (Antip. Thess.), 5.10.1 (Alc. Mess.).

τολμαρέ: "rash one". For the Doric long alpha cf. e.g. Theoc. 2.55 ἀνιαρέ. A prosaic and comic word (poetic is τολμήεις), but found also in Eur. *Supp.* 305, Heitsch 62.78 (Andromachus), Opp. *Hal.* 1.10, [Opp.] *Cyn.* 3.420, and often in Nonnus *D.* Adonis is θρασύς in Nonnus *D.* 29.135, and his overboldness is implicit in Ovid *Met.* 10.708–9; see Reed (1995) 336.

κυνάγεις: imperfect. This word too is prosaic. On Adonis' death in a boar hunt see 7 n.

61 καλὸς ἐών: Aphrodite hints that beautiful creatures have an obligation to take care of themselves.[106] To call the participle concessive might be too explicit; English when-clauses, informally used, can be similarly vague.

R has τοσσοῦτον, V has the unmetrical τοσοῦτον. V is just as likely to have omitted a sigma as R is to have restored one, but the repetition produced by Koechly's emendation τί τοσοῦτον is quite Bionean, and he may be right.

ἐμήναο: the middle aor. form (necessary for MS ἔμηνας) is post-Classical: Moschus fr. 2.2; [Theoc.] 20.34; *A.P.* 6.309.3 (Leon. Tar.), 9.35.2 (Antiph. Byz.) and 345.1 (Leon. Alex.); anon. *A.Pl.* 106.1. It was proposed by Brunck III.2.88, who, however, rejects it for Callierges' implausible ἔμεινας, "sustinuisti".

Understand ὥστε before θηρὶ παλαίειν, as in e.g. Mel. *A.P.* 12.147.2 τίς τόσος ἀντᾶραι καὶ πρὸς ἔρωτα μάχην, [Moschus] 3.111–12 τίς δὲ βροτὸς τοσσοῦτον ἀνάμερος ἢ κεράσαι τοι | ἢ δοῦναι καλέοντι τὸ φάρμακον (cf. Goodwin §600). μαίνομαι "desire madly" + inf. is attested late, e.g. E.N.A. 30–1 (spoken by the boar that killed Adonis) γυμνὸν τὸν εἶχε μηρόν | ἐμαινόμαν φιλᾶσαι, Timothy of Gaza (Cramer *Anec.* IV.264.12, on the he-camel) ἐν τῷ ὀχεύειν ἐὰν ἴδῃ ἄνθρωπον μαίνεται ἀνελεῖν; but that usage would leave τοσσοῦτον weak here.

παλαίειν: lit. "wrestle", here "fight, grapple with" (as possibly in *SH* anon. 901.9). Bion's inspiration may be Pind. *P.* 9.27, where Cyrene literally wrestles a lion.

The sentiment is imitated by [Tib.] 3.9.7–8 "quis furor est, quae mens densos indagine colles | claudentem teneras laedere velle manus?" (where the speaker, Sulpicia, has just implicitly compared her beloved to Adonis; see Tränkle *ad loc.* and F. Wilhelm, *RhM* 61 (1906) 96), and by Nonnus *D.* 11.288 (Dionysus to the dead Ampelus) τί χρέος ἦν, ἵνα ταῦρον ἀμείλιχον ἡνιοχεύσῃς;

62 ὧδε marking the end of a speech is Hellenistic (Führer 37 n. 14; in Homer ὧδε normally introduces speech). Cf. Alex. Aet. fr. 3.26 *CA*, Callim. *H.* 4.274, Leon. Tar. *A.P.* 7.731.5, [Theoc.] 23.49. Homeric is ὥς: cf. the very similar lines, concluding laments and introducing antiphonal mourning, at *Il.* 24.746, 760, 776.

64–6 Ahrens's doubts about the authenticity of these lines, based on diction and appropriateness to their place in the poem, are unfounded.

[106] Compare the emphasis on beauty in Ach. Tat. 1.14.2 ἐγὼ δὲ ὁ κακοδαίμων ἐχαριζόμην θηρίον μειρακίῳ καλῷ (Clinias berates himself for giving Charicles the horse that killed him).

Lang 205–6 finds that the metamorphoses make a welcome transition from Aphrodite's emotionally high-pitched lament to the more low-key details of the laying-out (cf. Buecheler (1863) 109).

64 δάκρυον: the sing. often occurs in poetry where we expect the pl. (e.g. *Il.* 16.11, *Od.* 4.153), and although we might sometimes explain it as a poetic sing. for pl. (cf. 11, 83), Greek could treat "tear" in the sing. as a collective substance (like most liquids); cf. e.g. [Hippoc.] *Pror.* 2.18.7 εἰ δὲ τὸ δάκρυον χωρέει πουλύ, *Loc. hom.* 13.9 δάκρυον ὀλίγον ἄγειν. Here with τόσον it must be so treated; Ahrens's δάκρυα δ' ... τόσσ' (prompted by δάκρυα in 66) is unnecessary.

Gods rarely weep; never at all, according to Ovid *Met.* 2.621–2, *Fasti* 4.521 (cf. Eur. *Hi.* 1396, Ovid *Am.* 3.9.46). Other exceptions are *Il.* 1.413, Callim. *H.* 6.17 (cf. *Il.* 16.459, Ovid *Met.* 4.426). Compare Aphrodite's anomalous bleeding in 22.

Παφία: Aphrodite is so called because of her famous cult in Paphos on Cyprus (cf. *Od.* 8.362–3). She is *pa-pi-a* in Cypriot cult inscriptions (O. Masson, *Les inscriptions chypriotes syllabiques* (Paris 1961) 418 s.v. Παφία); the title is first found in literature as an epithet (Aristoph. *Lys.* 556), and by the Hellenistic period was being used alone (e.g. Asclep. *A.P.* 5.158.2; Hedylus *HE* line 1839; Polystr. *A.P.* 12.91.6; [Theoc.] 27.15, 16, 56).

ἐκχέει: R has τόσον ἐγχέει, V has the unmetrical τόσσον ἐγχέει. Bion is unlikely to have written ἐγχέει ("in" what? The prefix is always felt in this compound, which usually refers to drinks), and most recent editors have trusted V's τόσσον and followed J. P. d'Orville, *Miscellaneae observationes criticae* IV (Amsterdam 1734) 367 in emending the verb to χέει. The prefix must be accounted for, however, and we had better accept (with Ahrens and Gallavotti) Heinsius' ἐκχέει and regard V's τόσσον as an error (cf. his τόσσον for τὸ σὸν in 70). Note that τόσον ἐκχέει produces a line beginning with four dactyls – Bion's favourite pattern – whereas τόσσον χέει yields the pattern DDSD..., which he avoids in this poem (though it occurs seven times in the frr.). If the poet had wanted χέει he could have written δάκρυον ἁ Κυθέρεια τόσον χέει. For ἐκχέω used of tears see Plato *Symp.* 215E μοι ... δάκρυα ἐκχεῖται (cf. *Tim.* 68A, Plut. *Alc.* 6.1), Ap. Rh. 3.705 τὸ δὲ πολλὸν ὑπεξέχυτ' αὐτίκα δάκρυ (which incidentally gives an example of "tear" in the sing. with an adj. of quantity; cf. above).

For the prosodic variation between the correlatives see fr. 11.3 n.; cf. 46 above.

65 χέει: for the repetition of a compound verb by a simple see on 2 ὤλετο.

τὰ δὲ πάντα: suggesting the individual teardrops and drops of blood.

ποτὶ χθονί: the phrase occurs in *Od.* 8.378 and *H.H.* 3.459 (both times in this position); v.l. at *Il.* 21.426. Here pregnant with a sense of motion: "once they reach the ground".

66 On contrastive δέ not preceded by μέν see Denniston 165 (cf. fr. 15.1).

Flower metamorphoses seem to have first gained literary currency in the Hellenistic period (Forbes Irving 129). A more widespread story than Bion's was that Adonis' blood produced the anemone; cf. Nic. fr. 65 Schneider = Schol. Theoc. 5.92F, Ovid *Met.* 10.728–39. Adonis and anemones may have been connected in *SH* 902.16–18 (P. Hamburg. II 201, second century B.C.), a very fragmentary hexameter poem in bucolic dialect. The Adonidian origins of the anemone, in fact, may go back to one of his Near Eastern counterparts: in Arabic the flower is called *shaqâ'iq an-Nu'mân*, of which the second term (the first is obscure) contains the title "pleasant" given to Western Semitic gods (W. F. Albright, *History, Archeology, and Christian Humanism* (New York 1964) 172–3). Bion has transferred the source of the anemone to the tears of Aphrodite and perhaps invented the story of the rose (unattested before him; Servius mentions it on *Ecl.* 10.18) in order to accommodate two flower-myths, and thus to assimilate the goddess to her beloved as often (see on 25). The growth of the rose may also suggest why it is Aphrodite's special flower (Forbes Irving 129).

A late αἴτιον, influenced by Bion (cf. line 22), holds that roses first acquired their redness from the blood shed by Aphrodite as she ran through the briars on her way to the dying Adonis: Aphthon. *Prog.* 2, Philostr. *Epist.* 4, *Perv. Ven.* 22–3, Claudian *Rapt.* 2.122–3 (see J.-L. Charlet, *InvLuc* 9 (1987) 39–44), Procop. *Epist.* 8, *Anth. lat.* 85 and 366.3–4 Riese, *Geop.* 11.17. Philostr. *Epist.* 1 refers to both Bion's version and the other: ὑπόδεξαι αὐτὰ (sc. roses) εὐμενῶς, ἢ ὡς Ἀδώνιδος ὑπομνήματα, ἢ ὡς Ἀφροδίτης βαφήν.[107]

68 **ἐνὶ δρυμοῖσι:** see 20 n. [Theoc.] 20.35–6 (Aphrodite) τὸν Ἄδωνιν | ἐν δρυμοῖσι φίλασε καὶ ἐν δρυμοῖσιν ἔκλαυσεν is an allusion (also to lines 13–14). Bion's phrase recurs in Triph. 369, Colluth. 357.

τὸν ἀνέρα: cf. 29.

μύρεο: transitive ("weep for") also in Ap. Rh. 3.657, [Moschus] 3.73

[107] Tzetzes' report on Lycophr. 831 that Adonis' blood changed the anemone from white to red when he fell dying on it sounds like a confusion of Nic. frr. 65 and 120 Schneider, influenced by the fable of the rose.

(cf. 27), Heitsch 30.82 (P. Berol. 10559B, fourth century A.D.), Greg. Naz. *A.P.* 8.134.4.

This verse, reprising and echoing line 3, marks the fulcrum of the chiasmus that structures the poem: the movement from the palace out into the wilderness and into mourning now turns back to the palace. Cf. 79 n.

69 The sense of 69–70 is clear: it is improper to let Adonis lie on the forest floor; he must have a proper bier. The MSS state "a lonely pile of leaves is a good bed for Adonis". This is obviously wrong, and Ahrens, diagnosing dittography, emended the first ἐστι to οὐκ. Trouble still lies in the word στιβάς, however, since this normally denotes an improvised bed of leafy branches or a humble pallet (cf. *GP* II.121), and so is poorly differentiated from φυλλάς. στιβάς = κλίνη in Agathias *A.P.* 5.267.4 and 9.643.7; but here we want a term without humble connotations (could στιβάς, originating as a gloss on φυλλάς, have ousted another word?). Ahrens (1854) 67 seems to take φυλλὰς ἐρήμα in apposition to στιβάς (with a comma after Ἀδώνιδι): "A mere στιβάς, a lonely pile of leaves, is not good for Adonis". For the gender of predicate ἀγαθά in this case (one would expect ἀγαθόν) see West on Hes. *Th.* 864, *Op.* 279 (where he cites Theogn. 1171) and 471–2.

ἐρήμα: "lonely, desolate", esp. of things in the wilderness, e.g. Callim. *H.* 4.243 ἐνὶ σπιλάδεσσιν ἐρήμοις, *CA* lyr. adesp. 7.3 ἐρῆμον δρίος.

70 νῦν: V has the unmetrical νῦν δέ, R has τὺ δέ (whence Morel's τόδε) with the rest of this line and the next addressed to Adonis: Triclinius found νῦν δέ in his exemplar and did some rewriting to repair the metre. I have rejected Hiller's emendation καί for νῦν δέ (p. 87: "νῦν δέ war ursprünglich übergeschrieben, um das logische Verhältnis zwischen V. 68 f. und V. 70 zu verdeutlichen"; cf. 13, 74) on the ground that καί is unlikely to have attracted such exegetical attention. We should take δέ as an error (cf. Wilamowitz (1900) 35) and accept νῦν alone as what Bion wrote, emphasizing the contrast between present and past and the fact that Adonis is now definitively dead. Construe νῦν closely with νεκρός: "now that he is dead" (thus avoiding a strong word-break after contracted fourth biceps).

71 καὶ νέκυς ὤν: concessive. The phrase reappears in anon. *A.P.* 7.319.1 and *GVI* 2040.14 (Pergamum, first–second century A.D.), the latter an imitation of Bion (preceded by οἷον δὲ ὑπνώων). νέκυς = νεκρός. The nom. and acc. sing. forms with short upsilon are un-Homeric and are attested first in Euripidean lyric (e.g. *Supp.* 70, *Alc.* 94 and 599), but may be original (R. S. P. Beekes, *Glotta* 51 (1973) 236–8); they are common in Hellenistic poetry (e.g. Theoc. 22.177, Ap. Rh. 4.480), regular in the *Anthology*.

καλός ἐστι, καλὸς νέκυς: repetition of καλός registers ecstatic admiration (cf. 1 n.): Callim. *A.P.* 12.43.5 (see Koenen 87) and 51.3, [Theoc.] 8.73, Euphor. fr. 175.1 *CA*, Mel. *A.P.* 12.154.3, anon. *A.P.* 12.62.1 and 130.1. For the persistence of beauty after death, a motif that appears first here, cf. Virg. *Aen.* 11.70, where the dead Pallas is compared to a plucked flower "cui nec fulgor adhuc nec dum sua forma recessit"; Longus 4.8 ὑπήνθει καὶ ἔλαμπε καὶ ἦν ἔτι καλὸν καὶ κείμενον (of an uprooted flower: cf. Ach. Tat. 1.13.3); Philostr. *Im.* 2.4.4; Nonnus *D.* 11.250 and 280–7, esp. 282 καὶ νέκυός περ ἐόντος ἔτι στίλβουσι παρειαί; Quintus 1.659–68. The motif can be understood as a typically Hellenistic revaluation of *Il.* 22.71–3 νέῳ δέ τε πάντ' ἐπέοικεν | ἀρηικταμένῳ ... πάντα δὲ καλὰ θανόντι περ (cf. Tyrt. fr. 10.27–30 *IEG*), where the emphasis is not on the sensual beauty of the corpse, but on the physical properties that mark an able warrior in his prime.

οἷα καθεύδων: "as if asleep" (for this sense of οἷα cf. e.g. Callim. *H.* 6.89). For the comparison of death to sleep (first in *Il.* 11.241, 14.482–3; cf. *Od.* 13.79–80) see M. B. Ogle, *MAAR* 11 (1933) 81–117; Lattimore 164–5. Cf. the metaphorical use of κοιμάω and εὐνάζω, e.g. Soph. *O.T.* 961 σμικρὰ παλαιὰ σώματ' εὐνάζει ῥοπή. The trope is esp. popular in the Hellenistic period (e.g. Asclep. *A.P.* 12.50.8; Theoc. 22.204; Callim. *A.P.* 7.451.1, 459.4, 725.3; [Moschus] 3.104). The identification of sleep, death, and love, whose common locus for Adonis is Aphrodite's bed, is also old (e.g. Alcman *PMG* 3.61–2); see Vermeule 145–77, 243 n. 1. Cf. 73.

72 κάτθεο: for the sense of "laying out" a dead body cf. *Od.* 24.190 (and 24.44, where the verb is active).

V's abbreviation for νιν here looks very much like his abbreviation for καί, and so gave rise through an intermediary to Aldus' καί (X, also descended from V, has νιν).

μαλακοῖς ἐνὶ φάρεσι: μαλακός is a standing epithet of bedding; cf. e.g. *Il.* 9.618, *Od.* 20.58, *H.H.* 5.158, and esp. Theoc. 15.125, where the covers on Adonis' nuptial bed are μαλακώτεροι ὕπνω and πορφύρεοι (as in 79 below). For φάρη as bedcovers see 3 n.

φάρεσι τοῖς: for Meineke's emendation see his first ed., *Theocriti Bionis et Moschi carmina* (Leipzig 1825) 151.

For the image in this line and the next cf. Virg. *Aen.* 6.221–2 (of the dead Misenus) "purpureasque super vestis (cf. 79), velamina nota, | coniciunt".

73 τοῖς: we could alternatively read οἷς here with Wakefield and φάρεσιν οἷς in 72 with Stephanus (mismatched relatives – οἷς ... τοῖς – are unlikely). The repetition is characteristic, and is esp. like that of ὡς in 43–4, introducing and then expanding upon an idea. Emendation to ὥς "when", proposed by Buecheler (1863) 110 and accepted by Gow, is paleographically unfounded, and a defining temporal clause is not needed or wanted. The imperfects in 72–3 are habitual: "Lay him down in the soft sheets in which he used to spend the night, in which at your side he laboured through holy sleep".

τεῦς: Bion's avoidance of hiatus makes it likely that the more familiar σεῦ has replaced an original τεῦς (or elided σεῖο, as M. L. West suggests to me).

ἀνὰ νύκτα: the striking phrase, "through the night" = "all night long", derives from *Il.* 14.80 οὐ γάρ τις νέμεσις φυγέειν κακόν, οὐδ' ἀνὰ νύκτα, where, however, the preposition is spatial, not temporal, and recalls the conception of νύξ as a space of darkness like its occasional synonym σκότος (cf. the Homeric phrase διὰ νύκτα); see R. Dyer, *Glotta* 52 (1974) 31–6. The phrase recurs in Bion's sense at [Theoc.] 20.45 μώνα δ' ἀνὰ νύκτα καθεύδοι (possibly an imitation of Bion), Strato *A.P.* 12.11.1, John of Gaza *Anacr.* 6.93 (Bergk 348).

τὸν ἱερὸν ὕπνον ἐμόχθει: "laboured through holy sleep" (on the verb cf. fr. 8.3 n.). Doubts that ὕπνον is to be taken literally, which go back to R's gloss συνεγένετό σοι, are unjustified ("Nocturnas Veneris et Adonidis voluptates castissimis verbis designat poeta": Heskin).[108] The comparison of death to sleep that governs lines 70–1 is furthered here: as David Leitão observes to me, ἐμόχθει boldly evokes the restless tossing and turning of a body asleep, and thus the contrast between the life coursing through Adonis then and his deadly stillness now, despite the constancy of his superficial appearance.[109] For the phrase ἱερὸν ὕπνον see Callim. *A.P.* 7.451.1, there a euphemism for death; here sleep is ἱερός because it was beside a goddess (see on 22).

74 παγχρύσῳ: Wilamowitz's παγχρυσέῳ would be the regular form in hexameter verse (πάγχρυσος is used in lyric and drama, though also,

[108] The literal meaning is also primary in [Bion] 2.26 σπεύδων κοινὸν ἐς ὕπνον, though more than sleep is implied there. Voss's syntactically impossible ἐμίχθη (p. 194), accepted by many, was doubtless the brainstorm of a moment, best forgotten.

[109] Recall that Hellenistic art often characterizes sleepers – e.g. Ariadne and the "Barberini Faun" – as surprisingly restless. Fantuzzi's hesitant suggestion that Adonis suffered from insomnia due to the distracting presence of the goddess at his side is trivial and ignores the governing metaphor.

very late, in Agathias *A.P.* 9.153.3 and Macedonius *A.P.* 11.380.3; cf. Bulloch on Callim. *H.* 5.31), but Bion elsewhere eschews an epic form for another (cf. 56 ἀκόρεστον). Note, however, that Wilamowitz's emendation without synizesis might give a more dactylic line, since the upsilon of χρύσεος is sometimes short in choral and tragic lyric (LSJ s.v.; for the possibility in Callim. *H.* 2.99, 3.111, and 4.39 see Hollis *Hec.* 19 n. 29); the pattern SSDS ... is paralleled in Bion only by fr. 8.9 (with the same pattern of word-breaks as here).

The furnishings of divine beings are naturally as elaborate as the human imagination allows: cf. the golden floor and drinking vessels of the gods in *Il.* 4.2–3, their golden equipage in Callim. *H.* 2.32–4 and 3.110–12, and Adonis' bed at Theoc. 15.123–7. Cf. Verdenius on Pind. *O.* 3.19. Perhaps it is especially appropriate that Aphrodite's bed be "all-golden", since χρυσῆ is an old epithet of hers (*Il.* 3.64, *Cypr.* fr. 5.4 *EGF*, Mimn. fr. 1.1 *IEG*, etc.). Her παστάς (cover or canopy for the marriage bed) is golden in Moero *A.P.* 6.119.1; her θάλαμοι are golden in Asclep. *A.P.* 5.194.2.

κλιντῆρι: attested in early poetry only at *Od.* 18.190, but common in the Hellenistic period, e.g. Theoc. 2.86 and 113, 24.43; Callim. fr. 191.41; Ap. Rh. 3.1159; Antiph. Byz. *A.P.* 7.634.1.

πρόθες: second pers. sing. aor. act. imper. of προτίθημι, "lay him out". In contrast with κάτθεο in 72, πρόθες emphasizes the placing of the corpse on view and in effect means "prepare him for the *prothesis*" (the lying in state: D. C. Kurtz and J. Boardman, *Greek Burial Customs* (London 1971) 143–4; Alexiou 5–6; R. Garland, *The Greek Way of Death* (London 1985) 23–31), which will soon be described. This conjecture of Edward Courtney improves on Platt's πόθες ("receive" or "admit" him to your bed), which puts Aphrodite herself in the bed (and as Platt admits we would expect the paleographically less likely middle ποθοῦ).[110] Platt rightly scorns attempts to attach παγχρύσῳ κλιντῆρι to the previous sentence and make the bed the subject of V's ποθεῖ. Fantuzzi (punctuating after κλιντῆρι, not after ἐμόχθει) accepts R's imper. πόθει; but the commands in this section concern the laying-out rituals, not the proper emotional state of the bereaved (and has she not made it abundantly clear that she does love and miss him?). The corruption will have been partly psychological, due to the mood of πόθος throughout the poem (cf. 58).

καί: "although". Cf. 71.

στυγνόν: "to be shuddered at, horrendous" (cf. 52 n.). The adj.

[110] A. Platt, *JPh* 34 (1918) 149.

reflects Aphrodite's viewpoint and continues the contrast between the dreadful (though still beautiful: 71) corpse and the splendid bed in which it is nevertheless to be laid (cf. 70–1). There are imitations in [Moschus] 3.67 καὶ στυγνὸν (PS alii: στυγνοὶ LVR) περὶ σῶμα τεὸν κλαίουσιν Ἔρωτες (in a comparison of Bion to his own Adonis) and E.N.A. 3.

Consideration should be given to Stier's proposal (p. 17) to read line 71 (καὶ νέκυς ὢν καλός ἐστι, καλὸς νέκυς, οἷα καθεύδων) after 74. Placed here, 71 would serve to correct the impression created by στυγνόν and would nicely sum up the comparison of sleep to death in 68–74. That νέκυς in 71 picks up νεκρός in 70, however, argues in favour of the traditional order.

75 βάλλε δέ νιν στεφάνοισι καὶ ἄνθεσι: cf. Pind. *P.* 8.57 Ἀλκμᾶνα στεφάνοισι βάλλω, denoting pelting. The idea here is the heaping up of the corpse with flowers (cf. Virg. *Aen.* 6.884, quoted below). Consideration, however, should be given to the emendations of Briggs, who would keep MS ἐνί and change the datives to accusatives, so that we could read a much smoother passage:

> παγχρύσῳ κλιντῆρι πρόθες καὶ στυγνὸν Ἄδωνιν,
> βάλλε δ' ἐνὶ στεφάνως τε καὶ ἄνθεα πάντα σὺν αὐτῷ·
> ὡς τῆνος τέθνακε καὶ ἄνθεα πάντ' ἐμαράνθη.

This relieves the awkward intrusion of the ὡς clause and the clumsy reinception of the sentence in 76; καὶ ἄνθεα πάντα in the same position two lines in a row is characterisic (cf. on 30 καλόν). The accusatives would have been changed to datives through a failure to understand the adverbial function of ἐνί ("on the κλιντήρ"; cf. *Od.* 18.190, Theoc. 2.86); an obstacle to the emendations is that πάντα would have been left intact (though it could have re-entered from 76).

σὺν αὐτῷ: cf. 31, [Moschus] 3.11. Wilamowitz (1900), followed by Gow, punctuates both after ἄνθεσι and at line-end, translating "die sind schon bei Adonis" (cf. pp. 46–7); but this makes poor syntax and poor sense.

For the custom of laying garlands on a corpse see e.g. Eur. *Phoen.* 1632, *H.F.* 526, *Tro.* 1143–4; Lucian *De luctu* 12. Brenk 223 sees here a possible source for Anchises' words on the death of Marcellus "manibus date lilia plenis, | purpureos spargam flores animamque nepotis | his saltem accumulem donis" (*Aen.* 6.883–5); for Virgil's habitual recourse to Bionean imagery when the death of a youth is his subject see Introd. VIII.

76 ὡς: "as" or "since"?

καί: "also".

ἐμαράνθη: "have wilted"; cf. 41 n. "An quisquam credet", demands Ahrens (1854) 70, "serta et flores, quibus spargebatur Adonis, jam flaccuisse, antequam spargerentur?" No doubt the flowers have died in sympathy with Adonis and so must join him on the bier (cf. the universal sympathy in 31–9, and see on 12 θνᾴσκει); the conceit is strained, but our author and his audience liked such rhetorical effects (cf. the reddened flowers in 35). The imitation in [Moschus] 3.32, ending τὰ δ' ἄνθεα πάντ' ἐμαράνθη, discourages emendation of the verb to a command form,[111] attractively parallel to ὀλλύσθω in 78. C. Hartung's ἀλλά for πάντα in 75 (*Philologus* 41 (1882) 348), effecting a self-correction by the narrator ("on second thought, *don't* strew flowers ..."), is unnecessary.

Fantuzzi sees an aetiology-producing allusion to the ritual "gardens of Adonis", potted seedlings that decorated his Athenian festival and were then left to wilt (in imitation of the dead youth, according to [Diogenian.] 1.14 (L–S 1.183)); these seedlings, however, are identified as fennel and lettuce (Hesych. and *Suda* s.v. Ἀδώνιδος κῆποι) or wheat and barley (Schol. Theoc. 15.112/113), not flowers.[112] More pertinent are internal connexions: imagery elsewhere in this poem associates Adonis' life and death with those of flowers (11, 35, 41); for the metaphor cf. *Il.* 8.306–8, Virg. *Aen.* 9.435–7, Lattimore 195–7, Alexiou 195–6.

Bion likes the repetition of πάντα: see on fr. 2.17.

77 Συρίοισιν: in place of the unmetrical μύροισιν of V, which has intruded from line-end, one expects an epithet for ἀλείφασι, but the bland καλοῖσιν of R is only the unimaginative guess of one who saw μύροισιν in his exemplar. "Syrian" is a standing epithet of perfumes and incense: cf. e.g. Aesch. *Ag.* 1312, Eur. *Ba.* 144, Theoc. 15.114 (at the Adonia), Philod. *A.P.* 11.34.2. Syria was famous for perfumes of many kinds (Apollonius of Herophila ap. Ath. 15.689A).

Note the elegant variation: ἄλειφαρ and μύρον both designate oils used to protect the skin from the dry climate; they were scented from earliest times and were in effect perfumes. For ῥαῖνε ... μύροισι see

[111] Most plausible is J. Sitzler's aor. act. imper. πάντα μαρᾶνον "make all flowers wilt too" (*JAW* 178 (1919) 146). Cf. J. M. Edmonds, *CR* 27 (1913) 77.

[112] Cf. Reed (1995) 319 n. 11, 323–8, 338–40. In the Imperial period we hear of galleries of potted flowering plants called "gardens of Adonis", unconnected to the cult: Philostr. *Vit. Ap.* 7.32, *SEG* 7.72; cf. Atallah 225–6.

Polyb. 30.25.17 μύροις ἔρραινον, Mel. *A.P.* 12.132A.5 μύροις δ' ἔρρανε. For redoubled ῥαῖνε see Posid. *A.P.* 5.134.1–2.

For the custom of anointing a corpse cf. e.g. *Il.* 18.351 (Patroclus' wounds are covered with ἄλειφαρ), C. W. Shelmerdine, *The Perfume Industry of Mycenaean Pylos* (Göteborg 1985) 125–7. Aphrodite's anointing of Adonis (dead or alive?) with nectar is alluded to in Nossis *A.P.* 6.275.4.

78 ὀλλύσθω: "be spent, used", like Lat. *pereo*, with the notion of squandering and wasting. This is how perfumes "die". Cf. on 12 θνᾴσκει.

μύρον: a term of endearment – e.g. "let all sweet things die; your sweetheart has died" – as in Marc. Arg. *A.P.* 5.113.3–4 ἡ δὲ πάρος σε καλεῦσα μύρον καὶ τερπνὸν Ἄδωνιν | Μηνοφίλα νῦν σου τοὔνομα πυνθάνεται, anon. *A.P.* 5.90 πέμπω σοι μύρον ἡδύ, μύρῳ τὸ μύρον θεραπεύων (the latter parallels Bion's pun). Cf. Plautus *Most.* 309 "vin unguenta? – quid opust? cum stacta accubo". The idea of smell used in this way is no more bizarre than that of taste in our "honey" or "sweetie-pie" or the like (or in Lat. *mel*); its origins are suggested in Marc. Arg. *A.P.* 5.118.1 δεκάκις μύρον ὄσδεις (cf. anon. *A.P.* 5.91).[113]

Ahrens conjectures a scene-changing repetition of line 6 after this line to break up the description of the laying-out between 68 and 86 (cf. 6, 15, 28, etc.); Matthews (1991) prefers a repetition of 28.

79 ἁβρός: the epithet comes from Sappho fr. 140A.1 L–P ἄβρος Ἄδωνις. In Sappho's poetry ἀβροσύνη is a key value, connoting Eastern sensuality and high-class pleasure (cf. frr. 2.14, 58.25, 128.1; see L. Kurke, *ClAnt* 11 (1992) 91–120, esp. 91–101); the most suggestive parallel to her application of the term to Adonis is fr. 44.7 L–P ἄβραν Ἀνδρομάχαν: the poet sees in the new bride of Hector and in the minion of Aphrodite the same voluptuousness she prizes. Adonis is ἁβρός also in Nonnus *D.* 6.365 and Proclus *H.* 1.26 (ἁβροκόμης in [Orph.] *H.* 56.2).

εἵμασι: here "bedcovers", lit. "garments"; cf. φάρεσι in 3 and 72.

πορφυρέοισιν: see on 3. Crimson-dyed covers, richly coloured and having royal and divine connotations, may have been traditional for the bed of Adonis; cf. his marriage bed in Theoc. 15.125. In Virg. *Aen.* 6.221 *purpureae vestes* cover the bier of Misenus. For the whole expression cf. (of clothing) *SH* 958.15 π]ορφυρέοισιν ἐν εἵμασι; [Manetho] *Apot.* 1 [5].101, 5 [6].259 Koechly.

[113] The same notion underlies given names like "Myron", and so must be old; for names derived from perfumes see Bechtel 602.

This line, echoing 7, helps effect the chiasmus that structures the poem (cf. on 68): then he lay on the mountainside, now he lies amid the luxury of Aphrodite's palace. Note that whereas κεῖται in 7 connoted "he lies dead", κέκλιται is lit. "he has been made to recline"; ἁβρός and the crimson-dyed sheets reinforce the softer image.

80 ἀναστενάχουσιν: for intensive ἀνα- see LSJ s.v. G.2 (though Thesleff §255 disputes that the prefix is truly intensive, maintaining that in such verbs as this it connotes rather "a 'breaking forth' of a sound"). For the verb used of antiphonal lamentation at the *prothesis* see *Il.* 18.315 (cf. στενάχοντο in 24.722, 746).

81 ἐπ': "over, in honour of" a deceased person, as in e.g. *Il.* 23.776 οὖς ἐπὶ Πατρόκλῳ πέφνεν πόδας ὠκὺς Ἀχιλλεύς. For hair-cutting as a mourning ritual (of both sexes) see e.g. *Od.* 4.198 and 24.46, Soph. *El.* 448–50, Eur. *Tro.* 480, Callim. *H.* 3.126 κείρονται δὲ γέροντες ἐφ' υἱάσιν; cf. Garvie on Aesch. *Cho.* 6.

81–5 χὢ μὲν ... ὃς δ' ... κτλ.: juxtaposition of demonstrative ὅ and relative ὅς used demonstratively occurs as early as Phocyl. fr. 1.1 (= Demodocus fr. 2.1 *IEG*), but is mostly a later affectation. Fantuzzi (on 81; cf. A. Naeke, *Opuscula philologica* II (Bonn 1842) 179) notes the popularity of the figure among epigrammatists of the second–first centuries B.C., e.g. *A.P.* 6.14.5 (Antip. Sid.), 12.94.3–4 (Mel.), 6.187.5–6 (Alph. Mit.); in bucolic Ameis *De art.* 7 notes [Theoc.] 27.69–71, [Moschus] 3.76–7. For later examples see Nonnus *D.* 17.145–9, 38.368, 47.119–20; Macedonius *A.P.* 11.27.5–6.

In this scene Bion is adapting an artistic motif; cf. Aëtion's painting of the marriage of Alexander and Roxane (described by Lucian *Herod.* 5), where a flock of winged Erotes assists at the nuptials, each with his own task. Longepierre, comparing Theoc. 15.120–2, suggests that Bion is reflecting festal scenery. A series of paintings that may in turn take inspiration from Bion's description are those Pompeian frescoes of the dying Adonis in which one Love supports Adonis' arm, another squeezes a sponge over a basin, and so on (*LIMC* I.1.226 no. 35). Cf. E.N.A. 11–14. For a similar scene of activity around a bier cf. Virg. *Aen.* 6.218–19 (on Misenus; 220–2 may echo Bion 79) "pars calidos latices et aëna undantia flammis | expediunt, corpusque lavant frigentis et unguunt".

82 ἐπὶ ... ἔβαλλ': tmesis. The verb is used of strewing hair on the corpse of Patroclus in *Il.* 23.135; here the Loves strew their own instruments on the bier as funeral offerings, as in the imitation by Ovid *Am.* 3.9.7–8 (at the pyre of Tibullus) "ecce puer Veneris fert eversamque pharetram | et fractos arcus et sine luce facem". The Loves' equipment is now worthless, like Aphrodite's κεστός (see 60 n.).

I have preferred Koennecke's emendation to Wilamowitz's ἔβαλλεν ὃ as being closer to the implausible MS reading ἐπὶ τόξον ἔβαιν' "went onto the bow",[114] though less dactylic; note that ἔβαλλ', ὃ δ' ἐΰπτερον (for the diaeresis see Antip. Sid. *A.P.* 9.603.5, Nonnus *D.* 39.324) would give a purely dactylic line – Bion's favourite pattern – whereas in this poem he avoids the opening DDSD (cf. 64 n.). The violation of Meyer's second law (prohibiting word-break at the second trochee before masculine third-foot caesura) is palliated both by the elision and by a strong sense-break at the caesura (cf. Introd. VI.3).

ὃς δ' εὔπτερον ἄγε φαρέτραν: "... and this one brought his feathered quiver ...". This reading, with the second Aldine's emendation of R's ὃς δ' εὔπτερον αὖ γε, has lost favour since the nineteenth century.[115] The reading of the Juntine and of recent editors, ὃς δὲ πτερόν, ὃς δὲ φαρέτραν (based on the more sincere V) is attractive, since bow, quiver, and πτερόν (usually "wing", here presumably "feather") are conventional attributes of Eros in Hellenistic poetry (e.g. Asclep. *A.P.* 12.75.1, Mel. *A.P.* 12.144.1–2, *Anacreont.* 33.17–18); Mel. *A.P.* 12.76.1–2 offers an especially close parallel to this reading: εἰ μὴ τόξον Ἔρως μηδὲ πτερὰ μηδὲ φαρέτραν | ... εἶχε.... Nevertheless it entails problems. The first involves the aptness of the feather plucked from the Love's wing, a touching personal gift, but one that, as Hopkinson notes, "does not fit well with the other articles of equipment". More seriously problematic is the supposition that Triclinius read ὃς δ' ἔπτερον ὃς δὲ φαρέτραν in the hyparchetype of V and R, did not realize that the only difficulty was with a word-break, and emended ἔπτερον into an epithet for the quiver, replacing the intelligible ὃς δέ with a bit of particular fluff (αὖ γε).[116] It is surely more plausible that ὃς δέ is a careless repetition of

[114] Editors before Wilamowitz took this to mean "trampled the bow", seeing the Loves "vim et violentiam inferentes armis illis, quae exitium Adonidi adduxerant" (so Schmitz 17, as if Adonis had been hunting the boar with a bow and arrows).

[115] Commentators used to mistranslate ἄγε as a Doric imperf. of ἄγνυμι (surely ἄγνυ) and take it as part of the Loves' mistreatment of the weaponry (see n. above). Cf. Pope's allusion in *Pastorals* 4.24 "And break your bows, as when Adonis died".

[116] Cf. his αὖ γε at Aristoph. *Ran.* 437 (found in MSS derived from his second edition), where he was supplying *missing* syllables to complete the metre. I owe this information to Kenneth Dover. Cf. Campbell on Moschus 2.34.

something V had already written twice in this line (cf. his ἅδ' ἁ in 52); it is also easier to explain the corruption of δ' εὔπτερον, involving the omission of upsilon, than that of δὲ πτερόν to δ' ἔπτερον (note esp. the accentuation). The corruption of ἆγε to αὖ γε will have been easy. Thus on balance it is safer to take Meleager's parallel as a misleading coincidence, or as a witty adaptation of our passage to an epigrammatic convention. Bion's Loves bring arrows, bow, and quiver (the last with a neat epithet): we can dispense with the incongruous feather.

εὔπτερον: "feathered", for the exposed fletching of the arrows inside, or more learnedly "full of arrows" (see Eur. *Hel.* 76 for πτερόν = "arrow"). The epithet is applied to arrows themselves in [Opp.] *Cyn.* 1.153, Nonnus *D.* 39.324. For the pattern adj. + φαρέτρα in this position cf. e.g. *Il.* 1.45, Theoc. 17.30, [Theoc.] 25.206 and 265.

ἆγε: this metrical position is normal for the imperf. of ἄγω.[117] In the sense "bring" the verb most often takes an animate obj. (cf. Ammonius *Diff.* 4 ἄγεται μὲν γὰρ τὰ ἔμψυχα, φέρεται δὲ τὰ ἄψυχα), but cf. e.g. *Il.* 11.632 δέπας περικαλλές, ὃ οἴκοθεν ἦγ' ὁ γεραιός.

φαρέτραν: Ahrens incorrectly reports this as R's reading (R uses a different final sign for -αν). The Doricized form is first printed by Brunck, but Ahrens (1854) says that it occurs in a marginal note in the copy of the Juntine edition that he inspected at Leipzig.

83–4 In this description of a Love or Loves bringing water in a golden bowl or bowls the two principal MSS give widely divergent readings:

V ὃς δὲ λέβητος | χρυσίη φορίησιν ὕδωρ.
R ὃς δὲ λέβησι | χρυσίοις φορέοισιν ὕδωρ.

There is only one bowl: Triclinius is more likely to have adjusted λέβητι to λέβησι to conform to his χρυσίοις (i.e. χρυσείοις) than V is to have changed an original λέβησι to the gen. sing. (his λέβητος is due to a repetition of -ος from ὅς or Ἀδώνιδος). R's χρυσίοις in turn[118] is a reconstruction of an original χρυσίης; V copied unquestioningly but omitted the final sigma. Thus the reading of the hyparchetype was:

ὃς δὲ λέβητι | χρυσίης φορίησιν (or -έοισιν) ὕδωρ.

χρυσίης may anticipate φορίησιν; the original form was of course χρυ-

[117] Cf. D. L. Hersey, *"To Lead," in Greek Epic: Oral Versification Technique Connected with the Verb Ago* (diss. Stanford 1995) 245–53.

[118] "χρυσείοις oder χρυσίοις" notes Hiller 35; but the first iota is clearly that, not a compendium for ει.

σίῳ (i.e. χρυσείῳ). The plural form of the verb (see 84 n.) necessitates Graefe's οἳ (p. 119), corrupted to ὅς under the influence of the many instances of ὅς in these lines. At least two Loves are thus bringing a golden bowl full of water too heavy for one to carry in flight:

οἳ δὲ λέβητι | χρυσείῳ φορέοισιν ὕδωρ.

83 πέδιλον: presumably both shoes are meant (cf. χείλεος in 11), as with σάμβαλον in Callim. fr. 631. The term can denote any type of footwear; in art Adonis is commonly depicted wearing laced hunting boots, which Atallah 77 wishes to identify as the eponyms of ἀδωνάρια (a kind of boot, usually derived from alpha privative + Lat. *donaria*; see LSJ s.v.).

λέβητι: "a basin, a big bowl". Cf. *Od.* 3.440–1 χέρνιβα ... ἐν ἀνθεμόεντι λέβητι | ἤλυθεν ἐκ θαλάμοιο φέρων. For the custom of washing the corpse cf. e.g. *Il.* 18.349–50, 24.587; *Od.* 24.44–5 and 189. Without more information it is hard to support Vox's characterization of this passage (p. 141) as a polemic against Euphor. fr. 43 *CA* Κώκυτος ⟨...⟩ μοῦνος ἀφ' ἕλκεα νίψεν Ἄδωνιν, an isolated line.

84 φορέοισιν: the second Aldine's φορέησιν (< V's φορίησιν) is defended as an instance of the *schema Ibyceum* by G. Giangrande, *Hermes* 98 (1970) 266 (following P. Buttmann, *Ausführliche griechische Sprachlehre* 1^2 (Berlin 1830) 498), but that *schema* is an epic third pers. sing. subj. in -ησι (Goodwin §544–5, Chantraine *GH* 1.461); grammarians like Heraclides (ap. Eustath. *Od.* 1576.56) who claim an indicative function for it may be confusing it with the -ησι of Aeolic contract verbs.[119] R's φορέοισιν, with Graefe's οἳ in 83 (cf. on 83–4 above), is correct here. No other extant bucolic poem uses the Aeolic third pers. pl. ending (cf. 94 ἀνακλείοισιν); Bion may have taken it from the literary Doric of Pindar by analogy with bucolic participles in -οισα (cf. on fr. 3.1 Μοίσας). Cf. Aeolic ἐμμί in 53, 56.

μηρία: this diminutive of μηρός is normally used of the thighbones of sacrificed animals, but that its literal meaning was never lost to view is shown by Sor. *Gyn.* 1.100 εἶτα στρέφειν τὸ βρέφος καὶ ... ἀποκαθαίρειν τὰ μηρία (cited by Fantuzzi, who implausibly takes μηρίον as a medical term). Here the diminutive is another sentimental touch (cf. on παῖδα and φίλοι in 18).

[119] Alleged examples of indicative -ησι in Homer can be explained as subjunctives of generality in an epic simile (Chantraine *GH* II.253; for the difficult *H.H.* 31.16 see Càssola *ad loc.*). The eponymous Ibycean examples (*PMG* 303) are subjunctive as well; cf. Bacchyl. 19.4, fr. 20B.7 Maehler.

85 ἀναψύχει: lit. "blows air on" (cf. on 9 ἀποψύχων). The Love stands behind Adonis' head (ὄπιθεν) and fans him with his wings, evidently in order to dry the corpse after it has been washed (cf. Hesych. ἀναψύχουσα· ξηραίνουσα). Cf. [Liban.] *Ecphr.* 30.18 (VIII.546.6 Foerster) Ἔρως ... παρὰ τῇ κόρῃ τὸ πτερὸν ἡδίστως ὑπέσεισε (Foerster: ὑπέσυρε codd.) καί πως ἔρωτι τὰς παρειὰς ὑπηνέμωσε, *Anacreont.* 31.9–10 (see M. L. West, *CQ* n.s. 34 (1984) 211).

87–90 The theme of the dead young person cheated of marriage is common, esp. in grave inscriptions; as here, the funeral is often treated as a travesty of a wedding, with various *topoi* played upon (see Lattimore 192–4). The treatment of the torches (87) symbolizes the unhappy change in e.g. *GVI* 1005.3–4 (Rheneia, first century B.C.), Mel. *A.P.* 7.182.7–8, Ovid *Her.* 11.101, Ach. Tat. 1.13.6; cf. Nonnus *D.* 7.52–4. For the interruption by death of the wedding song, or the changing of the wedding song into a lament (88–90), cf. Soph. *Ant.* 813–16, *GVI* 1470.3–5 (Crete, second century B.C.), [Erinna] *A.P.* 7.712.7–8 (imitated by Mel. *A.P.* 7.182.5–6), Ach. Tat. 1.13.5, Musaeus 278. For more citations see Fantuzzi on 87 and 89.

For the marriage of Aphrodite and Adonis, celebrated in Near Eastern cult ceremonies (esp. at Byblos), see Lucian *Dea Syr.* 6, Heitsch 10.24 (P. Brit. Mus. 2103, second century A.D.), Nonnus *D.* 42.268. Theoc. 15.112–31 describes a Ptolemaic celebration of the hierogamy. Bion may intend this whole section as an aetiology of the laying-out of the effigy of the dying god in the temple of his mighty paramour, her "house", as in Lucian. On Near Eastern cult elements in this poem's reflexion of the Adonia see Introd. III.

87 φλιαῖς: the term can denote any of several parts of the door-frame, most often the doorposts (Gow on Theoc. 2.60), to which the torches that Hymenaeus douses were presumably fastened.

Ὑμέναιος: the god of marriage. He is typically represented, as here, as a wedding attendant, garlanded and holding a torch (Roscher 1.2803; *LIMC* V.1.583, V.2.401). The reading is due to the Juntine and Calliergian editions (1516). V clearly reads ὑμεναίοις; as Hiller 35 notes, the abbreviation in R could as well be read ὑμεναίως (thus a misspelling of the true reading) as -οις, but in view of V's reading it probably signifies the latter.

The "sine luce facem" in Ovid *Am.* 3.9.8 (Cupid's; see on 82) may be borrowed from this line, though also from Tib. 2.6.15–16 by an adroit combination.

88 ἐξεπέτασσε: can ἐκπετάννυμι (lit. "to fling open wide") be used in the sense required here, "undo" the garland? The conjecture of Pierson 56, ἐξεκέδασσε, is what we might have expected, but Hesychius' gloss ἐξεπέτασεν on ἐξεκέδασεν suggests that "fling open" could in some contexts cover the sense "scatter" (if, however, Hesychius is glossing this very passage or one like it we must go with Pierson).

γαμήλιον: for the pattern noun–verb–γαμήλιος in this position cf. Mel. *A.P.* 6.163.7 οἷς θάλαμον κοσμεῖτε γαμήλιον and Colluth. 30 καὶ στέφος ἀσκήσασα γαμήλιον ἤλυθε Πειθώ, the latter of which imitates Bion, as does perhaps Nonnus *D.* 47.326 γάμιον στέφος (with influence also from Moschus 2.124 γάμιον μέλος).

"For the incompatibility of garlands with mourning see Eur. *Hipp.* 806, Diog. L. 2.54, Ath. 15.675A" (*HE* II.19, on Alc. Mess. *A.P.* 7.412.3).

88–9 ὑμὴν ὑμήν: Ahrens was first to print the exclamation thus, not in his 1854 edition of the *Adonis* (where he prints the second Aldine's ὑμὰν ὑμάν, a pseudo-Doricism unattested elsewhere), but in his 1855 edition of the collected bucolics and in his second Teubner edition. The forms already appear as corrections in Vat. gr. 1379. For the traditional wedding cry see Maas (1907); this form of it is found also at Eur. *Phaethon* fr. 781.14 Nauck = 227 Diggle. The upsilon is long first in Theoc. 18.58 (Maas (1907) 593). For the personification of marriage changing his celebration into a lament cf. *CEG* 587.1–2 (Athens, fourth century B.C.) οὔ σε γάμον πρόπολος, Πλαγγών, Ὑμέναιος ἐν οἴκοις | ὤλβισεν, ἀλλ' ἐδάκρυσε ἐκτὸς ἀποφθιμένην.

For reiteration of οὐκέτι or μηκέτι see Theoc. 1.116–17 (with the same collocation as here); *A.P.* 7.8.1 (Antip. Sid.), 7.223.5–6 (Thyillus, with the same collocation as here), 7.518.3 (Callim.), 9.87.1 (Marc. Arg.). On the type of repetition here, epanalepsis, see on fr. 1.3 χρῖεν.

89 ἄειδεν ἑὸν μέλος: Koechly (p. 9) bases his emendation of MS ἀειδονέος μέλος partly on the appearance of the phrase ἑὸν μέλος (in the same metrical position) in Ap. Rh. 4.1301. Meineke in his commentary proposes ἀείδει, attractive because of the present tenses in 91–5, but farther from the MS reading. Cf. the tense-changes in 79–85.

ἀλλὰ καί: most editors have restored verbs of utterance for MS ἄλλεται. The emendation ἀλλ' ἔλεγ' by Maas (1907) 591 is made plausible by the appearance of λέγειν αἰαῖ in 93 (cf. 5 n.), and was accepted by Gallavotti and Gow despite its multiplication of paleographical assumptions.[120] A verb, however, is not necessarily wanted here, since

[120] Maas supposes haplography of -λε-, dittography of -αι-, and misreading of majuscule gamma as tau. Of other conjectures, Cal-

ἄειδεν can easily continue governing this line and the next, and I have ventured to print emphatic ἀλλὰ καί "but rather" (cf. Soph. *Aj.* 1313, *Phil.* 419; Callim. *H.* 5.60; perhaps Bion fr. 5.2). Legrand emends to ἀλλ' ἀεί; corruption of neither should be too surprising in these very corrupt lines.

90 "αἰαῖ" καὶ "τὸν Ἄδωνιν": Wassenbergh (ap. Valckenaer) emends to "αἰαῖ καλὸν Ἄδωνιν", but τὸν Ἄδωνιν is quoted as a constituent of the full exclamation αἰαῖ τὸν Ἄδ. or ὢ τὸν Ἄδ. (cf. 32 n.). Estevez 41 takes τὸν Ἄδωνιν as "the Adonis-song", parallel to ὑμέναιον (see Gow on Theoc. 15.96 μέλλει τὸν Ἄδωνιν ἀείδειν), but it is doubtful whether that was a standard term, intelligible outside the Theocritean context.

ἤ: Valckenaer bases his emendation on the translation of E. G. Higt (posthumously printed with Valckenaer's edition). Hiatus after ἤ is common in princeps even in poets who avoid hiatus; see West *GM* 15 and 156, who suggests that such cases are elisions of ἠέ.

ὑμέναιον: some read exclamatory acc. Ὑμέναιον, parallel to τὸν Ἄδωνιν. Aeolic ὑμήναον is a nuptial exclamation in Sappho fr. 111 L–P (normally voc. Ὑμέναιε; see Maas (1907)), but here the term more likely = "nuptial song", ἑὸν μέλος (89), which the god no longer sings. He cries αἰαῖ etc. even more (i.e. more loudly?) than he had sung the nuptial song.

[Apolinar.] *Ps.* 70.30 Ludwich καί οἱ αἰνετὸν ὕμνον ἔτι πλέον ἢ πρὶν ἀείσω may be an imitation.

91 The Graces are frequent attendants and companions of Aphrodite (cf. Verdenius 103–4). R. M. R. Fernandes, *O tema das Graças na poesia clássica* (Lisbon 1962) 278 recognizes their role here as that of divine counterparts (or precursors?) to the women who mourned Adonis at his yearly festival.

τὸν υἱέα τῶ Κινύραο: a grand periphrasis in the epic style, giving information irrelevant to the present situation (contrast 24). Cinyras, who first appears in Greek literature as a legendary ruler of Cyprus (*Il.* 11.20–3, Alcman *PMG* 3.71; see C. Baurain, *BCH* 104 (1980) 277–308 on his role in mythology), was especially famous as the ancestor of the hereditary priest-kings of Paphian Aphrodite, the Cinyrads (cf. T. B. Mitford, *AJA* 65 (1961) 136–7). Because of the connexion of that Cyp-

lierges' ᾄδεται (for the middle form see *H.H.* 17.1, 20.1) would produce harsh asyndeton (MS ἄλλ- more likely conceals ἀλλά) and is not as close to the MS reading as its proponents think. Ahrens's paleographically more distant ἀλλ' ἐπαείδει eliminates the reiteration of αἰαῖ, which reiterated ὑμήν supports.

riot cult with a lamented young god, he was made the father of Adonis in one version of the myth (first attested in Plato Comicus fr. 3 *PCG*, Antim. fr. 102 *IEG*).

92 ἐν ἀλλάλαισι: "among themselves". An antiphonal lament is presumably meant (cf. 2 n.). For the Doric long alpha (first printed by Brunck) cf. fr. 13.5.

93 Pierson's conjecture αἰαῖ ("in schedis suis" according to Valckenaer) for MS αὐταί (cf. Lennep's αἰαῖ for αὐτάν in 86) is necessary, since ὀξύ "shrilly" should go with a verb meaning "lament", not just "say"; λέγειν "αἰαῖ" is semantically equivalent to αἰάζειν (cf. on 5, 32). Cf. 23.

πολὺ πλέον: cf. fr. 8.3 n.

πολὺ πλέον ἤ τύ, Διώνα: Dione, properly Aphrodite's mother, is Aphrodite herself here, as perhaps in Theoc. 7.116 (see Gow *ad loc.*) and often in Lat. (e.g. Catull. 56.6; Ovid *A.A.* 3.3 and 769). M. E. Grabar'-Passek, *Feokrit Mosx Bion* (Moscow 1958) 319 suggests that the mother appears in order to share in her daughter's grief (cf. *Il.* 5.370–4), but an address to her, when Aphrodite has so often been addressed, would be too abrupt. The sentiment is a hyperbolic compliment (to Adonis), like the model, Theoc. 2.79 στήθεα δὲ στίλβοντα πολὺ πλέον ἤ τύ, Σελάνα[121] (for πολὺ πλέον ἤ in this position see also Theoc. 5.80, [Moschus] 3.68 (cf. 87), Marc. Arg. *A.P.* 7.384.1; cf. 90). Ahrens's emendation ἢ παιῶνα – which he construed with Vulcanius' Μοῖσαι in 94 as subject of λέγοντι – is unlikely in view of the model. Acc. τυ (suggested by Schmitz 18–19 and R. Matthews, *CR* n.s. 38 (1988) 218) is syntactically impossible.

94 χαἰ: the article is not necessary (cf. fr. 8.14), but Meineke's emendation (first in his second ed., Berlin 1836) nicely correlates Μοῖραι with αἱ Χάριτες in 91.

ἀνακλείοισιν: for the Aeolic ending see on 84 φορέοισιν. Act. or mid. ἀνακαλέω is a technical term for summoning the dead back to life, as in e.g. Plut. *Gen. Soc.* 585F ἀνακαλούμενος τὴν Λύσιδος ψυχὴν κατελθεῖν; see Alexiou 109, who also observes that it was used less ambitiously "of the persistent calling of the dead by name during the supplication at the tomb" (cf. e.g. Anyte *A.P.* 7.486.3). Here the funereal and magical senses coincide.

[121] The impolitic hyperbole works better for the besotted adolescent Simaetha than here: why should anyone lament Adonis more than Aphrodite? Cf. the criticism of P. Maas, *CR* n.s. 4 (1954) 11 = *Kl. Schr.* (Munich 1973) 97.

Rather than the Μοῖραι, vainly working *against* destiny, Vulcanius conjectures the Μοῖσαι; the presence of the latter is plausible (for the close association of the Muses with the Graces see West on Hes. *Th.* 64, Verdenius 104), and the emendation should be considered. Μοῖραι, however, is *difficilior*, and produces a more interesting (and not less plausible) scenario. The Greeks pictured the Fates as having power not only over sending people down to death, but over bringing them back up to life as well. They assist at the yearly resurrection of Persephone in [Orph.] *H.* 43.7, where the Seasons preside as they preside over the resurrection of Adonis in Theoc. 15.103–4 (cf. on 96 below); perhaps such a role was traditional for the Fates too. Hyg. *Fab.* 251.4 lists Adonis among those "qui licentia Parcarum ab inferis redierunt"; Bion alludes to this version of the myth only to contradict it, making the power of Persephone greater even than that of fate.[122]

The echoed name simulates the repetitive cries of the mourners. Attempts to attach the second Ἄδωνιν to the next sentence[123] are needless in view of Bion's love of repetition, and the emendations of Palmerius 817 (ἐν Ἄιδω) and Wilamowitz (ἐν Ἄιδᾳ) make it sound as if the Fates themselves were in Hades (we could not interpret as τὸν ἐν Ἄιδω), whereas they seem to be present at the bier with Hymenaeus and the Graces.

95 ἐπαείδουσιν: refers to the uttering or singing of incantations. The verb is normally intransitive; cf. Aesch. *Ag.* 1020–1 ἀνδρὸς μέλαν αἷμα τίς ἂν πάλιν ἀγκαλέσαιτ' ἐπαείδων (on ἀνακαλέομαι see 94 n.), Theoc. 2.91. Here transitive: "they cast spells over him" (but C. Hartung, *Philologus* 41 (1882) 350 proposes dat. οἱ for MS μιν).

On the lengthening of the unaugmented first syllable of ἀείδω in princeps (commonest in Callimachus) see Gow on Theoc. 7.41.

οὐχ ὑπακούει: "does not heed, respond" (cf. Theoc. 3.24, ending οὐχ ὑπακούεις) is correct for MS οὐκ ἐπάκουει "does not hear", since the next line indicates that Adonis *does* hear; ἐπακούω has the right sense only with gen. or dat. of things (cf. e.g. Anacr. *PMG* 357.8 εὐχωλῆς ἐπακούειν).[124] ἐπ- has intruded from ἐπαείδουσιν. Stephanus suggests the emendation on the last page of the Prolegomena to his 1579 edition.

[122] Cf. Claudian *Rapt.* 305–6 (Pluto to Proserpina) "accipe Lethaeo famulas cum gurgite Parcas; | sit fatum quodcumque voles".

[123] 95 καί μιν codd.: καλὸν Heskin: αἱ μὲν S. Wyngaarden, *Acta literaria societatis Rheno-Trajectinae* 1 (1793) 190–1.

[124] Plato *Soph.* 227c καί μοι ... ἐπάκουε, cited by Fantuzzi in support of the MSS, means simply "listen to me".

In a Mesopotamian text Adonis' counterpart Tammuz laments, "Woe, I am become a ghost, I am not one who can answer my mother" (T. Jacobsen, *The Harps That Once. . . .* (New Haven 1987) 76).

96 οὐ μάν: corrects an impression one might have received from what has just been said (Denniston 335–6); the classic instance is Sappho 105A.3 L–P.

οὐ μὰν οὐκ ἐθέλει: "not that he is unwilling". The first negative adv. negates the whole phrase οὐκ ἐθέλει. Stier 23–4 recognizes adherescent οὐ forming with ἐθέλει a single word-group meaning "is unwilling" (cf. fr. 9.4); for the negation of this expression he adduces *Il.* 4.223–4 ἔνθ' οὐκ ἂν βρίζοντα ἴδοις Ἀγαμέμνονα δῖον, | οὐδὲ καταπτώσσοντ', οὐδ' οὐκ ἐθέλοντα μάχεσθαι; Xen. *Hell.* 5.2.33 οὐκ ἐπὶ μὲν τὸν ἐν Πειραιεῖ δῆμον . . . οὐκ ἠθέλησαν συστρατεύειν; ("did they not refuse . . . ?" in C. L. Brownson's Loeb translation).

Κώρα: "the Maiden", i.e. Persephone. For the title in verse see Eur. *Alc.* 852, *H.F.* 608, *Supp.* 34; [Moschus] 3.119, 4.75. Persephone's tenacity (cf. 54–5) recalls the legend – no doubt intended to explain Adonis' annual "death" – that she and Aphrodite divide his year between them. The story is originally Sumerian (A. Falkenstein, *Bibliotheca Orientalis* 22 (1965) 281; cf. Burkert (1979) 110) and first appears in Panyassis fr. 22A *EGF* = [Apollod.] *Bibl.* 3.14.4 (see Reed (1995) 330–1); later in Cyril *Comm. Is.* (*PG* 70.440–1; cf. 53 n.); cf. Theoc. 15.136–7, Schol. Theoc. 3.48, Alciphr. 4.14.3; *PGM* 4.2903 (fourth century A.D.), Agathias *A.P.* 5.289.9.

97 λῆγε γόων: in this position also in anon. *A.P.* 7.667.3 (from a tomb in the church of St Anastasia in Thessalonica, according to the Palatine corrector). The phrase is frequent in tragedy, e.g. Aesch. *Pers.* 705 κλαυμάτων λήξασα τῶνδε καὶ γόων; for the behest to cease lamentation in grave inscriptions see Lattimore 217–20. Here the wording alludes to the parallel motif in Theocritus' Daphnis-lament λήγετε βουκολικᾶς, Μοῖσαι, ἴτε λήγετ' ἀοιδᾶς (Theoc. 1.127, 131, 137, 142).

τὸ σάμερον: "for today". For the Doric form cf. fr. 11.6.

ἴσχεο κομμῶν: lit. "hold yourself back from . . ."; i.e. "refrain from" (an esp. Homeric use of the middle: LSJ s.v. I.2). Cf. Philetas *A.P.* 7.481.3 ἴσχεο λύπας (gen.). The κομμοί (< κόπτομαι) are the rapid beatings of the breast referred to in 4–5 and 25–7; the word is also a technical term for a lament on the tragic stage (Aristot. *Poet.* 1452B24), but here the more concrete meaning is right.

98 εἰς ἔτος ἄλλο: for this temporal use of εἰς see LSJ s.v. II.2 (cf. Dover on Aristoph. *Nub.* 562). Cf. Soph. *Ant.* 340 ἔτος εἰς ἔτος, Theoc.

18.15 κῆς ἔτος ἐξ ἔτεος (also Ap. Rh. 4.1774), [Theoc.] 25.124 ἐξ ἔτεος . . . εἰς ἔτος, Callim. *H.* 6.123 ἔτος δ' εἰς ἄλλο (perhaps Bion's model), [Moschus] 3.101 εἰς ἔτος ἄλλο (imitating Bion). For the sentiment of this line (and the previous) see Mnasalces *A.P.* 9.70.3–4 τίπτε παναμέριος γοάεις ἀνὰ δῶμα, χελιδοῖ; | παύε', ἐπεί σε μένει καὶ κατόπιν δάκρυα (cf. *Il.* 24.618–20, Callim. *H.* 5.68).

The end of the poem completes a ring-composition: Aphrodite is bidden to end her laments as she was bidden to begin them in 3–5. That all the consonants of line 1 reappear here (with the one addition of [r]), some in combination with the same vowels, is noteworthy and may underscore the ring-end. The commands effect an aetiology of the Adonia (cf. Ovid *A.A.* 3.85 "ut Veneri, quem luget adhuc, donetur Adonis"); Will 100 (cf. 103) sees here a reflexion of a Near Eastern ritual "farewell until next year", attested also in Theoc. 15.143–4 and 149, where Adonis is bidden farewell and his return the following year anticipated. Note, however, that Bion is silent on the possibility of a return (cf. on 53, 96).

APPENDIX A

Comparison between numerations of Bion's fragments in widely used editions since Ahrens. For a fuller list see Gow OCT 186.

A	**B**	**C**	**D**
1	14	11	16
2	15	3	17
3	16	14	18
4	1	15	2
5	2	13	3
6	6	16	4
7	4	7.1	5
8	5	7.2–15	6, 7
9	6	6	8
10	7	5	9
11	8	9	10
12	9	8	11
13	10	4	12
14	11	10	13
15	12	17	14
16	13	12	15
17	17	18	19

A This edition, Beckby, Gow, Gallavotti (following the order of Stobaeus)
B Legrand, Wilamowitz (1910)
C Edmonds, Ziegler, Meineke (1856)
D Ahrens

APPENDIX B

Comparison of sigla used for the manuscripts of the *Epitaph on Adonis*.

	A	B
Vat. gr. 1824	V	23
Paris. gr. 2832	R*	M
Vat. gr. 1311	X	11
Ambros. (104) B 75 sup.	C	c
Vat. gr. 1379		18
Paris. gr. 2812A**		K
Laur. gr. xxxii.43		r
Paris. Coisl. gr. 351		Z

A This edition, Fantuzzi, Beckby, Gow, Gallavotti, Wilamowitz

B Hiller, Ziegler, Ahrens

* Wilamowitz (followed by Gow and Fantuzzi) uses Tr for Paris. gr. 2832.

** Variously numbered by editors; see p. 74 n. 141.

INDEX LOCORUM

INDEX LOCORUM

INDEX LOCORUM

INDEX LOCORUM

INDEX BIONEUS

* refers to an adopted conjecture, (m) to an unadopted manuscript reading, † to a dubious manuscript reading. Dialectal forms are as given in the text.

GENERAL INDEX